Waterfalls

of the White Mountains

Waterfalls
of the White Mountains

◆

30 Trips to 100 Waterfalls

Bruce and Doreen Bolnick

Photographs by the authors
Illustrated by Doreen Bolnick

Backcountry Publications
The Countryman Press
Woodstock, Vermont

© 1990 by Bruce and Doreen Bolnick, Sixth Printing, 1997
Line illustrations © 1990 by Doreen Bolnick
Published by The Countryman Press, PO Box 748, Woodstock, VT 05091
Distributed by W.W. Norton & Company, Inc., 500 Fifth Avenue, New York, NY 10110

Library of Congress Cataloging-in-Publication Data
Bolnick, Bruce R.
    Waterfalls of the White Mountains : 30 trips to 100 waterfalls /
Bruce and Doreen Bolnick ; photographs by the authors ; illustrated
by Doreen Bolnick.
        p. cm.
    Includes bibliographical references.
    ISBN 0-88150-160-3 :
    1. Hiking—White Mountains (N.H. and Me.)—Guide-books.
    2. Waterfalls—New Hampshire—Description. 3. Waterfalls—Maine—
Description. 4. White Mountains (N.H. and Me.)—Description and
travel—Guide-books. I. Bolnick, Doreen, 1948- . II. Title.
GV199.42.W47B65 1990
917.42—dc20   89-18636
                                                                     CIP

Printed in the United States of America by McNaughton & Gunn
Typesetting by NK Graphics
Text and cover design by Ann Aspell
Maps by Doreen Bolnick, © 1990 by Backcountry Publications
Cover photograph of Crystal Cascade by Bruce and Doreen Bolnick

Frontispiece: Giant Falls in spring runoff

With all our love, we dedicate this book
to our son, Daniel

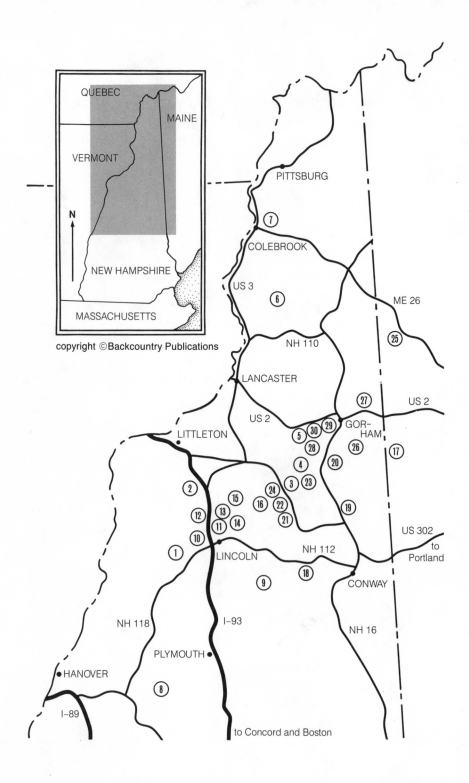

copyright ©Backcountry Publications

Contents

———◆———

Foreword

If you have ever wanted to find your own special place in this world, a specific place where you could sit quietly, be one with nature, and approach oneness with the plan of the Creator, I encourage you to make these writings on waterfalls an important part of your search. Bruce and Doreen Bolnick, who have explored exciting mountains on most of the world's continents, truly *love* waterfalls. They have explored, studied, and researched the waterfalls for this book, and have presented them with a blend of history, lore, myth, and water-fall-ology that speaks to the completeness of one's feelings for water-falls.

What do you *feel* when you stand beside a waterfall in the mountains? All of us would have different answers to that question, and each one's answer would vary depending upon whom one was standing next to, what time of year it was, and what the weather had been yesterday. But the authors have captured the personality of these waterfalls so completely that you will begin to experience the romance of your waterfall feelings while reading through their descriptions, long before you actually arrive at the waterfall.

I was coincidentally asked to write this foreword only a few days after my daughter, my son-in-law, and I had enjoyed a long lunch while relaxing on the granite beside Thoreau Falls (Chapter 16). What a delight it was to read the draft and to see such an accurate, romantic, and deep description of the waterfall that we had so thoroughly enjoyed together only a few days before.

I want to compliment Bruce and Doreen for the evocative prose and depth of feeling in describing each waterfall, and for the superlative artwork and fine photography which accompany the text. And I want to thank them for maintaining the ideals of conservation by pointing out proper low-impact trail etiquette, and the joys and hazards of bushwhacking trips. Thanks are also due for reminding us that the Wilderness Experience is for all to enjoy, by pointing out the availability of wonderful outdoor opportunities that are, in many cases, very easy to reach.

Francis J. Kelliher
President, Appalachian Mountain Club (1987–1988)

An Invitation to the Reader

Over time trails can be rerouted and signs and landmarks altered. If you find that changes have occurred on the routes described in this book, please let us know so that corrections may be made in future editions. The author and publisher also welcome other comments and suggestions. Address all correspondence to:

Editor
Waterfalls
Backcountry Publications
P.O. Box 175
Woodstock, Vermont 05091

Acknowledgments

This book could not have been written without a great deal of help. Without a doubt the most critical assistance came from the organizations that have established and maintained the superb network of White Mountain hiking trails. Our project would have been virtually unthinkable without the accumulated efforts of both paid staff and volunteers who have worked with the Appalachian Mountain Club, the U.S. Forest Service, the Randolph Mountain Club, the Chatham Trail Association, the Waterville Valley Athletic and Improvement Association, and the Dartmouth Outing Club. The AMC and the Forest Service also made vital contributions through their publications, particularly the AMC *White Mountain Guide* and a large stack of Forest Service public-information materials.

Another major debt is owed to the staff of the Reading (Massachusetts) Public Library, the source of most of the research material for the book, either directly or through interlibrary loan.

One other organization that deserves heartfelt thanks is Boy Scout Troop 702, led by Mr. George Taylor. It was on Scout trips to the White Mountains that the seed for this book germinated and took root. The critical catalyst was seeing how much the Scouts enjoyed visiting waterfalls.

Many other individuals made important contributions to the project. The order of citation here bears no implications about the importance of the contributions. The following people provided valuable information, suggestions, and encouragement at an early stage of the project: the late Malcolm Choate, one of the original conspirators behind the formation of the AMC's 4000-Footers Club; John Derby, retired public information officer for the Forest Service, whose own love of the waterfalls was highly contagious; Daniel Doan, author of *Fifty Hikes in the White Mountains* and *Fifty More Hikes in New Hampshire* (both from Backcountry Publications); our old friend Dr. Pancras van der Laan, of Lancaster, a storehouse of north-country hiking knowledge; and Sharon van der Laan, who sheltered our son on occasions when he wanted to be with his friends rather than hike.

Robert Donovan kindly and generously served as technical adviser

xi

on photography and provided a tremendous amount of help with printing the photographs. The late Ed Lee also helped with prints before he passed away. Robert Lautzenheiser, retired New England climatologist for the U.S. Weather Bureau, was our resource for weather statistics. Professor Wallace A. Bothner of the Department of Earth Sciences at the University of New Hampshire provided invaluable comments on the geology of the White Mountain waterfalls. Professor Malcolm Hill of the Geology Department at Northeastern University also answered numerous geological questions. Captain Henry P. Mock, Chief of Law Enforcement, New Hampshire Fish and Game Department, let us spend a day looking through the state's search-and-rescue files for information on accidents. Robert Trevor provided technical advice on mapping. Douglas Philbrook of Gorham, and Ned Therrien, public-information officer for the U.S. Forest Service, went out of their way to track down information. To all of these people we offer special thanks.

We also want to express our gratitude to others who provided useful information, including: Gary W. Carr, District Manager, White Mountain National Forest Androscoggin District; Roger Collins, Ammonoosuc District Ranger; Eugene S. Daniell III, editor, *AMC White Mountain Guide*; Barbara Eastman, Librarian, Chatham; Frances N. Haynes, Librarian, Colebrook; Earl Jette, Director, Outdoor Programs, Dartmouth College; Barry Kelley, White Mountain Lumber Company; Kenneth Kimball, Director of Research, AMC; Arlene Lewis, Librarian, Lunenburg, Vermont; Henry Murphy; Frank Rymes, of Scout Troop 119, Lexington, Massachusetts; Robert Walker, Saco District Ranger; Laura and Guy Waterman; Ken Wiley, Regional Park Supervisor, Maine Department of Conservation; and Eileen Woodland, U.S. Forest Service.

It seems to be a tradition to thank one's editors near the end of the list of acknowledgments. This custom certainly does not reflect their role in putting the book together. We owe a great deal to many people at The Countryman Press, including: the project editor, Castle Freeman; the production manager, Jeanie Levitan; Vice President Chris Lloyd; and most of all Vice President Carl Taylor, who managed the project from start to finish with enormous goodwill and encouragement.

Finally, we want to thank our son, Daniel, who put up with all of our compulsiveness during the three years it has taken to pull the book together. Probably he is used to it, since we started dragging him along on hikes when he was young enough to fit into a parka pocket—at age eleven weeks. We coaxed him up his first hike on his own power, to Lonesome Lake, with Tootsie Roll bribes at age twenty-one months. Now that he is a teenager we can't push him around so easily, but he continues to be a wonderful hiking companion and a very best friend for us. To him we dedicate this book.

Introduction

———◆———

They left their home of summer ease
Beneath the lowland's sheltering trees,
To seek, by ways unknown to all,
The promise of the waterfall.

Some vague, faint rumor to the vale
Had crept—perchance a hunter's tale—
Of its wild mirth of waters lost
On the dark woods through which it tossed.

Somewhere it laughed and sang; somewhere
Whirled in mad dance its misty hair; . . .
　　　—"The Seeking of the Waterfall,"
　　　John Greenleaf Whittier, 1878

This book is the first guide dedicated to the waterfalls of the White Mountains, which rank among the finest of New England's outstanding scenic attractions. The book is meant also as an *invitation* to seek out the waterfalls. We invite you to linger at the falls, to explore the ledges and ravines, to watch the sun-light flicker on ripples in the clear mountain pools, to lose your thoughts in the swirling currents, and to mingle in the company of the streams and forests.

The waterfalls are gifts from the clouds to hikers and tourists, youngsters and oldsters, artists and photographers, and all who take pleasure in the song of a tumbling brook. Some falls are miniature treasures hidden in deep forest, while others strike boldly down high mountain walls. Some are itinerant fountains that vanish and reappear with the rains. Others surge with vitality throughout the summer. Each has a personality of its own.

How many waterfalls, cascades, and cataracts can be found in the White Mountains? There is no single answer. Counting every spot where the descent of a rushing stream is beautiful enough to attract admirers, the total would be many thousands. Well over a hundred are notable enough to have been named or specially identified. (An alphabetical inventory of these landmarks is presented in the master list at the end of the book.)

This book describes thirty waterfall trips, each covering from one to as many as a dozen waterfalls that can be visited in a single outing. Each chapter includes information on how to reach the falls, trail conditions, and highlights by the way, as well as descriptions of the falls themselves. Do you want to know which cascades have wonderful swimming holes with good sunlight? Which waterfalls are great for exploring? Which are well suited for children? Which are easy to reach and which require strenuous hikes? Which are crowded and which are isolated? Which are tallest? Which lose their flair during dry spells? Which have etched deep gorges or fascinating contours in the bedrock? You will find the answers here.

In all, sixty-two waterfalls and cascades are described thoroughly. Excursions to another forty-one falls are discussed more briefly. (This tabulation is problematic, however, since it is not always clear what to count. For example you can get a higher total by counting individually each of the lovely cascades on Cascade Brook in Kinsman Notch.)

Every chapter also includes a "historical detour," which relates some of the rich history of the White Mountain region: the Indian wars; the heroic explorers; the indomitable settlers; the elegant Victorian inns; the coming of the railroads; the devastation of vast forests by logging and by fire; the birth of environmental awareness; the blossoming of winter sports; the once-flourishing towns that have disappeared. When visiting the waterfalls you can often sense ghosts of the past if you know to watch for them.

In geographic scope the book is restricted to waterfalls of the White Mountain region, but the region is defined generously. As shown on the map opposite the Table of Contents, the waterfall trips range from Mount Cardigan in the southeast to Colebrook in the north and to Grafton Notch, ME, in the east. The trip chapters have been grouped in four sections, reflecting nature's division of watersheds. The rains, snows, and mists that water the region all flow to the sea by one of four major rivers: the Connecticut, the Pemigewasset/Merrimack, the Saco, and the Androscoggin. Within each watershed section, trips appear roughly in upstream order—as if to lead you on

Watersheds of the White Mountains

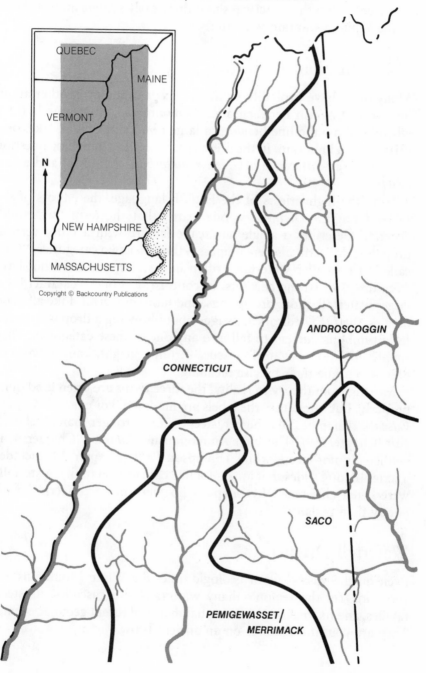

QUEBEC

MAINE

VERMONT

N

NEW HAMPSHIRE

MASSACHUSETTS

Copyright © Backcountry Publications

ANDROSCOGGIN

CONNECTICUT

SACO

PEMIGEWASSET / MERRIMACK

an adventure up the waterways that drew early settlers into the heart of the White Mountain wilderness.

Waterfall Nomenclature

Many of us have probably wondered at one time or another about how to distinguish between a small mountain and a large hill. Or where to draw the line between a large pond and a small lake, or a drizzle and a light rain. In the present context the compelling question is: what's the difference between a *waterfall*, a *cascade*, and a *cataract*?

From the high priests of the English language, the editors of the *Oxford English Dictionary*, one learns that the term "waterfall" generally describes a single landscape feature with a fairly vertical drop. But this term also encompasses the other two categories. "Cascades" are smaller waterfalls, often in a series, and need not have steep drops or strong currents. In contrast, a proper "cataract" is a larger waterfall, more precipitous, and more powerful. Like all good oracles, the *OED* editors are vague about how big a drop is required for a tumbling current to fall into any one of these categories. They simply note that a waterfall issues "from a height," and leave it to others to argue their precise meaning.

Moving from theory to reality, the three terms are often used quite properly. But often, too, the labels are muddled. For example Crystal *Cascade* (Chapter 20) is bigger, steeper, and stronger than Hitchcock *Fall* (Chapter 29). The First Ammonoosuc *Cataract* (Chapter 4) is neither big nor steep, while Thompson *Falls* (Chapter 20) includes a series of long slides that look a lot like cascades. Happily, waterfalls were often christened by people who were more concerned with poetry than pedantry.

Waterfall Origins

Even on the vast scale of geologic time, the White Mountains are very old. Yet the region's many waterfalls and cascades, its steep ravines, and its towering cliffs are hallmarks of recent geologic events. They are youthful features on an ancient brow.

The oldest exposed bedrock formations originated from sandy sediments deposited on the floor of the Iapetus Ocean, an ancestor of the modern Atlantic Ocean that covered the region 600 million years ago. A period of volcanic activity ensued, burying the sands under a sheet of ash perhaps a mile thick. Later, more sediments of silt, sand, and impure limestone were added to the pile.

The mountain-building activity began about 470 million years ago. Fueled by enormous convection energies within the earth, Africa and Europe crept toward North America, slowly and intermittently closing the Iapetus Ocean over a period of nearly 100 million years. Under titanic pressures the accumulated bedrock strata were crushed, uplifted, folded, tilted, and stacked by the continental collision. Compression also recrystallized the original minerals to form new metamorphic rocks from the ancient sediments. Bedrock clues today reveal a "tectonic hinge" running laterally through the White Mountains toward the northeast. This hinge formed a buttress against which the encroaching land mass from the east collided, about 410 million years ago. Geologists speculate that land east of the hinge today might be a fused remnant of Africa.

After a long period of stability and erosion, the tectonic forces shifted into reverse about 190 million years ago. The continents began to pull apart to create the modern Atlantic Ocean, a process that continues today. During this period of extension, large volumes of pressurized magma welled up through fractures deep in the earth's crust and gradually cooled to form bodies of granite that are seen today at many waterfalls. (Similar "plutonic events" had taken place earlier.)

The magma intrusion ended more than 100 million years ago. With it ended the buildup of the White Mountains. Subsequent erosion has stripped off *miles* of overlying rock, exposing a quiltwork of ancient metamorphic formations and newer granite bodies that were tempered far beneath the earth's surface.

During the ensuing 100 million years of geologic stability, erosion and sedimentation produced a mature White Mountain landscape, with rolling hills, well-graded valleys, rounded ridges, and deep soils. Through the eons the mountain streams gradually eliminated virtually all the discontinuities in their line of descent. As one geologist visualized the conditions, "Very probably there were no falls or rapids and certainly none in any of the major valleys." (Chapman, 1974).

Then came the Great Ice Age. As the earth's climate began to cool about two million years ago, accumulating snows formed Alpine glaciers on the flanks of the higher White Mountain summits. These local glaciers carved out great basins, or *cirques*, like Tuckerman's Ravine and the Great Gulf.

The continental ice sheet arrived in the area around 50,000 years ago. More than a mile thick, the vast river of ice covered the entire landscape, including the Presidential summits. With its great weight and the abrasive power of grit and stones caught in its grip, the creeping ice mass scoured the region clean of soil, and then carved its signature in the bedrock. Moving across the mountains, it plucked off huge blocks of stone, leaving precipitous cliffs. Passing through the valleys, it sheared off side walls, creating the deep U-shaped notches that now characterize the region.

A mere 15,000 years ago the ice sheet began to recede, taking perhaps 3,000 years to melt away. It left behind a rejuvenated landscape, dotted with young waterfalls and cascades. Some, called "hanging waterfalls," were produced because the glaciers obliterated their formerly mature streambeds. Instead of descending gradually to the valley floor, the waters now plunged over sheer notch walls. Exemplifying this category are the high waterfalls of Crawford Notch (Chapters 3, 21, 22, and 24).

Other displaced streambeds were rerouted over smaller cliffs where they cut new gorges, as at Glen Ellis Falls (Chapter 20). In places displaced streams crossed narrow bands (called dikes) of soft basalt, where magma had once spurted through fissures in ancient rock beds. These dikes eroded quickly, creating flumes, such as the famous Flume gorge in Franconia Notch (Chapter 11) and the gorge at Sabbaday Falls (Chapter 18).

Some small but very beautiful waterfalls were formed when gritty outwash from receding ice surged across bared ledges of granite. In spots, abrasive turbulence produced fascinating potholes and gorges, such as those seen at the Basin (Chapter 12) and Screw Auger Falls (Chapter 25).

Waterfalls usually developed at a contact between tough and less resistant rock. Moriah Gorge (Chapter 26), and Cold Brook Fall

(Chapter 30) are clear examples. In some cases glaciers displaced a stream over a boundary contact that had not previously been eroded. Elsewhere the ice carried away sediments that had filled in ancient waterfalls. In the millions of years to come the sediments will be replaced, and the stubborn rock walls will erode away. Most of the waterfalls will again disappear. Look closely, and you can see that the work is under way.

In Annex A you will find a table of technical information on the bedrock geology at many of the waterfalls. If you are interested in learning more about the region's geologic history, refer to the relevant sources cited in the bibliography (Annex C).

Waterfalls in the Book

For every major waterfall covered in the text there is a summary of Hiking Data showing:

- *Distance, parking area to falls:* The number given is the approximate *one-way* hiking distance in miles. A familiar rule for calculating hiking *time*—including brief rest stops—allows one hour for every 2 miles, *plus* thirty minutes per 1000 feet of ascent. A hiker in good condition carrying a light pack can move faster. Then again, a hiker who wants to enjoy the excursion can move slower! We recommend taking time to explore the woods and streams and to linger at the waterfalls.
- *Altitude gain:* The figure given is the approximate *net* altitude difference (in feet) from trailhead to waterfall, based on contour

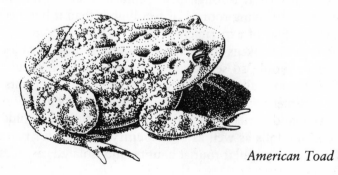

American Toad

counts from topographic maps. The figure excludes ups and downs along the trail, and is generally rounded to the nearest 50 feet.

• *Difficulty:* This subjective hike rating factors in distance, vertical climb, steepness, and quality of the walking surface. You may interpret the ratings by the following criteria. EASY means that a septuagenarian in reasonable health can make the trip (as confirmed by my parents). So can a cooperative four-year-old child. STRENUOUS means that even experienced hikers in fit condition will find the trip quite fatiguing—though their efforts will be amply rewarded. MODERATE means neither easy nor strenuous.

The waterfalls themselves are described in the text. One key characteristic of each waterfall and cascade is its height. The height figures provided in the text are based on reports found in other documents. Only in a handful of cases did we find any indication that a waterfall actually had been *measured.* Typically, the source documents state the height without explanation. Such figures were accepted and used here if they were confirmed by a visual check in the field.

For some falls different sources report different heights. For others the reported figures appeared implausible in the field. And in many instances no height reports were found at all. In all such cases we report best guesses based on visual comparisons with two familiar standards: a basketball hoop and our 35-foot chimney at home. One attempt was made to be scientific. We invested in an expensive altimeter that claimed accuracy to 10 feet. For practice we calibrated the instrument to the altitude of our living room. That night a low-pressure system passed through town, and in the morning the altimeter showed the living room 110 feet higher than it had been the evening before. End of experiment.

Our field work took us to far more waterfalls and cascades than could fit in the book, so selectivity was required. A few cuts were easy, because some falls were not worth the hike. Other cuts were matters of judgment. Generally, the final selection was based on both intrinsic value and variety. By design the trips selected include convenient roadside falls as well as backcountry beauties for marathon hikers. They cover popular tourist haunts, and isolated cascades that you might well have all to yourself. The tallest falls are here, together with many small charmers.

Regrettably, the mightiest cataracts on the main rivers of the White Mountains could not be included in the book, because years ago they were tamed by dams. Of Berlin Falls on the Androscoggin River, King (1868) wrote: "We do not think that in New England there is any passage of river passion that will compare. . . ." Fifteen Mile Falls below Dalton, according to Pike (1967), contained the most treacherous drop on the Connecticut River log drives. To see these powerful waterfalls today, however, you will have to visit the library, not the mountains.

Visiting the Falls

◆

The vast majority of White Mountain waterfalls and cascades are easily accessible to casual hikers, tourists, and families, as well as seasoned trail veterans and energetic mountaineers. Even for dedicated peak baggers the waterfalls are refreshing excursions on sweltering summer days, and days when the summits are locked in clouds or gripped by ice and snow. This section provides information that may be helpful for anyone setting out on a waterfall trip.

Trail Maps

The maps and trail descriptions in Part Two of the book provide all the information you will need to reach the waterfalls. But a good topographic map should be consulted for a complete picture of the local geography and the web of connecting trails, especially when hiking alternate routes or hiking beyond the falls. There are three popular topographic map resources for the region:

- *Appalachian Mountain Club (AMC) Trail Maps*: Long the standard for White Mountain hikers, these maps come packaged with the invaluable *White Mountain Guide* published by the Appalachian Mountain Club. The maps are also sold separately at some outlets. They are compact, lightweight, durable, and easy to read. I carry the pertinent AMC map on virtually every hike.
- *DeLorme's Trail Map and Guide to the White Mountain National Forest*: This handy publication has a regional topographic map on the front, and thumbnail trail descriptions on the back. It is like a compact, one-sheet version of the AMC trail-guide package, but the map cuts off some outlying areas, its contour lines are hard to read, and hiking routes are drawn less precisely in areas with dense trail systems.
- *U.S. Geological Survey quadrangle maps*: The USGS maps, which are available for every part of the region, use fine contour

10

intervals that reveal more detail than the AMC and DeLorme maps. But each quadrangle covers a limited area, so many hikes sprawl over more than one map. Also, the USGS maps are less durable, more bulky, often less up-to-date, and less readily available than the others. (To order USGS maps, call 1-800-USA-MAPS.)

Each chapter heading in Part II of the book includes a Map note showing the trip's location on the appropriate AMC map and on the DeLorme map. For trips not covered by the AMC and DeLorme maps, USGS map information is provided instead.

Waterfall Moods

> But what folly to attempt to draw in words the curves and colors, the coyness . . . , the flashes and the moodiness, the laughter and the plaints of these daughters of the clouds!
> —*King, 1868.*

At best, descriptions and photos on the flat pages of a book only hint at the spirit of a waterfall. Moreover each waterfall's demeanor varies from year to year, and even from day to day, depending on the weather. Over the course of a year, however, the mountain streams exhibit a regular cycle of moods.

Spring, the time of rebirth of the forests, is the season for mesmerizing, torrential currents. Streams and rivers swell with melting snows and seasonal rains, transforming waterfall lambs briefly into wolves. The mountains throw an aqueous extravaganza, sprouting waterfalls in gullies where one finds nothing but damp rock two months later.

Spring in the north country does not adhere to the calendar. At the equinox the mountain streams are often still tight in the grip of winter. Beginning in early April spring unfolds northward, climbing gradually to higher elevations. Once the mountains are in full thaw, the period of high water can last one to two months, depending on the rains. When the radio brings news of spring floods in the north country, then the show is at its climax!

Spring is a season of colorful wildflowers, opening buds, migrating warblers, and cool, invigorating air. It is also a season of mud-wallow trails that are highly vulnerable to erosion, of pools too icy for swimming, of clouds of spray that bar photography at the largest waterfalls, of wet or icy rocks too treacherous for exploring. And beginning in late May, it is the season of black flies (see "Hazards" below).

In summer the waterfalls put on a gentler face, and their mood grows playful. This is the season when the roar of the current is muted, the pools are deliciously clear and refreshing, the sun is high and bright, the rocks are dry and warm, and the days are long and lazy. Though more spectacular in the spring, the waterfalls are more fun in the summer. And more crowded, too.

Summer visitors do have opportunities to see the mountain streams in full surge. Two or three days of rain or evening thunderstorms are enough to restore spring conditions, temporarily. The amount of runoff at any particular waterfall depends on the pattern of precipitation (thunderstorms can be highly localized), the soil moisture conditions, the local bedrock structure, and the shape of the watershed. Chart 1 shows how the volume of water in the Ellis River swelled and ebbed following some summer rains.

If you want to time a summer trip to catch the waterfalls after a rain, be sure not to confuse the weather in the mountains with the weather at home. Coastal storms, for example, can soak the Boston area without touching the White Mountains. And vice versa. During August 1988, while southern New England suffered through a serious drought, Mount Washington had over 11 inches of rain (4 inches above normal). The waterfalls were in splendid form!

In early autumn the mood of the waterfalls reflects the luxuriant hues of the foliage. Northernmost sections of the region begin donning fall outfits in early September and reach a brief peak of vivid color shortly after the equinox. The color burst moves gradually southward, like the ebbing tide of forest life that rolled in the previous spring. This is the time of year when the waterfall scenery is most dazzling in the hardwood forests at lower elevations, and at higher points with panoramic views.

By mid-October the vivid display has usually ended. The brightest leaves have dropped to the forest floor, where they form a crisp, thick carpet underfoot. More subdued tones of birch and oak leaves linger a few more weeks on the bough. Then the trees grow bare, the days grow short, the sun hangs lower in the sky (when it shines at all),

CHART 1

Hydrograph for the Ellis River
Near Jackson, NH

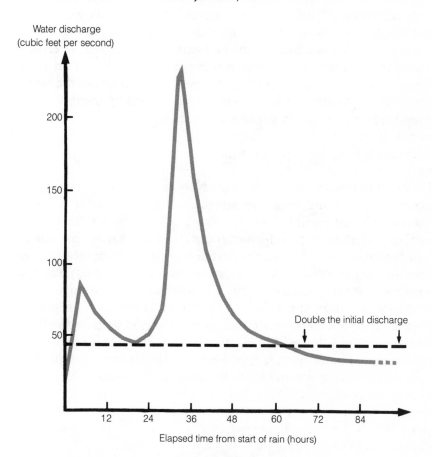

Water discharge
(cubic feet per second)

Double the initial discharge

Elapsed time from start of rain (hours)

This hydrograph shows the volume of the water flow in the Ellis River at Jackson during and after a period of summer rain. Time zero marks the onset of a moderate rainfall that caused the river to rise for four hours, beginning at 1800 hours on August 28, 1988. Then, beginning at 1700 hours on August 29, the river volume rose sharply for more than twelve hours. Over the two-day period precipitation at Pinkham Notch totaled just over two inches of rain, while 1.4 inches fell at North Conway. After peaking, the river took 29 hours to drop back to *double* its initial water volume. After 96 hours (four days) the river was back down to its initial level. We are grateful to Frank Blackey of the U. S. Geological Survey office in Bow, NH, for providing data for this graph.

and the nights are visited with hard frost. As autumn turns to winter the waterfalls become cold, gray, and rimmed with veils of ice. Their mood is more somber, and yet still beautiful.

Like the black bear, the waterfalls are usually hibernating by the winter solstice. If winter's cold arrives before deep snows, as often is the case, the waterfalls are transformed into fascinating blue-ice sculptures. Frigid currents can be heard under the winter crust or seen through windows in the ice. Huge icicles dangle from ravine walls. Gradually, snows blanket the forest and hide all but the highest and steepest waterfalls from view—while storing up the moisture to replenish the mountain streams come spring.

White Mountain Weather

With confidence we can predict that New England weather will amaze onlookers and confound forecasters. As Mark Twain put it, "There is a sumptuous variety about the New England weather that compels the stranger's admiration—and regret." All this variety has considerable significance for your waterfall trips. Afternoon weather may be completely different from morning weather. Three-day forecasts may be wrong as often as right. The weather in the mountains may be entirely unlike the weather three hours away. And in general, weather statistics are nearly useless for trip planning. In the White Mountains in July you can encounter anything from subzero wind-chills (on summit ridges) to torrid heat, and in January anything from 30 below (*before* wind-chill) to 60 above zero Fahrenheit.

Paper Birch (left), Yellow Birch, Heart-leaved White Birch

This having been said, Chart 2 presents average weather statistics for three White Mountain locations. For more timely information, call the Concord office of the National Weather Service at 1-603-225-5191. Or call the Appalachian Mountain Club information service in Pinkham Notch, at 1-603-466-2725.

Beyond this basic weather briefing a few points should be noted relating to waterfall trips in particular.

- Other things being equal, the daytime temperature drops as you gain elevation. Sunlight heats the earth's surface, which in turn warms the air. As the warm air rises, it cools by roughly 5 degrees Fahrenheit per 1000 feet of altitude.
- Waterfalls often have their own microclimates created by evaporating mists, shady forest cover, damp mosses and rocks, and cool breezes fueled by temperature differentials along the streambeds. Even on the hottest days some waterfall ravines are too chilly to encourage swimming.
- The microclimate is also affected by the exposure to the sun and the amount of adjacent open ledge. Southern slopes tend to be considerably warmer than northern slopes, and wide beds of rock can absorb enough heat to be wilting on a cool autumn day.
- Wind is often more important to your comfort than temperature. A stiff breeze on an exposed outcrop may refresh you on a hot day or chill you to the bone on a cool day. It is always a good idea to bring along a windbreaker.
- Finally, for those who enjoy quantifying conditions, tiny zipper-pull thermometers are not very accurate, but most camping-goods stores sell full-size thermometers in protective pocket-clip tubes that can be taken along on any excursion.

Hiking Tips

The most important rule of hiking is the familiar refrain: *pack out what you pack in.* Keeping the waterfalls and trails litter-free is everybody's business. An updated version of the old rule is to pack out *more than* you pack in. Rather than gripe about litter, why not pack some out and leave the forest cleaner than you found it?

CHART 2

White Mountain Weather Statistics

	Jan	Feb	Mar	Apr	May	Jun	Jul	Aug	Sept	Oct	Nov	Dec
Temperature (F)												
Mean daily high												
Mt. Washington	13.4	13.1	19.1	28.9	40.7	50.7	54.4	52.7	46.3	36.5	26.9	17.0
Pinkham Notch	25.9	27.8	34.9	46.8	60.5	69.3	73.1	71.0	64.3	54.9	40.4	28.8
Woodstock	29.5	32.5	41.1	53.9	65.6	76.0	80.5	78.7	70.7	61.4	45.4	32.2
Mean daily low												
Mt. Washington	-3.3	-3.4	4.7	15.9	28.1	38.4	42.9	41.5	34.9	24.5	13.8	1.2
Pinkham Notch	5.6	6.8	16.2	27.9	38.3	48.3	52.7	50.7	43.8	34.4	24.2	10.9
Woodstock	8.3	9.9	19.3	29.9	39.8	48.7	53.4	51.5	44.7	35.0	26.9	12.7
Mean no. days high > 90												
Mt. Washington	0	0	0	0	0	0	0	0	0	0	0	0
Pinkham Notch	0	0	0	0	0	0	0	0	0	0	0	0
Woodstock	0	0	0	0	0	2	2	2	1	0	0	0
Mean no. days low $<$ freezing												
Mt. Washington	31	28	31	28	20	7	2	3	12	23	28	31
Pinkham Notch	31	28	30	23	8	0	0	0	3	14	24	30
Woodstock	31	28	29	20	6	1	0	0	0	0	0	6
Mean no. days low $<$ zero												
Mt. Washington	18	16	11	2	0	0	0	0	0	0	4	14
Pinkham Notch	11	8	2	0	0	0	0	0	0	0	0	6
Woodstock	10	7	2	0	0	0	0	0	0	0	0	6
Record Low												
Mt. Washington	-47	-46	-38	-20	-2	8	25	20	11	-5	-20	-46

Mean

Mt. Washington	7.3	8.0	8.2	7.0	6.5	7.0	6.9	7.6	7.2	6.7	8.5	8.9
Pinkham Notch	4.0	4.8	4.8	4.2	4.4	4.8	4.8	4.5	4.4	5.1	6.5	5.6
Woodstock	3.3	3.1	3.1	3.8	4.0	3.7	4.9	3.4	3.9	3.7	4.8	3.4

Greatest, one day

Mt. Washington	4.9	10.4	4.0	8.3	4.6	6.5	7.4	5.2	5.4	7.0	6.1	8.6
Pinkham Notch	2.4	4.5	2.9	4.1	3.0	4.1	7.0	4.4	4.0	9.0	4.4	3.7
Woodstock	2.0	1.7	1.8	1.6	2.4	2.1	2.8	3.1	3.4	4.1	3.3	3.0

Snowfall, inches

Mean

Mt. Washington	39.7	40.5	42.5	29.5	10.6	1.1	0.0	0.2	1.7	11.7	30.7	42.7
Pinkham Notch	31.4	38.2	34.2	16.0	2.1	0.0	0.0	0.0	0.0	2.2	14.6	35.5
Woodstock	15.7	24.3	17.6	3.7	0.3	0.0	0.0	0.0	0.0	3.0	12.0	15.5

Maximum for month

Mt. Washington	94.6	172.8	98.0	89.3	52.2	8.1	1.1	2.5	7.8	34.4	86.6	103.7
Pinkham Notch	83.0	130.0	61.5	51.5	11.0	0.0	0.0	0.0	0.0	11.5	37.2	72.3
Woodstock	47.7	42.8	43.8	18.7	6.0	0.0	0.0	0.0	0.0	0.3	6.3	19.7

Notes:

* = melted equivalent

Mount Washington summit statistics are from National Oceanic and Atmospheric Administration, 1987 *Local Climatological Data: Mount Washington Observatory, Gorham, New Hampshire.* All figures are for 55 years of observations except snowfall, which is from 30-year table.

Pinkham Notch statistics are from National Oceanic and Atmospheric Administration, *Climate of Pinkham Notch,* 1975. All figures are for 24 years of observations.

Woodstock statistics are from U.S. Weather Bureau, *Climatological Summary, Woodstock, N.H.,* 1964. All figures are for 22 years of data.

We thank Robert Lautzenheiser, New England Meteorologist (retired) for the Weather Service, for providing these statistics. According to Mr. Lautzenheiser, differences in measurement periods have only a negligible effect, except perhaps for figures on extremes.

On a related theme, hikers should be aware that tramping feet contribute to erosion and destruction of plant life on the forest floor. We all share a responsibility to minimize the adverse effects of our presence in the forest by staying on trails wherever possible, and by being sensitive to the erosion problem when we do venture off trail. Sometimes "leaving nothing but footsteps" is leaving too much. Similarly, hikers must exercise extreme caution with fire.

Another basic precept is the old Boy Scout oath: *Be prepared.* For anything more than a very short hike it is important to have:

- comfortable, appropriate footwear that has been broken in;
- clothing suitable for weather conditions and activities;
- rain and wind gear;
- a first-aid kit;
- a map and compass;
- more than enough water or other nonalcoholic liquids (our most common regret on hikes is having along too little to drink);
- snacks;
- insect repellent and sun screen;
- an agreed-upon route, and clear plans on where to meet if the party gets separated;
- plenty of time to finish the hike and return before dark.

That may sound like a lot of preparation, but the essential items fit easily into a small day pack or a large fanny pack, and the precautions are simple enough. The effort to gather gear together will be repaid many times over if it proves to be needed just once. Also, before going on a long hike into an area that is not heavily traveled, you are wise to let someone know your plans. Then assistance can be mobilized in the unlikely event of an accident.

Yet another fundamental rule of hiking is: enjoy yourself! Allow time for resting, communing with the waterfall, studying the flora, examining the rocks, stalking the songbirds, sleuthing animal signs, and simply watching the clouds drift by. It is a proverbial shame to miss the forest for the trees; likewise, it is a shame to miss them both for want of time. To enhance your enjoyment you may wish to consult some of the nature guides listed in the bibliography (Annex C).

Finally, it should be noted that winter waterfall hikes require special equipment. At a minimum you should have layered clothing that will keep you dry and comfortable, boots with liners, snowshoes with crampon bindings, and some means to keep your drinking water from freezing.

Drinking Water

Unhappily, even the purest-looking running water in White Mountain streams is *not guaranteed safe to drink* without being treated, filtered, or boiled. The problem is microscopic organisms, and the villain is human and animal waste. One organism in particular, *Giardia lamblia*, has become a significant health hazard. When ingested it causes an extremely unpleasant intestinal disorder called giardia.

Despite a major public education campaign that has been continuing for years, people still frequently drink from White Mountain streams—especially at waterfalls where the running currents and clear pools give a false appearance that the water is spring-pure. We once approached the leader of a party of young campers at Franconia Falls to suggest that because of giardia it was not safe for the kids to be filling canteens from the stream. He replied that giardia "can't be a problem here" because there were no beaver ponds on the stream. He was wrong on two counts. First, there were large beaver ponds farther upstream that he did not know about. And second, the spread of giardia does not require beavers. We hope the youngsters were lucky enough to avoid the disease, but it would have been better not to have relied on luck.

If you do drink untreated water and come down with serious intestinal problems a week or two later, make sure your doctor tests for giardia. Otherwise you may suffer up to six weeks of distress.

Giardia is easy to avoid. First, carry enough liquids so you will not be tempted to drink from the streams. Second, be careful not to ingest stream water if you go for a swim or dunk your head. Third, use treatment tablets (Potable Aqua is a widely available brand) or a filter system (such as First Need) if you must drink stream water, as on overnight trips. But be certain to use a brand that is labeled as effective against giardia and other waterborne bacteria.

Finally, avoid contributing to the spread of giardia. Be absolutely certain when hiking or camping not to deposit human or pet wastes within 100 feet of open water (preferably 200 feet). Wastes should be buried 6 to 8 inches deep, where soil organisms for decomposition are most effective.

Other Hazards

Apart from possibly contaminated drinking water, what sorts of hazards does one face on a waterfall hike? Do people fall off cliffs? Are people mauled by bears? Poisoned by snakes? There are indeed hazards, and being aware of them can help keep your waterfall trip trouble free.

The northern mountain forests are basically benign. They harbor no poisonous snakes (any more), virtually no poison ivy (or poison oak, or poison sumac), and no disease-bearing ticks (yet). Some wild animals—such as black bear, wildcat, eastern coyote, porcupine, and even the gentle moose—are potentially dangerous at times, but they are rarely seen. No instances have been recorded in many years of unprovoked wild-animal attacks on hikers. If you chance to see wildlife, just leave it alone. Above all, don't go out of your way to bother the animals.

Insect pests, in contrast, can be extremely troublesome. The most hated is the black fly, which generally prowls for warm flesh from late May until early July. (We have run into them in isolated locations, especially at higher elevations, into August.) When at their worst, black flies are a swarming "malediction," to use Drake's apt description (1881). An early White Mountain explorer, John Josselyn, found in 1672 that "Black flies were so numerous in the country that a

Common Garter Snake

man cannot draw his breath but he will suck them in." (Quoted in King, 1868.) *Most* years, however, the black flies are no more than a nuisance that can be controlled by wearing a long-sleeved shirt, long pants tucked into socks, and bug dope. For good measure you can also carry along a net helmet and cotton gloves. Reportedly black flies don't bite through clothing, but they do have diabolical ways of sneaking in for a meal.

A much less common insect hazard is bee sting. Hives are not often found by trails, but we have experienced or seen enough stings to urge caution, especially when hiking off trail. Bee hives may be located in holes in the ground, rock crevices, old stumps, or fallen tree trunks. Being reasonably watchful will prevent most painful encounters. Individuals who experience severe bee-sting reactions must carry medication on hikes.

Judging from rescue records compiled by the New Hampshire Fish and Game Department, as well as news reports over the years, the most prevalent cause of serious injury on waterfall trips is slipping and falling. This happens most often on the trail, but serious falls also occur when individuals recklessly climb steep, dangerous ledges at the waterfalls themselves. Rescue records attribute these accidents to factors such as fatigue, intoxication, carelessness, and pre-existing medical problems.

Injuries from falling often result in broken bones. We know of only one instance of a fatality from falling during a visit to a waterfall. In October 1986, a party returning by way of Frankenstein Cliff from Arethusa Falls (see Chapter 22) was overcome by darkness on a wet, cloudy evening. One member hiked out to fetch a flashlight. On returning he fell off Frankenstein Cliff to his death.

Drownings have been more numerous. At high water, currents can be overpowering and life-threatening. A whirlpool undertow at Upper Falls of the Ammonoosuc claimed a number of victims before swimming and trespassing were prohibited by the landowners. Other drownings have occurred at swimming holes along the Pemigewasset River. Even river crossings can be dangerous in high water. Hikers have slipped and drowned while fording the notorious Dry River (Chapter 23).

One other fatality in conjunction with a waterfall trip occurred when a youth separated from his party and lost his way returning from No. 13 Falls (Chapter 15). He died of exposure before rescue teams could find him. We have not seen any record of other fatalities from exposure on waterfall hikes, but exposure (hypothermia) is certainly a serious hazard, particularly above tree-line. Most fatalities on Mount Washington have resulted from hypothermia, typically caused when hikers were caught unprepared by violent storms. Getting wet in a cold wind is a perfect recipe for rapid loss of body heat, and disaster.

To avert nearly all the major hazards, all one needs is common sense. Remember that carelessness or horseplay can spoil an otherwise wonderful outing. So if currents look at all dangerous, stay out of the water. If ledges look steep and dangerous, avoid them. If the weather is threatening, stay away from exposed ridges, and have proper gear for unexpected storms. Avoid hikes that exceed your physical condition. Keep an eye on your children. Plan your trip so you have ample time for rests to avoid fatigue, without getting caught by darkness. Don't let your party get separated deep in the backcountry.

Notably, the NH Fish and Game Department has recently begun to bring criminal charges of reckless conduct against individuals whose thoughtless behavior or intoxication necessitated rescue operations that endangered others.

Regrettably, a final hiking hazard is the risk of having valuables stolen from automobiles, particularly at isolated trailheads out of view from the road. This is not a common occurrence, but it happens enough to warrant caution against leaving valuables in your car.

Camping Information

Annex B presents a table listing all the roadside campgrounds in the White Mountain region that operate under the auspices of the United States Forest Service or the State of New Hampshire. The table also matches campgrounds to nearby waterfall trips, by chapter number. During the summer and on fall foliage weekends, these campgrounds are often full by midafternoon. If you intend to camp, it is a good idea to reach the campground around midday. A few campgrounds (as noted in Annex B) permit advanced reservations, which can be made by phoning 1-800-283-2267.

One can also spend overnight in the backcountry. The most comfortable facilities by far are the Appalachian Mountain Club huts (also listed in Annex B). Each hut offers exhilarating mountain views, air so fresh that you want to bottle it and take it home, hearty meals, and warm comradeship. In addition, by providing meals, a bed and blanket, and a roof over your head, the huts make it possible to penetrate the mountain wilderness without having to lug a full pack. You need to carry only day-hike supplies, warm clothing for the cool mountain evenings, and a sleeping bag or sheet. The huts are usually booked up well in advance. For information and reservations call the AMC at 1-603-466-2727, or write Reservations, AMC Pinkham Notch Camp, Box 298, Gorham, NH 03581.

Less luxurious are the dozens of backcountry campsites and shelters along various trails in the White Mountain National Forest. These facilities are for self-contained backpackers. If that's your style, consult the *AMC White Mountain Guide* for details about site locations. Bear in mind, too, that these facilities are available on the basis of first come, first served. There is a good chance that after slogging with a full pack all the way in to a campsite, you will find it full. If so, you have to seek a suitable and permissible tent site off in the woods.

Camping is permitted anywhere in the White Mountain National Forest *outside designated "Restricted Use Areas," or RUAs.* The RUA regulations are designed to prevent degradation of the forests along popular trails, and to help restore areas that have been damaged by overuse. Consequently, camping tends to be prohibited in precisely the places you would find most convenient for pitching a tent. Generally, RUA rules prohibit camping within a quarter-mile of designated roads, trailheads, and backcountry facilities, or within 200 feet of designated trails. At certain locations, such as Sabbaday Falls (Chapter 18) or anywhere above tree-line, camping is prohibited altogether.

These regulations are in effect from May 1 to November 1, although a few restrictions apply year-round. You can obtain detailed information on prevailing RUA regulations from the U.S. Forest Service (see Annex B). Pertinent restrictions are also posted at all trailheads. If you will be backpacking, check out the RUA restrictions and plan ahead accordingly. Incidentally, be prepared for difficulty in finding a suitable tent site, because many locations have thick underbrush, tangled timber blow-down, unsleepable slopes, or marshy soils.

Keep in mind that important conservation motives underlie the RUA rules. The same concerns imply that backpackers should be familiar with *low-impact camping* methods. The ideal today is to camp in a manner that leaves the forest looking as if no one had camped there. Formerly routine practices are now frowned upon, like creating fire circles of blackened rock, digging trenches around tents, and cutting wood for campfires. In addition, it is every camper's responsibility to deal properly with human wastes (see *Drinking Water* above), to exercise extreme vigilance with fire, and to carry out what you carry in.

Swimming Tips

It is hard for me to imagine anything more exhilarating than a dip in a crystal-clear mountain pool below a beautiful cascade on a hot summer day. Over half the waterfall trips in the book reach swimmable holes of one sort or another. But there are a few quirks about mountain pools that are worth mentioning before readers rush off into the woods with their beach towels and swimsuits.

The single most important quirk is that the water may be COLD! Even in midsummer we have measured the water temperature in some pools in the upper forties. Fahrenheit. Though the water may appear exquisitely inviting, it is a major shock to jump in. A toe-dip test can help you distinguish between water that is deliciously cold, bitingly cold, and painfully cold. In fact many people don't actually swim in most of the White Mountain pools. More often they jump in, take a few desperate strokes, and climb out before their skin gets bruised by goose bumps. How wonderful!

One does see swimmers, though. Many youngsters, for example, seem to be too hot-blooded or too numb to be discouraged by cold water. Besides, at some pools on open ledges with a southerly exposure, the water can be in the balmy mid-70-degree range, varying with the sun and recent rains. A few well-bleached waterfalls, like Lower Falls (Chapter 18) and Jackson Falls (Chapter 19), seem designed for water sport. Others, such as Bridal Veil Falls (Chapter 2) and No. 13 Falls (Chapter 15), have superb pools but very cold water. There are waterfalls in shady ravines on northern slopes that never feel the full warmth of the sun, and still others on streams that feed public water supplies, where even wading is prohibited. The trip descriptions in Part Two will help you sort out all the variations.

More seriously, there are dangers to swimming at waterfall pools. As pointed out in the *Hazards* section, strong currents during periods of high water are life-threatening, and people have been injured climbing the steep and often slippery ledges that abut many pools. Diving, too, can be dangerous because refraction and shadows make it difficult to see underwater boulders or to judge their depth. Furthermore, it is obviously foolish to play in the currents *above* the lip of a waterfall, or to get one's clothes soaking wet on a cold day miles up a mountain trail. As it says on a sign at Franconia Falls (Chapter 14): SWIM AT YOUR OWN RISK.

None of this, however, detracts from the tremendous thrill of a brisk, refreshing—and safe—jump into a shimmering mountain pool. Even people too sensible to try swimming should at least practice a few head dunks on a hot day.

Photography Tips

In his splendid book of White Mountain photography, Alan Nyiri (1987) confesses to spending nearly all his time visiting waterfalls during his first two weeks in the mountains. *Homo photographicus* is certainly a common breed at the waterfalls. Every shutter bug dreams of capturing the dynamics of the tumbling stream, the contours of the granite ledge, and the soft texture of the mosses and ferns. Waterfall photography can be tricky business, however. We are in no position to offer professional wisdom, but we do want to share a few easy-to-use tips accumulated from conversations with professional photographers in the course of working on the book. The following comments deal only with color photography, since this is by far the most popular, judging from the film inventories at White Mountain tourist shops.

Our first and best photography lesson was to bracket exposures. Light meters can be misled by glare and strong reflections off the water and wet rocks, especially when the glare is juxtaposed with dark forests and patches of deep shade. If the light meter reads bright spots, the dark zones will be underexposed. If the light meter reads dark zones, bright spots are washed out. Bracketing simply involves taking a number of frames at different exposures. You might shoot one frame at the light-meter reading, and then one or two letting in more light (slower shutter speed or larger aperture opening) or less light, as conditions warrant. This requires manual adjustments to the camera settings. Fully automatic point-and-shoot cameras cannot be manipulated this way. Bracketing greatly improves the odds of capturing your favorite shot at the proper exposure.

Regardless of the camera being used, being aware of the glare and contrast problems can come in handy. If direct sunlight makes it difficult to get a proper exposure, then you can get better shots when the problem is less severe. A light overcast is easier to work with than bright sun. On sunny days you can improve your odds by using an inexpensive polarizing filter. You can also wait for a passing cloud to cut the glare. Using a lens shade helps, too. Finally, the time of day makes a big difference in the quality of sunlight. At midday the lighting is intense and flat. Early morning or late afternoon sunlight produces far more interesting shadow patterns and colors.

A second invaluable lesson was learning to bring along a tripod (or a monopod, which is more convenient but less stable). This is worth the extra effort. At fast shutter speeds you will get sharper images using a tripod, while at slow shutter speeds a tripod makes all the difference between blur and success. It is difficult to get a crisp exposure with hand-held shots at under 1/60 second. Moreover slow shutter speeds (that is, relatively long exposures) often turn out to be what you end up using for waterfall photos. Many waterfalls are located in glens or ravines that are shaded most of the day. Lighting may be so dim that you either use a slow shutter speed or you don't take a picture. It may seem logical to use a fast film (like ASA 400) to overcome this problem, but a number of professional photographers insisted that a slower film (like ASA 64) produces better shots. Only after many disappointing rolls of slides did we follow their advice. It worked, but the slow film made long exposures—and therefore a tripod—indispensable.

A slow shutter speed is also useful for visual effect. Nearly every art photo of waterfalls that we see is shot at a very slow speed to

Black-capped Chickadee

make the currents appear streaked, thereby capturing a flavor of motion. We have read recommendations for shutter speeds of one second or more. From our own experience fairly natural effects are often achieved with a shutter speed of 1/15 to 1/30. A faster shutter freezes falling water, which in many cases ruins the effect. Furthermore setting a slow shutter speed permits you to use a smaller aperture opening (higher f-stop), which improves your depth of field. In short, attractive shots often require slow exposures. And again, this necessitates using a tripod.

A slow shutter speed does complicate matters in certain respects. For example, it is nice having people in the picture, but they usually come out blurred when photographed at 1/15-second. Similarly you will often find a breeze wafting along a cascade, setting the foliage asway. If so, the flora around the waterfalls will be blurred at slow shutter speeds.

Composition, of course, is essentially a matter of taste. At some waterfalls, however, a full view is difficult to achieve because it is not possible to back off to a proper angle without encountering obstructions in the line of vision. Another problem is that shots taken at the foot of a waterfall will foreshorten its height. This is an effective way to make a 60-foot waterfall appear insignificant.

Finally, all but the geniuses among us have to accept the fact that snapping two-dimensional, point-in-time photos will not capture the spirit of a mountain cataract. No photo album or slide show will convey the soft touch of the breeze, the faint rustle of hemlock boughs, or the pulsing rhythm of the cascade. The best way to share the experience of a waterfall trip with friends is to invite them along.

Map Legend

▄▄▄▄▄ Main road
▄▄▄▄▄ Side road
— — Jeep track, logging road or Forest Service road
▄ ▄▄ ▄ Main waterfall trail
········· Other trail
A   Appalachian Trail
AMC   Appalachian Mountain Club
✶   Waterfall, cascade
▲   Mountain summit
△   Cliff, ledge

The Connecticut
Watershed

◆

Bridal Veil Falls

CHAPTER 1

Beaver Brook Cascades

—————◆—————

Location
Kinsman Notch, on NH 112, west of North Woodstock.

Map
AMC Chocorua-Waterville Map: I-3.
DeLorme Trail Map: J-2.

Hiking Data
Distance, parking area to:
   bottom of the cascades .... 0.3 mile.
   top of the cascades..................................... 1.1 miles.
Altitude gain: 1300 feet (to altitude 3200 feet).
Difficulty: MODERATE; short, but very steep.

———————————————◆———————————————

Just after the turn of the century, loggers had reduced the vicinity of Kinsman Notch to "a wilderness of devastation," in the words of Karl Harrington (1926). Yet today the Beaver Brook Trail from the Notch to the summit of Mount Moosilauke is a virtual stairway to heaven. In less than a mile the trail climbs the equivalent of 130 stories of rock stairs, with each landing graced by lovely cascades.

The trail does have a few unheavenly features, though. First, there are some very steep stretches where the footing can be quite treacherous when the ground is wet or glazed with ice. Handrails and steps are bolted to the ledge to help you past the worst sections. Second, on the genuine stairway to the Pearly Gates, swimming would not be prohibited. Since Beaver Brook feeds a public water supply, though, visitors must keep out of the stream. Anyway, the water is too busy falling to form good pools.

A visit to the beautiful cascades on Beaver Brook can be combined

31

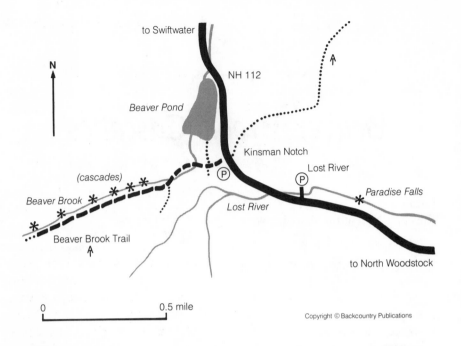

to Swiftwater

N

NH 112

Beaver Pond

Kinsman Notch

(cascades)

Lost River

Beaver Brook

Paradise Falls

Lost River

Beaver Brook Trail

to North Woodstock

0   0.5 mile

Copyright © Backcountry Publications

with a number of excellent side excursions. These include continuing up the trail to the summit of Moosilauke, finding Lost River and Paradise Falls, or stopping to admire the Indian Leap at Agassiz Basin.

The Trail

The Beaver Brook Trail begins at the height of land on NH 112 in Kinsman Notch, 6 miles west of North Woodstock center. A bright-green Appalachian Trail sign on the north side of the road marks the spot where AT trampers exit from the Kinsman Ridge Trail and begin their climb up Mount Moosilauke, en route to Georgia. There is no parking lot, but the gravel shoulder on the south side of the road has room enough for many cars.

Beginning at the Beaver Brook Trail sign by the road, the path into the woods is quite clear. The trail soon crosses the brook on an impressively sturdy footbridge, beyond which it forks. Keep left at the fork, following the white blaze. The right-hand fork leads over to Beaver Pond, where the waters of Beaver Brook pause before proceeding down the Wild Ammonoosuc River to the Connecticut.

Shortly the trail crosses a second footbridge and forks again. This time stay right. The left-hand fork leads to a shelter maintained by the Dartmouth Outing Club, the oldest college outing club in the country. A sign informs visitors that the DOC maintains 120 miles of trail, including 70 miles of the Appalachian Trail from this point south. A second sign explains the system of trail blazes. Yet another cautions hikers to "take special care at cascades to avoid tragic results." Amen.

The trail is essentially level over the first 0.3 mile, as the forks are negotiated. It then climbs and climbs and climbs alongside a nearly continuous chain of delightful cascades. After 0.8 mile the cascades taper off, but the climbing continues. For a short distance the trail stays by the brook, now just a gurgling, mossy stream. It then veers left up a small feeder stream toward the saddle between Mount Jim and Mount Blue, 1.9 miles and 2500 vertical feet from the highway. The final 1.5 miles to the Moosilauke summit climbs only 500 feet more and includes a mercifully level stretch along the rim of Jobildunk Ravine.

It is worth noting that Mount Moosilauke, first climbed in 1773, boasts one of the most beautiful (and windblown) summits in the White Mountains. Sunset watchers found accommodations on the summit as early as the 1840s. A carriage road provided easy access from Warren after 1870. These amenities are gone now, but the views remain.

The Cascades

By some counts over a dozen lovely, unnamed cascades adorn the precipitous ravine of Beaver Brook. To describe them all one by one would be tedious, but a sampler can provide a taste of what lies along the trail.

Shortly after the trail starts climbing, a set of bolted wooden steps leads up a slab ramp to the brink of a narrow chute that cuts through a deep cleft in the bedrock. Immediately above the chute is a small but very pretty ribbon cascade, and above this two more cascades can be seen awaiting your arrival. This prospect of cascades is characteristic of the trail: because the ravine is so steep, as you visit one cascade you also get a preview of the coming attractions.

Farther along the falls become more impressive. At one inviting snack stop you find a lovely cascade where the brook drops over a wall high overhead, slides down a long sloping ledge, and then drops again before disappearing over the rim of the next cascade below.

Higher, a sparkling, transparent sheet ripples across a smooth slab, while 100 feet above, bright ribbons of white pour through channels in a dark wall. At your approach the ribbons turn into beautiful falls. Continuing up a short switchback, you then encounter a sheer 80-foot drop where the stream breaks into a maze of channels as it tumbles down the fractured ledge. And so it goes, a kaleidoscope of waterfall patterns.

Depending on the water level there may be a few spots, especially higher up, where some scrambling is possible. In fact a few fine cascades higher up the ravine can be seen only by scrambling over to the brook from the trail at opportune points. But keep in mind the DOC warning sign, as well as the restriction on swimming or bathing.

Eventually the trail enters a zone of white birch with a thick undergrowth of fir. The footing changes to a long set of irregular boulder steps, and the shoulder of the ravine becomes visible above. This is where the brook changes from cascades to gurgling stream, though there is one final treat—a small horseshoe falls cut in brown ledge—at the point where the brook divides and the trail turns toward the Jim/Blue saddle.

It may be hard to imagine, but this is one long, steep climb that you will be sorry to see ending.

Bonus Falls

A half-mile east of the Beaver Brook Trail on NH 112 is the Lost River Reservation, one of the most popular natural attractions in the White Mountains since before the First World War. If you are not heading for the summit of Moosilauke after visiting the Beaver Brook cascades, there should be time to see Lost River while you're in the neighborhood. For waterfall chasers the lure of Lost River is *Paradise Falls*, and a small but extraordinary underground waterfall (once called the *Falls of Proserpine*) in a boulder cave named the Judgment Hall of Pluto.

At least an hour is required to visit Lost River gorge, and triple

Beaver Brook Cascades

that if you also take advantage of the Geology Center, Ecology Center, Nature Garden, and Ecology Trail, as well as the gift shop and cafeteria. All of these facilities are owned and maintained by the Society for the Protection of New Hampshire Forests.

The Lost River Reservation is open to the public from mid-May through mid-October from 9:00 A.M. to 5:30 P.M. For the trip through the gorge (as of 1988) there is a charge of $5.00 per adult and $2.50 per child. (For comparison, the fee was 25 cents back in 1938.) Off-season and off-hour visits are not permitted. The Lost River trail starts near the gift shop, descends 300 feet, and then climbs wooden stairs and walkways through the fascinating gorge. Overall the circuit is about 0.75 mile in length.

Paradise Falls is located near the base of the gorge. Emerging from the caverns, the stream drops over a small dike wall and then plunges over a higher wall to a large pothole pool below. The Lost River brochure claims that the falls are 35 feet high, but a 1938 pamphlet calls it 20 feet, which seems to be a more accurate figure. In any case the beauty of Paradise Falls is in its magnificent setting, not its height.

A boardwalk spur provides a head-on view of the falls from across the pool, while the main trail climbs a narrow stair to a bridge above the falls. The bird's-eye view from this bridge is especially attractive. Paradise Falls was even more exciting for early visitors, who toured the gorge in reverse. The falls greeted them as they emerged into daylight—along with the stream—after penetrating the dark, narrow caverns of the gorge.

The underground Falls of Proserpine are located farther up the gorge along one of the many side paths leading into the wonderfully shaped caves and crevasses. This particular cave (labeled Number 16) is just barely big enough for the plume of water that gushes from a hole in the roof 15 feet overhead. In fact during high water there is no room for visitors, and the cave is closed off.

Over the decades the pothole below Paradise Falls and the floor of the Judgment Hall of Pluto have both been filling with silt and gravel. Perhaps some great storm will wash out the gorge and add 10 feet to each of the falls.

On the drive between North Woodstock and Kinsman Notch one more waterfall merits a visit: *Agassiz Basin*, or Indian Leap. This is located right behind Govoni's Restaurant, 1.7 miles west of North Woodstock center. Don't use the restaurant parking lot, unless of course you are hungry.

Agassiz Basin is a small, exquisite gorge of water-sculpted granitic bedrock (actually, Kinsman quartz monzonite), with a surging 10-

foot waterfall at the head of the formation. The waters that carved the gorge also undercut a rock platform immediately below the falls, nearly forming a natural bridge above the swirling currents. It is said that Indians leapt across the 5-foot gap to prove their courage.

There is another roadside waterfall to visit if you are heading west from Kinsman Notch. *Swiftwater Falls* is located just below the long covered bridge in the village of Swiftwater, 2 miles east of the terminus of NH 112 at US 302 in Bath. Swiftwater Falls lacks the natural elegance of the other waterfalls and cascades mentioned in this chapter, but on a hot summer's day this is the one to visit. Remember to bring your swimsuit!

Historical Detour

Kinsman Notch, like other major notches in the region, was carved and smoothed by passing glacial ice sheets. Its beautiful gorges were etched within the past 15,000 years by silt-laden meltwaters of the receding glaciers. Interestingly, the discovery of the Ice Age is generally credited to Louis Agassiz, a Swiss scientist after whom Agassiz Basin is named. In 1837, Agassiz shook the scientific world with a speech outlining geological evidence that Europe's land forms had been shaped by an ancient ice sheet. On a visit to New England in 1847 Agassiz found confirming evidence of a great Ice Age. He then settled into a faculty position at Harvard, as his remarkable thesis gradually gained adherents. This required profound changes in thinking. To accept Agassiz's evidence, scholars had to reject the biblical doctrine that land forms were products of the great Deluge—and that the earth had been created only 6000 years before.

Kinsman Notch itself is named after Asa Kinsman, a pioneer who received a grant of land in Easton, NH, in the 1780s. On his way north with his wife and an ox cart laden with possessions, Kinsman took a wrong turn at Plymouth. Instead of retracing his route to reach the road through Warren, he stubbornly hacked his way through the dense forest across the notch to his homestead, assisted by two strangers recruited in the valley.

For the next century Kinsman Notch was largely bypassed by the developments that flooded the White Mountain region with tourists. Thomas Starr King, for example, wrote lavish praise of the Pemigewasset valley and Franconia Notch in 1859, but he knew nothing of what lay up "Moosehillock Brook." Neither Kinsman Notch nor even Kinsman Mountain had yet been named.

The Notch did receive at least a few visitors, however. Two boys from North Woodstock, Royal and Lyman Jackman, went fishing up that way in 1855 when Royal fell through a hole and discovered Lost River. Years later, Royal cut a footpath to the gorge, and began leading tours in 1893. Lost River and Kinsman Notch quickly gained celebrity.

The area around the Notch also gained the attention of the loggers. A very limited amount of logging had been taking place long before 1907, when timber baron George L. Johnson began building the Gordon Pond Railroad from the valley up to the Notch. A large logging camp was established at Beaver Meadow, in the heart of the Notch. Wholesale destructive cutting ensued, stimulating early conservationists to undertake an effort to save Lost River. In 1912, the newly formed Society for the Preservation of New Hampshire Forests purchased the gorge and surrounding property from the timber baron, establishing the Lost River Reservation—but not before all the virgin spruce had been removed and logging roads had been cut all the way to the top of the Beaver Brook cascades.

In 1916 the Notch road was upgraded for autos. In that same year the major logging operations in the vicinity ceased. Kinsman Notch then began its slow readjustment from "waste land" to the beautiful natural attraction we enjoy today.

CHAPTER 2

Bridal Veil Falls

◆

Location
Off NH 116, south of Franconia village.

Map
AMC Franconia Map: H-4.
DeLorme Trail Map: F-4.

Hiking Data
Distance, parking area to falls: 2.5 miles.
Altitude gain: 1100 feet (to altitude 2100 feet).
Difficulty: On the light side of MODERATE.

◆

Does the name Bridal Veil Falls sound familiar? If so, you may be thinking of the famous waterfall in Yosemite valley, where Bridalveil Creek plunges dramatically more than 600 feet to join the Merced River. Its humble namesake on the western flank of Cannon Mountain in Franconia simply channels Coppermine Brook down 80 feet of drops and slides.

Nature, though, does not equate size with pleasure. A wildflower can be as engaging as a sequoia; a warbler can outsing a condor; and a waterfall can brighten your smile without requiring that you wrench your neck to see the top. For awesome scale, book a flight to California. But for a delightful waterfall, complete with fine pools, a hanging garden, and a long waterslide, hike up the Coppermine Trail to New Hampshire's version of Bridal Veil Falls.

One indication of the appeal of Bridal Veil Falls is the character of the trail. The 5-mile round trip leads to no summits or panoramic overviews. The trailhead is located off a quiet country road rather than a major traffic artery, with no roadside sign to publicize the hike. And yet the trail is very well used. Coppermine Trail is exclusively for hikers out to visit a beautiful waterfall; many return over and over again to enjoy Bridal Veil Falls.

The Trail to the Falls

To reach the trail, head south from Franconia village along NH 116, passing the Franconia airport and a zone of development properties. At the airport one can arrange a short flight over the mountains in a small plane, or a quiet soar in a glider! Just under 3.5 miles from Franconia village, Coppermine Road leads left into a private development. This is your turn. If you are approaching from the south, the turn will be on the right, 0.75 mile past the Easton–Franconia town line.

Park on the shoulder of Coppermine Road along the 100-yard stretch between NH 116 and the sign that warns "No Parking Beyond This Point: Tow-away Zone." On foot now, head straight up the dirt road, passing a left turn into the Coppermine Village development. Shortly thereafter the trail forks to the left, as indicated clearly by an arrow beneath a U.S. Forest Service "hiker" sign. After passing a logged clearing, the trail forks right and follows an old road into the woods. This second fork is marked only by yellow paint blazes on the trees. From here on, however, the route is very straightforward and well marked.

The old road ascends steadily but gently through mixed forest. Among the many trees and wildflowers by the trail, watch for samples of striped maple. Apart from the white birch, this slender understory tree has the most attractive bark in the woods: a pattern of meandering vertical stripes of light green and white. Moose allegedly find its smooth skin especially succulent, giving the tree the nickname "moosewood." The broad three-lobed leaves of the striped maple are also quite striking.

Nearly 1.25 miles from the highway, the murmur of rushing water begins to mix with the rush of the breeze. Soon, Coppermine Brook appears below a large shelf on the right. The shelf, which has been used as a campsite, hides a small cascade and a pretty pool. Camping is also permitted just below the main waterfall at a Forest Service shelter, though there is little flat terrain in the vicinity of that site.

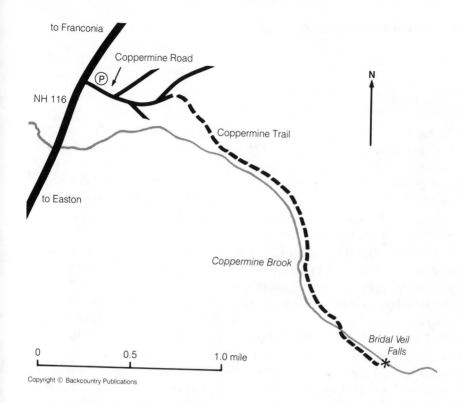

to Franconia

Coppermine Road

NH 116

to Easton

(P)

N

Coppermine Trail

Coppermine Brook

Bridal Veil
Falls

0   0.5   1.0 mile

Copyright © Backcountry Publications

A few minutes farther along, the trail touches the edge of the brook
at a point where the old road once crossed a wide slab of bedrock
to the far side of the streambed. The trail, though, remains on the
north bank here, climbing a bit more steeply and never straying far
from the brook. At mile 2.2 the trail finally crosses to the south bank
of the brook by a wooden footbridge. A sign indicates that the Forest
Service shelter is only 0.1 mile away and the falls 0.2 mile; that first
tenth is a long one, however. Still, you quickly reach the shelter, from
which point the falls can be seen ahead through the trees. For its
final leg the trail dips to recross the brook, and ends at the edge of
a pool below the falls.

Years ago the Coppermine Trail was maintained as a ski trail,
which linked to other winter runs on the northern flank of Cannon
Mountain. Today one can still ski in nearly to the falls, but the
Coppermine Trail is an almost unrelieved ascent. In addition, the last
mile has pitches that are steep enough to require a lot of tiring
herringbone to climb on cross-country skis—and narrow enough to
be somewhat tricky to descend.

The Falls

Bridal Veil Falls has a split personality. Viewed from the base, a feathery cascade is seen in the background, but the predominant feature is a broad, smooth bank of granite ledge that slopes down to a green pool at the foot of the falls. As the brook spreads across the face of the ledge to slide to the pool, the water takes on the appearance of a thin, rippled veil, like fine gossamer. It is this feature for which the waterfall was named.

A wholly different view of the falls is obtained from a wide terrace at the top of the waterslide. The terrace can be reached with only moderate difficulty by climbing carefully up the left corner of the lower ledge, or by a steep footpath in the woods farther to the left. Cupped in the terrace slabs is a second pool that is not visible from the base of the waterslide. This second pool is larger and lovelier than the one below. From the terrace the waterslide is now almost an incidental feature. Dominating the view is a 50-foot wall with a wide, overhanging midriff bulge. At the back corner of the wall, the brook plunges across the mouth of a large, dark cave situated beneath the bulge, and then cascades down steep, angled ledges to the terrace pool.

To the left of these upper falls the wall is dry and bare, except for closely cropped lichen. In contrast, the high wall to the right of the falls has a northern exposure that keeps the surface damp and shady. Here a garden of wildflowers, grasses, and ferns clings to cracks and sloping surfaces. Yellow birch trees line the brow of the wall.

Except when the sun is at its midsummer peak, the high wall behind the terrace keeps the upper falls and most of the terrace pool in the shade. Also, on sunny days the temperature differential between the cold currents and the sunny ledges alongside the pool causes a cool breeze to drift across the terrace. The combination of shade, breeze, and cold water is enough to chill a hiker's ardor for swimming. Still, some hardy visitors can't resist the temptation to play in the inviting pools—a temptation heightened by the waterslide feeding into the bottom pool. The last dozen feet of the slide are negotiable if you take care to stay in the smooth part of the channel.

There is temptation for scramblers, as well, namely to find a way up and around the high wall to the top of the waterfall. This is indeed possible, but the route is quite steep (we have seen technical rock climbers on sections of the cliff). For extra adventure you can search for two obscure small waterfalls lying higher up Coppermine Brook. The two are identified as *Holden Falls* and *Noble Falls* ("well above Bridal Veil Falls") in old photos that appear in Welch's *History of Franconia* (1973).

Historical Detour

Whereas the Franconia Notch side of Cannon Mountain has been a major tourist attraction since the first rough road from Plymouth was cut in the early nineteenth century, the western slope along the Ham Branch of the Gale River was more hospitable to the settlers and industries that built the town of Franconia. The first settlement in 1774—when the area was known as Morristown—was located just south of the present Coppermine trailhead.

The settlers turned immediately to farming, supplemented by good fishing, plus intermittent (and quickly depleted) supplies of bear, deer, moose, beaver, and other wildlife for hunting and trapping. In addition, maple sugar could be obtained from the trees, and meager rations of edible plants and berries could be gathered, in season. Yet it took rugged, determined people to struggle against the wilderness in a land of long, bitter winters and glacial-till soil that never was suited for plowing.

Ernest Poole provides a marvelous description of the life of the Ham Branch hill farmers in his book, *The Great White Hills of New Hampshire* (1946). The pioneers cleared the wild forests for land on which to build their sturdy homes, plant their corn and potatoes, and graze their sheep and cattle. The women gardened, cooked, raised the children, and kept the family stocked with necessities such as candles, clothes, soap, baskets, blankets, and hooked rugs.

Dismayed by paying taxes to finance the coastal barons who controlled the state's plutocratic government, the farming communities west of the mountains actually chose to secede from New Hampshire and join the independent republic of Vermont after the Revolutionary War. George Washington settled this early tax revolt in 1782 by negotiating with the counties along the east bank of the Connecticut

The slide below Bridal Veil Falls

River to rejoin New Hampshire, while Vermont remained independent until 1791.

Although grouped into small communities, the hill farmers remained virtually self-sufficient well into the nineteenth century. No one would hop into the family buggy for a trip to town to buy milk or to purchase a new coat. Apart from the trading activities at the annual county fair market, the farmers' only regular commercial contacts were with itinerant peddlers who offered such commodities as hardware, tobacco, medicines (including 120-proof alcohol and opium gum) and dyes, as well as ballads and devious swindles.

Farming continued to be a major industry in the hill country west of Cannon and Kinsman mountains until about the time of the Civil War. The farm economy languished when the Erie Canal brought competition from the lush soils of the Midwest, and the war lured farmers' sons to the battlefields and the cities.

For the town of Franconia, though, the primary source of prosperity was iron. Directly across the valley northwest of the Coppermine trailhead is Ore Hill, where a large vein of iron ore was discovered in the early 1800s. It was said to be the richest ore in the country at the time. The ore was dug from shafts blasted out of solid granite and gneiss, and then transported 3 miles to foundries in town. The New Hampshire Iron Factory Company, incorporated in 1805, built a large iron works in town, complete with a blast furnace and forge. Another similar facility was built a few years later by the Haverhill and Franconia Iron Works Company. Today, it is hard to envision that Franconia was once a flourishing center for iron smelting!

Iron was not the only ore extracted in the region. You may have guessed by now that Coppermine Brook was named for a copper mine. The mine was worked during the years before the Civil War, when a shaft penetrated 100 feet below the brook. Other copper mines dotted the surrounding hills. Like the iron ore, the copper ore was smelted and forged in the Franconia foundries. The hills were also mined for lead, zinc, silver, tin, cobalt, garnet, quartz, and mica.

And gold. Although the iron works were put out of business by 1865 as a result of competition from the Midwest, that year John Henry Allen dug up gold-bearing quartz crystals near Lisbon, across Ore Hill. A brief gold boom ensued. No major veins were ever discovered, but diligent prospectors continue to find placer deposits and small nuggets in rivers of the area to this day (Foley, 1980).

The region's most enduring treasure, though, is undoubtedly the beauty of the mountains, the forests, and the watercourses. Treasure-seekers will find an especially nice nugget up at the end of the Coppermine Trail.

CHAPTER 3

Waterfalls at the Gate of the Notch

Silver and Flume Cascades
Beecher and Pearl Cascades
Gibbs Falls

◆

Location
Head of Crawford Notch on US 302.

Map
AMC Mount Washington Range Map: G-7.
DeLorme Trail Map: E-9.

◆

Andrew Jackson was in Washington awaiting his inauguration when the first hotel opened its doors at the Gate of the Notch—the height of land separating the Ammonoosuc and Saco watersheds. America then was on a binge of economic growth, geographic expansion, and demographic mobility. The frontier was luring pioneers westward, while "the White Mountain Notch" was attracting more and more tourists to its spectacular cliffs and beautiful cascades. One unique attraction at the Gate of the Notch was the path that Abel and Ethan Allen Crawford had blazed to the summit ridge of the Presidential Range in 1819.

The growing traffic of tourists and teamsters prompted the Crawfords to open a hotel near the Crawford Path trailhead in early 1829. In 1852 the Crawfords began building a larger hotel next door, but

46

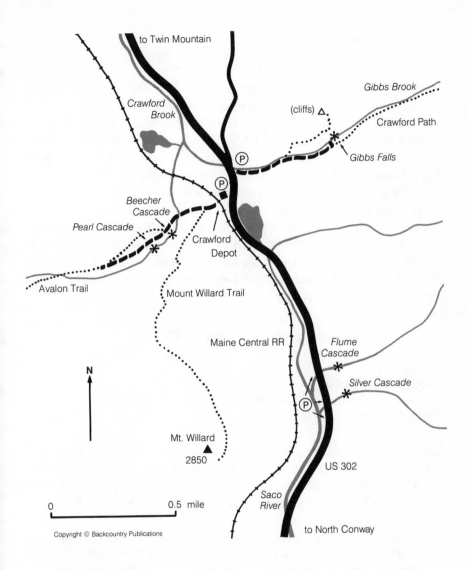

to Twin Mountain

Crawford
Brook

Gibbs Brook

(cliffs) △

Crawford Path

Gibbs Falls

Beecher
Cascade

Pearl Cascade

Crawford
Depot

Avalon Trail

Mount Willard Trail

N

Maine Central RR

Flume
Cascade

Silver Cascade

Mt. Willard
▲
2850

US 302

0   0.5 mile

Saco
River

to North Conway

Copyright © Backcountry Publications

financial difficulties forced them to sell out to J. L. Gibb, after whom Gibbs Falls and Gibbs Brook are named. Gibb completed construction of the larger hotel, later called Crawford House. One of his early guests, Reverend Henry Ward Beecher, popularized a nearby cascade that now bears his name.

The cascades at the Gate of the Notch were major drawing cards for nineteenth-century tourists. Silver and Flume cascades, hardly a mile down the road, ranked among the most famous of the White Mountain waterfalls. Gibbs Falls and Beecher Cascade were popular as short strolls for the gentlemen in bowler hats and ladies in hooped skirts who frequented the luxurious Crawford House hotel.

Today the Notch is named for the Crawfords. Crawford House is gone, having burned down in 1977. Yet visitors still flock to the Gate of the Notch to view the cliffs and waterfalls, and to hike up Crawford Path. Somehow the waterfalls seem less remarkable now than they must have appeared 150 years ago when the first hotels were literally carved out of the wilderness. Many travelers zoom past Silver and Flume cascades at 55 miles per hour with hardly a glance, and the smaller cascades are often treated by hikers in the same category as a convenient boulder—a spot for a quick rest en route to the summits. But the falls at the Gate of the Notch are always charming, often very pretty, and fun to explore.

Silver and Flume Cascades

Hiking Data
Distance from parking area to falls: Roadside.
Altitude gain: Zero (altitude 1700 feet).
Difficulty: EASY.

Side by side on the eastern wall of Crawford Notch, the Silver and Flume cascades feed the nascent Saco River less than a mile below the Gate of the Notch. Early writers were exceedingly impressed by the scenery here. Benjamin Willey, for instance, wrote in 1856 that:

> The sublime and awful grandeur of the Notch baffles all description. . . . [N]o words can tell the emotions of the soul, as it looks upwards and views the almost perpendicular precipices which line the narrow space. . . .

Willey claimed that the cascades were "unrivalled in their romantic beauty," and that Silver Cascade, in particular, was to be considered "one of the most beautiful in the world." His florid description is rather difficult for a modern reader to stomach.

Other nineteenth-century accounts described Silver Cascade as a long, graceful silver braid gliding down the sheer cliffs of Mount Jackson. (The mountain is named after geologist Charles T. Jackson

Silver Cascade in autumn

not President Andrew Jackson.) The cascade was variously reported to be anywhere from 300 feet to 1000 feet in height. When the railroad opened in 1875, Silver Cascade was called its "brightest jewel." Observation cars provided passengers with full views from across the valley—views sullied only by smoke and cinders blown back from the locomotive. Ladies wore veils to keep the grit out of their eyes.

More objectively, the Silver Cascade is attractive, but far from world-class. To reach the falls, park at either of the two large lots on the west side of US 302, 0.9 mile below Crawford Depot. The foot of the cascade is just across the highway. From the roadside Silver Cascade appears as a long, slender ribbon that glides down the ledges, dropping from one inclined terrace to the next, and finally rushing through a bedrock chute under the highway.

To see more of the cascade or simply to get a better look, take a short hike up the rocky ledge to visit the lower falls. With some effort, plus a dash of daring, you can transform a two-minute "Oh-my-isn't-that-nice" waterfall into an enjoyable adventure.

The same comment applies even more strongly to Flume Cascade. This meager waterfall is hardly worth a bother if you only want a quick view from the roadside, but a careful scramble up the ledge can be rewarding. The prettiest sections are higher up the headwall and barely noticeable from the road.

Dr. Timothy Dwight, president of Yale, had the right idea when he visited Flume Cascade back in 1797:

> ... alighting from our horses, [we] walked up the acclivity, per-haps a furlong. The stream fell from a height of 240–250 ft. over three precipices. . . . It is impossible for a brook of this size [puny!] to be modelled into more diversified or delightful forms.

Beecher and Pearl Cascades

Hiking Data
Distance from parking area to Pearl Cascade: 0.4 mile.
Altitude gain: 200 feet (to altitude 2100 feet).
Difficulty: EASY.

The name Beecher's Cascades (plural) originally referred to a series of small waterfalls and pools along Crawford Brook, which descends from Mount Field and runs past Crawford Depot to join the Am-monoosuc River at Bretton Woods. Nowadays the name Beecher Cascade (singular) applies to a particular waterfall near the bottom of the hill. Just upstream, a second small waterfall now bears the name Pearl Cascade, while the rest of the lot are unnamed.

Reverend Henry Ward Beecher, the famous abolitionist pastor of the Plymouth Church in Brooklyn, was the first to describe in writing this "avenue of cascades." A guest at Crawford House in 1856, Beecher had fled the city to escape his hay fever. He later spent every summer in the fresh mountain air, and drew hundreds of worshippers to Sunday sermons held under a great tent at Twin Mountain. Beecher was a fine writer as well as a powerful speaker. In one delightful passage from his essay on the cascades, he captured perfectly the sensual thrill of swimming in a mountain pool:

> This was my pool. It waited for me. How deliciously it opened its flood to my coming. It rushed up to every pore, and sheeted my skin with an aqueous covering, prepared in the mountain water-looms. Ah, the coldness;—every drop was molten hail. It was the very brother of ice.

To reach Beecher's Cascades (plural), park at the Crawford Depot, where the AMC runs an information center. The Avalon Trail begins across the railroad tracks behind the depot. After 100 yards the Mount Willard Trail splits off left and climbs to the brink of spectacular cliffs at the head of the Notch. This trail, a former carriage road constructed by Thomas Crawford in 1846, is perhaps the best short hike in all of the White Mountains.

The Avalon Trail continues ahead, soon crossing Crawford Brook. About 200 feet farther on a side loop trail forks left to the cascades. After a brief, easy climb you reach a small sign pointing left to a spur path for Beecher Cascade. The spur emerges on a weathered ledge of pink-brown Conway granite. The stream funnels through a narrow channel and tumbles 30 feet down a chute into a rock-bound glen. If the water is not running high adept scramblers can climb down into the glen or explore up the ledges and waterslides above the cascade.

Continuing up the loop trail 0.1 mile, you come to another sign on the left pointing to an overlook below Pearl Cascade. Except when the water level is unusually low, Pearl Cascade is quite beautiful. A 20-foot-high cone of bubbling water dances down a mossy headwall at the back of a small gorge. The stream then traverses the gorge in a series of short steps before pouring over a 4-foot ledge into a broad pool. If it's a hot day, take off your shoes and wade right up the waterfall—taking care, of course, to gain secure footing on wet surfaces.

Above Pearl Cascade the path loops up to rejoin the Avalon Trail. This junction is clearly posted. More of Beecher's Cascades (plural again) appear farther up the trail. About 0.2 mile above the junction, where the trail once more touches the brook, is an unnamed twin of (the) Beecher Cascade. In some ways this one is even more attractive than the original down below. It has wider "sittin' rocks," and a splendid rifle-barrel-shaped pool at the foot of the chute. Without going into detail, suffice it to say that enterprising explorers will find other fine, nameless cascades along the streambed.

Beyond the cascades the Avalon Trail climbs steeply to Mount Avalon (at 1.8 miles) and Mount Field (2.8 miles). Unless you are bagging 4000-footers, Mount Avalon is an excellent destination—a rocky spur with panoramic views of the Notch and the Presidentials, plus good blueberries in August.

Gibbs Falls

Hiking Data
Distance from parking area to falls: 0.4 mile.
Altitude gain: 400 feet (to altitude 2300 feet).
Difficulty: EASY, but a bit of a climb.

Gibbs Falls is a short walk up Crawford Path, which begins directly across the highway from the AMC hostel beside Crawford Depot. There is trail parking on both the east and west sides of US 302. Since Crawford Path is heavily used as a route to the summit ridge of the Presidentials (2.9 miles), as well as access to Mizpah Springs Hut (2.7 miles), the parking lots are often jammed.

The hike to the falls is a straight climb at a steady, moderate grade. Until late summer, the soft murmur of Gibbs Brook is accompanied by robins and Swainson's thrushes singing from the thick forest. At 0.2 mile a side trail diverges left. This side trail crosses the brook and climbs steeply for 0.5 mile to an overlook atop Crawford cliffs. Another 0.2 mile along Crawford Path, you reach the short spur down to Gibbs Falls.

The spur descends into a lovely glen, shaded by virgin spruce and yellow birch. The waterfall—a sparkling silver feather ornament on a dark gray wall of ancient gneiss—lies at the back of the glen, across a small triangular pool lined with smooth stones. Starting from ledges hidden behind a protruding knob above the pool, Gibbs Falls drops about 35 feet. The brook first sweeps through a cleft wrapped around the base of the knob, and then spills down the wall to the pool.

Even on the hottest summer day the glen is refreshingly cool. (On one of our trips the temperature at the depot was nearly 100 degrees, but the glen was a comfy 75 degrees.) The ledges just above the falls are open and sunny, though, with fine channels and small pools in which to swim—including one incredible chest-deep, lime-green pothole bathtub. This pool can make your day!

The problem is reaching the upper ledges. When dry, the channel to the right of the falls has just enough toeholds for an experienced friction climber to scramble up, exiting onto the knob in front of the first spruce tree. More prudent visitors, though, will prefer to hike up Crawford Path another 100 yards to a point where the ledges can be seen through the woods *below*. You can then pick your way down through the prickly spruce and fallen logs.

One word of warning: if you are continuing up Crawford Path to Mount Washington, don't linger too long at the falls. The summit is still 7.8 miles (and nearly 4000 vertical feet) away.

Historical Detour

Along with exhilarating scenery the road through the Gate of the Notch also has a fascinating history.

Although there are indications that Crawford Notch was used by the Indians to transport captives during the French and Indian War, discovery of the notch is generally dated to 1771. That year Timothy Nash of Lancaster spotted the narrow gap in the wall of mountains to the southeast while out hunting moose on Cherry Mountain. He worked his way through the dense forest wilderness to explore the gap, and continued all the way down the Saco to the coast.

Nash reported his discovery to New Hampshire Governor Wentworth, who immediately recognized the enormous value of a direct route from the Maine coast to the upper Connecticut valley. He asked Nash to prove his claim by leading a horse from Lancaster to Portsmouth. With a friend, Benjamin Sawyer, Nash succeeded in dragging a horse down the notch, even though doing so required using a rope cradle to ease the poor animal over steep slabs at the Gate. Nash and Sawyer were rewarded with a 2000-acre grant of land just above the notch and, some say, a bag of gold.

One condition of the land grant was that a road be built. By 1785 a rough route had been constructed, but very badly. The route zigzagged across the river no less than thirty-two times, and was so steep in sections that horses and wagons still had to be pulled up with ropes. The first trade commodity to pass along the road was a barrel of rum that Captain Eleazer Rosebrook, of Guildhall, Vermont, hauled from Portland to Lancaster to exchange for a barrel of tobacco.

In 1792, the same enterprising captain moved with his family to a small log cabin at what is now Fabyan. He cleared over 100 acres of wilderness for a farm, and began taking in travelers. The log cabin had first been occupied by Rosebrook's son-in-law, Abel Crawford. But that pioneering settler soon moved 12 miles down the notch, "rather than to be crowded by neighbors." There he welcomed travelers, guided hikers, and later built the first hostel in the notch, which became known as Mount Crawford House.

The attrocious condition of the original road led in 1803 to the incorporation of a turnpike authority, which rerouted and improved the road at a cost of $40,000, raised by a lottery. The new road cut the Portland to Lancaster round trip from twenty-two days to as few as eight. Thus, despite travelers' having to pay turnpike tolls, the volume of traffic through the notch grew rapidly. Even in winter, half-mile-long lines of horse-drawn sleighs laden with pork, cheese, butter, lard, and other freight could be seen fighting the bitter northwest winds on their way up the turnpike.

For nearly three quarters of a century, the turnpike was the main thoroughfare through the mountains. The turnpike's importance waned—and tolls disappeared—only after the Portland & Ogdensburg Railroad (later the Maine Central) pushed a rail line through from Bartlett to Fabyan in 1875. The track up the side wall of the notch was in operation for over a century before succumbing to the internal-combustion engine and modernization of the highway.

Because the glaciers left the Gate of the Notch only 26 feet wide, the railroad builders blasted a *second* gate just to the west. Sweetser (1887) mentioned a proposal to span the two gates "by a double triumphal arch" commemorating victory over the mountain barrier, first by ice and later by man. The true victory is that the beauty of the Gate managed to survive the onslaught.

CHAPTER 4

The Ammonoosuc Ravine Trail

---◆---

Location
From Mount Washington Cog Railway base station.

Map
AMC Mount Washington Range Map: F-8/9.
DeLorme Trail Map: D-10.

Hiking Data
Distance, hikers' parking area to:
Gem Pool .... 2.1 miles.
The Gorge .... 2.3 miles.
Upper ledges .... 2.5 miles.
Altitude Gain: 2000 feet to the ledges (altitude 4500 feet).
Difficulty: MODERATE to Gem Pool; STRENUOUS beyond.

---◆---

When the AMC opened the Ammonoosuc Ravine Trail in 1915, the trail was intended to provide visitors to Lakes-of-the-Clouds Hut and hikers along Crawford Path with a badly needed escape route from the alpine zone during the frequent bouts of extreme weather. Indeed the early AMC trail descriptions were written from the hut down; it was presumed that trampers would be discouraged from ascending the steep, rough grade in the vicinity of the Gorge except in an emergency.

But the normally restrained AMC guidebook also mentioned that the trail had "spectacular" views, a "sensational" 600-foot water-slide, "precipitous" ledges, and "a beautiful pool at the foot of some

55

fine little cascades" (AMC, 1922). In addition, the new trail provided one of the shortest routes to the summit of Mount Washington. Little wonder, then, that the emergency escape route turned into one of the most heavily used paths in the Whites.

The Trail to the Falls

The usual route to the Cog Railway Base Station (also called Marshfield) is by the Base Road that runs north from US 302 at Fabyan. Alternatively, one can take the Mount Clinton Road north from US 302 at Crawford Depot, intercepting the Base Road 1.5 miles below Marshfield. Driving along the Base Road, you will see a U.S. Forest Service parking lot for hikers on the right 0.5 mile before the Cog Railway station. If you are willing to pay a moderate fee to save 0.5 mile and 200 vertical feet of fairly dull walking, continue on and park at the Base Station. There, you will have excellent mountain views (on a clear day), a close look at the fabled Mount Washington Cog Railway, and access to the facilities. After seeing the noisy locomotive billow gritty black smoke about milling crowds of tourists at the Base Station, you will be happy to proceed up the mountain on foot.

From the Base Station parking lot, walk up to the complex of buildings and head into the woods behind the cabins on the right. A sign behind the Cog Railway Museum points the way, or you can climb the steps next to the gift shop. If you choose to park at the free hikers' lot, the trail proceeds through the woods, crosses a brook, and by-passes the Base Station. The two approaches merge 1 mile from the hikers' lot (0.3 mile above the Base Station). Continuing up the south bank of the Ammonoosuc, the gradient is steady but moderate. The footing, however, is rough and uneven much of the way.

The river here has the appearance of a typical tumbling stream, dotted with small pools and strewn with rocks. Streams on the far side of the Presidential range drain enormous glacial bowls and therefore tend to flow strongly much of the year. In contrast the streams on the western slopes did not benefit from glacial excavation. They have carved steep V-shaped ravines that generate a high spring runoff but less water volume later in the season. The shade of the narrow ravine encourages a rich growth of moss, sorrel, and fern beneath the boreal forest.

Near the top of this lower stretch of trail the steep headwall of the Ammonoosuc ravine comes into view at points where snow slides and heavy rains have mowed down swaths of timber. At 1.4 miles from the Base Station (2.1 miles from the free parking) the trail crosses the Ammonoosuc—now just a small stream—at the foot of Gem Pool and the first cascade. This idyllic scene is a good place to rest, because the trail immediately becomes very steep, climbing 1000 vertical feet in the next 0.4 mile. If you like scaling long flights of stairs, you should enjoy the next leg of the hike. And if not, just plod on step by step, pausing for frequent sips of water. Your effort will be amply rewarded.

The side path over to the Gorge is on the right 0.2 mile above the pool (though it feels farther). Don't be fooled by dead-end side paths tramped down by wishful thinkers who felt they had reached the Gorge path. The correct path is marked by a carved wooden sign placed on a tree at head level, where it will not be noticed by hikers who are busy watching their footing. Fortunately the side path itself is easy to spot.

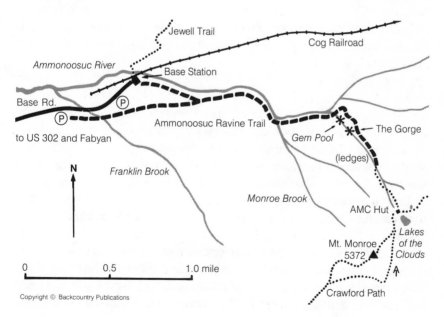

The main trail continues steeply up the ravine headwall. Soon you are scrambling up slabs of bedrock instead of dirty boulder steps. At one point a rock ramp leads to the edge of a precipitous drop down to the Gorge. As the trail flattens out, it reaches the first of the upper ledges, with superb views to the west. On a clear day you can see all the way across to the dark ridge of the Adirondack Mountains in New York.

As the ledges broaden out, the trail crosses back over the Ammonoosuc, now just a pretty rivulet cascading over high rock walls. The trail then passes into stunted evergreen forest and turns left to follow the course of the stream up the ledges. Looming above, the massive rock-pile cone of Mount Washington appears deceptively near at hand.

Although the waterfall excursion ends at the ledges, the trail continues up to Lakes-of-the-Clouds Hut, 0.6 mile beyond the stream crossing at the ledges. At the hut you can rest, have a snack, buy a souvenir T-shirt, and decide whether to push on farther. The summit of Mount Washington, with its buildings, crowds, parking lot, and rail terminal, is still a stiff hike of 1.4 miles and 1200 vertical feet. Those continuing toward the summit can make a long loop by returning to the Base Station via the Jewell Trail to the north. An excellent alternative hike is the jaunt up to the craggy summit of Mount Monroe, just south of the hut.

The Falls

Curiously, the three sets of waterfalls along the Ammonoosuc Ravine Trail have no proper names. Yet each is distinctively beautiful.

Gem Pool, just before the trail steepens, might well be the pool you see when you close your eyes to daydream about mountain streams. Its clear, shallow waters form a perfect crystal fan, bound in banks of ancient rock. The handle of the fan is a silvery cascade that emerges from the forest through a narrow chute carved in the ravine wall.

Lying in a shady hollow that opens toward the northwest, Gem Pool gets little direct sunlight. Also, the pool often harbors a fair supply of black flies, making it difficult to linger too long in its grace. Fortunately, though, there is a lot more to see farther up the trail.

The Gorge is one of the finest waterfall spectacles in the White Mountains. Here the river, a sparkling ribbon of water, completes a 600-foot tumble in a long series of bold leaps down the lofty headwall of the ravine (only a portion of which is visible from the rocky rampart at the Gorge). The cascade terminates with a straight plunge into the corner of a dark pool at the base of the Gorge's sheer walls of weathered schist. From the left a small side stream mimics the main cascade, tumbling down its own narrow channel of the headwall to join the Ammonoosuc at the pool. If the rocks are dry you can scramble down to the poolside to inspect the Gorge and the talus pile that dams the stream's outlet in low water.

One feature contributing to the spectacle is that you get a very intimate view of the Gorge from atop the crag opposite the falls. It is like looking at a splendid work of architecture from a third-story window across a narrow street—with the glistening pool serving admirably as the street. Don't miss it, especially if there has recently been rain.

The hike's third waterfall formation is less clearly demarcated. It begins where the trail crosses the stream at the upper ledges and continues for about 0.3 mile. Here, the pint-sized stream teams up with rugged, crystal-embedded schist and quartzite ledges to form a long, variegated series of thin falls, waterslides, and cascades. Add in bracing mountain air, warm sunlight bathing the smooth rock, and panoramic vistas, and you have a captivating spot for a hiker's picnic!

At the ledges the water flow is highly variable. During dry spells the upper cascades can slow to a trickle. But the ledges themselves are ever beautiful. And unlike the confined conditions in the ravine below, the ledges offer room to explore.

Historical Detour

The name *Ammonoosuc* is derived from the Abnaki Indian word for "fish-place." To the early settlers this name was quite appropriate; the river provided a bounty of trout and salmon, as well as a favorite hunting ground. Ethan Allen Crawford is reported to have pulled 600 to 700 pounds of trout and salmon out of the river each year to serve to his family and guests. Today the river below Marshfield

The Gorge after a summer thunder storm

remains a favorite spot for anglers. Recent years have even seen the return of the salmon as a result of successful pollution-control efforts and stocking by the state Fish and Game Department.

The value of the Ammonoosuc Ravine as an emergency exit from the alpine zone at Lakes of the Clouds (then called Blue Pond) was evident almost as soon as Abel Crawford cleared the first path from Crawford Notch to the summit ridge in 1819. In her *History of the White Mountains*, Lucy Crawford describes how two "gentlemen from Boston" were forced down what they called "Escape Glen" to retreat from a storm in 1823. One nearly lost his life when a tree root came loose at the top of a 50-foot precipice. Two years later the noted biologist William Oakes also fled down "Amanoosuc" ravine, which he referred to as "the most villainous break-neck route."

Another climber cited by Lucy Crawford wrote in 1825 of the fearsome weather encountered above the tree-line:

> I have experienced gales in the Gulf Stream, tempests off Cape Hatteras, tornadoes in the West Indies, and been surrounded by water spouts in the Gulf of Mexico, but I never saw anything more furious or dreadful than this.

One of the earliest recorded fatalities among White Mountain climbers occurred on an emergency retreat down the Ammonoosuc Ravine. In October 1851, the son of an English member of Parliament died trying to escape from snow and high winds that he encountered during a hike up Crawford Path.

It is surprising, then, that no formal route down the ravine was established until the AMC opened both the trail and the Lakes-of-the-Clouds Hut in 1915. This is especially so considering that Ethan Allen Crawford cut a path up what is now the Base Road all the way back in 1823. This road provided a means of ascending Mount Washington—essentially establishing the Cog Railway route—that was more protected than the Crawford Path. The latter continued to be popular, though, and the new path was on the wrong side of the summit to provide a quick exit when storms struck the ridge.

One early hiker to ascend the route from the Base Road was Sylvester Marsh, a Campton native who made a fortune in meat packing in Chicago. His climb in 1852 inspired the idea of building a Cog Railway to the summit. Marsh convinced the New Hampshire legislature to grant a charter in 1858. Construction was then delayed by the Civil War, but the line was completed and opened to the public in 1869. A small hotel was established at Marshfield station, which lodged logging crews during the winter months. For nearly fifty more years hikers climbed alongside the railbed, and the waterfalls of Ammonoosuc Ravine continued to be neglected.

Bonus Falls of the Ammonoosuc

Between Marshfield and the Zealand Campground (on US 302) the picturesque Ammonoosuc River is graced with long stretches of rapids, etched exposures of fine granite, beautiful pools, small cascades, and two excellent waterfalls that were once major attractions in their own right.

The *Upper Falls of the Ammonoosuc*, beside the Base Road 2.3 miles from US 302 (no sign post), is a strong candidate for the most beautiful formation in the whole region. But it is on private land and posted: "Notice and Warning to the Public: No Trespassing, No Swimming." Here the river has chiseled the fine-grained granite with a dazzling composition of potholes, grottoes, and curved walls, including a unique underwater arch. The clear waters surge down a smooth chute and leap into a deep pothole about 20 feet in diameter. According to one forest ranger a number of people drowned here,

Mountain Ash

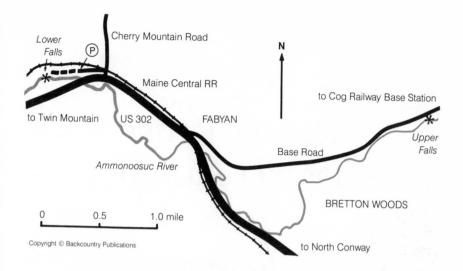

Lower
Falls Ⓟ

Cherry Mountain Road

N

Maine Central RR

to Cog Railway Base Station

to Twin Mountain US 302 FABYAN

Upper
Falls

Base Road

Ammonoosuc River

BRETTON WOODS

0 0.5 1.0 mile

Copyright © Backcountry Publications

to North Conway

before swimming was prohibited, when pinned underwater by powerful whirlpool currents beneath the falls.

The *Lower Falls of the Ammonoosuc* is reached by turning north off US 302 onto the Old Cherry Mountain Road, 0.9 mile west of the Base Road, and 1.4 miles east of Zealand Road. There is a sign for the falls, but you need keen eyes to spot it. A large parking area is located at the end of a paved road on your left immediately after the turn off US 302 (before the railroad tracks). Hiking along the dirt road at the end of the parking area, you will find the river sandy and shallow at first. Only 0.1 mile from the parking area the current quickens. Large boulders appear in the riverbed, and then smooth reddish-brown ledges mark the top of the falls. Access is easiest at the foot of the falls, 100 yards farther down the road.

At Lower Falls the river glides down a long, broad channel of gently sloped granite shelves, deeply undercutting a granite wall that is jointed like fine masonry. Though the biggest single drop in the river is not more than 3 feet high, the overall effect is quite beautiful. Because of the shallows above the falls and the broad, sunny ledges, the water temperature here is much less frigid than farther upstream. On the other hand the water is also less clear, and the ledges tend to be slippery.

Moses Sweetser, writing in 1887, warned tourists to stay away from Lower Falls because a nearby sawmill ruined the view. This early case of overdevelopment has long since disappeared, so tourists today are warned not to miss this easy side trip.

CHAPTER 5

Cascade Ravine
(Mount Adams)

◆

Location
From Bowman, on US 2 on the west side of Randolph.

Map
AMC Mount Washington Map: 9-E.
DeLorme Trail Map: 10-B.

Hiking Data
Distance, parking area to:
First Cascade .... 2.5 miles.
Second Cascade .... 2.7 miles.
Altitude gain: 1500 feet to the Second Cascade (altitude 3000 feet).
Difficulty: MODERATE, but the last mile is rough.

◆

Cascade Ravine is a narrow cut on the steep northwest shoulder of Mount Adams, separating the tongue of Israel Ridge from the broad massif of Nowell Ridge. Cascade Brook dashes down the ravine to join Castle Brook and form the Israel River. Both the ravine and the brook take their name from a long string of cascades that line a band of exposed ledges tucked in high virgin forests midway up the mountain flank.

The Israel Ridge Path to the cascades was cut in 1892 by J. Rayner Edmands, a researcher at the Harvard Observatory and an early president of the Appalachian Mountain Club. He was also the premier trail-builder of the Presidential range. In addition to the Israel Ridge Path up Mount Adams, Edmands established the Gulfside Trail along the summit ridge; the Randolph Path to the saddle (now Edmands Col) between Mount Adams and Mount Jefferson; the Edmands Path up what is now Mount Eisenhower; the Link trail that slabs up the northern slopes, connecting all of the trails out of Randolph; and the West Side Trail around Mount Washington's summit cone. Much of this work was done largely at his own expense.

Edmands had explored Cascade Ravine in 1868 while still a student at the Massachusetts Institute of Technology. Later he devoted special efforts to helping others enjoy the ravine and its attractive cascades. Although the cascades were already accessible as early as 1880 by a long spur off Lowe's Path, Edmands chose the Israel Ridge Path up Cascade Ravine as his very first trail project. At the foot of the Second Cascade he constructed Cascade Camp, with one cabin for the ladies and one for the gentlemen, along with a set of scenic trails that became known as the "pleasure paths in Cascade Ravine." One of these paths climbed along the brook past six cascades in the vicinity of Cascade Camp. Edmands also routed his Link trail past the cascades, providing a well-graded route from the old Ravine House in Randolph, a favorite stopover for visiting mountaineers.

The cabins at the Second Cascade were highly popular until they were swept away by floods and slides unleashed by a severe storm in November 1927. Hardly a decade later the pleasure paths of Cascade Ravine were obliterated by the Great Hurricane of 1938, which closed 700 miles of trails throughout the White Mountains.

Today only the First Cascade and Second Cascade remain acces-

Young Male Moose

sible by trail. Even these cascades, which saw a lot of traffic around the turn of the century, are infrequently visited. Cascades three through six can be reached only by a rough bushwhack. The pleasure path has not been restored.

The Trail to the Cascades

The hike begins on the Castle trail from Bowman, a tiny settlement where US 2 edges the Boston and Maine railroad track 1 mile west of Lowe's Store, and 4.3 miles east of the junction with NH 115 at Jefferson Highlands. A small "hiker" sign on the south side of US 2 marks the turn-off. There is also a trailhead sign for the Castle Trail beside the gravel parking area between US 2 and the railroad track.

After checking to make sure your car lights are off (a step we once forgot!), walk across the tracks and follow the right-hand gravel driveway, which has a wonderful view of the twin ravines and the Castellated Ridge up to Mount Jefferson. The ravine on the right is Castle Ravine; that on the left is Cascade Ravine, your objective.

The Castle Trail quickly turns off the driveway and enters the woods. The property owners have posted very conspicuous signs to make sure that you spot the turn. In about 100 yards the trail passes into the national forest and soon crosses a powerline clearing. The Israel River is just past the clearing. The trail follows the river a short distance before crossing (at mile 0.4). In high water the crossing is quite tricky to manage with dry feet.

The Castle Trail climbs gradually through the hardwood forest by an old logging road to a fork (mile 1.3) where the Israel Ridge Path begins. The river runs parallel to the logging road out of view. Listen, though, for the rush of the Israel Rapids off to the left about 0.2 mile after the initial river crossing. There is no path down to the river here, but this lovely run of small cascades and pools is well worth a short detour. In its trail guide the Randolph Mountaineering Club commends the rapids for trout fishing and picnicking.

From the trail junction the Israel Ridge Path splits off to the left on another logging road and soon recrosses the river. If there has been much recent rain, this second crossing may require wading. After an extended heat wave had been broken by thundershowers in August 1988, the water was a bone-chilling 49 degrees Fahrenheit

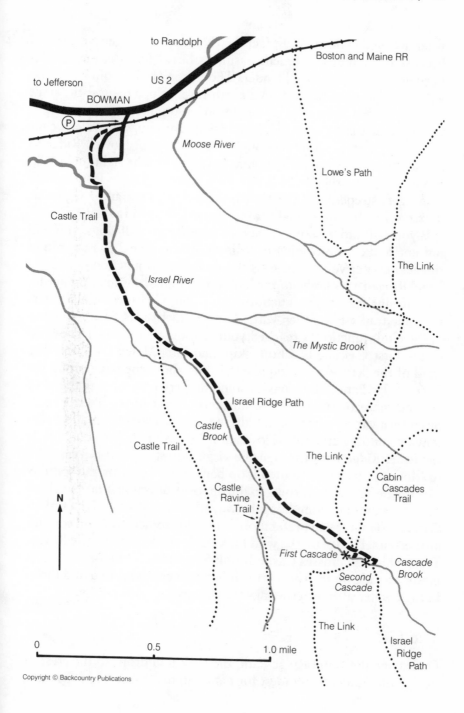

to Randolph

Boston and Maine RR

to Jefferson

US 2

BOWMAN

Ⓟ

Moose River

Lowe's Path

Castle Trail

The Link

Israel River

The Mystic Brook

Israel Ridge Path

Castle Brook

Castle Trail

The Link

Cabin Cascades Trail

Castle Ravine Trail

N

First Cascade

Second Cascade

Cascade Brook

The Link

Israel Ridge Path

0   0.5   1.0 mile

Copyright © Backcountry Publications

when we waded through. In fact the river here never gets very warm because of its high catchment basin, its heavy forest cover, and its northern exposure. Betty Flanders Thompson (1958) points out that a gradient of just 5 degrees on a north-facing slope reduces the sun's intensity to the equivalent of conditions 300 miles farther north.

On the east bank now, the Israel Ridge Path hugs the river's edge for a short distance and then angles up the foot of Nowell Ridge to a junction where the Castle Ravine Trail forks to the right (mile 1.7). From this point the Israel Ridge Path enters Cascade Ravine. The climb gets steeper, and the path becomes narrower and rougher as it ascends high on the flank of the sharp V-shaped ravine.

If you fall into a hiking trance on sustained uphill slogs, you will not notice the Link coming in from the left at mile 2.5. But around the next corner you won't miss the well-marked junction where the Israel Ridge Path climbs to the left and the Link continues on ahead. A confusing sign at the junction, "To Cabin-Cascades Trail," refers to a side trail a few dozen yards up the Israel Ridge Path.

Once this junction is reached your work is nearly done. The head of the First Cascade is a hop, skip, and jump down the Link. The head of the Second Cascade just 0.2 mile above the junction up the Israel Ridge Path, which passes some slippery ledges along the way.

The maze of trails on the northern apron of the Presidentials provides a variety of attractive alternatives to a simple up-and-back-down-again day trip to the cascades. For example you can follow the Israel Ridge Path through the virgin forest beyond the cascades to Mount Jefferson, and then loop back to Bowman by the spectacular Castle Trail. Or, turning in the opposite direction, you can climb Mount Adams and loop home by way of Lowe's Path and the Cabin-Cascades Trail. If you prefer more brookside scenery you can contour around Israel Ridge on the wild Link path and descend Castle Ravine Trail. This trail crosses Castle Brook four times, and passes a small, pretty cascade on the short stretch between crossings two and three. In high water all four crossings require getting your feet wet.

The Cascades

On leaving the Israel Ridge Path, the Link trail drops to the crest of the First Cascade, the boldest formation in the ravine. Here Cascade

Brook tumbles out from a thick cloak of forest, rushes over a narrow rim where the trail crosses, and bounds down a long flight of giant bedrock steps totaling roughly 100 feet in height. The view across the ravine from the top of cascade ledge is as fresh and unspoiled as the cool breeze that drifts down the bed of the brook.

From top to bottom the pitch of the cascade is about 45 degrees, but each individual step is a steep drop. This means that the bottom of the cascade is hidden from view, and it isn't easy to scramble down the ledge. With a bit of pluck, a few rock-climbing moves, and a considerable amount of caution, it is possible to clamber down the eastern (near) corner of the ledge. It is unfortunate that the scramble is so treacherous, because the loveliest cascades are at the base of the formation.

The Second Cascade runs down another long, broad slab of ledge. This one slopes much less steeply, and lacks the staircase plunges that characterize the First Cascade. Consequently, the Second Cascade is not as lofty or as dramatic as the First, but it is a much friendlier place to stop for a fig bar, to bask in the sun, and to explore. With little difficulty one can scramble from the narrow crossing at the top of the cascade all the way to the small pool at the bottom, where Cascade Camp was located. The cascade itself tumbles past large boulders below the trail crossing, and then slides down the corner of the long ledge below a rocky bank hedged with small birch, mountain ash, spruce, and fir.

The Second Cascade is high enough up the ravine to offer an excellent view out to the northwest. From the ledge one can see across Israel Ridge to Jefferson and across to the Pliny Range. This is also a good place to admire the bedrock. At this altitude the rock consists of interbedded quartzite and schist, both metamorphic descendants of ancient seabed sediments. Curved pressure patterns are clearly visible, along with veins of minerals such as mica, garnet, and silli-manite. This tough, weathered rock becomes very slippery when wet.

To reach the Second Cascade it is not necessary to stay on the Israel Ridge Path to where it crosses the brook. In fact the easiest access is to step out onto the shoulder of the broad ledge when it is first seen off to the right, just before the point where the trail mounts a bare slab of rock set with spikes (showing that there used to be wooden steps bolted to the rock).

Boulders at the top of Second Cascade

Cascades three through six, which once were reached by Edmands' Pleasure Path, have returned to a state of wild splendor. They are crowded closely by dense forests, strewn with timber felled by decades of storms and carpeted with thick beds of lush, fragile moss. Unless and until the old Pleasure Path is restored, these upper cascades will remain inaccessible to all but experienced and well-prepared bushwhackers. If you continue up the Israel Ridge Path, however, you can catch a glimpse of the top cascade. About 0.6 mile and 900 feet above the Second Cascade you can look across the ravine and see in the distance a silvery plume dashing grandly down the dark facade of the remote headwall.

Historical Detour

The Israel River forms at the confluence of Cascade Brook and Castle Brook. The Indians' name for this river was some variation of Siwoog-a-nac, or Singrawac. These names have been translated to mean "a place where we return in the spring" or "foaming stream with white rock." Either interpretation makes clear that the Indians considered the river to be a place of great beauty. The English renamed the river for a pioneer named Israel Glines, who visited the region to hunt and trap along its banks sometime before 1750.

Prior to the end of the French and Indian War in 1763 there were no settlements in the north country. Yet legend has it that in 1759 nine men met their doom somewhere up in a deep ravine at the head of the Israel River—where, it is said, they may have concealed a silver statue of the Virgin Mary weighing as much as eight pounds.

The legend is well grounded in historical facts, which are recounted in Solon Colby's *Indian History*. In September 1759, two British officers who had been sent to Saint Francis, Quebec, to request neutrality of the Indians were imprisoned and turned over to the French. In response, the angry General Jeffery Amherst issued orders to a company of two hundred elite fighters led by Major Robert Rogers to punish the Indians for their maltreatment of the emissaries and to inflict revenge for many years of Indian raids.

Although spotted and pursued, Rogers' Rangers succeeded in taking the Indian village at Saint Francis by surprise in a dawn raid. The raiders killed dozens of Indians and destroyed the village—

wherein they found hundreds of poles bearing white scalps. Among the buildings destroyed was an elaborately decorated chapel. Before burning the chapel the raiders cleaned it of valuables, including the silver icon. It is said that by raiding this chapel the rangers brought on themselves a curse that haunted their return to British territory.

Evading both French and Indian forces on their tail, the retreating rangers detoured toward the Connecticut River. With supplies running low and the weather deteriorating, the company split up into small groups. Along the way some men died of starvation and some of exposure, while other rangers were overtaken by pursuing Indians. One group of nine men—the group with the silver statue—planned to follow the Israel River and escape through Jefferson Notch. According to Colby, they were never seen again, though their rusted muskets and rotting knapsacks were later found along the banks of the Israel River. Over the years many objects stolen from the church at Saint Francis have been found at various locations around northern Vermont, but the icon of the Virgin Mary was never seen again.

Some of the details omitted by history have been filled in by legend. A deceitful Indian guide, it is said, misled the company bearing the silver statue. He brought them high up the Israel River into a ravine where he poisoned the leader with a rattlesnake fang. The other men scattered and perished in the early winter snow. By some accounts one man managed to reach a settlement, where he told the story of his comrades' fate and revealed that the silver statue lay hidden in a cave, high in the unmapped ravine.

The raid on Saint Francis and its aftermath are all the more tragic because the decisive battle in the French and Indian War had already been fought and won when Rogers' Rangers fell on the Indian village. On the very day that orders were issued for Rogers to proceed north, the British forces under General James Wolfe were defeating the French at Quebec.

Even if a silver statue does lie buried in Cascade Ravine it is not likely ever to be found, unless some future landslide happens to unearth the cache. Until that day, however, the silver cascades themselves are a treasure we all can enjoy.

CHAPTER 6

Pond Brook Falls

$\blacklozenge$

Location
Nash Stream valley, north of Stark (via NH 110).

Map
USGS Percy Quadrangle.

Hiking Data
Distance, parking area to falls: 0.1 mile.
Altitude gain: 100 feet (to altitude 1500 feet).
Difficulty: EASY.

$\blacklozenge$

If certain European financiers had not decided to liquidate some corporate assets, this waterfall trip might have remained a north-country secret. Therein lies a tale.

When work on this book was beginning I asked a friend from the north country to pick his favorite White Mountain waterfall. His response was quite unexpected: "The cascades off Nash Stream. Wonderful place!" I had never heard of it. "Not many people have," he explained, "and it's hard to find unless you know where to look." He was vague on the directions: a crude footpath up a side stream north of Percy Peaks.

A few weeks later, in mid-August, I hiked up Percy Peaks with a visitor from Boston. I promised him that the mountain's immense granite dome would be bursting with juicy blueberries. The views would be splendid. And, I added, we could explore a wonderful waterfall nearby. The hike went according to plan, but our exploration of side streams north of Percy Peaks turned up only muck and briars. My waterfall notebook sums it up concisely: "Nope." Further investigation revealed that none of the guidebooks, old or new, mentioned any such cascades or falls off Nash Stream. Nor was any waterfall shown on any maps. Surely we hadn't missed much.

Then a second friend identified the same spot as her favorite White Mountain waterfall. She was reluctant to elaborate, because she did not want the secret publicized. Anyhow, she pointed out, the waterfall did not belong in this book because the property was private timberland.

Enter the financiers. Since the turn of the century the Nash Stream watershed had been owned and logged by timber companies. The most recent owner was Diamond International, which in turn was acquired by Generale Occidental, a European conglomerate. In 1987 the corporate financiers concluded that the Diamond properties were worth more in cash than in trees. Consequently, in May 1988, over 67,000 acres of Diamond forestlands in northern New England were sold to Rancourt Associates, a land developer. Gravely concerned conservation groups and public officials quickly organized a scheme for public acquisition of 45,000 acres of prime recreation land including the Nash Stream watershed. (More on this below.)

Since the Nash Stream lands were about to become a public reserve, the elusive waterfall regained the list of prospects to be explored. A bit of map detective work revealed that the most likely location for the waterfall was on Pond Brook, a feeder stream draining four ponds cupped in a high valley between Long and Whitcomb mountains

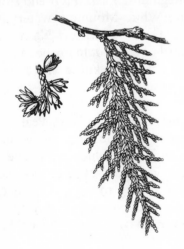

Northern White Cedar

(obviously not household names). On my initial venture I had not driven far enough north of Percy Peaks. A second trip, though, revealed a backcountry bonanza.

The Route to the Cascades

From Groveton follow NH 110 east for 2 miles through the winding valley of the Upper Ammonoosuc River to a left (north) turn onto Emerson Road. After 1.25 miles Emerson Road crosses the river and turns sharply to the right. When the road turns right a second time at an intersection 2.2 miles from NH 110, you turn left (north) instead. This turn takes you onto a logging road that penetrates a dozen miles up the remote Nash Stream valley. The surface is rough dirt and gravel, but the road is generally passable after the spring mud season ends.

At 2.8 miles along the Nash Stream Road, you will pass the trailhead for the hike up Percy Peaks. Prior to 1989, the only marking for the trailhead was a large rock overgrown with vegetation. Now a signpost marks the beginning of the trail.

The climb up north Percy Peak is just over 2 miles long by the Notch Trail, with some steep and slippery stretches along the way. The West Side variation becomes especially treacherous when wet. The summit offers a spectacular panorama of the north country, with excellent views south across the Pilot Range to Mount Washington. Consult the AMC guide for a detailed trail description.

Beyond the Percy Peaks trailhead the logging road continues north through the narrow valley, passing forests in various stages of regeneration. This mixed habitat is excellent birding territory. Our visit seemed to coincide with an abundance of yellow-shafted flickers. Other visitors have reported numerous hawks and falcons, perhaps feasting on scrumptious flickers.

If you stop alongside Nash Stream to birdwatch or to explore, you may notice that the banks are stony and denuded of soil. In May 1969—after a hard winter with more than 7 feet of snow accumulation—meltwater and rain burst a dam that held back 240 acres of Nash Bog Pond. It is said that a 20-foot-high wall of water surged downstream to Groveton, scouring everything in its path. The scars remain visible today.

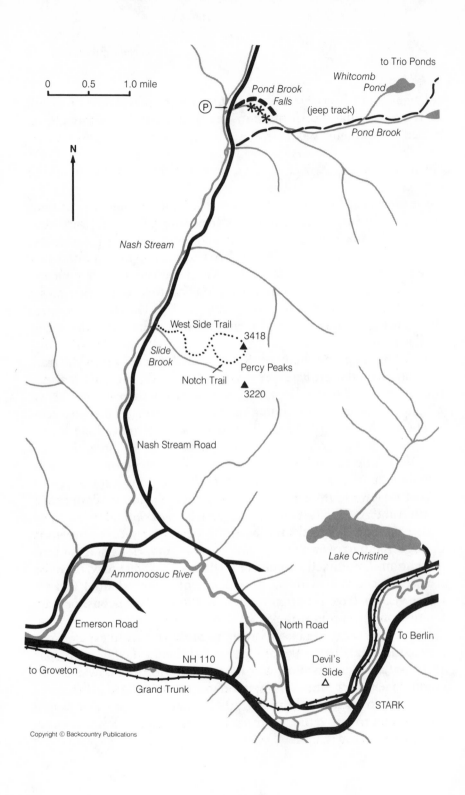

to Trio Ponds

Whitcomb Pond

Pond Brook Falls

(jeep track)

Pond Brook

0   0.5   1.0 mile

N

Nash Stream

West Side Trail

3418

Slide Brook

Percy Peaks

Notch Trail

3220

Nash Stream Road

Lake Christine

Ammonoosuc River

Emerson Road

North Road

To Berlin

to Groveton

NH 110

Devil's Slide

Grand Trunk

STARK

Copyright © Backcountry Publications

At mile 4.2 (measured from the turn off of Emerson Road) a dirt track diverges up a ridge to the right. This rugged jeep track leads to Little Bog Pond and Trio Ponds. It is *not* passable in standard vehicles. At mile 4.8 Nash Stream Road crosses a culvert over Pond Brook. Park just before the culvert on either side of the road, taking care to leave room for logging trucks.

A crude footpath follows the side of the brook, but it is easier to walk up the main road 30 yards beyond the culvert and turn right (east) up an old logging track. A field of brush and slash beside the track is a playground for sparrows and wrens. Where the track veers left at 0.1 mile, take the path that continues ahead into the woods. The path makes a soft right turn and soon reaches the foot of the lower cascades.

As a detour, consider driving a few miles out of your way to see the village of Stark. Dwarfing the picturesque hamlet is Devil's Slide, a massive ledge rising nearly 800 feet above the constricted valley of the Upper Ammonoosuc River. During World War II Stark was the site of a German prisoner-of-war camp, an interesting account of which can be found in the recent book *Stark Decency*, by Allen Koop. Today it is best known for its annual fiddler's festival.

The Waterfall

A "wonderful place," my friend said. Take him at his word. Pond Brook collects the waters of numerous feeder streams and four remote trout ponds that cover more than 120 acres of highland shelf. On exiting its mountain vale the brook tumbles and slides down a long corridor of granite ledge, creating a fascinating tapestry of cascades and small waterfalls.

The initial view you get of the waterfall is merely a pleasant teaser. The path first reaches a minor cascade pouring through a sluice at the back of a pothole pool, churning the tea-colored waters to a white foam. By scrambling up one tier of granite blocks, you reach a small waterslide terminating in another sparkling pool, where the brook undercuts a large table rock to form a low, dark grotto.

One tier higher the falls change character entirely. The brook spreads out and crisscrosses an angular banked ledge 75 feet in width and triple that in length. The granite is fashioned with assorted

Bruce Bolnick at Pond Brook Falls

scoops, dips, ridges, and flakes. In spots the rock itself ripples under a glassy liquid veil. On one side of the ledge a long "ski jump" contour sweeps down from the forest crest. The inner edge of the ski jump drops off abruptly, forming an unusual lateral water curtain in the middle of the broad ledge. Though the polished granite is not steep—it inclines about 25 degrees—the surface is quite slippery when wet, so caution is required when exploring the formation.

Climbing farther to the top of the ski jump ledge, you will reach a marvelous water plume that actually spouts above the horizontal. Higher still, a lacy curtain of water drapes across the mouth of a deep cavern. Capping the display are waterfalls draped over large angular blocks of granite. Surely these falls were meant for frolicking woodland elves.

The path to the waterfall runs up through the woods all the way to the top, allowing one to explore without scaling slick granite ramps and tall boulders. The upper ledges offer secure perches from which to enjoy the view across Nash Stream valley to the long ridge of Stratford Mountain and the 3701-foot summit of Sugarloaf Mountain.

Above the topmost falls the gradient of Pond Brook eases, and the ledge narrows. Spruce, birch, and maple trees press against the banks. If you are curious to explore upstream, Little Bog Pond is 2 miles and 500 vertical feet farther on. You can hike on the jeep track much of the way. The trout will be waiting for you, and perhaps a few moose as well.

Our visit to Pond Brook Falls took place in late August on a day when the forecast called for sunny weather and highs around 70 degrees. It turned out to be cloudy and 49 degrees. In better weather the open ledges get plenty of sun to encourage visitors to test the chilly pools, showers, and slides.

Historical Detour

> The narrow valley of Nash's Stream is cloven through this rugged and desolate region. . . . The character of the view in this direction is wild and primeval, the mountain forests being as yet unbroken by tilled clearings or roads, and no vestige of civilization is visible.
>
> —*Moses Sweetser, 1887*

While settlement and development spread quickly along the Connecticut River valley after the French and Indian War, only a trickle of migration reached the isolated town of Percy (later Stark), which was incorporated in 1795. For three generations the quiet village remained the domain of remote hill farms and small local mills.

The town's quiet isolation ended when the Atlantic & St. Lawrence

Railroad ran its Portland-to-Montreal trunk line through the valley in 1852. (The following year the Grand Trunk Railroad took over the line.) Stark was transformed into a railroad boom town, and heavy logging began consuming the neighboring forests. Sweetser's description of the view north from Percy Peak, quoted above, indicates that the remote kingdom of spruce and pine along Nash Stream did not succumb quickly to the woodsman's axe, but these forests were not long to remain "wild and primeval."

Shortly after Sweetser climbed Percy Peaks, the era of the great log drives reached the north country. (See Chapter 7). Like other backcountry watercourses Nash Stream became a spring thoroughfare for the winter's harvest of softwood logs. According to Robert Pike in *Tall Trees, Tough Men*, the Nash Stream valley was logged initially by the Odell Manufacturing Company, a predecessor of the Groveton Paper Company. Later the Groveton operations were acquired by Diamond, which retained the land until 1988.

As modern forestry practices evolved after the turn of the century the timber companies proved to be capable stewards of the northern woodlands. John Porterfield explains in a recent *New Hampshire Spirit* article (January/February 1989) that "paper company ownership of the land meant stability." Indeed he describes the Nash Stream "wildlands" as "untamed, defiant of the 20th century realities south of the notches"—echoing Sweetser's words a hundred years earlier.

Because Nash Stream was still untamed, its sale in May 1988, along with the other Diamond timberlands, produced an anguished outcry of concern. Conservation groups and public agencies had been negotiating with Diamond to acquire the Nash Stream property, but they were outhustled and outbid by Rancourt Associates, who offered over $19 million for 67,000 acres of forestland—far more than the land's appraised value. When Rancourt announced that all but 2,000 acres would be auctioned off that September, subdivision and development seemed imminent, and more threatening to public recreation than the destructive logging that occurred back around the turn of the century elsewhere in the White Mountains.

Even politicians disinclined to accept government interference in private markets joined hands with conservationists to protect Nash Stream. Senator Warren Rudman introduced legislation in Congress raising the threat of federal eminent domain. Governor John Sununu worked to arrange state funding for land purchases, while pressing Rancourt to reach an accommodation.

An expensive bargain was struck. The state of New Hampshire purchased 45,000 acres for $12.75 million, of which $7.65 million would come from the state's Land Conservation Investment Fund and the balance from the federal purchase of a conservation easement to the land. Interim financing was provided by the Society for the Protection of New Hampshire Forests, a pioneer in preserving the state's natural treasures, and by the Nature Conservancy.

Part of the cost will be recovered through a lease of the gravel and timber rights. This means that forest harvests and gravel mining will continue in the Nash Stream valley. Still, the public achieved the single most important purchase of recreational forestland since the north-country wilderness was sold to private interests more than a century ago. On October 27, 1988, the title changed hands.

We all enjoy happy endings, but the Nash Stream acquisition is not the end of the saga. Faced with a combination of take-over threats and rising development values for timberlands, edgy corporate managers are likely to place other large tracts of timberland on the auction block in the future. As one executive explained to the *Boston Globe* (September 14, 1988), "The MBAs come into the paper companies and say we've got to make the assets perform." A concerted and sustained effort will be needed to ensure that the public interest in forest recreation land is expressed effectively in the market.

Back in 1832 the town of Percy was renamed Stark in honor of General John Stark, the hero of Bunker Hill and the Battle of Bennington. It was General Stark who uttered New Hampshire's state motto: "Live free or die." In a way, the state's purchase of the Nash Stream watershed extends the principle to the great wildlands and forests of the north country.

CHAPTER 7

Beaver Brook Falls

◆

Location
On NH 145, just northwest of Colebrook.

Map
USGS Dixville Quadrangle.

Hiking Data
Distance, parking area to falls: Roadside.
Altitude gain: zero (altitude 1200 feet).
Difficulty: EASY.

◆

The main tourist centers of the White Mountains are concentrated to the south of US 2, which runs from Lancaster through Gorham. The entire White Mountain National Forest lies to the south of NH 110, which runs from Groveton to Berlin. But in terms of both tradition and at least some geology books, the White Mountain region extends up through the vast timberlands of northern New Hampshire.

The mountains of the far north are quite different from the great peaks in the tourist centers to the south. Summits are generally rounded and wooded, and few points north of the Nash Stream headlands (see Chapter 6) exceed 3000 feet. Even by these modest northland standards the low hills above the Connecticut River valley outside Colebrook are hardly more than bumps on the map. This is not a setting where one would expect to find a major waterfall, any more than one would expect the sparsely populated north country to field a baseball team to compete with the Red Sox. Yet Beaver Brook Falls matches up well against the major-league waterfalls of the higher White Mountains. And it is conveniently located alongside one of the few paved roads in the district.

To avoid confusion it is important to distinguish our present subject, Beaver Brook Falls in Colebrook, from the Beaver Brook Cascades covered in Chapter 1. There are at least five Beaver Brooks scattered throughout the state, so it is not entirely coincidental that two important waterfalls share the Beaver label.

Judging from the frequent use of this name, it would appear that the pioneer settlers were far more impressed with the beaver than with other common denizens of the mountain streambeds, such as black flies, bullfrogs, or kingfishers. (Although one obscure waterfall is named Muscanigra, after the black fly; see Chapter 29.) This is no surprise, considering how important the cute rodent was to early inhabitants of the north woods. The beaver supplied meat, clothing, barter pelts, and medicines to the Indians. Early settlers so prized the pelt that they hunted the poor *Castor canadensis* nearly to extermination in the region. Only in recent decades has the beaver returned in significant numbers. Today, the animal is valued for its ecological contributions more than its fur. Beaver ponds regulate the water flow in mountain streams and create excellent habitat for a variety of wildlife. But when beavers move too close to human activity, their dedication to cutting trees and building ponds can be a terrific nuisance. There was even a train wreck in Vermont a few years back that was blamed on a beaver pond undermining the railbed.

Along with the moose, the beaver is a symbol of the north woods.

Beaver

So it is fitting that Beaver Brook Falls provides a handy excuse for waterfall seekers to visit the north country. To make the most of the long drive, a trip to the falls can be combined with a visit to Quebec Province (to practice your French), a canoe trip on the Connecticut Lakes, or a tour of Dixville Notch State Park. The Dixville side trip is described briefly below, because each wall of the notch hosts an attractive waterfall.

The Falls

The town of Colebrook is located 36 miles north of Lancaster on US 3, 10 miles below the Forty-Fifth Parallel (the halfway point between the Equator and the North Pole) and 11 miles from the international border crossing at Beecher Falls, VT.

To reach Beaver Brook Falls (heading north), stay on US 3 for one block beyond the junction with NH 26, Colebrook's main intersection. Then turn right onto NH 145, which is marked with a large sign for Stewartstown and Clarksville, and a small sign for the waterfall. Route 145 winds through the outskirts of town, with fine views to the high pyramid of Vermont's Mount Monadnock across the Connecticut River. The road then enters the shallow valley of Beaver Brook and reaches the waterfall 2.5 miles from US 3. Truly, you can't miss it. There is a large sign on the right saying "Beaver Brook Falls Scenic Area," a conspicuous pullout on either side of the road for parking, and a splendid view of the falls directly across a broad, terraced lawn.

Flanked by tall evergreen spires that climb the valley wall, Beaver Brook dashes down more than seven stories of dark ledge. The top half of the falls is quite steep, while the bottom portion is more of a cascade than a direct fall. During high water, the scene is especially beautiful as the brook spreads across the whole face of the ledge and plunges over the upper cliffs in a clear leap of nearly 30 feet. In more typical summer conditions the falls are less dramatic, but then recreational opportunities are at their best.

Below the foot of the cascade the brook runs 30 yards through weedy shallows and then turns a 90-degree corner to parallel the highway. It merges at this point with a side stream coming down from Stewartstown Hollow. Both below the cascades and around the

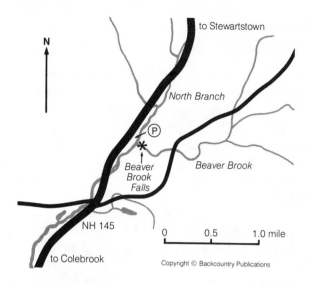

corner in the woods are wading pools where children can play safely, including spots with sandy bottoms. Keep an eye out for deer tracks along the banks. There are also interesting old foundations to investigate in the woods. These are the remains of an electric power-house built about 1890.

The Colebrook Kiwanis Club maintains picnic facilities for the public, as well as walkways along the stream to the foot of the falls. From the end of the walkways, informal paths climb through the forest on either side of the falls to the top of the ledge. These paths are steep and eroded, but passable. The one on the right provides the best views of the falls, since the foliage on this side has been trimmed. One reward for exploring up the falls is a close-up view of sinuous veins of quartz embedded in the ancient phyllite and schist ledge rock. Another bonus is the sweet, subtle fragrance of white cedar (arborvitae), which is abundant on the steep slopes alongside the falls.

Even though you can get a fine view right from your car, Beaver Brook Falls is not there just to *see*. It is also for picnicking, strolling, wading, swimming, and exploring. Have fun.

Side Trip: Waterfalls of Dixville Notch

Dixville, NH, had a population of only thirty-six people in 1980. Yet the town boasts four claims to fame: it is the home of one of the grandest resort hotels in the northeast, the Balsams, built in 1873; it is the first precinct in the country to finish counting ballots in each presidential election (always going Republican); it produces most of the nation's rubber balloons; and it encompasses a beautiful notch that is geologically unique among New England's mountain passes. Only Dixville Notch is cut from ancient shales that have been buckled to nearly vertical strata and eroded to create jagged walls and pinnacled ridges.

There are two picnic areas at the lower end of the notch—one on Flume Brook, which descends from the north, and one along Cascade Brook, which approaches from the south. As the names suggest each brook contributes a waterfall to the scenery of Dixville Notch.

To reach Dixville Notch from Beaver Brook Falls, double back to Colebrook and turn east on NH 26. The highway climbs gradually up the shallow valley of the Mohawk River for 11 miles to the height-of-land where the stunning Balsams Hotel is located. The Flume Brook picnic area is on the left 1 mile east of the height-of-land. The *Dixville Flume* is right beside the lower end of the picnic area. Although metamorphic schists and phyllites dominate the upper reaches of the Notch, here the brook crosses onto an intrusion of granite, carving a sheer gorge about 250 feet long and as much as 40 feet

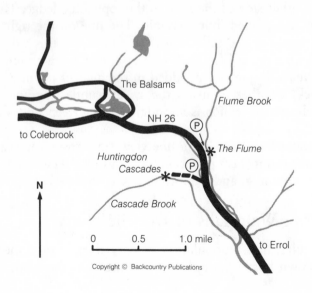

Copyright © Backcountry Publications

deep. Rushing through a narrow constriction at the neck of the flume, the brook tumbles down a series of cascades to an abrupt 15-foot drop over a bank of ledge. Since there is little underbrush below the thick canopy of conifers alongside the brook, one can walk along the rim of the gorge for a bird's-eye view of the waterfall.

Another 0.25 mile down the notch, at the lower boundary of the state park, a second picnic area lies off to the right (south) behind a green equipment shed. Cascade Brook is a 0.1 mile walk back into the forest. According to the 1896 edition of Sweetser's travel guide, excursion parties stopped to dine at this rest spot, and then walked up the brook for fifteen minutes to where "a cliff-side seat is reached, from which a noble series of falls are seen, descending sheer from the precipice above." These are called *Huntingdon Cascades*. Today, paths lead from the picnic area to a moss-lined ravine at the foot of a pretty set of small cascades. No "precipice" or "noble falls" is in sight. The position described by Sweetser might be higher up the ravine, but no maintained paths lead the way.

In addition to the two waterfalls and the spectacle of the notch itself there are a number of short hiking trails to outcrops or ridges with excellent scenic views. For example, the Sanguinari Ridge Trail leads from the Flume Brook picnic area to a pinnacle 1 mile up the ridge. For more information, consult the *AMC White Mountain Guide*, or stop for a map at the information booth across from the Balsams (summer season only).

Historical Detour

For White Mountain waterfall-seekers the trip to Beaver Brook Falls may seem a bit off the beaten path. This was literally true back around 1774 when Eleazer Rosebrook led his wife, Hannah, his two young daughters, and the family cow up the Connecticut River to settle in the Colebrook wilderness. Although a charter had been issued in 1770 to Sir George Colebrooke, chairman of the board of the British East India Company, no other settlements were to be found within 30 miles of Rosebrook's small log cabin.

A vivid portrait of the early settlers' isolated life at Colebrook is given by Rosebrook's granddaughter, Lucy Crawford, in her *History of the White Mountains*.

Their living was principally upon animal food. . . . The woods were beautiful and well stored with game, such as moose, deer, bears, etc., and hunters might, in a short time, kill and procure a sufficient quantity of this kind of food to supply their families a long time.

Lucy Crawford describes how Rosebrook once had to walk all the way to Haverhill to procure a bushel of salt—a round trip of 160 miles. But her greatest praise is reserved for Hannah Rosebrook: "What courage this woman must have possessed . . . changing [relatives, friends, and neighbors] for the woods!"

When the Revolutionary War was declared, Rosebrook moved his family down to Guildhall, VT, and went off to join the fight. Later, after his daughter Hannah married Abel Crawford, Rosebrook left his productive farm at Guildhall and once again took to the wilderness. This time he followed his pioneering son-in-law into the heart of the White Mountains, becoming one of the earliest and most prominent settlers in the vicinity of what later became Crawford Notch (see Chapter 3).

Despite losing the Rosebrooks, Colebrook soon attracted other settlers with its vast forests and rich river-valley sediments. The town grew and prospered on a foundation of dairying and potato farming. At one time it was a major producer of potato starch, with as many as eight factories. The town also became a trading center after the road through Dixville Notch was cut in 1804, creating a land route from "Upper Coos" to Portland.

Undoubtedly the greatest drama in Colebrook history, however, was the log drive that choked the Connecticut River each spring from 1868 to 1915. During most of this period the timberlands of the northern Connecticut River valley were monopolized by George Van Dyke, the most powerful of New Hampshire's often-vilified lumber kings. Van Dyke was known for his fondness of 160-proof "white wine," his unsavory business practices, and his motto: "Get out the logs"—often applied without regard for life or property. When he saw a worker fall into a logjam, Van Dyke would shout to the others, "To hell with the man. Save the cant-dog!" (This was a stout hooked pole used to turn and control logs on the river.) And when his log drives destroyed farm buildings and railroad bridges, Van Dyke an-

Beaver Brook Falls in spring runoff

ticipated modern business practice by endlessly delaying compensation payments through legal maneuvers.

Once, thirty Colebrook farmers claimed compensation for crop damage caused by the log drive. Van Dyke met with the farmers "with a pistol on his desk" and declared, "I ain't goin' to pay a cent" (Poole, 1946). It took the farmers years to recover their losses through the courts.

If Van Dyke was fascinating, his rivermen were legendary. For a few weeks each spring, rains and melting snows would raise the north-country streams and rivers high enough to bear along the winter's accumulation of logs, which were stacked on landings along the banks. With their nail-studded calked boots, the rivermen didn't simply joy-ride the logs down the Connecticut. Much of their time was spent breaking mountainous logjams, dynamiting icejams, anticipating and preventing jams, prying wayward logs off the banks or maneuvering them out of eddies, and generally cajoling the timber down the roaring river. In the process they spent long hours waist-deep in ice water, "flirted with death a dozen times a day," and slept it off each night in soggy clothes and wet blankets. Their work required an incredible mix of agility, balance, strength, and judgment, as well as 7000 calories a day of pork and beans, pea soup, molasses, bread, cakes, and pies. By comparison cowboys practically had desk jobs.

A single log drive from the north country to Van Dyke's mill at Holyoke, Massachusetts, could float fifty million board feet of softwood logs past Colebrook, with timber blanketing as much as 100 miles of the Connecticut River. When paychecks were handed out at the end of the drive, many of the men would head for the river towns and go on wild, drunken sprees that often lasted for weeks. Some men would spend everything they had earned on drink and women in a matter of days. And many would leave with indelible souvenirs in the form of spike marks from getting stomped in riotous brawls. In towns such as Woodsville and North Stratford it is said that gentler citizens barred their doors while the woodsmen partied in high gear.

Much of this information about the log drives, including the unattributed quotations, comes from Robert Pike's absorbing book, *Tall Trees, Tough Men*. Pike's accounts of the rivermen add an aura of adventure to the otherwise tranquil scenery along the Connecticut River en route to Beaver Brook Falls.

The Pemigewasset/
Merrimack
Watershed

◆

The Basin in April (The Basin–Cascades Trail)

CHAPTER 8

Welton Falls

———————◆———————

Location
On the Fowler River in Alexandria, just east of Cardigan State Park.

Map
AMC Cardigan Map: B-13.

Hiking Data
Distance, parking area to falls: 1.2 miles.
Altitude change: minus 300 feet (to altitude 1100 feet).
Difficulty: EASY.

—————————————◆—————————————

Admittedly, Welton Falls is not an official "White Mountain water-fall." As the raven flies, the falls are 10 miles south of the White Mountain National Forest. But it is far better to fudge the boundaries than to omit this "surpassing beauty"—as the falls are described in early editions of the *AMC White Mountain Guide*—on a geographical technicality.

The AMC Cardigan Lodge serves as home base for visiting Welton Falls. Set in a broad meadow in Shem Valley at the foot of Mount Cardigan, the year-round lodge also serves as a center for hiking, camping, snowshoeing, and cross-country skiing, as the weather permits. Mount Cardigan, which has top billing for most visitors, is a hiker's dream. The mountain's broad, bare dome dominates the local topography. On clear days the summit view encompasses a panorama of sparkling lakes, waves of forested ridges, and a serrated skyline of high peaks to the north. The climb from the lodge is a moderate 1700-foot ascent with well-graded trails and excellent loop routes. (Pick up a map at the lodge.) The excursion is especially rewarding

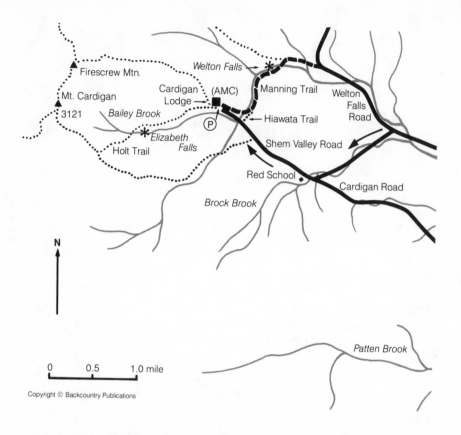

in August when the summit ridges host a carnival of fresh blueberries.
   With an early start, a moderately ambitious hiker can reach both
the mountaintop and the waterfall in a single day trip. The combined
tour can be under 8 miles long, depending on the route. In hot weather
it is best to schedule the climb in the cool morning hours, leaving
the afternoon for sampling the fine pools below Welton Falls.
   This chapter also describes *Elizabeth Falls*, which lies along the
path up Mount Cardigan. Though it is not a major attraction, Elizabeth Falls is interesting enough to have a look at if you happen to
be walking right by it anyway.

The Trail to the Falls

The most challenging aspect of a visit to Welton Falls is negotiating
the drive in to the lodge. Take NH 3A north from Bristol center for
2-plus miles to a left turn just past the large stone church at the

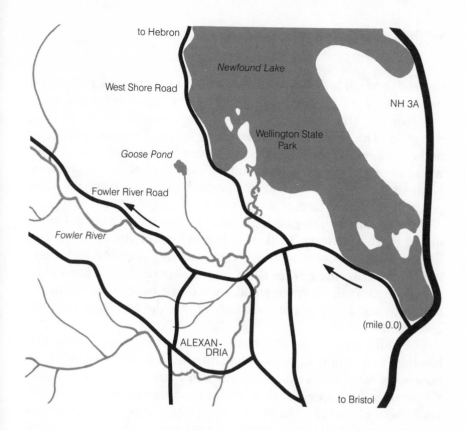

southern tip of Newfound Lake. A road sign at the junction points to Wellington State Park. Call this junction mile 0.0. After skirting the overly developed lakeshore, once a favorite Indian haunt, continue straight (west) when the main road turns to the north at mile 1.9. Again continue straight (west) at a fork to the left (mile 3.1). You are now on Fowler River Road. At mile 6.3, watch for an unobtrusive AMC sign indicating a left turn onto a dirt road. Ascend this road to an old red schoolhouse at mile 7.5, where a final right turn takes you across a low ridge into Shem Valley and the AMC lodge (mile 9.0). Warning: the last 2.7 miles require careful driving when the road is muddy or icy.

After pausing to admire the view of Mount Cardigan from the parking area, find the sign marking the Manning Trail to Welton Falls. The trail crosses the east lawn of the lodge toward a large cookout firepit and enters a grove of spruce, which conceals a number of campsites. After passing through the thick spruce stand, the path descends a small hill and swings left along a high shoulder above the west bank of the Fowler River. Clear yellow blazes mark the route.

A half-mile from the lodge the trail drops into the ravine to cross the river. The scene at the crossing is quite charming. Miniature potholes dimple colorful ledge shelves that border a narrow channel where the river's clear currents tumble over a series of tiny cascades. None of the riverbed clues at this point, however, presage the scene you will encounter farther downstream.

After fording to the east bank of the river the Manning Trail is joined by the Hiawata Trail, which provides an alternate route to Welton Falls for use when the river is running high. At such times it is best to cross the Fowler River on the auto road, and then follow the Hiawata Trail downstream along the east bank. When in doubt about the condition of the river crossing on the Manning Trail, inquire at the lodge.

The trail continues parallel to the river, passing through stands of hemlock and young hardwood forest. After a stretch of fairly level hiking, the trail climbs over a low ridge to a large, rocky knob, where the river gathers speed and slides into a gorge on the left. At the knob the trail makes a sharp right turn, while a spur path continues onto a narrow shelf that leads to a small cave notched in the face of a cliff directly above the falls! Sturdy cable fencing offers comfort and protection.

The Manning Trail, meanwhile, circles the rim of a deep chasm across from the waterfall and descends to the mouth of the formation (mile 1.2). Beyond the waterfall the trail continues downstream a few hundred yards, where it fords the river and terminates at an abandoned extension of Fowler River Road.

This northern tail of the Manning Trail is unmarked, unmaintained, and circuitous. But for those who are not prone to getting lost it provides a back door shortcut to Welton Falls. On the drive in, ignore the turn for the AMC lodge at mile 6.3 and bump along Fowler River Road another 1.2 miles to a sharp right turn up a hill. Here, an abandoned extension of the road runs straight into the woods. If your car has good clearance and the track is dry, you can drive in 100 yards and park just before a washed out gully. Otherwise, park and walk from the road. About 100 yards beyond the washout a path on the left leads down to the Fowler River. Ignore this turn, and continue 20 more yards to a second left turn onto an old logging road. This is the Manning Trail, which soon fords the river and follows along the east bank to Welton Falls. By this back door route the hike to the falls is 0.5 mile.

The Falls

To envision Welton Falls start with a deep pool 40 feet long and 20 feet wide, shaped like a wineskin. Its rock-bound mouth is narrow enough to jump across with only a touch of anxiety. Place the pool in a precipitous hollow with moss-covered cliffs rising 40 to 60 feet above the water. Line the rim of the hollow with a thick hemlock forest. Near the back of the ravine etch a narrow channel halfway down the cliff. Finally, send a river rushing through the channel and surging over the cliff in a foamy plume, stirring the pool to a slow swirl.

There are many vantage points for viewing Welton Falls. The most unusual is from a small cave in the face of the cliff directly above the falls. This is reached by the spur path mentioned in the trail description. Crouched in the cave with the back of your head scraping its dome, you feel like part of the landscape. From this point you have a clear view of the river sweeping around the base of the high knob and accelerating through a series of chutes and cascades to its dramatic plunge to the pool below.

More conventional views are obtained from the rim of the cliff across from the waterfall, and from the mouth of the ravine looking up to the falls.

Surely the most stimulating vantage point, however, is from the middle of the pool. This aquatic view is best appreciated in hot weather. With the waterfall facing east and the pool draining to the north, the ravine receives sunlight only in the late morning. The pool's deep water, therefore, never gets very warm.

For younger children and less adventurous swimmers the Fowler River provides a long line of shallow, tranquil pools below the waterfall gorge. Farther downstream past the lower river crossing of Manning Trail you will find small, delightful cascades and splendid rock-lined pools. Because the river swings around to the east here, the broad ledges benefit fully from the warm midday sun.

A pool downstream from Welton Falls

A Waterfall Side Trip

If you hike up Mount Cardigan from the AMC lodge you will probably pass within a stone-throw of *Elizabeth Falls*. The popular Holt
Trail crosses Bailey Brook immediately above the falls, an easy mile
from the lodge. Being only 1000 feet below the forest fringe that

encircles Cardigan's dome, Elizabeth Falls bears but a humble veil of water much of the year. The thin current spreads across dark slabs at the brow of a shady ravine, and then separates into fine strands that dangle over 40 feet of cliff before regrouping in a wide pool at the base of the ravine. Let the summit wait a few minutes while you stop to rest, have a snack, and feel the quiet pulse of Elizabeth Falls.

One minor route complication merits attention. The Holt Trail follows a forest road for over a 0.5 mile and then turns off to the right shortly before the road crosses Bailey Brook on a wooden bridge. If you happen to miss this right turn and reach the bridge you have accidentally gotten onto the Alexandria Ski Trail. You can double back to the Holt Trail or simply continue up the south bank of the brook to rejoin the trail just above the falls. In the latter case Elizabeth Falls will be in the ravine that drops away to your right as you are climbing.

Historical Detour

Although it is the southernmost of the major waterfalls of the White Mountain region, Welton Falls, ironically, was one of the last to catch the public eye. According to Bernard Shattuck, a town historian for Alexandria, local folk have enjoyed Welton Falls since shortly after the area was settled in 1769. In fact the waterfall takes its name from a family that once owned a nearby farm. But as a tourist attraction the falls remained virtually unknown until after World War I—decades after the high peaks of the White Mountains had become familiar terrain for hikers, and logging railroads had stripped the heart of the northern wilderness.

A rail branch reached the town of Bristol even before the Civil War, but neighboring Alexandria remained a quiet hill community of small farms and mica mines, off the beaten path for itinerant travel editors. Deep in the Alexandria's backwoods, Welton Falls was uniformly overlooked in nineteenth-century guidebooks for tourists and hikers. By 1920, 2,000 acres of land around Mount Cardigan had already been acquired as state forest, and yet popular guidebooks said not a word about the waterfall.

Welton Falls finally entered the limelight in 1923 when the state obtained more than 100 acres of land to create the Welton Falls

Reservation. A year later members of the AMC Merrimack Chapter built the Manning Trail from the Fowler River Road to the summit of Firescrew Mountain—named for a towering smoke spiral produced by the 1855 fire that bared the summit ledges. The first leg of the original Manning Trail was obliterated by timber operations after World War II.

The most significant development in the Mount Cardigan region occurred ten years later. Though the nation was mired in the misery of the Great Depression, interest in the novel sport of skiing was booming in New England. In a sense the economic trauma gave life to the new sport, since the Depression-born Civilian Conservation Corps (CCC) supplied the labor power for cutting the first ski trails.

True to its tradition of promoting mountain sports, the AMC was in the vanguard of the ski boom. In 1934 the club purchased over 500 acres of forest and abandoned farmland in Shem Valley (at under $2 an acre) to establish a ski center on Mount Cardigan. The purchase included a dilapidated farmhouse built before the Civil War—called the "old Shem Ackerman place," whence the name of the valley. Club volunteers set about converting the old farmhouse to "a modern ski lodge," as it was described in a Manchester *Union* article of January 11, 1935; the article is posted on the wall of the lodge.

Energetic club members promptly began building ski trails. In the words of the *Union* article, the result was "one of the most complete and satisfying winter sports centers in the state." The Cardigan Ski Reservation was such a hit that special trains were run from Boston to Canaan and Bristol. In those days a "complete and satisfying" ski center did not include a ski lift. Skiers were happy to ascend on foot. With the post-war advent of automatic lifts at commercial ski areas, the Cardigan Ski Reservation faded quickly from glory.

An article in *Appalachia* (Winter 1983–84) celebrating the fiftieth anniversary of Cardigan Lodge tells how the old Shem Ackerman place was occupied at the time of the AMC purchase by a bearded squatter, John Yegerman, and his old dog. Yegerman is described as a Latvian who had been imprisoned in Siberia and escaped by way of the Bering Strait to become a hermit in Shem Valley. To build the lodge the club had to evict Yegerman and his dog, who moved into a nearby shack—early victims of New Hampshire's ski-boom development.

CHAPTER 9

Waterville Cascades

◆

Location
Waterville Valley.

Map
AMC Chocorua-Waterville Map: J-7.
DeLorme Trail Map: L-7.

Hiking Data
Distance, parking area to foot of falls: 1.2 miles.
Altitude gain: 300 feet (to altitude 1800 feet).
Difficulty: EASY.

◆

Try a quick word-association test: What is the first thing that comes to mind when you hear "Waterville Valley?" If you thought "skiing," you should be in good company. The valley's winter sports facilities are undoubtedly its best-known attraction today. One tourist leaflet sets the tone by discussing alpine skiing, ski touring, and snowmobiling before mentioning any summer recreation at all. But down the list in small print under the heading "hiking," careful readers will notice "short walks to spectacular cascades," as well as hikes to beautiful mountain ponds and several 4000-foot peaks.

Prior to the introduction of modern alpine skiing facilities, Waterville Valley was best known for its summer mountain scenery. The village was a small, secluded resort with one large inn and a handful of cottages set in the deep bowl formed by Mount Tripyramid to the east, Mounts Osceola and Kancamagus to the north, Mount Tecumseh to the west, and Sandwich Mountain to the south. Early guidebooks commended Waterville Valley to "true mountain connoisseurs."

Along with excellent fishing and splendid mountain views, the hike along Cascade Brook was always a favorite attraction. Turn-of-the-century postcards highlighted the cascades; their grainy photographs show that a wooden footbridge once spanned the ledges above the bottom cascade. Had the word-association game been played a hundred years ago, the response to "Waterville Valley" might well have been "cascades." Or perhaps "trout."

The Trail to the Cascades

To reach Waterville Valley turn off I-93 at Exit 28 (Campton) and follow NH 49 for 11 miles up the valley of the Mad River. In the village, the turns become a bit more confusing. Stay on NH 49 as it swings to the left past a golf course and then makes a sharp right turn (where a side road continues straight) before reaching a large parking area beside the Finish Line Restaurant at the foot of the Snow's Mountain ski lift.

An alternative route into or out of the village is by the Tripoli Road (Exit 31 off I-93). This gravel road climbs through Thornton Pass, between Mount Osceola and Mount Tecumseh, and descends into the village only a few yards south of the Finish Line Restaurant.

The Cascade Path is maintained by the Waterville Valley Athletic and Improvement Association, which supports 22 miles of trails in the valley. The path begins at the north end of the parking lot beside a fenced horse paddock. A small sign post marks the trailhead. Initially the trail ascends a grassy ski slope before turning left into the woods. Don't take the first turn into the woods, which is marked by a brown sign bearing trail information for cross-country skiing. The correct left turn is 100 yards farther on, where the ski slope levels out a bit. There, a small, unobtrusive sign points in the direction of the Cascades. Once the path enters the woods intermittent yellow blazes painted on the trees mark the way.

At 0.5 mile from the parking lot the Elephant Rock Trail diverges to the right while Cascade Path continues straight on. The path contours around the flank of Snow's Mountain and then descends to a trail junction at Cascade Brook (mile 1.0). From this junction Cascade Path turns right and follows up the west bank of the brook. Although you are heading upstream here, the path is not steep at all. Cascade Brook looks like a very ordinary forest stream for the first

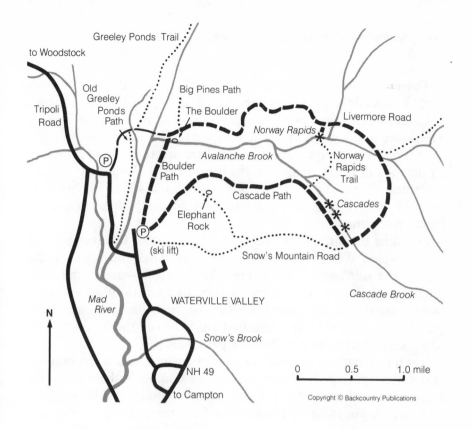

0.2 mile, at which point the trail passes a lovely pool—the first hint of more interesting sights just ahead.

Over the next 0.25 mile paths climb more steeply up both sides of the brook past a nearly continuous string of beautiful cascade scenery, ending at a bridge where the Snow's Mountain service road crosses the brook (mile 1.5). Judging from the trampled soil, most hikers stay on the west bank. The blazes indicate, however, that the official trail is across the brook on the east bank. It is the official trail that provides better views of the upper cascades and better access to the remarkable pools.

From the top of the cascades there are three ways to head for home. First, you can simply retrace your steps back along Cascade Path. Second, you can turn right above the cascades and follow the gravel road to the top of the Snow's Mountain ski lift. From there the ski slope descends directly to the parking lot at the Finish Line Restaurant. This route is shorter, only 2.5 miles for the circuit, and offers fine views across the valley from the top of the ski slope.

The third route is longer, but it complements the cascades with more brookside scenery. From the bridge above the top cascade turn left and descend the Snow's Mountain service road for 0.6 mile to Livermore Road, which you will intercept just beyond a sturdy bridge over Avalanche Brook. (These "roads" are dirt tracks used primarily by hikers and skiers; vehicle traffic is very rare.) Head west (left) on Livermore Road, and watch for a Norway Rapids Trail sign on your left after 0.2 mile. A short detour over to the *Norway Rapids* is highly recommended.

After the detour, follow the gradual descent of Livermore Road for 1.3 miles. When Avalanche Brook next comes into sight on the left, take a side path down to see "the Boulder"—one of the most immense glacial erratics in the region. (If immensity strikes your fancy, you should also watch for the Big Pines Path heading north off Livermore Road a few hundred yards before the Boulder turn. The name explains where this side path goes.)

If you can manage to wade across Avalanche Brook at the Boulder (a tricky proposition) you can pick up the Boulder Path on the south bank. This path provides a nearly straight 1-mile shot back to the parking lot. Finishing by the Boulder Path the complete circuit is a 4.5-mile hike. If you prefer to avoid fording Avalanche Brook at the Boulder, continue down Livermore Road 0.1 mile beyond the Mad River bridge. Then take the Old Greely Ponds Path south toward town. At the paved road, two quick left turns will take you back to the parking lot. This option adds an extra 0.25 mile to the loop hike.

The Cascades

Cascade Brook presents a visual symphony of variations on a theme. The theme is simple and appealing: pretty waterfall to a sparkling pool.

At the first cascade the brook sweeps through a high gate of heavily fractured bedrock (Norway quartz monzonite) and forms a cone of whitewater as it falls over 25 feet to a dreamy pool on the floor of a shady glen. The formation is not large, but it is compellingly lovely. Thus the harmonious theme, *con grazia*.

The first two variations are small, delightful waterchutes into rock-lined pools. Then comes a grand repetition of the first cascade; viewed

Bridge above the cascades on Cascade Brook in Waterville

from the west bank the high waterfall silhouettes an overhanging profile sculpted in the rock. Just above, a wide sheet of water fans across a granite ramp and slides into a deep pothole pool. Altogether the orchestra of rock and water restates the theme eight times, ending with surging crescent cascade sluicing into a glimmering green pool. And at the end of the performance, you can replay your favorites simply by returning down the path.

Many of the deep, clear pools formed by the cascades would make wonderful swimming holes except that the brook's northeast exposure provides little direct sunlight. Moreover, most of the cascade basins have steep banks that make it difficult to reach the pools.

For water play, your best bet is to route your return trip past Norway Rapids, as outlined above. At the rapids, Avalanche Brook slides over more than 100 yards of smooth, sloping, colorful ledges, forming small chutes, plumes, and pools. Best of all, the ledges lie east-to-west so they benefit fully from the midday sun. There is not really a waterfall, as such, at Norway Rapids, but on a warm summer day kids of all ages won't mind at all.

Historical Detour

A sculptor creating a statue honoring the founders of Waterville Valley might consider modeling two figures: Nathaniel Greeley and the brook trout. It was for fish and game that Indians from the lakes region and the Pemigewasset valley made excursions into the valley. The "brooks prolific in trout" also played a major role in the development of tourism. One early guidebook goes so far as to say that the valley "might have remained obscure and unknown until doomsday, had not a few anglers stumbled upon it while in pursuit of brooks and waters new" (Drake, 1881). The very name of the valley highlights the significance of the mountain streams.

In some White Mountain townships fishing was a primary source of food for the early settlers. A single spring day out on a mountain brook could yield literally hundreds of trout, as well as a crop of Atlantic salmon. By drying the spring catch, Indians and settlers could accumulate enough cured provisions to last through the hungry winter—at least in a good year.

It is said that in precolonial days, the salmon runs down on the Merrimack River had the appearance of a solid mass of fish. Indians even told of walking across Salmon Falls in the southern part of the state on the backs of the ascending salmon. By 1850, though, downstream dams eliminated the Atlantic salmon from the Pemigewasset

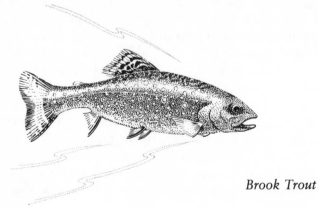

Brook Trout

watershed altogether. After the Civil War efforts were made to modify the dams in order to restore the salmon, but overfishing, new dams, and the modern scourge of pollution again killed off the species.

Since 1969, a group of federal and state agencies has worked to re-establish the Atlantic salmon in the Merrimack River system (as well as the Connecticut River). The Mad River is one beneficiary. In addition, the New Hampshire Fish and Game Department has been replenishing the Mad River system with trout stock since 1939. The stocking programs include rainbow trout and brown trout, but the eastern brook trout is the only species native to the cold White Mountain streams, where it rarely grows to as much as six inches in length.

And then there is Nathaniel Greeley, the most successful of the early settlers who tried carving farms out of the valley wilderness beginning in 1820. Considering the terrain, it is not surprising that most of these efforts failed. According to Anderson and Morse (1930), the town had only 20 acres of cleared land in 1831, when seventeen poll taxes were assessed. By 1833, the year Greeley began lodging boarders, the population was down to just six.

Eventually Greeley acquired all of the cleared land in the valley. In 1865 he opened an inn, which for many years was called Greeley's Summer Boarding-House, or simply Greeley's. A handful of cottages was added shortly thereafter, and a system of trails was developed, including the path to the cascades. This path was also the first leg of the original trail up Mount Tripyramid, the area's greatest marvel. Writing about it in 1881, Samuel Adams Drake was struck silly with awe: "Hail to thee, mountain of the high heroic crest. . . . None approach thy forest courts but do thee homage." Great landslides on Mount Tripyramid in 1869 and 1885 (hence the name Avalanche Brook) added to its renown.

The Cascade Path also connected Waterville Valley to the original Livermore Road when it opened in 1879, providing a direct bridle path from the valley to Mount Washington. An earlier Waterville-to-Crawfords path through Mad River Notch, cut in 1860, had been much more circuitous.

During Greeley's stewardship there was no problem of overdevelopment in Waterville Valley. The tourist facilities remained modest in scale, as Campton, not Waterville, received most of the traffic, most of the attention of the landscape painters and poets, and most of the ink in the tourist guides. Greeley's was considered a resort for fishermen and for those who sought "seclusion and fine mountain scenery" rather than comforts of a grand hotel.

Greeley was succeeded by Silas Elliot (the inn was called Elliot's Hotel for many years), and then by an association of guests who bought the property at the end of World War I. Throughout this era, development of Waterville Valley was evidently dominated by the philosophy of small is beautiful. From 1880 to 1930 the town's population merely swapped digits from 32 to 23 people, although a few new cottages were added to the village street map. Though much of the valley fell into the hands of timber interests, no logging railroads ever penetrated into the valley. The forests were still in healthy shape in 1928 when the government bought nearly 23,000 acres from the Woodstock Lumber Company for inclusion in the White Mountain National Forest. Not long thereafter the first ski slopes were cut to add a winter season to the mountain resort. The seeds of the modern Waterville Valley had been planted.

The end of the era might be dated, however, to the late 1960s when modern alpine skiing blossomed, the grand Waterville Inn burned down, and the first condominiums were built in the village. Since then the valley has developed rapidly. But with the National Forest owning most of the land in the township, Waterville Valley should still be a lure for the "true mountain connoisseurs" of future generations.

CHAPTER 10

Georgiana Falls

◆

Location
Just below the Indian Head Profile, south of Franconia Notch.

Map
AMC Franconia Map: I-4.
DeLorme Trail Map: H-4.

Hiking Data
Distance, parking area to:
Lower Georgiana Falls .... 0.8 mile.
Upper Georgiana (Harvard) Falls .... 1.3 miles.
Altitude gain: 600 feet (to altitude 1600 feet).
Difficulty: MODERATE.

◆

Visitors to Georgiana Falls face an unusual problem: locating the falls! The difficulty stems from the fact that different sources provide conflicting accounts about which of the waterfalls gracing the steep ledges along Harvard Brook is the real Georgiana. The recent *AMC White Mountain Guide* pins the label on the lower cascades, while using the name Harvard Falls for the uppermost drop. But the book's map, like most maps, locates Georgiana at the top of the ledges. Thomas Starr King's 1859 description ("One of the grandest cascades of the mountain region . . . making two leaps of eighty feet each, one right after the other") is a clear but exaggerated reference to the upper set of falls. Then again, the 1922 *AMC Guide* refers to both the lower and upper cascades as Georgiana Falls, while acknowledging that the latter is "sometimes known as Harvard Fall." Curiously, though, the 1922 map labels only the *bottom* as Georgiana.

An authoritative description by M. Isabella Stone in an early issue of *Appalachia* (Volume IV, 1885) indicates the genuine Georgiana Falls as the precipitous cascade at the top of the long ramp of ledge; the name *Harvard Cascade* was given to a beautiful small waterfall 0.2 mile farther up Harvard Brook. For clarity, the bottom section of the brook's rapid descent will be referred to here as lower Georgiana Falls.

Although labels have been applied inconsistently during the past century of maps and trail descriptions, there is no confusion about what you should see on your hike: you should explore the whole stretch of cascades. However, Georgiana Falls proper is certainly the highlight of the trip.

The Trail to the Falls

The first path to Georgiana Falls was cleared in 1877. Earlier in the present century the Forest Service maintained the Bog Pond Trail past Georgiana Falls. Today no official trail is maintained, but a good footpath still climbs alongside Harvard Brook up to the falls.

To begin the hike to Georgiana Falls you must first find Hanson Farm Road, which turns off of the west side of US 3 in North Lincoln, across from the Longhorn Restaurant. For orientation, the location is between Exit 33 on Interstate 93 and Exit 1 (for the Flume) on the Franconia Notch Parkway. Northbound drivers on I-93 can get a wide-angle preview of Georgiana Falls—a narrow white ribbon splitting a verdant expanse of undulating hillside—by scanning the ravines south of the Indian Head cliff from the top of the long hill above Exit 32 (one exit south of North Lincoln).

The footpath starts at an unmarked gravel parking area at the end of Hanson Farm Road, 0.1 mile west of US 3. Walk through the gate in the chain-link fence on the west side of the parking area and follow the dirt logging road through a pair of tunnels under I-93. About 0.3 mile beyond the highway, and 100 yards after crossing a metal culvert, you will reach a small grassy clearing where the path cuts into the woods on the left. Watch carefully, because the turn here is easy to miss. (The logging road continues climbing up to the right.) From this point red blazes mark the way.

Once off the logging road, you will find that the scenery changes to pretty-forest-with-tumbling-brook. The path is quite easy to follow as it parallels Harvard Brook upstream for 0.3 mile through a mixed

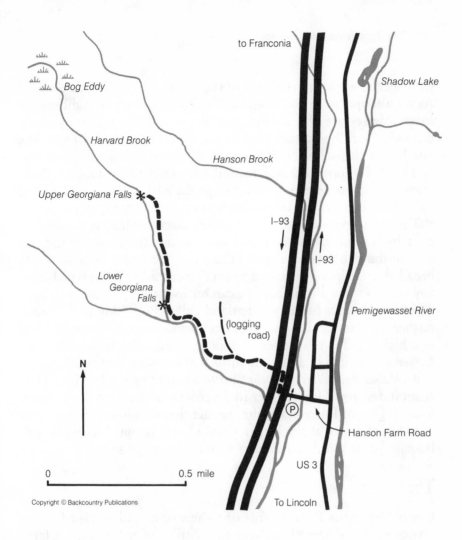

to Franconia

Shadow Lake

Bog Eddy

Harvard Brook

Hanson Brook

Upper Georgiana Falls ✱

I-93

I-93

Lower
Georgiana
Falls
✱

Pemigewasset River

(logging
road)

N

P

Hanson Farm Road

US 3

0   0.5 mile

To Lincoln

company of trees. Soon you arrive at the base of an open gray ledge encrusted with lichen and moss. The path climbs one flight of blazed rocks past some small introductory cascades to a broad shelf at the foot of lower Georgiana Falls.

According to a local fisherman who passed us on his way to Bog Pond to try his luck on the brown trout, most visitors stop at this point and turn back, not realizing that the main waterfall is higher up the trail. According to the old *Appalachia* article, hikers were making the same mistake a century ago!

Above the pool the blazed trail steepens considerably as it ascends through the woods to the right of the brook, with obstructed views. As an alternative to following the trail you can climb right up the ledges (if they are dry) to enjoy the line of cascades that runs nearly 0.5 mile from the bottom pool to the cliffs at Georgiana Falls. The last leg of this climb, however, is too sheer to negotiate without rejoining the footpath, which itself has some tricky footing. After maneuvering up a steep, wooded slope the path emerges atop a bluff that faces directly into the midsection of the main waterfall.

The path continues only a short distance farther. It descends a gully by the side of the falls and then mounts the corner of the cliff wall to the slabs above. Beyond this point the brook flattens out on broad, open ledges punctuated by smaller cascades. There is no longer any semblance of a trail, but one can bushwhack upstream with little difficulty. A tract of marshy flatland called Bog Eddy is 0.75 mile farther up Harvard Brook. Bog Pond is another 1.25 miles and 500 feet higher still. A long set of thin cascades—formerly called the *Upper Falls*—can be found about 0.5 mile below Bog Pond.

In *Walks and Climbs in the White Mountains* (1926), Karl Harrington devoted a full chapter to describing in great detail the entire hike up Harvard Brook, despite the fact that his photos show hardly a trickle of water at the Upper Falls! One is tempted to agree with Isabella Stone that "few visitors would care to go so far."

The Falls

Lower Georgiana Falls consists of a sheet of cascades draped across a wide ledge 30 feet high. Near the bottom of the cascade a large cleft boulder stands sentry above a tea-colored pool that is cupped in a broad shelf of bedrock. The rock here was described a century ago by Professor Huntington, the state geologist, as a breccia of gneiss, hornblende, and other silicates cemented by a light feldspar paste. Translated, this means that the tough ledge rock is embedded with a fascinating variety of minerals. It is also a very inviting ledge for brookside scrambling, and its sunny southeastern exposure creates a pleasant environment for a waterfall picnic.

Ascending the ledge one flight up from the bottom pool, you can see the brook gush through a chute that undercuts a bank of ledge before sliding into a second fine pool. Farther on, the waters have etched a narrow channel down the base of a large, steep slab. As you climb higher, the hemlock forest closes in more tightly on the ledge. Soon you reach a small, boulder-strewn pool at the foot of another narrow cascade. High above, a slender reed of whitewater angles across the dark forest backdrop. This is Georgiana Falls, from afar.

Farther up at the bluff you will be gazing straight into the heart of the falls with a full frontal view. The brook slides directly toward you over a sloping ledge before plunging down a sheer cliff into a deep, narrow chasm at your feet. Down in the confined basin the turbulent waters make a sharp right turn and embark on their long descent to the bottom pool. Beyond the bluff the footpath drops into a gully before climbing the corner to the top of the cliff. The gully offers an altogether different perspective on the waterfall: a close-up side view looking down the narrow basin and out across the Pemigewasset valley to the south.

The flat stretch of brook above Georgiana Falls is quite safe to explore, but the precipitous formation itself is not a good place for sporting. It is instead a visual and spiritual playground, offering the rugged geometry of rock and brook, the complex dynamics of the falls, and the tranquil valley panorama beyond.

When the brook runs high Georgiana Falls is quite a spectacle, with powerful currents surging across the full face of the steep cliffs. Viewing the falls from the bluff at such times, one can almost imagine how a small fish must feel looking into the baleen of an approaching whale's jaw. When the brook is low the falls are less commanding, but then there are better opportunities for exploring the ledges above and below.

Historical Detour

Georgiana Falls lies under the watchful gaze of the Indian Head on Mount Pemigewasset. Down in the valley, its waters swell the river bearing that same ancient Indian name (pronounced with a soft "g"). Like the exact location of Georgiana Falls, the name Pemigewasset is attributed to different origins in different books. Some sources claim that the name comes from an Indian tribe that lived near what is now Plymouth before fleeing to Canada following a massacre in

Upper Georgiana Falls in spring runoff

1712. Others recount the legend of a great chief, whose very profile is carved in the Indian Head cliffs on the nearby mountain that now bears his name. According to the legend Chief Pemigewasset used the top of this mountain as a lookout to watch for campfires of marauding Algonquins. In one version of the folktale, the chief died on the mountaintop one frigid winter while watching for his wife to return from a visit to her Mohawk homeland.

In more serious reference books, though, one finds no mention of Chief Pemigewasset, and the local Indian subtribe seems to have been named after the river rather than the other way around. The river, it seems, derives its colorful name from an Abnaki Indian word that simply means "swift, extended current," or "extensive rapids."

As for Georgiana itself, the source of the name is quite obscure. Might it have been intended as a feminized tribute to our first president? King (1859) merely lamented that the name was not very appropriate for such a grand cascade. Sweetser's usually informative guidebook (1887) is no more helpful, and indeed fuels confusion about what is Georgiana and what is Harvard Falls.

In his description of Georgiana Falls, Sweetser noted that "The Falls have been visited very rarely for several years past, on account of their secluded position." The "position" was not to remain secluded much longer. Even as Sweetser was writing, George B. James, of Roxbury, Massachusetts, was in the process of consolidating land holdings in order to sell large parcels to the loggers. According to Belcher (1980), George James was a self-proclaimed conservationist whose shocking strong-arm tactics in acquiring timberlands earned him the title of "Vampire of the White Mountains," among other epithets.

In 1896 the Boston and Maine Railroad was authorized to run a branch line from North Woodstock to a sawmill at Whitehouse Brook near the Flume. This indicates that logging operations had by that time penetrated into Franconia Notch. In 1904, George L. Johnson established a sawmill and a bustling company town (named Johnson) nearly at the base of the present trail to Georgiana Falls. Johnson's crews quickly stripped the timber in the surrounding territory, sparing only the trees that framed Indian Head. In 1907, after securing a ten-year contract to timber rights farther south, Johnson built the Gordon Pond Railroad to haul logs from the flanks of Kinsman Mountain. The trackbed ran right across the lower section of Georgiana Falls.

This railroad shut down in 1916, and the town of Johnson soon disappeared. Logging around Georgiana Falls continued many years thereafter but without the wholesale destruction wrought by the earlier operations. In 1983 the property around the falls was purchased by the State of New Hampshire, as part of the land acquisition for the Franconia Notch Parkway project.

Today, the resurgence of moose and beaver populations in the headlands above Georgiana Falls testify that the forests are regaining their health. Old Chief Pemigewasset must be pleased to gaze once again across verdant ridges rather than scrub and slash. One wonders, though, what his impression might be of the sprawling commercial developments in the valley below.

CHAPTER 11

The Flume–Pool Loop

---◆---

Location
Franconia Notch.

Map
AMC Franconia Map: H-4.
DeLorme Trail Map: G/H-4.

Hiking Data
Distance, parking area to:
Avalanche Falls .... 0.8 mile.
Liberty Gorge Cascade .... 1.4 miles.
The Pool .... 1.5 miles.
Full loop .... 2.1 miles.
(Subtract 0.5 mile from each figure if the shuttle bus is taken to Boulder Cabin.)
Altitude gain: 250 feet from covered bridge (low point) to Avalanche Falls (altitude 1500 feet).
Difficulty: EASY (particularly with shuttle bus to Boulder Cabin).

---◆---

"This natural curiosity fills the beholder with amazement and admiration." So Lucy Crawford, in her *History of the White Mountains*, reacted to the Flume. Ever since its discovery in 1808 the Flume has been a favorite tourist stopover. It has been celebrated by writers, artists, poets, photographers, post-card companies, and tour operators.

Flume formations are actually fairly commonplace in the White Mountains. Among the better known are those in Dixville Notch, at Sabbaday Falls, and on Kedron Brook in Crawford Notch. In geological terms a flume is formed from a narrow band, or dike, of softer rock such as basalt that has plugged a fissure in harder bedrock.

When exposed to running water the dike erodes much more rapidly than the surrounding bedrock. The result is a narrow, sheer gorge that is gradually widened by frost action. The Flume in Franconia Notch, therefore, is not really a curiosity. What accounts for its notoriety is its size: 800 feet long and 12 to 20 feet wide, with vertical walls 7 to 9 stories high.

Since the Flume gets so much publicity in its own right there is no need to discuss it at length in a book on waterfalls. There is a need, however, to tell about the three fine falls that lie along a pleasant loop hike, which just happens to pass through the Flume. It should be noted that these waterfall attractions are for spectators rather than explorers. The trail leads to overlooks offering excellent views, but off-trail recreational adventures are not permitted here due to the heavy tourist use of the area.

The Trail to the Falls

The Flume-Pool loop trail starts from the Flume Visitor Center, which is reached off Exit 1 of the Notch Parkway (I-93) or by US 3 from North Lincoln. From the vast parking area there are three ways to get to Boulder Cabin, 500 yards below the Flume.

First, when the state-operated Visitor Center is open (mid-May to mid-October, 9:00 A.M. to 5:00 P.M.) a 0.5-mile shuttle bus ride to Boulder Cabin is included in the entrance fee. In 1988 the entrance fee was $4—up from 25 cents in 1938. In addition to a ticket booth the Visitor Center has information exhibits, a gift shop, a cafeteria, and a short film on Franconia Notch State Park.

Second, you may prefer to leg it rather than ride the bus. Just follow the asphalt footpath to the left behind the Visitor Center. Continue down the gravel path to the covered bridge over the Pemigewasset River and then back up to Boulder Cabin.

Third, when the Visitor Center is closed—off season or off hours—the hike is a bit more circuitous. But these are the times when the area is less crowded and therefore especially engaging. (Offsetting this advantage is the fact that the boardwalk through the Flume is dismantled during the off season and barricaded off hours, so you can't see quite as much of the famous gorge.) Park at the highest lot and follow the asphalt bicycle path north into the woods. After 0.1

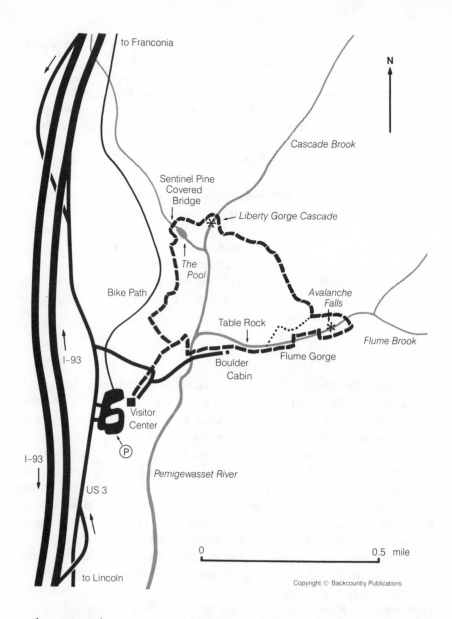

to Franconia

N

Cascade Brook

Sentinel Pine
Covered
Bridge

Liberty Gorge Cascade

The
Pool

Bike Path

Avalanche
Falls

Table Rock

Flume Brook

I-93

Boulder
Cabin

Flume Gorge

Visitor
Center

I-93

P

Pemigewasset River

US 3

0   0.5   mile

to Lincoln

mile, turn right onto a paved service road that runs from the Liberty Springs Trail parking lot to the back of the Visitor Center. Then proceed to Boulder Cabin along the footpath.

From Boulder Cabin the trail ascends sharply to Flume Brook, which it follows for a short distance upstream before crossing on a footbridge. Flume Brook at this point offers a splendid bonus attraction known as Table Rock. The glistening waters slip smoothly over a broad, sunny ledge of polished Conway granite: a total contrast to the damp, narrow gorge only yards upstream. Access to the steeper part of the ledge is restricted by a wooden rail fence.

Past the footbridge the trail splits. The fork to the right leads into the mouth of the Flume gorge. The fork to the left is the usual descent route from the head of the Flume. But when the Flume boardwalk is closed, take the left-hand fork to the head of the gorge for views of Avalanche Falls. It might be tempting in the off season to scramble up the gorge without benefit of the boardwalk. This is quite unsafe, though, because the rocks are slippery when wet and extremely treacherous when iced. Indeed in the winter fully equipped ice climbers can occasionally be found practicing technical moves on the tremendous icicles that drape the perpendicular walls of the gorge.

The boardwalk into the Flume traverses the length of the gorge to the foot of Avalanche Falls, where a ramp climbs to the outlet at the head of the falls. En route to Avalanche Falls the walkway passes two very pretty small cascades at the narrowest part of the gorge. From the steps at this point you can see a band of dark basalt in the gorge wall to the left.

At the top end of the Flume there is an interesting cave, which is guarded by jack-in-the-pulpits during the late spring. A wooden shelter provides a rest stop for weary visitors, and toilets are located behind the shelter. As you begin to descend from the shelter you will confront another fork in the trail. The path to the left returns to the bottom of the Flume and Boulder Cabin, while the wide dirt trail heading straight into the woods ahead is the loop trail to the Pool.

This trail contours around the side of a long ridge and then drops gently through a fine hardwood forest. The large trees include stately white ash, which can be recognized by their compound leaves and deeply furrowed bark. In the spring the forest floor is dotted with wildflowers, highlighted by bright white hobblebush bouquets. In the summer thrushes, robins, and chickadees fill the air with gay song. After just over 0.5 mile the trail crosses a stream and reaches a gravel path on the left, which leads down a set of steps to the overlook at Liberty Gorge Cascade.

Continuing along the main trail, you quickly reach a second set of steps on the left. These descend to a sturdily railed viewing platform perched atop a 130-foot-high cliff that forms the northeastern wall of the Pool. The trail then drops and curls around to cross the Sentinel Pine Bridge, a picturesque span over a gorge cut by the Pemigewasset as it cascades into the Pool. The bridge takes its name from a 175-foot-tall white pine that towered above the gorge until falling victim to the hurricane of 1938. This pine now forms the main beam for the bridge.

Across on the southwestern rim of the gorge a side path leads down to another railed platform with picture-perfect views across the Pool to the high wall of cliffs and the cascades beneath the Sentinel Pine Bridge.

To finish the loop just follow the main trail over a small ridge and back to the Visitor's Center (or to the parking lot, off season). This final leg of the hike features a garden of massive boulders called glacial erratics. These boulders were plucked off mountains and transported south by passing glaciers, then deposited at their present location when the ice sheets melted away.

The Falls

Avalanche Falls, once called Flume Cascade, is located at the head of the Flume. It is not a waterfall giant, but the setting is hard to beat. Flume Brook emerges from the woods on the hillside, dashes across bare slabs of smooth Conway granite, and plunges over the lip of the gorge. When the stream is low, the waters tumble steeply down large granite steps into an alcove carved in the side of the gorge, and then leap to the bottom of the Flume. When the stream is running high the waters surge over the edge in a single 45-foot drop. Viewed from alongside, on the ramp that leads out of the gorge, the falls form a sparkling mare's tail, with soft rainbows afloat in the spray.

In early winter or early spring, when the gorge is bedecked with ice, Avalanche Falls can be unusually beautiful. (Only tremendous self-restraint prevents us from calling it "gorgeous.") Frozen spray builds up to form a rippled translucent mask for the falling water. Ice and snow linger well into May in a deep cave just above the falls. The cave is formed by the collapsed wall of what was once an extension of the gorge. In the roof at the back of the cave there is a secret exit just large enough for kids to climb through.

Giant icicles in the Flume Gorge in spring

Liberty Gorge Cascade is generally overshadowed by its famous neighbors along the loop trail. Compared to the falls at the Flume and the Pool, the Liberty Gorge Cascade lacks drama. But this is easily the highest of the falls. The stairs from the trail lead to a railing set on a bluff halfway down a deep ravine. Across the ravine the cascades sweep in a long arcing chute down a steep cut of bedrock, framed with spruce, yellow birch, and hemlock trees. At the base of the long rock slab the waters fan out to form a broad sash that drops into a crystal pool. Below, the stream continues its steep tumble down the heart of the ravine. Unhappily there is not much to *do* at Liberty Gorge Cascade other than spend a few minutes admiring the scene from the viewing rail.

The Pool is not itself a waterfall. Rather, like the Flume, it is the name for a grandly impressive formation, with cascades at the upper end. Whereas the Flume is long and confining, the Pool is an enormous basin—150 feet in diameter, 40 feet deep, under granite walls 13 stories high. And whereas everyone expects to be impressed by the Flume, the Pool generally comes as a very pleasant surprise. As one young girl shrieked at first sight of the Pool, "Whooooa! That's beautiful!"

The best views of the cascades are from the middle of the breezy Sentinel Pine Bridge, from the trail on the side path just past the bridge, and from the viewing rail at the end of this side path. Seen across the waters of the Pool from a high viewing rail, the cascades may appear rather insignificant. But the ring of turbulent foam they stir up in the Pool suggests that the cascades would be impressive closer up, especially when the Pemigewasset River is running high. From 1853 to 1887 an eccentric country philosopher named "Professor" John Merrill earned a living operating a rowboat in the Pool, providing summer visitors with a close-up view of these cascades. Today visitors are essentially confined to sightseeing from various high perches.

Another effect of being high above the Pool, across from the cascades, is that their song is strangely muffled. John Anderson and Stearns Morse (1930) described the feeling: "It seems oppressively quiet, in spite of the noise of the water, as if some secret wood cult kept here a shrine of silence."

Historical Detour

"How wild the spot is!" exclaimed Thomas Starr King of the Flume, in his book *The White Hills*, published in 1859. Even then the statement was not meant in a literal sense. The Flume House, a hundred-room resort hotel, had been built in 1848 not far from the site occupied by the Visitor Center today. In fact King went on to caution his readers that the best time for a visit was in the early morning or the evening, "in order to be able to see the Flume without the large parties."

The Flume was discovered about 1808 by ninety-three-year-old Jessie Guernsey, who reportedly came upon the gorge while fishing up the brook from her pioneer homestead a mile south. At the Guernsey farm was a blockhouse where settlers reportedly fended off a fierce attack by Abnaki Indians from Canada, who allegedly had been incited by the British during the War of 1812. (Solon Colby, in his *Indian History*, denies that any Indian attacks occurred in New Hampshire during that war.) With construction of the road through the Notch—the bridge below Boulder Cabin dates back to 1820— the Flume and the Old Man Profile quickly became major attractions for nature-loving travelers and curiosity seekers.

Surprisingly the geological formation seen by early visitors to the Flume differed rather dramatically from what we see today. Most notably an enormous boulder was wedged between the narrow walls of the Flume until it was washed away by tremendous flood on June 20, 1883. Visitors walking along the crude plank predecessor to today's boardwalk would shudder as they passed directly under the massive boulder. The same storm cleaned out ages of accumulated rubble. This made the gorge longer and deeper—and gave birth to both Avalanche Falls and Table Rock. Even now the geology is visibly dynamic: visitors in the spring can see fresh flakes of granite lying on top of last fall's leaves.

The original Flume House burned down in 1870 but was replaced in 1872 with an even grander hotel. The latter, in turn, burned down in 1918. It was replaced by a restaurant, then a tourist center. The contemporary Visitor Center was built as part of the Notch Parkway project, in 1986.

CHAPTER 12

The Basin–Cascades Trail

◆

Location
Franconia Notch.

Map
AMC Franconia Map: H-4
DeLorme Trail Map: G-4

Hiking Data
Distance, parking area to:
The Basin .... 0.1 mile.
The Cascades .... 0.2 mile.
Kinsman Falls .... 0.5 mile.
Rocky Glen Falls .... 1.1 miles.
Altitude gain: 600 feet to Rocky Glen Falls (altitude 2000 feet).
Difficulty: EASY to Kinsman Falls; MODERATE thereafter.

◆

If there were a delight meter for measuring the splendor of waterfalls, its reading for the Basin would be surprisingly low, considering the spot's great popularity. This large pothole pool set in a riverbed sculpture of polished Conway granite is a fascinating natural feature, to be sure, but not much of a waterfall. Most visitors gaze at the swirling currents for a few minutes, snap a photo, and then tramp back to their cars. Adventurers who leave the crowds behind and forge up the Basin-Cascades Trail, however, quickly find their delight meter swinging high into the Lovely zone. Dr. William Prime, who was known as America's Izaak Walton for his popular nineteenth-century book *I Go A-Fishing*, called Cascade Brook "the finest brook in America for scenery as well as for trout."

Cascade Brook is a delight not only in terms of lovely views. The cascades and waterfalls that extend for a mile along the brook are also great fun to explore, offering a mixture of broad ledges, cool glens, and tempting pools. If you bring any rambunctious kids along it will be hard to hold them back! They'll find the urge to scamper up the ledges nearly irresistible. And on a warm summer day they might "accidentally" get pretty wet investigating the clear pools.

A visit to the falls can be combined with a hike to Lonesome Lake, which occupies a picturesque basin beneath the high bluffs of Cannon Mountain, 1000 feet above the floor of Franconia Notch. Best of all would be to combine the waterfall hike with an overnight stay at the Lonesome Lake AMC hut. The hut offers visitors hearty home cooking, fine hospitality, and a perfect view of evening alpenglow shimmering on the cliffs of Franconia Ridge across the notch.

The Trail to the Falls

Both lanes of the Notch Parkway (I-93) have large, well-marked exits to parking for the Basin. Heading north, you will reach the turn-off 1.5 miles past the Flume. A footpath passes through a tunnel under the parkway and then follows the Pemigewasset River—here just a sparkling stream—a short distance upstream. Cross the footbridge to the west bank for the best view of the Basin and access to the trailhead.

Driving southbound you will find the turn-off 1.5 miles below Lafayette Campground. The walk in from this direction is more interesting, as the Pemi here exhibits a fine collection of scoured granite molds—the best being the Basin itself. An asphalted path along the east bank of the river provides access to the Basin for handicapped persons. For the best view, though, cross the first footbridge and continue along the west bank path to the Basin. Anyone camping at Lafayette Campground can hike along the river all the way to the Basin, via the Pemi Trail.

After visiting the Basin follow the path across the footbridge behind the viewing deck, past an information sign about the nonhuman mammals of Franconia Notch. Dogleg to the right along the clearly marked pathway. Only about 50 yards from the Basin you will reach a large sign identifying the Basin-Cascades trailhead.

Very quickly after you start up the trail the lower ledges of Cascade

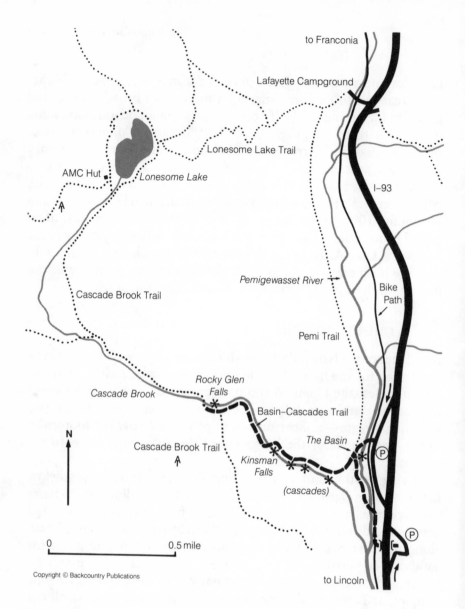

to Franconia

Lafayette Campground

Lonesome Lake Trail

AMC Hut

Lonesome Lake

I-93

Pemigewasset River

Bike Path

Cascade Brook Trail

Pemi Trail

Rocky Glen Falls

Cascade Brook

Basin–Cascades Trail

N

Cascade Brook Trail

The Basin

Ⓟ

Kinsman Falls

(cascades)

Ⓟ

0   0.5 mile

to Lincoln

Brook appear off to the left. Smooth granite slabs slope hundreds of yards upstream, bedecked with an assortment of cascades. The ledges can be reached from the trail almost anywhere along this stretch. In fact it is most enjoyable to leave the trail altogether and scramble up the sloping streambed or the woods immediately alongside. Since the trail parallels the cascades, meeting the ledge at a number of points, you won't get lost.

Immediately above the ledges Cascade Brook becomes a boulder-strewn mountain stream. The trail here slants into the woods and mounts the side of a ridge above the north bank of the brook, climbing steadily. At 0.4 mile from the trailhead a side path leads down to Kinsman Falls, which can't be seen until you reach the bottom of the ravine. Slightly farther up the main trail another side path runs to the top of the falls. Soon thereafter the trail crosses to the south bank of the brook on a narrow bridge—consisting of a log beam with a single rough handrail.

Beyond the log-beam bridge the trail becomes considerably rougher. Footing can be tricky in spots where the trail passes over slick roots, damp rocks, small side streams, or stretches of mud. To compensate for the poor footing you will find a running exhibit of brook treasures. There is a pretty cascade spilling over a steep granite wall into a shady gorge; a pool glittering like a tiny green starburst; a pothole tub serviced by a shower of cold stream water. Beside the trail the damp forest floor puts on its own display of mushrooms and mosses.

At 0.4 mile above the narrow footbridge a Forest Service sign nailed to a spruce points to Rocky Glen Falls. This is one sign that is hardly needed. It is not difficult to discern the identity of the formation to the right of the trail—a rocky glen split by a beautiful set of falls.

To reach the ledge platform atop the falls climb up through a damp cleft in the glen wall off to the left, being careful of slick footing. Just above Rocky Glen Falls the Basin-Cascades Trail merges with the Cascade Brook Trail. The latter proceeds across the brook and continues at a moderate grade another 1.4 miles to Lonesome Lake. The Cascade Brook Trail also links up with routes leading to the surrounding summits.

For a moderate 5.4-mile loop, you can hike up to the lake by the route just described and then descend by the Lonesome Lake Trail to the Pemi Trail, which returns to the Basin.

The Falls

Although the Basin is only a minor-league waterfall, it shouldn't be missed. Here the crystal-clear Pemigewasset—old guidebooks were fond of the adjective "pellucid"—funnels down a narrow chute into a deep pool. The force and angle of the cascade incessantly stir the pool's cold jade waters, creating a sweeping whirlpool that has undercut a granite shelf to form an elegant arched grotto. Watching the current revolve around the Basin pool, you can easily understand how water-borne sand and stones could carve such potholes in the solid granite bedrock. Geologists estimate that the Basin has been formed during the past 25,000 years, with most of the cutting being done as the retreating ice cap swelled the Pemi with grit-laden meltwater.

Whereas the Basin is for viewing, the cascades are for playing. For the price of a very short hike you get lovely, sunny ledges that have been bared by the stream and then scalloped, grooved, beveled, and polished by thousands of years of freshets. Near the base of the formation the stream is confined to a narrow channel along the left edge of the ledge (except when the water is high). Here the rock is smooth and level enough that even a toddler (under close supervision) can have a safe romp, in dry conditions.

Scrambling up and over a granite hump, you will find pretty waterslides and small, shallow pools dotting the long, sloped cut of rockbed. Higher, the views across the notch improve as the rock becomes more angular and ornamented with lacy cascades. Altogether there are more than a half-dozen distinct levels of cascades and pools stacked along the ledge. The entire stretch is custom made for exploring.

At Kinsman Falls exploring is less easy. The side path from the main trail descends steeply into a cool ravine. At the head of the ravine a 20-foot-high ribbon of whitewater pours through a narrow chute flanked by dark cliffs that rise nearly three stories above an oval pool. The ravine forms a cool, breezy amphitheater with the falls at center stage and a mural of mosses and lichens adorning the walls. Rounded boulders at the foot of the pool provide ample seating for the audience, which is generally quite small in number. Indeed you might have the theater all to yourself, even on days when the Basin below is jammed with tourists.

If you are not content being a spectator, it is possible to hop boulders to the left bank of the stream and climb carefully to the slabs atop Kinsman Falls. Considering the strength of the current and the dangerous plunge just below, attempts to leap the channel above the falls are definitely inadvisable.

Rocky Glen, the last of the waterfalls along the trail, is the most lovely of the lot—though it has keen competition for the honor. The dictionary defines a "glen" as a secluded, narrow valley. In this instance the valley is a narrow gorge carved into a large outcrop of frost-fractured rock. The formation looks as if some great force had pulled at the sides of the outcrop until it split along a zigzag fissure, providing a channel for the tumbling brook.

At the bottom of the falls you can approach the mouth of the glen and peer up the lower tongue of cascades, but the sheer cliffs make it difficult to get very far. The best view is obtained from the flat-topped boulders and ledges flanking the brook just above the falls. From this vantage point you can see the wide whitewater curtain cascading into the glen, forming a large pool at the center. The walls below amplify the lilting music of the brook. Altogether it is a wonderful place to sit a spell and absorb the woodland atmosphere.

Historical Detour

While Mount Washington attracted explorers within decades after the arrival of the Pilgrims, there is no record of Franconia Notch being explored until after the French and Indian War. Even the Indians seem not to have frequented the notch, perhaps because of their belief that the mountains were abodes of the gods. Since the township of Woodstock received its grant in 1763 and Franconia was settled in 1774, the Notch evidently had visitors already. But not until early in the nineteenth century was the first narrow road cleared through the primeval forest.

With the road came pony-express mail service to the north country, followed by stagecoach service from Plymouth (New Hampshire). With the coach service came the tourists. Just after midcentury, grand hotels were attracting thousands of well-heeled tourists to see the "savage and startling forms in which cliffs and forest are combined," as Thomas Starr King described Franconia Notch in 1859. King glowingly recounted for his readers the beauty of the Basin, and urged visitors to hike up the cascades "that slide along a mile of the slope of the mountain at the west." The formal trail, however, was not established for another century.

Anyone feeling that the natural serenity of the Basin is blighted today by the nearby traffic might find comfort in knowing that the problem is not exclusively a product of the auto age. King, too, remarked about the traffic more than a century ago: "if it [the Basin] did not lie so near the dusty road . . . ," he lamented.

As in most of the region, tourists were followed by loggers who gained access to the land when it was sold off by the state after the Civil War. In fact the Cascade Brook Trail up to Lonesome Lake ascends along old logging roads for much of its length.

After the elegant Profile House at the head of Franconia Notch was destroyed by fire in 1923, conservationists pressed for the property to be reacquired by the state for public recreation. In 1927 the notch became a forest reservation, financed by a grant of $200,000 from the state and matching contributions from the public—including a popular "buy-a-tree" campaign operated by the Society for the Preservation of New Hampshire Forests. The Forest Society managed the notch reservation until 1948, when it became a state park.

This entire span of history has been witnessed by a grand old white pine tree that still stands three fourths of the way up the lower cascades. The tree's tall spire, now barren, towers above the surrounding treetops. The purple-brown bark of its massive trunk (5 feet in diameter) is deeply furrowed with age. This forest elder is said to be one of the few precolonial white pines remaining in New England. In 1668, long before the White Mountain region was settled, all white pines large enough to be made into ship masts 2 feet in diameter and 72 feet long were claimed by the King for the Royal Navy. Thereafter deputies of the royal Surveyor General combed the countryside to brand the "mast pines," some of which were reported to be as large as 264 feet high and 7 feet in diameter.

The colonists, who did not accept royal directives complacently, generally cut what they liked anyway. They sometimes mobbed and beat royal agents who tried to enforce the mast laws. Robert Pike (1967) estimates that for every mast pine to reach England another 500 were cut for timber by the colonists. Pike contends nevertheless that resentment over the mast pine laws "did more to cause the American Revolution than the Stamp Act and the tea tax put together."

Today the White Mountain forests are graced by many tall and beautiful white pines, but the giants of the past have vanished.

CHAPTER 13

The Falling Waters Trail

◆

Location
Franconia Notch; trail begins at Lafayette Place parking lots.

Map
AMC Franconia Map: H-4/5.
DeLorme Trail Map: G-5.

Hiking Data
Distance, parking area to:
Stairs Falls . . . . 0.8 mile.
Swiftwater Falls . . . . 1.0 mile.
Cloudland Falls . . . . 1.4 miles.
Altitude Gain: 1100 feet to Cloudland Falls (altitude 2900 feet).
Difficulty: MODERATE.

◆

To summit baggers, Falling Waters Trail is the southern leg of a grueling but popular 8-mile loop traversing the craggy alpine ridge that runs across Mounts Lafayette, Lincoln, and Little Haystack. Even hikers preoccupied with thoughts of the spectacular summit ridge are captivated, however, by the beautiful waterfalls they encounter in Dry Brook ravine. They may pause at the falls only briefly on their long hike—time enough for a breather and a snack—but the spell of the waterfalls beckons them to return.

To travelers through Franconia Notch, Falling Waters Trail provides easy access to mountain forests, frolicking streams, and a string of fine falls and cascades, including Cloudland Falls, the highest in the vicinity. The hike could hardly be more convenient, with trailhead parking right off the Notch Parkway (I-93). Since we pass through the notch quite often, the convenience and beauty of Falling Waters has made it our most frequented trail. We have been drawn back over and over again to visit our pet falls in all their moods.

The Trail and the Falls

Traveling south, pull off the Notch Parkway at the sign for Lafayette Place, just under 2 miles past the Old Man viewing points. Swing to the right and park near the footpath tunnel that crosses under the Parkway to reach the trailhead. Heading north, watch for the Trailhead Parking sign about 1.5 miles beyond the Basin. There are picnicking facilities on both sides of the highway.

The Falling Waters Trail and the Old Bridle Path Trail (up Mount Lafayette) start together behind the hiker-information booth at the northbound parking area. If you are planning to hike beyond the falls to the summit ridge, check at the booth for a report on the mountain weather. One blustery July morning after the passage of a stormy cold front, we were informed that the summits would have below-zero (Fahrenheit) wind-chills all day with a chance of snow squalls. Clad in shorts, we were quite grateful for the news and altered our hiking plans accordingly.

At 0.2 mile the Falling Waters Trail splits off to the right from the Old Bridle Path across a footbridge over Walker Brook. Even if you intend to go no farther, it is worth a trip to the bridge just to spend a few moments listening to the brook's lilting music and watching its crystal-clear waters swirl over smooth boulders to small, sparkling pools. By bushwhacking 100 yards up the north side of the brook you can reach *Walker Cascades*. Here, clear brook waters slide 50 yards down sloping banks of burnished granite ledge, where a wide part in the forest canopy admits the noonday sun. The highest cascade is a 10-foot drop over a block midway up the ledge. Though not as grand as the well-known waterfalls along the Falling Waters Trail, Walker Cascades has better pools and fewer visitors. You might even find that you have the spot to yourself for a picnic or a cold swim.

Past the footbridge the Falling Waters Trail turns left and climbs parallel to Walker Brook for a short distance. Just off the trail near the top of this first hump, you can catch sight of silvery cascades below, but the descent to the brook from this point is rough. The trail then veers to the southeast, traversing a forest of slender hard-

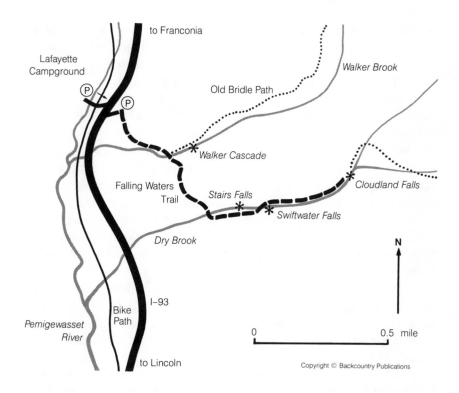

wood trees with an abundance of yellow birch and white birch. Apart from some muddy spots here, the trail is in fine condition all the way to the top of the falls.

Dry Brook is reached at 0.7 mile. Unless the brook is low some deft rock-hopping is needed to get across the series of small cascades and pools. The boulders here invite passers-by to pause and enjoy the woodland atmosphere.

Across the brook the trail climbs above the south bank, turns left, and ascends a short distance to the foot of Stairs Falls. This is the smallest of the three main waterfalls along the trail—not quite 20 feet high—but it is by far the prettiest. Here the brook spreads out and drapes a broad curtain of white ribbons over a tier of angular granite steps. An open patch of stony ground by the trail is a good place sit and meditate on the mantra of the falling waters. Another good rest spot is a rock perch on the smooth ledge at the top of the falls.

Above Stairs Falls the trail skirts a jagged rock wall known as the Sawteeth Ledges. Very quickly then you reach Swiftwater Falls, which churns down 60 feet of weathered bedrock chutes to a rippling pool that cuts directly across your path. To get to the granite ramp on the other side of the stream, you can either do another rock-hop or balance across on a birch log that spans the stream—if it hasn't yet washed away. Once across, be careful going up the rock slab; it is treacherous when slicked with spray, drizzle, or ice.

During dry weather Swiftwater Falls snakes down a long curved channel above the crossing, while in high water the brook splits to form a frothing white necklace around a large outcrop of rock at the top of the falls. Though Swiftwater Falls can be impressive at times it is less graceful than its neighbors above and below. Also, there is little room for scrambling around to explore the steep and confined ravine.

The trail next climbs steeply along the north side of Swiftwater Falls, providing an opportunity to clamber to a cluster of boulders midway up the falls. Some ledges at the top of the falls can also be reached with a bit of climbing. Above this steep pitch the trail steadily ascends the flank of a deep V-shaped ravine. Dry Brook tumbles down a long series of leaps and slides, usually well below the trail. At a few points the trail edges closer to the stream, providing access to fine "sitting rocks" with views up and down the ravine. One stretch of trail follows an old logging road, confirming that even the walls of the notch were invaded by the loggers around the turn of the century.

Because of the trail's steady grade, the hike above Swiftwater Falls seems longer than the indicated mileage. Just as you begin to doubt your guidebook, however, the trail crosses a rough outcrop of rock and descends to the climax of your waterfall hunt. In front of you *Cloudland Falls* tumbles over a fractured cliff, fanning into an endlessly animated white cone 80 feet tall. It is easy to scramble down the rocky bank to the streambed for a neck-stretching view from the bottom. When the water is high the cold draft of spray rushing down the narrow ravine and the echoing roar of the falls will chase you back onto the trail long before you tire of the view.

Although Cloudland Falls is the climax of the trip, don't stop at the bottom. The scene just above the falls is not to be missed. The

Swiftwater Falls in May

trail again becomes quite steep as it works its way up the left side of the falls beneath high overhanging ledges that sprout gigantic icicles from autumn until spring. The climb here makes it easy to appreciate the full stature of the falls, which may not look so tall when seen from below. At the top of the climb you will reach flat ledges that run out to the edge of the vertiginous lip of the waterfall ledge. This high terrace also provides an excellent view across Franconia Notch to the Kinsman ridge and the broad crest of Mount Moosilauke looming in the west. As a delightful bonus, a side stream gushes from the dark forest on the far side ledge and spills over a 15-foot-high wall to join the cascades and waterslides in the main channel.

The picturesque terrace above Cloudland Falls is a logical terminus for your waterfall trip. Beyond, the trail climbs alongside the north branch of Dry Brook and then crosses to a series of tedious, increasingly rugged switchbacks through dense evergreen forest. Until one reaches the stunted balsams just below the summit of Little Haystack, there is little more to see along the remaining 1.8 miles of the trail. The only exception is about 0.5 mile below the summit ridge, where a spur trail leads down to the base of a vast, exfoliated slab of bare granite, called Shining Rock. A trip to the summits would be incomplete without spending a few minutes investigating this impressive formation. Last but not least, the ridge across to the Lincoln and Lafayette summits is one of the most splendid walks in the White Mountains. From the north end of the ridge traverse you can descend by way of the AMC Greenleaf Hut (hot chocolate!) and the Old Bridle Path, arriving right back at your car.

In the winter the Falling Waters Trail usually has enough snowshoe traffic to permit anyone with warm, lined boots to hike in as far as Stairs Falls. Before being blanketed by deep snow, the molded green and blue ice formations of Walker Cascades and Stairs Falls are also fascinating to visit—carefully. Beyond Stairs Falls the steeper sections of trail generally require proper winter hiking equipment.

Historical Detour

Long after Crawford Notch began to suffer the blights of civilization—a turnpike, a railroad, logging operations, fires, landslides—Franconia Notch was still being celebrated for its "pleasing aspect of primeval quietude and tranquil beauty" (Sweetser, 1887). The Profile House at the head of Franconia Notch was one of the grandest and most elegant tourist hotels of the region, yet only a narrow

Balsam Fir

carriage road cut through the dense, undefiled forests of the Notch itself. Most visitors to Profile House arrived from the north by a narrow-gauge rail link out of Bethlehem. The railroad from Boston swung west from Plymouth through Warren and Haverhill, bypassing the high mountains.

Lafayette Place, at the base of the present Falling Waters Trail, is the site of a tavern built in 1835. Only ten years earlier the highest peak of the Franconia Range had been rechristened Lafayette in honor of the French general, who was visiting the United States at the time. Formerly it had been called Great Haystack, which explains why there is no big brother to Little Haystack along the ridge. Just before the Civil War the tavern was expanded into a tourist hotel called Lafayette House, which burned down only a few years later.

Most early guidebooks gave lavish and detailed descriptions of the Notch, the Flume, and the Basin, but said not a word about the waterfalls along the present Falling Waters Trail. The one early description is found in Sweetser's guidebook (1887), which referred collectively to the trio of falls along Dry Brook as "Walkers Falls." Thereafter the waterfalls seem to have disappeared from public view for nearly eight decades. Not even the *AMC White Mountain Guide* mentioned the falls until after the Falling Waters Trail was established in the late 1950s by Clyde F. Smith, a watchman at Cannon Mountain.

One cause for this long neglect was the devastating arrival of the lumberjacks in the forests and ravines on the western flanks of Franconia Ridge. Testimony to this effect is given in early editions of the AMC guide, which described how the Old Bridle Path from Lafayette Place had "long been disused and portions have been obliterated by logging." (This trail was reestablished in 1929.)

In 1918 the newly created White Mountain National Forest purchased the property up the ravine of Dry Brook from the Johnson Lumber Company (see Chapter 10). Franconia Notch itself was acquired by the State of New Hampshire in 1927. Since then Sweetser's "primeval quietude" has not exactly been restored, but you can once again enjoy the "tranquil beauty" of the regenerated forests and the long-lost waterfalls along the Falling Waters Trail.

CHAPTER 14

Franconia Falls

◆

Location
Off the Lincoln Woods Trail, which starts on the Kancamagus Highway east of Lincoln.

Map
AMC Franconia Map: H-5/6.
DeLorme Trail Map: H-6.

Hiking Data
Distance, parking area to falls: 3.2 miles.
Altitude gain: 300 feet (to altitude 1500 feet).
Difficulty: MODERATE. The round trip is more than 6 miles, but the trail is very level and easy.

◆

On a sunny summer's day when Franconia Brook is not running too high and the broad slabs of rock alongside the falls are dry, Franconia Falls is a perfectly delightful spot for a water frolic. You can take a quick swim in a cold, clear pool. Or you might muster the courage for a fast ride down a hip-wide water chute that spouts over the lip of a 10-foot-high cliff into the swirling current of a deep pothole pool. You can choose a cold Jacuzzi in the foaming wash at the base of a smaller cascade, or you can just take off your shoes and wade in more tranquil pools above or below the falls. Whatever your choice, the smooth, open ledges of colorful Conway granite soak up the warmth of the sun well past noon, providing a ready recovery from the chill of the brook waters.

At other times of the year you will be less inclined to go for a swim, but these beautiful falls are always a pleasure to visit and explore.

The Trail to the Falls

Traveling east along the Kancamagus Highway, the parking lot for the Lincoln Woods Trail will be on your left 4.7 miles east of Lincoln, immediately after the highway crosses the bridge over the East Branch of the Pemigewasset River. Although this trailhead lot is one of the largest in the White Mountains, it is often packed full—attesting to the popularity of the trails along the East Branch. With the rapid development of Lincoln and Loon Mountain, these trails have become as popular among cross-country skiers as among hikers. A forest service visitor center is located next to the parking lot.

From the parking area, cross the river on the footbridge. Pause at the center of the swaying bridge and watch the river's mesmerizing currents sweep through the maze of polished boulders below. At the end of the bridge, simply turn right and follow the trial for 2.8 miles to a smaller wooden footbridge spanning Franconia Brook, just past the Franconia Brook Campsite. Turn onto the spur trail that branches to your left just before this bridge. The falls are 0.4 mile up the spur. Each essential turn is clearly marked by a wooden sign.

You will notice that the Lincoln Woods Trail is unusually straight and level. The reason becomes apparent once you begin to see railroad ties down the middle of the trail: you are hiking the route of an old logging railroad. The route runs through mixed forest, essentially parallel to the East Branch of the Pemi. At spots where the river edges the trail you can walk to the bank and find large, smooth boulders to rest on, with views north up the riverbed toward the distant Bond ridge. In late July and early August another excellent place to stop for a rest, even if none is needed, is a huge raspberry patch on the left just past the Osseo Trail cutoff (leading up to the high peaks of Franconia Ridge) 1.4 miles from the parking lot.

One mile past the Osseo Trail, another trail branches off to the left. This one follows a small stream for 0.8 mile to tranquil Black Pond. Just beyond this turn for Black Pond, you reach the Franconia Brook Campground, amidst a stand of tall spruce, pine, and hemlock trees. The spur trail to Franconia Falls is only a hop, skip, and a jump ahead.

In the winter the Lincoln Woods Trail is heavily used for cross-

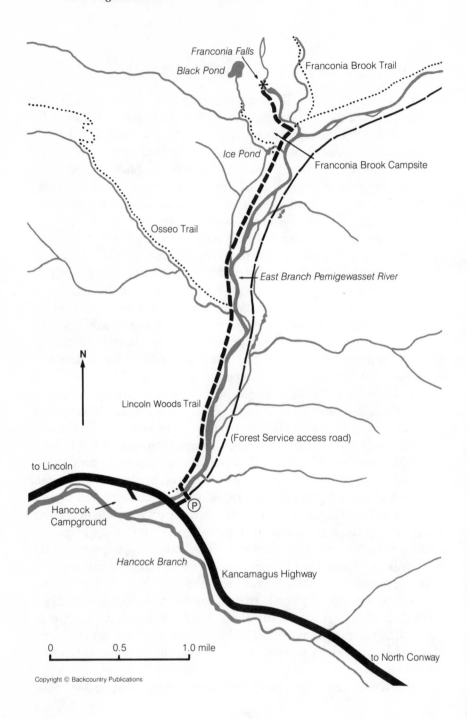

Franconia Falls

Black Pond

Franconia Brook Trail

Ice Pond

Franconia Brook Campsite

Osseo Trail

East Branch Pemigewasset River

N

Lincoln Woods Trail

(Forest Service access road)

to Lincoln

Hancock
Campground

Hancock Branch

Kancamagus Highway

0   0.5   1.0 mile

to North Conway

Copyright © Backcountry Publications

country skiing. The ski trip to Franconia Falls is very easy all the way to the lower section of the spur trail. The last 0.25 mile to the falls, however, is quite narrow and steep for negotiating on skis. It is also anticlimactic, since in mid-winter the falls are disguised under a thick mask of ice and snow. On one winter trip we encountered a party descending the spur trail. They told us that the trail was not passable far enough to reach the falls. Yet as they spoke the falls were less than 100 yards away, and their tracks confirmed that they had reached their destination without recognizing it!

The Falls

If it weren't for the bone-chilling water, you could hardly wish for a more fascinating waterfall playground than Franconia Falls. Here the crystal waters of Franconia Brook descend across an acre of smooth, sunny ledges in surging leaps and graceful slides, broken by deep, clear pools and gouged granite potholes, foaming with current.

The beauty of the entire formation lies in its long mosaic of narrow channels and silvery water veils cast amidst sculpted granite beds. The tallest free drop, midway up the cascades on the trail side of the ledges, is hardly more than 10 feet, yet it is of stunning design. A swift current rushes down from a small pool above and pours through a shallow water chute about hip wide and 20 feet long. At the base of the chute the water spouts over an abrupt drop into a deep, clear, swirling pool, ringed by steep, smooth granite walls on three sides. A second channel of water tumbles down another corner of the pool, its currents buffeting those spawned by the spout. Brave and hardy (or foolhardy?) adventurers enter the long chute well above the spout and ride the swelling current to the pool below. At the far end of the pool a fairly level slab offers the best exit. But be warned that the strong current in the pool is somewhat disorienting, and the pool's deep waters are shockingly frigid. When the water is high restrictions on swimming may be posted by the Forest Service. It is wise to check the information board in the parking area before hitting the trail.

Telling about Franconia Falls by describing the water spout is like telling about a three-ring circus by describing a favorite clown: there is a lot more to see as well. The ledges are custom made for careful exploring or carefree relaxing, with open views to the southeast

Franconia Falls

across the valley of the East Branch of the Pemigewasset toward Mount Hancock.

If you choose to explore, watch out for rock surfaces that have been polished by the current to the point of being slippery even when dry. This is not an idle warning. In August 1988, one woman slipped on a rock near the falls and broke her hip. If you are careful, however, and if the water level is not too high, you can negotiate your way safely up and down the full length of the falls, and beyond. For example, around a right-hand bend not far upstream from the falls, you can find an exquisite, crystal-green pool that has undercut a house-sized ledge to form a large grotto fringed with spruce.

Because of the gentle hike in, the campsite nearby, and the growth of tourism in the Lincoln area, you can expect to find a small crowd of visitors at Franconia Falls on any fine hiking day. There is room aplenty, however. Campers have the best opportunity to enjoy the falls at their leisure. The hike in to the Franconia Brook Campsite is one of the easiest trips for beginning backpackers. The campground has sixteen tent platforms, located very near the site of one of the old logging camps. Except at this national forest campsite, no camping is permitted within 0.25 mile of the Lincoln Woods Trail.

Historical Detour

The area you traverse to reach Franconia Falls has a fascinating history that dates back barely a hundred years. The description of the area in Moses Sweetser's 1887 *White Mountain Handbook* states simply that "this great wild land is virgin soil for the fisherman and hunter, and the brooks and ponds are swarming with trout." Though still pristine wilderness, the land was already in private hands as a result of a New Hampshire General Court decision in 1867 to sell off the state's undeveloped lands for a trifle, on the pretext of financing a fund for public schools.

After trunk-line rail links connected the White Mountain region with the major eastern urban markets, the loggers swarmed in to the backcountry. In 1892, virtually overnight, the present town center of Lincoln was transformed from the site of a small, remote mountain lodge amidst dense wild forests to the center of operations for timber baron—or wood butcher, depending on your point of view—James Everell Henry.

Earlier in life Henry had failed at drilling for oil in Canada, growing wheat in Minnesota, and scratching for gold in California, but his success at mining New Hampshire's forests was legendary. In his 1980 book on the old logging railroads, C. Francis Belcher cites a

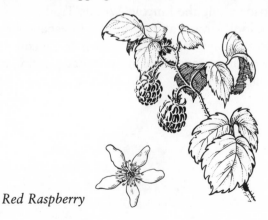

Red Raspberry

quotation attributed to J. E. Henry in a 1908 *Collier's* article: "I never see the tree yit that didn't mean a damned sight more to me goin' under the saw than it did standin' on a mountain." Whether the quotation is authentic or not, it certainly characterized Henry's attitude as he set about penetrating the wilderness with 72 miles of railroad lines to haul the timber out and supplies in. On summer Sundays Henry earned pocket change by running a flatcar full of "excursionists" into the heart of his mountain logging empire.

Incredibly, within fifteen years the area was virtually barren; it was first stripped clean of its towering spruce and fir, and then it was devastated by an awesome 1907 inferno that burned for over ten days on residual "slash" from the logging operations. Thereafter logging activity along the East Branch of the Pemigewasset ebbed. The federal government bought the land from near-bankrupt loggers in 1936, but only after more than one *billion* board feet of timber had been removed from the 66,000-acre watershed. The East Branch & Lincoln Railroad lines into the erstwhile wilderness continued to be used until 1948, when the last tracks were pulled up.

Equally incredible has been the verdant recovery of the East Branch forests so evident today. Indeed Belcher contends that the very deeds of "wood butchers" were the spark that ignited public opinion, leading to the passage of the Weeks Act in 1911 authorizing the federal purchase of land for the White Mountain National Forest. The story came full circle in 1984 when federal legislation established full wilderness protection for the Pemigewasset Wilderness area—erstwhile no longer.

As you stride along the Lincoln Woods Trail across the surviving hemlock ties, look around at the youthful forest and let your thoughts drift back to the days of the East Branch & Lincoln Railroad. One of the old workhorse engines can be visited nearby at the entrance to Loon Mountain.

CHAPTER 15

No. 13 Falls

———————◆———————

Location
In the Pemigewasset Wilderness, south of the Garfield ridge.

Map
AMC Franconia Map: G-5.
DeLorme Trail Map: F-6.

Hiking Data
Distance to falls:
    From Kancamagus Highway .... 8.0 miles.
    From NH 3 via Galehead Hut .... 7.3 miles.
Altitude gain from road to falls:
    From Kancamagus Highway: 600 feet (to altitude 1600 feet).
    From NH 3 via Galehead Hut: 0 feet (up a 2200 foot ridge then down
    2200 feet on the far side).
Difficulty: STRENUOUS.

———————————————◆———————————————

Around the turn of the century Camp #13 was the terminus of the
Franconia branch of the East Branch & Lincoln Railroad, which
hauled in supplies to the remote logging camp and hauled out the
timber. On occasional summer Sundays, flatbed cars carried tourists
on excursions from Lincoln into the interior. Gentlemen in dress
coats and ladies in ruffled blouses and full-length skirts would ride
into Camp #13 and marvel "at the completeness of the removal of
all [the trees] that once stood upon these mountains" (Harrington,
1926).
    Now that lightweight hiking boots have replaced flatcars as the
primary mode of transportation in the area, the falls and cascades
high on Franconia Brook still bear the name of the former lumber

camp. Located at the foot of Mount Garfield, deep in the heart of the Pemigewasset Wilderness, No. 13 Falls is the most remote of all the major waterfalls in the White Mountains. From the south the hike in is easy, but the round trip is 16 miles long; from the north the trail is very rough and only slightly shorter. Consequently, No. 13 Falls is impractical as a single day trip from the road for all but the hardy hiker who relishes a long, tiring trek.

For the rest of us, No. 13 Falls can best be reached by spending a night or two out on the trail. The most comfortable option is to establish a home base at Galehead Hut—itself the most remote of the AMC mountain huts—and then take a day hike down to the falls. If you stay more than one night at the hut you can also fit in a day trip up Twin Mountain and over to the summits of the Bond ridge. This is another superb excursion.

A second option for reaching No. 13 falls is to backpack and camp. There is a national forest tentsite with nine tent platforms right next to the falls. An easier alternative is to set up base camp at the Franconia Brook campground (see Chapter 14) and then make a pilgrimage to No. 13 Falls as a day hike. Experienced campers may prefer to push on into the Pemigewasset Wilderness to find an off-trail site for low-impact camping en route to the falls.

If you find yourself asking whether the trip to No. 13 Falls is worth all the trouble, the answer is a resounding "yes." The falls and cascades are beautiful, and there is a subtle magic to the wilderness. Also, your nights out in the mountains will be treasured memories. But be sure to pray for decent weather.

The Trail to the Falls

The easiest route in to No. 13 Falls is from the Kancamagus Highway via the Lincoln Woods Trail and the Franconia Brook Trail. The previous chapter described the first 2.8 miles from the trailhead parking lot to the footbridge over Franconia Brook. This time cross the footbridge to the Wilderness Trail and make a quick left turn onto the Franconia Brook Trail at mile 2.9.

The Franconia Brook Trail begins by climbing a low hill and entering the Pemigewasset Wilderness Area. For the next 3 miles the trail follows the gentle gradient of the old logging railroad track bed, except at stream crossings and at one rough detour just south of the Lincoln Brook Trail cutoff (mile 4.6). This detour bypasses the site of old Camp #9, which has been flooded by a beaver pond. Gray ghosts of trees killed by the rising pond waters are visible from the path. The detour is also the point where a young man lost his way returning from No. 13 Falls in July 1988 and died of exposure before being found. This tragic incident serves to remind us that the vast forest tracts of the Pemi Wilderness—though deeply satisfying to explore—are inhospitable places to get lost and dangerous places for parties to become separated.

Shortly after passing the Lincoln Brook Trail cutoff the Franconia Brook Trail edges another large beaver pond where the air is filled with swallows; kingfishers may also be seen perching on bleached gray snags. Look for the beavers' lodge, a mound of sticks and branches, in the middle of the pond. Beyond the beaver pond the trail passes through an *Alice in Wonderland* corridor beneath a canopy of spruce and fir trees, and then crosses Hellgate Brook (mile 5.4) and Redrock Brook (mile 6.4). Past Redrock Brook, where old Camp #10 was located, the trail climbs more persistently, though it never gets very steep. The crossing of Twin Brook at mile 7.4, near old Camp #12, marks the beginning of the home stretch to No. 13 Falls.

The alternative approach, from the north, ascends the Gale River Trail past Galehead Hut and then descends to No. 13 Falls by the Twin Brook Trail. To get to the Gale River Trail from US 3, watch for Trudeau Road about halfway between Franconia and Twin Mountain. A sign at this intersection points north to the Ammonoosuc district ranger station, where national forest information can be obtained. You want to turn south, however, onto the bumpy gravel road opposite Trudeau Road.

Once on the gravel road, continue straight for 1.35 miles to a right turn. From this turn it is just a 0.25-mile drive to the trailhead information sign and parking area. The Gale River Trail first passes through a broad belt of northern hardwood forest, crossing a sturdy footbridge over the North Branch of the Gale River at mile 1.5. This is a beautiful rest spot. Bear in mind, however, that the river feeds a public water supply, so swimming and wading are prohibited here. The trail gradient remains moderate for another 1.5 miles, during

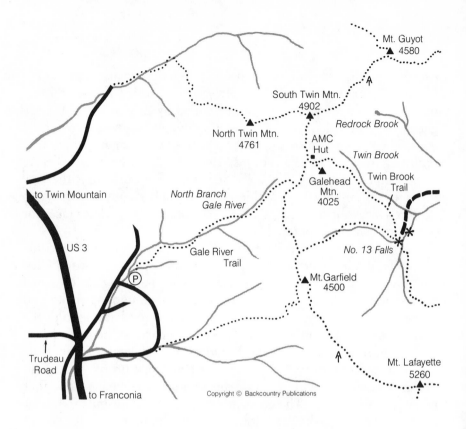

which the river is crossed back to the west bank. Gradually you will notice the forest being conquered by conifers. Then comes the crunch: a steep, rough, 1000-foot climb to the Garfield Ridge Trail (mile 4.1). At the top of the steep climb turn left. The hut is 0.5 mile farther on and 400 feet higher.

To reach the falls from the hut, start off on the Frost Trail, a short spur that brings 4000-foot-peak baggers up Galehead Mountain. In only 0.1 mile the Twin Brook Trail branches to the left. Pull up your knee bandages and head on down. It's a sustained drop of 2.6 miles and 2200 feet down to No. 13 Falls. Obviously this means you will have a hard slog back to the hut, but a hearty hut dinner and the panoramic twilight view of the Pemigewasset Wilderness should be enough to revive your spirits.

In addition to the two routes described above, No. 13 Falls can also be reached by the Lincoln Brook Trail, or by *descending* along the Franconia Brook Trail from the Garfield Ridge Trail just east of

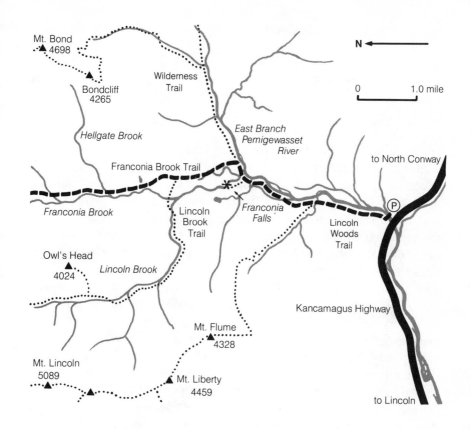

the Garfield Ridge Campsite. If you are interested in these alternate routes, consult the AMC *White Mountain Guide* for details.

The Falls

So what do you get in return for all the effort required to reach No. 13 Falls? Nothing grand or dramatic. Your reward is simply a delightful package of cascades, waterfalls, and pools, all wrapped in tranquil wilderness. In fact the very name of the place is often truncated to "13 Falls," which is descriptive of what you will find.

Approaching by the Franconia Brook Trail from the south, your first contact with the falls will be the muffled undertone of falling water harmonizing with the rushing breeze. Very soon the forest to the left opens up to reveal a broad, sloping ledge that invites you to climb down from the trail. Go right ahead and accept the invitation. You will be greeted by a long slide of water that tumbles down a smooth bedrock ramp and pours over a 10-foot block of ledge into a clear green horseshoe-shaped pool. Stop for a snack and a rest. Dunk your head in the cold stream, cool your tired feet, or take a quick dip in the pool. Then get ready for some exploring.

Upstream the exposed bedrock (metagraywacke and then Kinsman quartz monzonite) stretches on for hundreds of feet, providing a wide selection of small chutes and slides, shallow pothole pools, scalloped tubs, and sunning rocks on which to recover from a cold dunk. Partway up the sloping ledge the streambed forks. To the right—in the direction of the campground and the trail junction—a maze of thin cascades slips down a broad expanse of broken slabs. Here are found the sunniest and warmest basking rocks. Along the left-hand fork the ledge narrows. You can follow the slabs up alongside a waterslide to a lovely mare's tail waterfall 20 feet high. Above this the forest closes in more tightly, providing a deep green frame for a picturesque water spout that empties into a split-level pair of pools.

Now explore downstream. Just below the horseshoe pool a beautiful triple-ribbon cascade feeds into an enormous oval pool set in a cool glen. This is surely one of the most impressive pools in the whole region. We like to call it the Olympic Pool. Because it is so large and deep this pool is very cold; it would be wise to check with your cardiologist before going for a swim here. Below the Olympic Pool you will find the brook tumbling to one pool after another, splitting the forest with a deep ravine.

You can't help but enjoy yourself at No. 13 Falls. You can scramble around and explore the ledge, or splash around in the brook, or just bask in the sun and relish a hard-earned rest—while gathering strength for the long hike out.

Historical Detour

In addition to the railbed and the scars of old logging roads traced on the hillsides, physical remnants of the old lumber camps in the Pemigewasset Wilderness can still be found. At No. 13 Falls the most apparent sign is a set of thick iron spikes that protrude here and there from the ledge. Elsewhere we have stumbled on half-rotted spiked logging boots, a fancy cast-iron oven door, rusted iron wheels, and even a well preserved rail.

One of many cascades at No. 13 Falls

In his book *Logging Railroads of the White Mountains*, C. Francis Belcher describes the character of J. E. Henry's logging camps along the East Branch & Lincoln Railroad. A typical camp was a small community that included "stables, living quarters, cook shacks, blacksmith shops, and allied structures for many horses, 150 or so lumberjacks, and their bosses." All Henry's buildings were red-painted frame-and-board structures that could be dismantled and hauled by rail to another camp as logging operations shifted.

The barracks often slept 100 exhausted, snoring lumberjacks at a time, two per bunk. This was relative comfort compared to the primitive lumber camps portrayed by Richard Pinette in *Northwoods Echoes* (1986). In the earlier camps a dozen men slept on their sides stacked like spoons under a single quilt, conserving space and providing a feast for the lice.

The lumberjacks were well fed, with large variations in quality depending on the cook. Supply trains arrived each Tuesday and Friday, so fresh beef was available regularly. Meals were eaten in silence in compliance with the standard cook's rule: "Feed your guts and get through" (Poole, 1946). Other company rules were equally strict. Most dealt with the care of horses, with safety, and with economy. On the latter point, workers were routinely charged for broken equipment and fined for all manner of rule violations. Consequently the tough, spirited lumberjacks often found payday to be quite an unpleasant surprise. To settle any arguments over these punitive sanctions, it is said, J. E. Henry himself handed out the monthly paychecks armed with a gun.

Tote roads from the main camps were cut into the mountainsides during the summer, providing access to timber high up the slopes. Most of the actual logging was done in the winter when the tote roads were smoothed over with ice and snow. The 12-hour work days began and ended in frigid darkness. The job was physically demanding, tightly disciplined, and very dangerous.

In this context the hike into No. 13 Falls doesn't seem so tough, after all.

CHAPTER 16

Thoreau Falls

---◆---

Location
At the far end of Zealand Notch from Zealand Road, off US 302.

Map
AMC Franconia Map: G-7.
DeLorme Trail Map: F-8.

Hiking Data
Distance, parking area to:
Zealand Falls .... 2.7 miles.
Thoreau Falls .... 4.8 miles.
Altitude gain: 400 feet to Zealand Falls (altitude 2500 feet), but only 200
feet to Thoreau Falls (altitude 2300 feet).
Difficulty: MODERATE, but long.

---◆---

Henry David Thoreau, the renowned New England writer, naturalist,
and philosopher, is honored in the White Mountains by one wonderfully fitting tribute: a waterfall of sweeping beauty, located in the
most distant corner of the Merrimack watershed. Moses Sweetser
chose to name these falls for Thoreau in part because the poet of
Concord had "so often written lovingly of the Merrimack River and
its fountains in the wilderness."

Thoreau visited the White Mountains and climbed Mount Washington in 1839 and again in 1858, but never saw the particular
"fountain in the wilderness" that now bears his name. Although
Ethan Allen Crawford was leading parties to Ethan Pond as early as
1830, the vast forest tracts down the North Fork of the Pemigewasset
River's East Branch were still essentially *terra incognita*. Today doz-

ens of hikers visit the falls each weekend when the weather is clear and mild. Many even ski in during the winter.

Unlike Thoreau, we now have the advantage of a well-graded trail, as well as books and maps to direct us to the falls. But we are at a keen disadvantage as students of Nature. Who today can match Thoreau's patience and diligence in absorbing the lessons of the forest? In a eulogy delivered at Thoreau's funeral, Ralph Waldo Emerson described how his friend took to the woods:

> He knew how to sit immovable, a part of the rock he rested on, until the bird, the reptile, the fish, which had retired from him, should come back and resume its habits. . . . He knew every track in the snow or on the ground, and what creature had taken this path before him. . . . Under his arm he carried an old music-book to press plants; in his pocket, his diary and pencil, a spy-glass for birds, microscope, jack-knife and twine. He wore a straw hat, stout shoes, strong gray trousers, to brave scrub-oaks and smilax, and to climb a tree for a hawk's or a squirrel's nest. He waded into the pool for the water-plants. . . .

To Thoreau the wilds were a tonic. He found beauty at each step, heard music in the stillness of the forest, and delighted in fresh fragrances borne by the breeze. As much as the man himself, Thoreau Falls honors Nature—with a capital N.

One very enjoyable way to visit Thoreau Falls is to spend a night or two at the AMC Zealand Falls Hut. From that base Thoreau Falls is an easy day trip, leaving plenty of time for imbibing the heady tonic of the wilds.

The Trail to the Falls

The Zealand Road turns off of US 302 at the Zealand Campground, nearly midway between Twin Mountain and Bretton Woods. Drive in 3.6 miles to the parking area and trailhead sign at the end of the road. From there, the route to the falls runs straight through Zealand Notch for 4.6 miles via the Zealand Trail and then the Ethan Pond Trail. For the final 0.25 mile you follow the Thoreau Falls Trail down to the falls. An alternative route to Thoreau Falls is to start on the other end of the Ethan Pond Trail at Willey House Station in Crawford Notch. This hike is favored by many backpackers, who spend a night at the Ethan Pond shelter, but it is a bit longer than the hike through Zealand Notch and involves an extra 1400-foot climb over the Willey ridge.

From the end of the Zealand Road, the Zealand Trail crosses a bridge over Hoxie Brook and ascends slowly through evergreen forest. Look for blue blazes at spots where the direction of the trail is not readily apparent. At 0.7 mile the trail takes a hard right turn and picks up the smooth, well-graded bed of the old Zealand Valley logging railroad.

Soon the character of the forest changes dramatically as the trail approaches a marshy tableland at the head of the notch. Long sections of plank walkway bridge shallow beaver ponds where stunted but sturdy white birch and feathery mountain ash replace the conifers. In early summer redstarts and white-throated sparrows flutter in the undergrowth, whistling greetings. In the spring, when the wildflowers are in bloom, you might also surprise a garter snake out basking in the sun.

The woods soon open out to provide a magnificent view of Zealand Notch, a U-shaped gap carved out of an ancient mountain pass by the Pleistocene glaciers. This scene is what Franconia Notch must have looked like 200 years ago, before it was "improved" for tourists and travelers!

After passing the terminus of the A–Z Trail (from Crawford Depot) at mile 2.3, the Zealand Trail circles placid Zealand Pond. It is hard to resist stopping to take a photograph of the large beaver lodge in the foreground. On the forested slope behind the pond a dark green stripe of conifer spires marks the location of Whitewall Brook and Zealand Falls. At 2.5 miles the Zealand Trail ends, and the Ethan Pond Trail begins. To the right, the Twinway trail leads up a 10-story flight of steep rock steps to Zealand Falls and the AMC hut (0.2 mile).

Continuing along the Ethan Pond Trail, you now enter one of the loveliest forests in the region. All around you are gleaming white birch with twisted boughs—a legacy of catastrophic fires that ravaged the notch around the turn of the century. Soft yellow-green crowns of birch also blanket the steep mountain wall to the west, which is capped by the gray crags of Zeacliff, 1300 feet overhead.

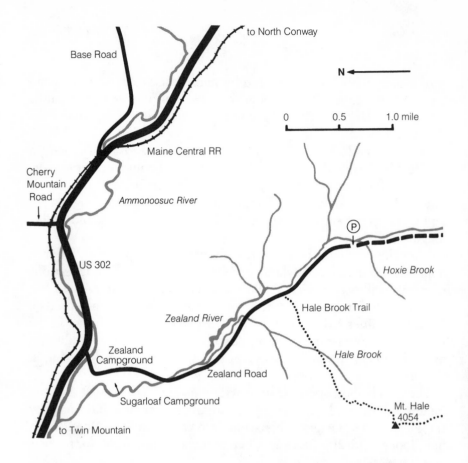

The trail contours along the eastern wall of the notch 200 feet above Whitewall Brook and 600 feet beneath the stark, crumbling cliffs of Whitewall Mountain. Although the path generally follows the old railroad grade it is not exactly level. Nearly a century of slides, storms, and rockfalls have buried some sections of the old railbed and washed away others. The slides also opened up superb views of the notch and created corridors where thrive a new generation of young spruce, blueberries (!), and colorful wildflowers such as the splendid rhodora. From one fresh rockslide you can even spot a huge (and heretofore undocumented) natural rock profile of a female moose at the crest of the Whitewall cliffs. Admittedly this requires a bit of imagination, as well as a proper angle.

The Zeacliff Trail cuts off right at mile 3.8 (just past the moose profile). Not far beyond, the notch widens out and the trail passes into immature boreal forest. Soon you reach the junction with Tho-

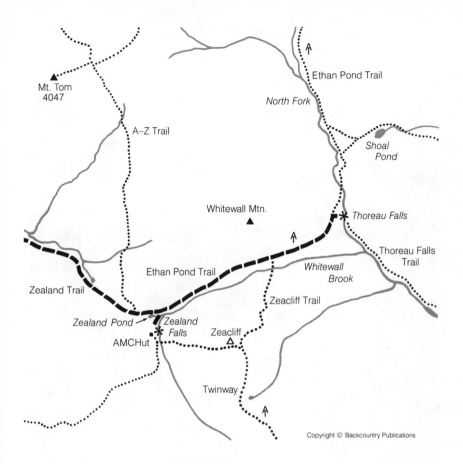

reau Falls Trail. The sign at the junction gives the distance to the waterfall as 0.3 mile, but it is even nearer than that.

The Falls

On a clear day your first impression at Thoreau Falls probably won't be of the waterfall itself, but rather of the magnificent view to the southwest across the deep, wild valley of the North Fork to the high ridge of Mount Bond. Very likely the second feature to catch your eye will be the clear stream sliding across broad, smooth shelf of Conway granite, dimpled with potholes. When you walk to the edge of the shelf, however, the waterfall will command your attention. At your feet the stream dances in a sweeping arc down long, sloping terraces of weathered granite, undercutting a high concave wall topped with slender birch that sway in the constant updraft.

Thoreau Falls

Sweetser (1887) described Thoreau Falls as being 200 feet high and 0.5 mile long. These figures might have included some of the cascades above and below the main waterfall, but they do convey the impressive scale of the whole formation. The grandeur of Thoreau Falls was extolled in Harrington's *Walks and Climbs in the White Mountains* (1926): "none of the others has the massive wildness, the long splashing descent . . . , the lonely isolation, the poetic atmosphere. . . ."

For the best view, work your way to the bottom of the ledge, from which point the long dogleg cascade is especially lovely. When the rock is dry, it is normally possible to scramble right down the ledge. In fact, the angle of the rock makes the scramble very delightful— or very scary, depending on your predilection! (The topmost incline is a bit steep, but it can be bypassed easily on the right.) If you prefer to avoid scampering down smooth, airy ledges you can reach the bottom of the falls by the trail, which crosses the stream at the top of the ledge and descends through the woods.

Exploring above and below the falls is great fun. There are small cascades with pretty pools, large tumbled boulders, and interesting rock formations. Downstream, watch for a natural bridge in the bed of the stream, and a large wedged boulder that appears to be supporting an overhanging outcrop.

Compared to Thoreau Falls, Zealand Falls is a minor attraction. It can be quite pretty with a good current, but you wouldn't want to walk a 6-mile round trip just for this. Still, Zealand Falls is a pleasant treat for hut guests and weary hikers passing by. The brook that tumbles down the ledges alongside the Zealand Falls Hut is named Whitewall Brook, which is a bit strange considering that Whitewall Mountain is on the *other* side of the notch. Maybe someone got tired of having everything named Zealand.

Spaced along the ledges beside the hut are small cascades, rippled waterslides, crystal pools, and etched channels that resemble miniature flumes. The open slabs also provide excellent views through the notch to distant Mount Carrigain. The main falls are below the hut, where the ledge abruptly drops two stories into a shady ravine. Large angular blocks of granite that have been wedged from the wall by frost clutter the base of the falls.

On a warm summer day the atmosphere at Zealand Falls is festive.

Kids ramble up and down the streambed, while the adults bask on the rocks or follow the youngsters around with cameras. Because the walk in is quite easy, Zealand Falls Hut is a great place for a family adventure.

Historical Detour

"Thank God they cannot cut down the clouds!" Thoreau said of the loggers—even before the arrival of the railroads and the advent of woodpulp paper making triggered destructive lumbering in the late nineteenth century. Along with Franconia Brook to the west, Zealand Valley epitomizes the cycle of devastation and regeneration. C. Francis Belcher's *Logging Railroads of the White Mountains* provides an authoritative account of the dramatic saga of the Zealand forests.

As late as 1887 Sweetser's *Handbook for Travellers* averred that the upper watershed of the East Branch of the Pemigewasset "is still in a condition of primeval wildness, and has not been invaded by clearings, roads, or trails." Actually his information was slightly out of date. J. E. Henry had begun construction of the Zealand Valley Railroad up to the notch in 1884, logging as he went. In these early days Henry was not clear-cutting. He concentrated on the larger spruce trees in what was then a conifer forest. Henry's base was the village of Zealand, which was located just west of today's campground. At that time Zealand was a sizable community complete with a railyard, a depot, a mill, homes, shops, and a school. Today, not a trace remains.

Rhodora

In 1886, a major fire consumed 12,000 acres of forest in the Zealand area, including virgin tracts well up into notch. Reportedly the fire was ignited by sparks from one of Henry's engines. In an 1891 speech the state fire commissioner described the effects:

> If there is any sight entirely disheartening, it is that of these fire denuded tracts, from which everything has been swept clean, down to the underlying rocks. . . . For seven miles up the valley, the fire swept resistless across it from crestline to crestline . . . (Belcher, 1980.)

Yet the logging continued, pushing farther up the notch. By the early 1890s logging trains ran 11 miles into the former wilderness, crossing the North Fork a short distance above Thoreau Falls. A large railroad yard was located where the placid beaver marshes now stand, just north of Zealand Pond. A writer in 1892 viewed the operations and called the Zealand Valley a "vast scene of waste and desolation."

That same year Henry moved his company to Lincoln (see Chapter 14), and by 1897 the Zealand railroad ceased operations. In 1903 the debris of slash from Henry's logging operations kindled a second intense fire that burned another 10,000 acres and transformed Zealand Notch into a "desolate ash wasteland."

Many feared that the notch, or "Death Valley," as one writer called it, would never again be able to support plant or animal life. But as Thoreau observed many years earlier: "How swift Nature is to repair the damage that man does!" A landmark date in the restoration of the forest is 1915, when the entire Zealand River watershed was purchased by the White Mountain National Forest.

By 1922 the AMC *White Mountain Guide* was still referring to "bare, fire-scarred walls of Zealand Notch," but it also reported that the old railbed was choked with young cherry trees. In 1926 Harrington found alders, poplars, and birch growing back as well. In 1933 the Zealand Falls Hut opened to the public. The "Zealand wilds" had been devastated and then reborn.

A similar story can be told of the forests around the North Fork, near Thoreau Falls—though without the fires. In 1907 the interior region was still all virgin forest, but by 1922 the lumberjacks were at work on the last major stands of old growth timber below Thoreau Falls. Hikers called this "the Desolation region." And now—well, see for yourself.

Thoreau supplied the tale with a fitting moral, which has become the motto of the Wilderness Society:

In wildness is the preservation of the world. . . .

The Saco
Watershed

◆

Arethusa Falls

CHAPTER 17

Waterfalls from Brickett Place

Mad River Falls / Bickford Slides

◆

Location
Southern end of Evans Notch, Route 113 between Chatham, NH and Gilead, ME.

Map
AMC Carter-Mahoosuc Map: F-12/13.
DeLorme Trail Map: C-15.

◆

High in Evans Notch, under the defiant cliffs of East Royce Mountain, the Cold River springs to life. For 3 miles the slender watercourse cuts through tangled forests, dropping more than 800 feet to the broad valley that bears its name. Because of the rugged headlands to the north, the Cold River valley never developed into a major artery for commerce or tourism. To this day it remains an oasis of tranquillity, unspoiled by crowds or commercialism.

At the tip of the Cold River valley, where Route 113 crosses the New Hampshire/Maine state line and begins ascending Evans Notch, there is a well-preserved red-brick farmhouse called Brickett Place. Starting at Brickett Place, the Bickford Brook Trail climbs Speckled Mountain (2906 feet) to the east of Evans Notch, while the Royce Trail mounts the abrupt ridges of Royce Mountain (3116 feet) on the western wall of the notch. Only 300 vertical feet up each of these two trails you will reach a lovely waterfall: to the east the shady

Mad River Falls during a heavy rain

ravine of Bickford Slides, and to the north the golden basin of Mad River Falls. Like the valley below, these waterfalls are balms for the spirit: serene, picturesque, and secluded.

Just 0.25 mile south of Brickett Place the Forest Service maintains the Cold River Campground and the adjacent Basin Campground, together totaling thirty-five sites. Set beside a reservoir in a deep valley lobe, the Basin Campground is especially lovely. (Swimmers be warned: the reservoir is said to have leeches.) These campsites provide an excellent base for exploring the eastern front of the White Mountains. Probably the most popular local hike is the circuit of spectacular Baldface Mountain, which starts on the west side of NH 113, 1.9 miles south of the Forest Service campgrounds.

Mad River Falls

Hiking Data
Distance, parking area to falls: 1.6 miles.
Altitude gain: 300 feet (to altitude 900 feet).
Difficulty: MODERATE.

The Mad River (not to be confused with the one in Waterville Valley) drains the eastern slope of West Royce Mountain and joins the Cold River about 1.5 miles above Brickett Place. The hike in to Mad River Falls simply accompanies the Cold River up to its junction with the Mad River and then climbs to the falls. Faded blue blazes mark the way.

A small white trail sign across Route 113 from Brickett Place locates the start of the Royce Trail. A few cars can squeeze onto the shoulder of the road at the trailhead, and more ample parking space can be found behind Brickett Place. For the first 0.25 mile the trail follows a level logging road over to the Cold River. Where the logging road enters a clearing and veers left, the trail heads straight down to the river and hops rocks across to the west bank. (After heavy rains all the river crossings on the Royce Trail may require wading through moderately strong currents.)

Apart from some irregular footing, the hike up the Cold River is quite easy and rather delightful. One treat for hikers is a wall of low cliffs on the east bank of the river where frost wedging has exposed clear fold patterns in the gray paragneiss bedrock that underlies the district. Beyond the cliffs the trail returns to the east bank and soon passes four pools separated by small slides and cascades, where the north-south line of the channel catches the warm midday sun. A scooped pothole in the bed of the third pool up is nearly irresistible for a quick swim—if you don't mind the cold water or the tiny trout that nibble at intruding toes.

Continuing north, the Royce Trail crosses a rock-strewn side stream and fords back to the west bank, passing more pools and small cascades. Promptly after this last zigzag across the Cold River the trail crosses the Mad River, feeding in from the west. Shortly the path begins climbing up a long, steep ridge. Summit-bound hikers have a hard slog ahead, but waterfall-seekers have to climb only 0.1 mile before reaching a small sign that marks the short spur path to Mad River Falls.

The spur path leads to an overlook at the edge of a precipitous basin. Fifty feet underfoot an amber pool sparkles with darting rays of sunlight that penetrate the high forest canopy overhead to cast a golden hue over the scene. At the far corner of the basin the waterfall slips in fine strands down channels of fractured bedrock flanked by tall sentinel cliffs. The rustling of the forest boughs muffles the gentle rush of the falls. From top to bottom Mad River Falls descends 100 feet over a receding series of drops and slides. In low water the falls are an ornament for the basin, like spun-glass artwork in a golden cathedral. After a storm, however, the falls roar headlong over the steep ledges and sweep across the basin floor. At such times the normally gentle stream earns its imposing name.

For a close-up view of the pool, the falls, and the fractured rock formations, you will have to climb into the basin. The word "climb" is used deliberately here because the descent is steep and tricky, with dirty footing. A few well-placed tree roots render the passage manageable, however, even for people who are not prone to accept foolish dares. Down in the bowl you will discover that you are not looking at a waterfall scene at all; rather, you are *in* a waterfall scene. It is the difference between watching a play and being in the cast. You are surrounded by the landscape and the music of Mad River Falls.

Of course if you are unsure of your scrambling abilities, you should heed the old cliché: better safe than sorry. Enjoy the view from the overlook and then backtrack down to play in the pools along the Cold River. Or head back to Brickett Place for Act II.

Bickford Slides

Hiking Data
Distance from parking area:
 0.7 mile to the first slide.
 1.1 miles to the upper slide.
Altitude gain:
 300 feet (to altitude 900 feet).
 500 feet to upper slide (altitude 1100 feet).
Difficulty: EASY to the lower slides, rougher above.

Two long buttress ridges fall toward Brickett Place from the summit ridge of Speckled Mountain. The buttresses terminate at high knobs called Sugarloaf Mountain and Blueberry Mountain. In the deep ravine between the two knobs, Bickford Brook has bared a series of bedrock ledges known as the Bickford Slides: Lower, Middle, and Upper. The brook has a very modest current for much of the season, but even when the water is low the slides are lovely.

Park behind Brickett Place, where a Forest Service sign to the right of the white garage marks the start of the Bickford Brook Trail. The trail enters the woods—a second-growth mix of scrubby trees—and immediately climbs 200 feet to join a well-graded Forest Service track. This grassy track then winds around the lower slope of Sugarloaf Mountain and climbs at a very moderate grade into Bickford Brook ravine. Here the forest changes to mature northern hardwoods that are dazzling during foliage season. Looking around, you will find it hard to imagine that only seventy years ago the AMC guide described these slopes as "steep pasture."

At mile 0.6 the Blueberry Ridge Trail forks off to the right (east) toward the Lower Slides. To see the whole set of slides you can hike a loop that consists of the two trails meeting here plus a rough Chatham Trail Association path up Bickford Brook. You can either turn at this first junction and then climb along the brook from the Lower Slides, or you can continue up the service road another 0.4

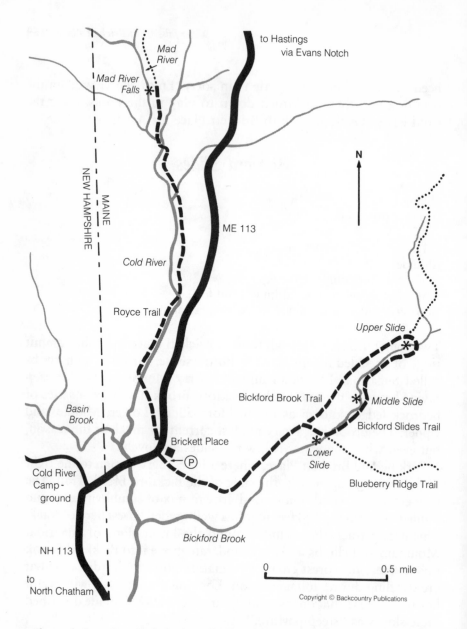

N

NEW HAMPSHIRE

MAINE

Mad River

Mad River Falls ✳

to Hastings via Evans Notch

ME 113

Cold River

Royce Trail

Upper Slide ✳

Bickford Brook Trail

Middle Slide ✳

Bickford Slides Trail

Basin Brook

Brickett Place

Ⓟ

Lower Slide ✳

Blueberry Ridge Trail

Cold River Camp-ground

Bickford Brook

NH 113

to North Chatham

0   0.5 mile

Copyright © Backcountry Publications

mile and then descend the brook from the Upper Slides. On the latter course watch carefully for a small sign saying "CTA Path, Upper Slides" on a tree to the right shortly after the track narrows. The route described below follows the first of these options.

Turn onto the Blueberry Ridge Trail, which descends directly to Bickford Brook. Beyond the brook the trail climbs steeply up Blueberry Ridge, which, as the name suggests, bursts with blueberries in early August. At the brook one sign points to the Lower Slides just below and another sign steers you to the left up the Bickford Slides Trail (not to be confused with the Bickford *Brook* Trail, which you were on a few moments earlier).

The Lower Slide begins with a 45-foot-long chute through a small flume overhung with slender oak, maple, hemlock, and beech trees. Below this flume, the brook flows across a small terrace and slips 25 feet down a steep wall of gneiss to an unusual trough pool in a very narrow gorge. Invisible from the trail above, this glistening pool is about 15 feet long but only 2 to 4 feet wide. Its sheer, smooth walls are sprinkled with clinging mosses and wildflowers. The ledge at the head of the trench can be reached most readily by walking down through the woods above the far (eastern) wall of the ravine to an obvious ramp that angles back into the gorge.

This first set of slides is entirely unlike the others higher up the brook. To see for yourself follow the Bickford Slides Trail (yellow blazes) up the ravine. For the first few rods the path is moderate and well trodden, but it soon becomes rough and steep. Evidently the Upper Slides don't receive so many visitors. After 0.25 mile of ascending through excellent mushroom and wildflower habitat (watch for purple flowering raspberries) the trail climbs a small ridge and descends to the Middle Slide.

Here you enter a shady glen at the foot of a transparent pool that mirrors the soft green radiance of the mosses on surrounding rocks and the dome of spreading hardwood boughs overhead. Forty feet above the pool Bickford Brook passes through a gate of dark gray cliffs and slides down a mossy bank of ledge, the slope of which is broken by small terraces cradling shallow pools. An eroded footpath circles to the left of the pool, skirts a deep cave under a precarious crag of fractured rock, and climbs alongside the cascades. This is not the proper route out of the glen, however. The Chatham Trail Association path exits up the opposite (east) wall.

Beyond the Middle Slide the path is narrow and overgrown as it parallels a shallow gorge that the brook is busy chiseling. After a long 0.1 mile you will approach the rim of another deep basin at Upper Bickford Slide. Here the gentle brook slips over a headwall carpeted with thick moss and gurgles down to a shimmering pool cupped in a narrow ravine. The path circles the rim of the slide basin, crosses to the west side of Bickford Brook just above the Upper Slide, and angles over to the main Bickford Brook Trail, only 100 yards away. You don't need a compass and map to figure out that *down* is the way back to Brickett Place.

Historical Detour

A primitive trail through the northern pass to the Androscoggin valley was established by the Pequawket Indians who inhabited the Cold River valley before the arrival of the Europeans. For the most part, though, colonial history bypassed the Cold River valley. It was the Saco River that served as a primary artery of exploration and migration. Like today's tourists, early adventurers were more interested in reaching the heart of the mountains than in exploring the frontal range. During the French and Indian War famous battles were fought to the south of the Cold River valley. In 1762 nearby Fryeburg became the first town chartered in the White Mountain region, and the following year it was the first town to be settled—beating Plymouth (NH) by one year on each score. Fryeburg soon became the foremost gateway to the White Mountains, but the Cold River valley slept under its blanket of wilderness forests.

A few early settlers did travel up the Cold River and across the old Indian trail to Gilead and Bethel. The first settlers to cut homesteads from the great forests of the upper valley itself arrived in 1781, fourteen years after Chatham was chartered. That same year Captain John Evans was put in charge of protecting settlers in the region following an Indian raid on Bethel (see Chapter 27). Evans Notch now honors his name.

John Brickett arrived in 1803. He settled in a log cabin on the Cold River, cleared farmland for corn and potatoes, and burned hardwood logs to make potash, which, among other things, was used for fertilizer and soap making. The farmhouse now called Brickett Place was built in 1812. Brickett used bricks, which he fired himself, to avoid having to make long trips to the nearest planing mill down on the Saco River. His family lived in this house for generations; in fact direct descendants still live in the neighborhood.

According to local folklore John Brickett played a unique role in preserving the serenity of the Cold River valley. When the Portland & Ogdensburg Railroad line up the Saco River valley was being planned, the company was daunted by the prospect of building a track through Crawford Notch. As an alternative the railroad considered routing the line over Evans Notch to the Androscoggin valley. Legend has it that Brickett was hired to survey the route. Unhappy at the prospect of having trains thundering past his front door, he measured the slope of the notch from the floor of valley to the top of Royce Mountain! The gradient he reported was too steep for the railroad, so the engineers turned their attention back to Crawford Notch. Characteristically, the only railroad ever to penetrate the Cold River valley was a quiet one: the Underground Railroad for runaway slaves in the 1840s and 1850s.

Victory over the great iron horse may have nothing to do with it, but the Brickett family earned a permanent spot on the map: 2 miles to the south, off the Mount Meader Trail, you can find *Brickett Falls*. Despite its handsome rock wall, Brickett Falls did not make the final cut for this book because in dry weather it has only a trickle of water.

By World War I, when the White Mountain National Forest acquired Brickett Place and the surrounding properties, the old brick farmhouse had fallen into disuse and disrepair. It was renovated during the Depression by Civilian Conservation Corps workers who also built the highway through Evans Notch. Brickett Place was used as a ranger station for a number of years, and since around 1960 it has been leased by a scout troop from Lexington, Massachusetts. The house is now a registered National Historic Building.

There is no room left for the Bickford story, which is just as well, since no one seems to know it!

CHAPTER 18

Roadside Falls of the Eastern Kancamagus

Lower Falls
Rocky Gorge (Upper Falls)
Sabbaday Falls

◆

Location
Kancamagus Highway in the vicinity of Passaconaway, west of Conway. (No gas stations between Conway and Lincoln!)

Map
AMC Chocorua-Waterville Map: I/J-8/9.
DeLorme Trail Map: J-9/10/11.

◆

Three fascinating waterfalls lie within an easy stroll of the Kancamagus Highway as it winds along the route of an old logging railroad through the valley of the Swift River. Starting from Conway, the first two falls—Lower Falls and Rocky Gorge (also called Upper Falls)— carry the powerful waters of the Swift River itself. These falls are the largest drops in 12 miles of rapids formed by the Swift, which tumbles nearly 700 vertical feet from the flatlands of Passaconaway (Albany Intervale) to the Saco Valley. Along this stretch of road one can stop at almost any parkable shoulder and descend the rugged river bank to see fine rapids. One rapid, called The Gorge, located about 2.5 miles below Lower Falls, is notorious among spring white-water paddlers.

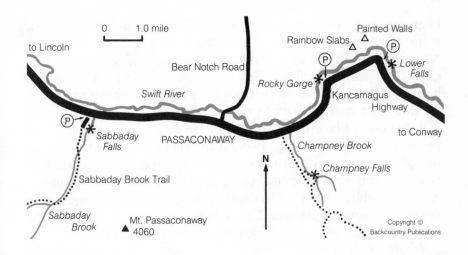

The third falls, Sabbaday, interrupts Sabbaday Brook as it descends the steep eastern slopes of Mount Tripyramid to join the Swift just west of Passaconaway. Though less powerful than the first two, Sabbaday Falls has long been a favorite of tourists and artists. Over a hundred years ago the New Hampshire State Geologist, Professor J. H. Huntington, described the falls as "a picture of beauty, which, once fixed in the mind, is a joy forever."

Another nearby trail, not described in detail here, leads up Mount Chocorua past *Champney* and *Pitcher Falls*. This is a longer hike (1.6 miles each way), and the falls have little water except in the spring or after periods of heavy rain, at which times they are very beautiful.

Lower Falls

Hiking Data
Distance, parking area to falls: Roadside.
Altitude gain: zero (altitude 1000 feet).
Difficulty: EASY.

If it's a warm day, bring along a swimsuit and a bottle of sun screen when you visit the Lower Falls Recreation Area on the Kancamagus

Highway, just over 7 miles from its terminus at Conway. This spot is the closest thing to Coney Island that you will find in the White Mountains, complete with parking-lot jams, changing rooms, picnic tables, and (small) sandy beaches. There are fast currents and foaming basins for thrill-seekers, as well as quiet eddy pools above and below the falls for tamer souls and small children.

If you don't like crowds you may have to visit Lower Falls when the weather is less inviting. Even in the chilly days of early spring, though, you may have a lot of company. When the currents are high and fast from snowmelt and spring rain, the Swift River becomes a mecca for whitewater paddlers and curious spectators. Along a river famous for smashing boats, Lower Falls and Rocky Gorge are the two spots that even expert kayakers usually prefer to portage.

Whatever the timing of your visit, Lower Falls is a compelling sight. Here the collected waters of the entire Swift River basin surge through a maze of channels, slides, chutes, curtains, and spouts arrayed across a broad band of polished ledges and boulders. Though the river drops only 10 feet, you have a front-row view of panoramic cataracts and colorful rock gardens, framed by birch and conifer. The view ranges from lovely to thrilling depending on the level of the river, which rises and falls quickly after heavy rains.

Across the river, Moat Mountain rises more than 2000 feet above the valley floor. This mountain contains a large remnant plug of volcanic rock thousands of feet thick, evidence of an 80-million-year epoch of volcanism that began as the North American crustal plate pulled back from a primeval collision with Europe or Africa. The entire White Mountain region was once blanketed by a similar deposit of ash and magma. In most places the soft volcanic rock has weathered away completely over the past 100 million years. Here the volcanic remnant was preserved when a large caldera sank into an underlying body of magma, like a cork falling into a bottle. The magma then cooled to form a protective ring of granite. Just upstream from the parking area some of this granite is on display in a huge amphitheater of colorful ledges known as the Painted Walls.

Rocky Gorge (Upper Falls)

Hiking Data
Distance, parking area to falls: 0.1 mile.
Altitude gain: zero.
Difficulty: EASY.

Rocky Gorge is located 9 miles from Conway and just over 3 miles east of the Bear Notch Road. At this point the Swift River flows north, but it curves sharply around to flow south at nearby Lower Falls. A sharp turnabout also distinguishes the character of the two waterfalls. Whereas Lower Falls consists of a broad cataract, at Upper Falls the river surges through a narrow gorge.

Each of these two waterfalls has a vertical drop of just over 10 feet, but Upper Falls is more dramatic. Indeed to early writers Rocky Gorge was "the" Swift River Falls. Sweetser's popular nineteenth-century guidebook described the formation in typically graphic terms:

> The river plunges downward . . . through a series of boiling eddies, and is narrowed into a straight passage between regular and massive granite walls about twenty feet high and several rods long. The stream roars down through this contracted gorge, and overflows during high water.

A short path leads down from the parking lot to the falls across open ledges edged with wildflowers such as goldenrod, blue aster, and pearly everlasting. The walkway crosses the bleached granite shoulder of the river channel to a footbridge that provides a bird's-eye view of the mesmerizing waterfall, the steep, scoured granite walls of the gorge, and the turbulent currents racing through the channel below. The bridge also provides access to the far bank, where you can explore the woods up and downstream, walk to nearby Falls Pond, and escape the transient crowds that congregate at the gorge.

Though swimming is prohibited in the gorge itself, excellent pools have been chiseled into the broad, sunny ledges along the river's edge above the falls. Depending on the water level, you should be able to find channels out of the main current that are safe enough for even

Rocky Gorge (Upper Falls)

(supervised) tots. Swimming is also permitted below the gorge, but access there is more difficult, the currents are stronger, and the steep walls block the sun.

If you do go into the water above the falls, be triply careful not to take any chance of getting caught in the main current and dragged into the powerful waterfall. A 1949 *Reader's Digest* article tells the miraculous story of a young woman who foolishly tried to wade across the river just above Rocky Gorge and was swept away by the current. Hours later she was found—alive—in an air pocket under the waterfall, dangling headfirst by an ankle that had wedged in the rock!

Like Lower Falls, Rocky Gorge has been developed as a National Forest Recreation Area, with a large parking lot, picnic tables, and pumped drinking water to go along with the splendid scenery.

Sabbaday Falls

Hiking Data
Distance, parking area to falls: 0.3 mile.
Altitude gain: 100 feet (to altitude 1400 feet).
Difficulty: EASY.

Sabbaday Falls has been a prime scenic attraction ever since the Passaconaway area began welcoming tourists after the Civil War. To reach the falls watch for a large Forest Service sign announcing the Sabbaday Falls Picnic Area on the south side of the Kancamagus Highway, 3.4 miles west of Bear Notch Road, and 3.9 miles east of the Livermore Trail and Lily Pond.

From the picnic area a gently graded gravel path leads south to Sabbaday Falls. The path is broad and well marked, with information signs posted along the way. Among them, one warns that NO SWIMMING is permitted at Sabbaday Falls or within 500 feet above or below the falls. The prohibition applies to "entering or being in the water," under threat of fines, imprisonment, or both. Clearly Sabbaday Falls is reserved for spectators, not bathers.

Sabbaday Falls consists of three separate drops combined in an enchanting display of natural architecture. The waters of Sabbaday Brook pour through a smooth channel chiseled in the ledge and then cascade into a bubbling emerald basin, molded smooth and undercut by the swirling currents. From this basin the waters slide down a shallow chute and tumble as a broad, glistening curtain over a 25-foot-high wall of broken granite. At the base of the drop lies a deep pool where the water "boils and roars and is churned into a foam" (Beals, 1916) before turning at a right angle to surge through a beautiful flume.

The flume itself is a chasm about 10 feet across. On the far side perpendicular cliffs rise 50 feet, wet with spray and ornaments of dripping moss. This flume is the result of a dike of volcanic basalt that penetrated vertical cracks in the tough granite bedrock, only to be worn down by erosion. A distinct vein of dark basalt can be seen embedded in the ledge at the mouth of the chasm.

The flume is the first part of Sabbaday Falls that you see when you approach from the picnic area. Stepping from the trail to the edge of the clear pool below the flume, you can examine a perfectly formed pothole that has been gouged out of the flat ledge by swirling waterborne sand and stones. The pothole is known as "the devil's wash basin." Above the pool the trail mounts a set of steps onto a walkway along the rim of the flume to the rest of the waterfall. The walkway is guarded by a sturdy log rail. Beyond the falls the path loops back to the Sabbaday Brook Trail. To the left the trail climbs to the summit ridge on Mount Tripyramid, 4.6 miles from the trailhead. To the right the trail returns to the parking area.

The waterfall was named Sabbaday because a party of settlers who were trying to cut a road to Waterville abandoned their arduous labor nearby the brook one Sabbath day as winter was approaching. In his 1887 guidebook Moses Sweetser tried to introduce the name "Church's Falls on Sabbaday Brook," in honor of Frederick E.

Velvet-leaf Blueberry

Church, a famous landscape painter. This noble effort failed to pass the test of time.

The hike to Sabbaday Falls is very popular, so expect company if you visit during tourist season.

Historical Detour

> Look where the braves are gathered
> Like the clouds before a flood!
> And Kancamagus' tomahawk
> Is all athirst for blood!
> —*Mary Wheeler, "Warsong of Kancamagus"*

To Indians who lived along the Saco River, the valley of the Swift River was a favored hunting ground teeming with deer, bear, beaver, and otter. They called the river Chataguay. Today the highway and the mountains to the south stand as monuments to the Indians, and their story adds a fascinating dimension to this waterfall trip. The historical information presented here is drawn primarily from *Passaconway in the White Mountains*, by Charles Edward Beals, Jr. (1916).

The source of the Swift River is located on Mount Kancamagus, which Professor Huntington named for the last *bashaba*, or great chief, of the Pennacook people. Before the Pilgrims arrived the Pennacook confederation of small New England tribes had been unified by Kancamagus' legendary grandfather, Passaconaway, for defense against raiding Mohawks. It is said that Passaconaway possessed magical powers. Early colonists recorded hearing stories that "hee can make water burne, the rocks move, the trees dance." This magic was ineffectual, though, against the white man and his feared "iron pipe." So Passaconaway fervently preached peace, and kept his people out of the early Indian wars against the colonists.

According to Pilgrim accounts, Passaconaway was already about sixty years old when he visited the Plymouth plantation in 1623. Yet he remained chief of the Pennacook until 1669, and lived until 1682—long enough to see his land taken, his tribe pauperized, many of his braves shipped as slaves to the Caribbean, and his people dispirited by rum and commercial exploitation. Today both the intervale between Sabbaday Falls and Rocky Gorge, and the 4060-foot mountain looming to the south honor the name of Passaconaway, "Son of the Bear."

Kancamagus succeeded his uncle Wonalancet as *bashaba* in 1684 and sought revenge for the humiliations suffered by his people. In 1689 he led a bloody attack on Dover but was pursued into Maine and forced to entreat for peace in 1691. Not long thereafter the Pennacook emigrated to Quebec, leaving behind only scattered bands.

One such band was headed by Chocorua. Chocorua lived in peace with early settlers of the Swift River valley until around 1761 when, according to legend, his son was accidently poisoned while in the care of Cornelius Campbell, a local farmer. Enraged, Chocorua massacred Campbell's family and was pursued to the summit of the mountain that bears his name today. There he died after issuing a chilling "curse upon ye, white man!"

When the town of Albany was chartered in 1766 the intervale was still wilderness forest uninhabited by white men. The first intrepid settlers who moved into the intervale after the Revolutionary War found their lives beset with tragedies that were attributed to Chocorua's curse: illness, sick cattle, floods, hurricane winds, wild animal attacks, and winter storms. By 1815 the intervale had been abandoned. In 1821 Professor Dana, of Dartmouth, found that the history of illness in the intervale had been caused by "muriate of lime" in the waters, not by an Indian curse. The valley was resettled shortly thereafter and became a popular summer resort after the Civil War.

As elsewhere in the White Mountains, loggers followed the Indians and settlers into the virgin forests of the Swift River valley. A railroad through Bear Notch and a second that ran south from the Sawyer River brought loggers to the area around Sabbaday Brook beginning in 1877. The most destructive logging occurred after the Swift River Railroad was run 20 miles up the valley from Conway in 1906—the route now followed by the highway. With conservationist momentum building, the loggers resorted to cut-and-run tactics "so that not even a bush could be seen" on the slopes of Mount Paugus above Passaconaway. In 1912 forest fires and floods swept the valley. From this devastation has emerged the lovely national forest that visitors enjoy today.

CHAPTER 19

Jackson Falls

Diana's Baths

◆

Location
Jackson village.

Map
AMC Mount Washington Map: H-10.
DeLorme Trail Map: F-12.

Hiking Data
Distance, parking area to falls: Roadside.
Altitude gain: zero (altitude 900 feet).
Difficulty: EASY.

◆

The village of Jackson has been called a plaza in the city of mountains. Many plazas have a pond or fountain where folks can cool off and kids can play. But none can match Jackson, with its acres of waterfall playground on the colorful ledges of the Wildcat River.

By the same token, purists may grumble about devoting a chapter of a book on *mountain* waterfalls to a *downtown* waterfall. Let them grumble, while the rest of us enjoy the finest waterfall in the North Conway–Jackson area. Then again, Jackson Falls alone does not make for a very full waterfall trip—unless you are an ardent sun bather who can spend the whole day baking on sunny ledges. So, to fill out the trip and to add a woodsy dimension to the chapter we include an excursion to a very pretty waterfall not far down the road at *Diana's Baths*.

A few words should be added about two duds that keen observers

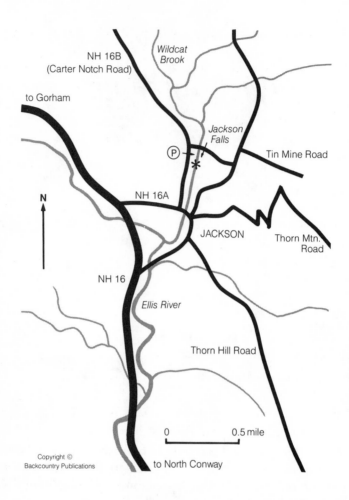

might notice on maps of the North Conway–Jackson area. The first is *Goodrich Falls*, which is located below the Ellis River bridge on NH 16, 1.6 miles south of Jackson. Goodrich Falls was once quite a spectacle, but, alas, an 80-foot drop of the powerful Ellis River was too good to remain undisturbed. More than a century ago the waterfall was dammed, first for a mill and later for electricity. Today the dull blank wall of a concrete dam overshadows a remnant of this once-glorious waterfall. There is no public trail to the falls, and no view from the road.

The second is *Artist Falls* in North Conway. Despite its fetching name, this was never much of a spectacle. The name dates to the nineteenth century when North Conway was a flourishing art center. Artist Falls was a favorite subject for painters who preferred a short walk to a teensy waterfall over a long walk to something worthwhile. Evidently it is easier to embellish a painting than to tote art supplies over mountain trails.

If you spot Goodrich Falls or Artist Falls on a map, head for Jackson Falls.

The Falls

The village of Jackson lies just off NH 16 about 10 miles south of Pinkham Notch and less than 3 miles north of US 302. Two ends of NH 16A 0.5 mile apart, lead east into Jackson from NH 16. Take the northernmost of the these for 0.4 mile to a left turn onto Carter Notch Road, just before crossing the Wildcat River, which, in 1988, was designated as one of the nation's Wild and Scenic Rivers. Carter Notch Road penetrates more than 5 miles up the picturesque river valley, but to reach the waterfall—which can be seen from Jackson village—simply drive up the first hill and park at the dirt pullout. The distance is 0.4 mile.

Jackson Falls is not so much "a waterfall" as a maze of cataracts and pools spread across an enormous ledge of beautiful pink granite (technically, it is porphyritic quartz syenite). In some spots the ledge is smooth and polished, while elsewhere it is more fractured and scattered with broken boulders. The ledge is so large that if pulled flat and smoothed over it could easily accommodate landing aircraft. So there is plenty of room for exploring.

The crown of the ledge is a fairly level platform the size of a football field. Along this platform the river drops only a few feet at a time, though some of its pools are large enough to be envied by most hotels and many municipalities. The riverbed is also graced with pothole tubs, slides, and small showers. It has an open southern exposure that soaks up the sun and warms the water, at least in comparison to most other mountain streams.

The top platform ends at a hillside where the ledge banks down sharply—though not too sharply for careful scrambling. Here the river shoots down long cascades, selecting from a multitude of bed-

Pothole at Jackson Falls

rock channels depending on the volume of water. Two slender cascades race lengthwise down sloping corners that cut laterally across
the wide riverbed, like huge, tilted stairs climbing down from the
woods on the east bank.

On our first visit to Jackson Falls we were accompanied by three
Boy Scouts coming home from a camping trip. In view of the long

drive ahead, we made it quite clear to the Scouts that we were stopping to investigate the falls, and *not* to swim. But once the kids were out on the sunny ledges scampering around the cascades and pools, no warnings could keep them from accidentally getting, *oops*, soaking wet—at which point they entreated us successfully to let them go for a swim. The anecdote serves as a warning: Jackson Falls is so much fun that restraint and discipline may suffer. (Be sure that everyone understands the hazards of wet, slick rocks; it isn't fun to slip and break an arm or a leg.)

Diana's Baths

Location
Access is from West Side Road in North Conway, near Cathedral Ledge.

Map
AMC Mount Washington Map: I-10.
DeLorme Trail Map: H-12.

Hiking Data
Distance, parking area to falls: 0.5 mile.
Altitude gain: 100 feet (to altitude 700 feet).
Difficulty: EASY.

Diana's Baths is described in many tourist guidebooks as a fascinating collection of potholes and ledges on Lucy Brook, near North Conway. The brook is also adorned with a long sash of pretty cascades and a very beautiful small waterfall.

Finding the trail is the hardest part of the trip to Diana's Baths. The trailhead is only 5 miles south of Jackson as the crow flies, but earthbound vehicles are confined to a circuitous route that doubles that distance. Taking NH 16 south from Jackson, turn right (west) on US 302. After 2 miles the highway crosses the Saco River, and 0.25 mile later West Side Ride branches off to the left at a very acute angle. Turn onto this road, which winds along the Saco back downstream past Humphrey Ledge. On your right (west) less than 0.5 mile after passing the Bartlett-Conway town line, you will see two fenced meadows and a white farmhouse posed in the foreground of a superb view of Cathedral and Whitehorse Ledges. Turn onto the gravel road between the two meadows and park on the shoulder. No sign marks this turn, but a small hiking sign at the far end of the gravel road confirms that you are at Moat Mountain Trail, which leads to Diana's Baths.

An alternative route from Jackson is less scenic and 1 mile longer, but great for shoppers. Take US 302 into North Conway. After shopping, turn onto the road to Echo Lake State Park, at the north end of town. Across the Saco River, keep right at the first fork. A half-mile later turn right onto West Side Road. The two fenced meadows and the gravel road for trailhead parking are on the left after 0.7 mile.

From the end of the gravel road the Moat Mountain Trail enters the woods and follows a wide, smooth forest road through young deciduous woods interspersed with handsome specimens of mature ash, hemlock, and pine. The trail spans a small side stream, passes a stand of tall red pines alongside Lucy Brook, and then enters a clearing (posted: no camping). At the edge of the clearing, beside the brook, you can find the remains of an old water-powered grist mill, overgrown with brambles. Above the mill site, Lucy Brook cascades down more than 200 yards of granite terraces.

To reach the cascades take any one of the short side paths to the left after the clearing. Once you reach Lucy Brook it is easy to explore up and down the ledges or on the paths through the woods alongside. (The main trail continues to North Moat Mountain and a long traverse of the Moat summit ridge.) Starting at the bottom of the cascades you come first to a sloping waterslide 15 feet high, then to an abrupt 8-foot fall, and then to a feathery waterspout gushing from a chute etched in the bedrock.

Next comes the main attraction. It was described in 1881 by Samuel Adams Drake as "a solid mass of granite, more than a hundred feet across the bed of the stream, and twenty feet high," with crystal streams slipping down the face "into basins they have hollowed out. It is these curious, circular stone cavities, out of which the freshest and cleanest water constantly pours, that give to the cascade the name of Diana's Baths." According to legend the ledges were inhabited by goblins who bedevilled the Pequawket Indians of the Saco River valley. Heeding the Indians' prayers, a mountain god swept

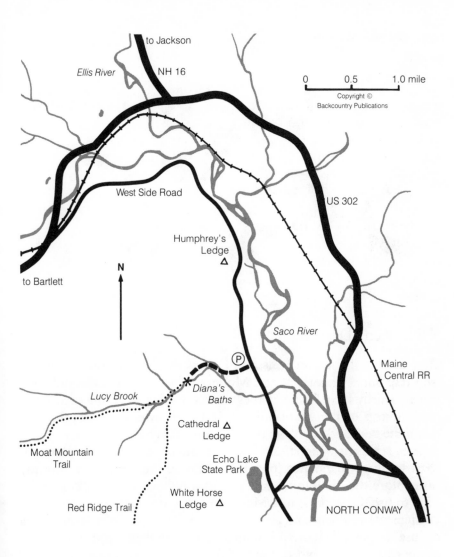

the goblins away in a flood. From this legend the cascade was originally called "The Home of the Water Fairies."

Above the broad granite wall at Diana's Baths, the incline of the
molded ledge and the cascades both become more gentle, but still
great fun to explore. Above the main falls, however, you will also
see signs posted: No Swimming: Public Water Supply. The Forest
Service assures us that the public water supply intake pipes are located
above the falls. Therefore, swimming is indeed permitted in the sparkling pools at Diana's Baths, *below* the waterfall.

Belted Kingfisher

Historical Detour

The waters of Jackson Falls and Diana's Baths feed into the major thoroughfares of early White Mountain history: the Ellis and Saco rivers. Darby Field followed these rivers on his pioneering expedition to "the top of the white hill" in 1642. He was guided by Indians from the Pequawket village (what is now Conway), though only two braves set aside superstition and accompanied him to the summit. Nearly thirty years later John Josselyn used the same river highway to explore the mountains. His account, published in 1672, was the first to use the name White Mountains. He also described the Indian settlements in detail and recorded the Indian legends. The first man to use the name Mount Washington, Jeremy Belknap, followed the same rivers on his expedition in 1784.

Later, at the end of the French and Indian War, these rivers became major thoroughfares for settlement. Fryeberg, ME, drew the first White Mountain settlers in 1763. Only two years later Conway was incorporated; the grantee, Daniel Foster, became the first settler at North Conway in 1766. Soon the former Indian meadowlands were flooded with new arrivals.

It took twelve more years before settlement penetrated the Ellis River valley. Sturdy Benjamin Copp moved his family to the junction of the Wildcat and Ellis rivers in 1778. Although trout and moose were abundant in season, the Copp family suffered terrible hardships living alone in the dense forest wilderness until 1790, when five more families moved to what was then called New Madbury. (The town's name was changed to Adams in 1800, to honor John Adams, and then to Jackson in 1829, as a statement of support for Andrew Jackson over John Quincy Adams.)

One new settler was Captain Joseph Pinkham, whose ten-year-old son Daniel grew to become a pioneer of what is today called Pinkham Notch (see Chapter 20). Although it was early April when the Pinkhams moved to Jackson, the valleys were still blanketed with 5 feet of snow. This made it very difficult to pull the hand sled on which all their stocks and supplies were drawn. As an experiment the children hitched the family's one hog to the sled. "Though less fleeting than the horse, and less powerful than the ox, he did us good and sufficient service," Daniel later wrote. The crude log house his father had built the previous autumn—with no chimney, no stove, no floor, and no windows—was half buried in snow when the family arrived.

After ushering explorers and settlers into the mountain region, these river valleys later became highways of development. The first road through the mountains followed the Saco into Crawford Notch in 1785, creating a trade route that stimulated development of the north country. The road also spawned the first small inns for teamsters. The earliest tourist hotels also took root in the upper Saco valley, beginning around 1812. By 1825—decades before the grand hotels were established at the major notches—North Conway had five lodges and regular stage coach service. Guidebook writers gushed about the beauty of the mountain views, the towering ledges, and the nearby cascades. Landscape artists were soon drawn to the village "like bees to the sweetest flowers."

Jackson developed more slowly as a tourist center. The first hotel (Jackson Falls House) was not built until 1858. Thereafter the popularity of the "enchanted valley" grew quickly. Jackson has also been slow to follow the lead of North Conway in terms of commercial development. Rather than becoming a plaza of factory outlets and tourist shops, the village remains a quiet plaza in the city of mountains.

CHAPTER 20

Short Walks at Pinkham Notch

Glen Ellis Falls / Crystal Cascade
Thompson Falls

◆

Location

Pinkham Notch is the height of land on NH 16 between Gorham and Jackson, on the eastern flank of the Presidentials.

Map

AMC Mount Washington Range: F/G-9/10.
DeLorme Trail Map: D-11.

◆

> Almost everything in nature, which can be supposed of inspiring ideas of the sublime and beautiful, is here realized. Aged mountains, stupendous elevations, rolling clouds, impending rocks, verdant woods, crystal streams, the gentle rill, and the roaring torrent, all conspire to amaze, to soothe and to enrapture.
> —*Jeremy Belknap, 1792 (as quoted in Anderson, 1930)*

In describing his 1784 expedition to the mountains that local Indians called Agiochook, the Reverend Dr. Jeremy Belknap did not name the "roaring torrent" that so impressed him. Clearly, though, the "sublime and beautiful" scenery was in Pinkham Notch, where Belknap's party established camp between Glen Ellis Falls and Crystal Cascade (to use the modern appellations). Dr. Belknap was not a moon-struck prose poet, but a careful historian who renounced the "temptation to romance" in recounting his expedition. The quotation above reveals that scholarly objectivity proved no match for the romantic allure of the notch's mountains, woods, and watercourses.

Today, despite its picture-book familiarity and its traffic, Pinkham Notch still conspires to amaze, to soothe, and to enrapture visitors. Among the most popular attractions in the notch are two roaring torrents: Glen Ellis Falls and Crystal Cascade. Glen Ellis Falls is queen of the region's waterfalls in terms of power, form, and setting, while Crystal Cascade is unexcelled in graceful beauty. The third waterfall of the chapter, nearby Thompson Falls, is not in the same league with its famous neighbors in terms of splendor or popularity. In fact it isn't even in the same watershed, since it lies on the Peabody River side of the notch. What Thompson Falls offers is a taste of seclusion, excellent views across to Mount Washington, and 0.25 mile of tumbling cascades.

Each hike is easy and accessible, so all three falls can be seen in a day without difficulty. Accommodations are available at the AMC guest lodge at Pinkham Notch Camp. (For reservations, call 1-603-466-2727, or write to Reservations, Pinkham Notch Camp, Gorham, NH 03581.)

Glen Ellis Falls

Hiking Data
Distance, parking area to falls: 0.2 mile.
Altitude gain: −100 feet (altitude 1850 feet).
Difficulty: EASY.

The Ellis River is formed by the confluence of the New River and the Cutler River, which gather the waters of the great glacial cirques on the eastern wall of Mount Washington: Huntington Ravine, Tuckerman Ravine, and the Gulf of Slides. From its point of origin the Ellis River skirts the ragged cliffs of Wildcat Ridge and then races through a narrow chute that discharges over the precipitous headwall of Glen Ellis. As if being poured from a giant pitcher, the seething spout of whitewater plunges 64 feet into the deep basin. For its appearance the waterfall was called Pitcher Falls until 1852, when the name Glen Ellis Falls was suggested by Henry Ripley (whose name was tagged to an even loftier waterfall; see Chapter 24).

At the bottom of the Glen Ellis basin, swirling currents have hollowed out a dark green pool that is bound on three sides by high, tree-capped crags. Piled at the pool's outlet are large boulders that centuries of frost have wedged from the cliffs. To Moses Sweetser, editor of the best-known nineteenth-century guidebook to the region, Glen Ellis Falls was "probably the finest in the White Mountains." This assessment is widely shared.

The well-marked turn-off to Glen Ellis Falls is 0.7 mile south of Pinkham Notch on the west side of NH 16. The same parking area also serves the Glen Boulder Trail up Mount Washington (via Slide Peak and Boott Spur) and the Wildcat Ridge Trail to the east. A sign at the parking lot explains that the Forest Service acquired the area around the falls in 1915 after the surrounding forests had been devastated by fire.

To reach the falls, pass through the pedestrian tunnel to the east side of the highway and turn right onto the smooth gravel path along the bank of the Ellis River. Very shortly you will reach a small cataract above a glistening pool, with a backdrop of 20-foot cliffs. Some writers have given the name Upper Glen Ellis Falls to this first cascade. Immediately below the pool large, angular, rust-hued boulders channel the rushing waters to the lip of the main waterfall. An overlook at this point (with sturdy masonry protection) provides a bird's-eye view of the river's seething plunge. There is also an information sign here summarizing the geological history of the glen.

The footpath then descends to the foot of the gorge by way of a long, winding flight of regular stone steps. Just before the descent bottoms out, a short spur of steps on the left climbs to a second overlook midway up the falls. The view here can be mesmerizing: you can easily imagine being suspended above the swirling currents of the pool, watching the falls surge past. Continuing to the bottom of the stone staircase, you will reach a third viewing point beside the outlet of the basin pool. This vantage provides an unexcelled view of Glen Ellis Falls and the rugged cliffs of the glen. You also have access to the spray-dampened slabs alongside the pool—a favorite spot for snapshots.

On one trip to Glen Ellis Falls we watched a grandfatherly visitor,

Glen Ellis Falls

evidently quite out of condition, accompany his family down the long flight of steps to the base of the falls. Approaching the last corner he grumbled, "This had better be worth it!" But the moment the waterfall came into view, one of the children cried out "Awesome!" and the others simply nodded in quiet consent.

The glen opens to the south, inviting the sun to paint subdued rainbows in the fine spray from the falls. When the river thunders with spring snowmelt, however, the spray is so heavy that the area is doused with mist, rendering photography all but impossible. It is said that the spray reveals ghostly forms of two young lovers holding hands. According to an Indian legend a local chief promised his beautiful daughter to a warrior, but the maiden fell in love with a brave from a neighboring tribe. A bow-and-arrow contest was arranged to settle her fate. When the warrior won the contest the maiden fled with her lover, and the two leapt to their death, hand in hand, over the brink of the falls.

Most visitors go no farther than the terminus of the maintained trail at the base of the falls. After all, that's the main attraction. A short distance farther down the gorge, however, you can find a delightful sideshow of cataracts, pools, and sunny ledges to explore. An informal path runs through the woods alongside the river. Not far downstream a table ledge provides the safest crossing to the east bank of the river, where more paths run through the woods along the east bank.

Even if you are not in top condition for climbing stairs, do pay Glen Ellis Falls a visit. Just take it easy on the stairs and rest as often as you wish.

Crystal Cascade

Hiking Data
Distance, parking area to falls: 0.3 mile.
Altitude gain: 200 feet (altitude 2200 feet).
Difficulty: EASY.

To reach Crystal Cascade, park at the AMC Pinkham Notch Camp and get onto the path that passes to the left of the Trading Post (where you can obtain maps, books, snacks, minor supplies, and information). This is start of the Tuckerman Ravine Trail, the most popular trail up Mount Washington. Keep to the right on the main trail when the Old Jackson Road forks off to the right a few dozen yards from the trailhead. After a few hundred more yards of very easy walking the trail bridges the Cutler River above a pretty cascade. If you look upstream from the bridge you can see the river tumbling out of a deep ravine that narrows to a dark gorge. Crystal Cascade is at the head of this gorge.

Continue up the trail past the bridge. The path gets considerably steeper now, but you have only 100 yards to go before reaching a side path to a set of steps leading up to the rim of the gorge. Directly across from this vantage point the Cutler River—named for the Reverend Dr. Manasseh Cutler, a botanist whom Belknap accompanied in 1784—emerges from a canopy of thick forest to tumble down a steep bank of dark rock in a series of lively leaps. To Thomas Starr King (1859) the cascade's sprightly descent gave the impression of "graceful and perpetual youth." The cascade is 80 feet high, in two drops. First, a broad curtain of dancing whitewater falls 60 feet to a small ledge, followed by another 20-foot plunge. On both sides are dark cliffs, hemmed with moist green boughs of spruce, fir, birch, and mountain ash. At the bottom of the narrow gorge the river churns through an abrupt right-angle turn.

The geology at Crystal Cascade is quite unlike that of any other waterfall in the area. Its dark rockbed is a remnant volcanic vent that intruded into the surrounding field of schist and quartzite during relatively recent geological times. Another small volcanic vent is exposed at the footbridge below the cascade; Billings, *et al.* (1979) explain that the formation is distinguished "by angular fragments of dark rock embedded in a dark-greenish base."

In some respects, it is a misfortune for Crystal Cascade to be located on the Tuckerman Ravine Trail. Visitors make a special stop to admire Glen Ellis Falls, but Crystal Cascade is often rewarded with little more than a passing glance by hikers en route to or from the summit of Mount Washington. Evidently many visitors to the mountain palace are not distracted by the dazzling jewels when they have an audience with the king!

Crystal Cascade did not always play second fiddle to the summit.

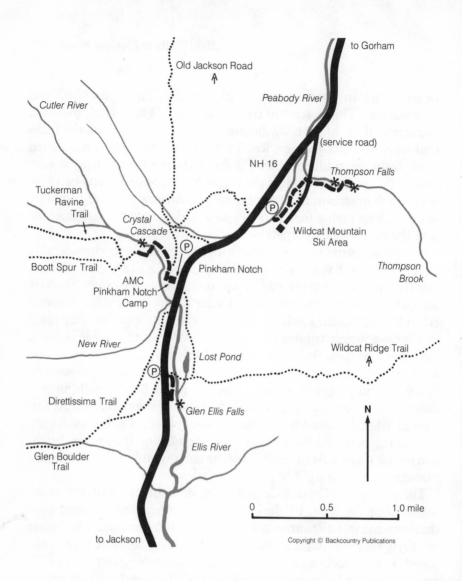

to Gorham

Old Jackson Road

Cutler River

Peabody River

(service road)

NH 16

Thompson Falls

Tuckerman
Ravine
Trail

Crystal
Cascade

Wildcat Mountain
Ski Area

Boott Spur Trail

Pinkham Notch

Thompson
Brook

AMC
Pinkham Notch
Camp

New River

Lost Pond

Wildcat Ridge Trail

Direttissima Trail

Glen Ellis Falls

N

Glen Boulder
Trail

Ellis River

0   0.5   1.0 mile

to Jackson

Before Tuckerman Ravine Trail was established the footpath from
the notch stopped at the cascade. Carriage rides to see Crystal Cascade and Glen Ellis Falls were favorite excursions for the well-heeled
guests who lodged up the road at the elegant Glen House. Samuel
Drake (1881) devoted three doting pages to describing Crystal Cascade, and Julius Ward (1890) picked it over Glen Ellis as "perhaps
the most beautiful of the White Mountain falls."

Beautiful though it is, Crystal Cascade suffers another ill effect
from being located on the Tuckerman Ravine Trail: heavy foot traffic

has led the Forest Service to post notices for hikers to stay on the trail. This means that exploratory side trips are expressly discouraged. Consequently there is not much to do at Crystal Cascade except enjoy the view. Unless, of course, you join other hikers and head up to Tuckerman Ravine, where you will find some of the most inspiring scenery in the region. The ravine, a superb glacial cirque that is famous for its spring skiing, lies 3 miles of steady climbing farther along. During the spring and after heavy rains, its precipitous head-wall is laced with white ribbons of cascading waters, which early guidebooks called the *Fall of a Thousand Streams*. Alternatively, a right turn onto the Huntington Ravine Trail, 1 hard mile beyond Crystal Cascade, leads past numerous small cascades en route to one of the steepest headwall trails in the White Mountains. The summit of Mount Washington is the ultimate side trip, 4 miles and 4000 vertical feet above Crystal Cascade.

Thompson Falls

Hiking Data
Distance, parking area to falls: 0.7 mile.
Altitude gain: 100 feet (altitude 2000 feet).
Difficulty: EASY.

Unlike its esteemed neighbors on the south side of Pinkham Notch, Thompson Falls doesn't appear at the top of anyone's list of the most beautiful waterfalls in the White Mountains. Most Guidebooks over-look it altogether. Books that do mention Thompson Falls are usually referring to a less interesting waterfall of the same name that is located behind White Horse Ledge in North Conway.

While exaggerating the mileage, Sweetser's reliable old *Handbook for Travellers* (1887) points readers in the right direction. Sweetser describes Thompson Falls as:

> a chain of cascades 1/2 M. long, sweeping down through pretty forest scenery, and furnishing rich ground for pleasant rambles. The view of Mount Washington and its E. ravines, from the head of the main fall, is one of the best in the mountains. . . .

The falls are on Thompson Brook, which flows off of Wildcat Mountain into the Peabody River just north of the Wildcat Ski Area. The hike begins at the main Wildcat parking lot, 0.8 mile north of the AMC Pinkham Notch Camp and 2 miles south of the Mount Washington Auto Road. Cross the footbridge over the narrow Peabody River directly behind the Wildcat Base Lodge and look for the "Way of the Wildcat" Nature Trail. This self-guided trail parallels the river for 0.25 mile and then loops back to the lodge. The path to Thompson Falls diverges from the nature trail at the far end of this loop.

The Thompson Falls Trail proceeds on level ground through cool forests for 0.25 mile before crossing a gravel service road that leads to the Wildcat C parking lot. It is a bit disconcerting that the only trail indicator here is a small weathered sign bearing an indistinct painted arrow. Be sure to stay on the east bank of Thompson Brook when you cross the service road. From this point the trail ascends gently for another 0.25 mile, crosses a small rise, and descends into a lovely glen, which encloses a large, shady pool. At the head of the glen a 12-foot-high ribbon of water spills across the mouth of a giant clam-shaped ledge and splashes off the lower "lip" of the clam into the pool. The pool is an especially inviting place to swim, but the water is bitterly cold. We have noticed that Boy Scouts can tolerate the cold water on a dare, but most sensible people will settle for a quick footbath.

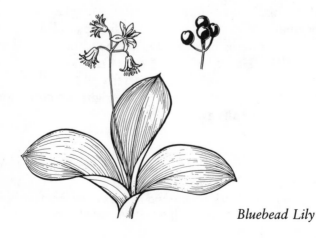

Bluebead Lily

The quality of the path indicates that most visitors proceed no farther than the glen, perhaps under the impression they have seen Thompson Falls. Actually this is just the last of a long string of cascades. To explore the rest of the waterfall, follow the rough path to the right of the giant clam falls and cross the ledges to the north side of the stream. The path then stays on the north bank, passing a succession of charming waterfalls, mossy pothole basins, and crystal-clear cascades sliding down open ledges. The uppermost ledge provides the best views across the Peabody valley to Mount Washington. Be sure to bring binoculars along on this hike!

In addition to the waterfall and the views the hike also offers a handsome mix of trees, a host of wildflowers in the late spring, and an easy escape from the Pinkham Notch crowds. This is not the same wild forest that Sweetser found so endearing, since the area was logged clean prior to World War I. But even having lost its wilderness spirit, the forest retains a sense of solitude and charm.

Thompson Falls and Thompson Brook are both named in honor of Colonel J. M. Thompson, the first proprietor of Glen House, which opened in 1853. The Glen House became one of the grandest of the White Mountain inns, with a dining room for two hundred guests, a parlor a hundred feet long, and a stable of more than a hundred horses. Glen House coaches, drawn by eight white horses, would transport guests in style to and from the train depot at Gorham. Thompson was also a trail-builder. In addition to trails to nearby waterfalls he cut the first bridle path up Mount Washington—the predecessor of today's Mount Washington Auto Road.

Tragically, Thompson drowned in the swollen Peabody River during a severe storm in 1869. The original Glen House burned down in 1884. An even more luxurious replacement was reduced to ashes in 1893, and a third, more modest, Glen House burned down in 1967.

Historical Detour

At the time of Belknap's expedition in 1784, Pinkham Notch was simply known as the "eastern pass." A rude trail, called the Shelburne Road, had been blazed through the pass by a Captain Evans, who served as Belknap's guide. More than forty years later the state contracted Daniel Pinkham, son of Jackson's pioneer settler (see Chapter 19), to improve the path through the notch so it could accommodate wagon traffic between Conway and Gorham. In return for this service Pinkham received a grant of land extending 0.25 mile on each side of the road, from Glen Ellis Falls to just above Glen House. In short, he was granted the notch that now bears his name.

Pinkham's Grant was never incorporated as a town, and the only early development in the vicinity—the Glen House site, cleared in 1853—was located just outside the grant boundary. The Appalachian Mountain Club began developing hiking trails in the notch shortly after the club's founding in 1876, but the district was essentially undeveloped when the AMC acquired its Pinkham Notch property in 1915. The first structures to be built, in 1920, were two log cabins. The road then was just a gravel track that closed each winter. Under the guiding hand of Joe Dodge, who took on the job of hutmaster in 1922, the Pinkham Notch Camp developed into the center of AMC operations and activities in the White Mountains.

Let your visit to the waterfalls of Pinkham Notch serve as a tribute to the Appalachian Mountain Club for its dedication to enhancing the accessibility of New England's natural treasures, while protecting the region's great beauty.

CHAPTER 21

Nancy Cascades

◆

Location
Nancy Pond Trail, off US 302 below Crawford Notch.

Map
AMC Mount Washington Range Map: H-8.
DeLorme Trail Map: G-9.

Hiking Data
Distance, parking area to cascades: 2.4 miles.
Altitude gain: 1500 feet (to altitude 2400 feet).
Difficulty: MODERATE.

◆

From the serene waters of Nancy Pond, high in the mountains above Notchland, Nancy Brook flows for less than 2.5 miles to the Saco River, 2100 feet below. The brook begins its short run to the valley floor by meandering quietly through a broad, moss-carpeted headland of virgin spruce forest. The meandering ends abruptly at the head of a deep ravine where the brook tumbles down 400 feet of steep ledges, forming the long line of lacy waterfalls called Nancy Cascades.

Although Nancy Brook was christened in the earliest years of the republic, the lofty cascades on the mountain headwall seem to have been unknown until after the Civil War. When Benjamin Willey described Nancy Brook in 1856—"the eye is never weary in gazing upon the cascades and deep transparent basins"—he was referring only to the bottom mile. Between US 302 and the Saco River, Nancy Brook races through a small gorge that encloses a set of minor cascades. In Willey's time a carriage road crossed this gorge on a wooden span called Nancy's Bridge. So these minor cascades were familiar, while the brook's upper reaches were merely "unknown heights in the dark forest above."

Only since 1960 has a maintained trail reached Nancy Cascades. More accurately, a trail was established by the AMC in 1938, but destroyed within months by the Great Hurricane which struck New England that autumn. In 1960 crews from the Pasquaney Camp at Newfound Lake restored and extended the Nancy Pond Trail. Perhaps because the trail does not reach any summits, and perhaps because the hike to Nancy Cascades is a solid climb, there are not usually many hikers here. The sparsity of visitors makes this major cascade all the more attractive.

The Trail to the Cascades

The Nancy Pond Trail begins from a gravel roadside parking area on the west side of US 302, 1 mile below the Notchland Inn and 3 miles north of the Sawyer Rock Picnic Area. The small trailhead sign at the entrance to the forest path is easily visible from the road. Directly across the highway there is a larger dirt parking area. A path

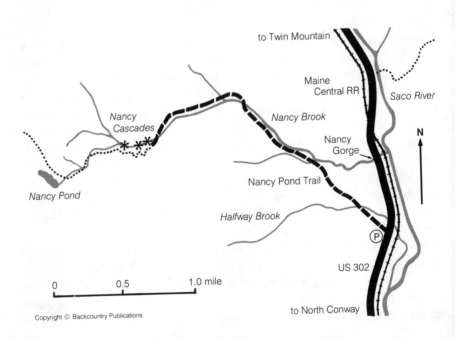

to Twin Mountain

Maine
Central RR

Saco River

Nancy
Cascades

Nancy Brook

Nancy
Gorge

N

Nancy Pond Trail

Nancy Pond

Halfway Brook

P

US 302

0   0.5   1.0 mile

Copyright © Backcountry Publications

to North Conway

from this lot leads down to the Saco River at a point called Rowan's Rapids, which is popular with spring whitewater paddlers. The beautiful pool here is deliciously refreshing on a hot summer's day. In fact you can find numerous swimming holes along the Saco on a hot day just by watching for concentrations of parked cars along the highway.

To bypass private property, the trail starts 0.75 mile south of Nancy Brook, and therefore begins by angling northwest back to the brook. After starting out on a wide forest road, the trail quickly turns left into the woods and climbs a small rise to a second logging road. This road climbs gradually for about 0.5 mile through handsome beech forest before crossing Halfway Brook, where we once saw two toddlers squealing with delight in a small pool—under the watchful eyes of their parents. Less than 1 mile from the highway an ugly red-painted cairn marks your entrance into the national forest. From here to the shallow col between Mounts Nancy and Anderson the trail traverses the Nancy Brook Scenic Area, a 460-acre protected zone established in 1964.

The trail parallels Nancy Brook on a ridge well above the south bank before crossing to the north bank at mile 1.6. To this point and a short distance beyond, the trail is easy to follow, well-graded, and clearly blazed. Much of the route is on old logging roads and a forest road that once served a fire tower on Mount Bemis, which flanks Nancy Brook to the north. During the early part of this century logging roads penetrated most of the area. AMC guidebooks before World War II described the range as having been heavily lumbered from both east and west, "leaving in many places a mere fringe of trees along the crest of the ridge." The stand of virgin spruce beside Nancy Pond is one spot they missed, though it was extensively damaged by the 1938 hurricane.

Immediately past the Nancy Brook crossing, the trail turns left off the old Mount Bemis service road onto another logging road that ascends along the north bank. After passing the remains of an old mill, the trail becomes narrower, rougher, and steeper as the beech forest gives way to birch and then to conifers. A number of slides cut across the path, contributing to the rough footing. Here you may notice that the water has a distinct teakish tint, and that a brown foam accumulates in eddy pools along the brook. Both are natural effects of acids generated by the decay of organic matter in the stagnant water in and around Nancy Pond. The foam is caused when the acids weaken surface tension and allow turbulence from the cascades to form small bubbles.

After 0.5 mile of steady climbing the trail crosses back to the south bank and soon thereafter approaches the shimmering white curtain of Nancy Cascades. From this bottom cascade (at mile 2.4) the trail switchbacks up the steep headwall of the ravine to the top of the cascades (mile 2.8). The last 0.6 mile to Nancy Pond passes through an enchanting conifer forest and a wild highland marsh. Backpackers can continue over the height-of-land and down into Carrigain Notch in the Pemigewasset Wilderness.

The Cascades

Stepping down from the trail to the base of the first cascade, you come to the edge of the large, rippling pool. Across the pool a tapered curtain of whitewater ribbons leaps down a steep bank of weathered gray gneiss that is eight stories high and 30 feet wide. With either a few brisk strokes across the pool, or a careful barefoot scramble around the perimeter, you can clamber onto the base of the ledge and play under the waterfall. You have to be tough to go in the water, however, because the glen is well shaded, and cooled by a draft that rides down the cascade. Kids can be lured into the cold water by the prospect of having their picture taken. Most visitors, though, will be content just to soak in the spectacle from a dry perch on the boulders at the foot of the pool.

What you see from the base pool is only the first in a long line of impressive cascades. A detailed account of an early exploration of Nancy Brook (*Appalachia*, 1883) described four distinct cascades totaling over 300 feet of vertical drop. Modern topographic maps indicate that the drop is closer to 400 feet.

Climbing one long switchback farther up the trail, you will reach a platform with a stunning view of the middle cascades. From heights above, the water rushes down a nearly continuous series of chutes and slides to a brown pool on a small shelf below—which forms the *crest* of the bottom cascade. After a few more steep switchbacks you will come to the brink of the top cascade and another spectacular

Bottom of Nancy Cascades

view. From a secure aerie you can watch the brook tumble headlong down a steep corridor of ledge, framed by feathery boughs of mountain ash. Out beyond, you can trace the winding ravine back down to the Saco River valley and across to the Montalban Ridge, the long southern leg of Mount Washington. The spot is truly idyllic, as is Nancy Pond farther up the trail.

Although some hikers bushwhacked up the cascades before the present trail was established, the scrambling opportunities are poor on the sheer ledges. Not only is the rock steep and treacherous, but a thick copse of spruce and fir trees blocks the passage up the falls. By far the best spots for exploring the streambed are above and below the headwall.

The gray gneiss (pronounced "nice") bedrock that is exposed at Nancy Cascades is one of the oldest rock forms in the region. This tough metamorphic rock began as silt at the bottom of a shallow sea more than 500 million years ago. After being compressed by millions of years of overlying sediments the rock was contorted and subsumed by movements of the earth's crustal plates. The resulting pressure and heat recrystallized the ancient sediments (and also destroyed any fossil records in the formation). Later intrusions of magma produced the attractive granites that are found in much of the region, but here— and in the Presidential range to the north—all of the overlying rock has eroded away to expose the ancient metamorphic foundation.

Historical Detour

Nancy Cascades, Nancy Brook, Nancy Pond, Mount Nancy, Nancy's Bridge. If you suspect that there is a Nancy story behind all these names, you're right. It is one of the most widely known tales in White Mountain history and one of the few that is a romance, albeit a tragic one.

The story begins with a Colonel Joseph Whipple, who was the first settler to pass north through the White Mountain Notch (Crawford Notch, today) after the passage was discovered in 1771. As the pioneer settler in the town of Jefferson, Whipple gained control of vast tracts of land over which he exercised autocratic, though benign, authority. As one example of his noblesse oblige, he refused to sell any of his grain to starving farmers from Bartlett in order to conserve supplies for his dependent neighbors in Jefferson. His noncommercial exploits included piloting Jeremy Belknap's 1784 exploration of what was later named Mount Washington, and escaping from Indians who had been sent by the English to capture him during the Revolutionary War.

Nancy Barton (the surname is uncertain), a servant girl at Whipple's manor, fell in love with one of the colonel's farmhands. The two lovers arranged, so Nancy thought, to accompany Whipple to Portsmouth on his annual trading trip in the late fall of 1778, and there to be married. But after Nancy entrusted two years of savings to her lover, he and the colonel set out for the coast while she was off in Lancaster. Nancy was frantic when she heard about their departure, and assumed that the two men had left her behind mistakenly. Resolving to catch up with the party and be reunited with her lover, Nancy tied together a small bundle of clothes and set off toward the White Mountain Notch in deep snow and a bitter northwest wind.

Though poorly clad for the wintry storm, Nancy managed to tramp over 20 miles down into the notch, only to arrive at Colonel Whipple's campsite a bit too late. The party had moved on, though the embers of the campfire were still alive. After warming herself briefly by the dying embers Nancy pushed on in desperation, having eaten nothing since leaving Jefferson. When she crossed the Saco River, her clothes got wet. Exhausted and cold, Nancy collapsed in the snow, where a search party from Jefferson found her, frozen, the next day.

Her lover, it is said, went mad after hearing of her death and died only months later. Some say, as well, that the lover's wails can still be heard when the winds sweep across the place where Nancy died.

In memory of the tragic tale of this love-struck young woman, Nancy Brook took its place in the geography of New Hampshire decades ahead of Mount Washington or Crawford Notch, and a century before the cascades were first described. It might be noted, too, that nothing of any significance today bears the name Whipple.

CHAPTER 22

Arethusa Falls

◆

Location
Western wall of Crawford Notch, just inside the southern boundary of the
state park.

Map
AMC Mount Washington Range Map: H-8.
DeLorme Trail Map: F-9.

Hiking Data
Distance, parking area to:
Bemis Brook Falls and Coliseum Falls .... 0.5 mile.
Arethusa Falls .... 1.3 miles.
Altitude gain: 750 feet to Arethusa Falls (altitude 2000 feet).
Difficulty: EASY to Bemis Brook Falls and Coliseum Falls; MODERATE
to Arethusa Falls.

◆

In early editions of the *AMC White Mountain Guide*, Arethusa Falls
was described as being "about 140 ft. high." More recent editions
have the falls stretching to "over 200 ft. high." An average of these
two estimates comes close to what was reported in 1875 by M. F.
Sweetser and Professor J. H. Huntington, who named the falls and
measured its height as 176 feet. Even their figure is not clear cut,
however, since the measurement depends on exactly where the observers spotted the top and the bottom of the falls. All agree, though,
that Arethusa Falls is the highest single drop in New Hampshire, as
well as one of the most spectacular—especially when Bemis Brook
is running high.

Along with a grand main attraction, this trip also features a delightful side show of delicate miniatures. Bemis Brook Falls and Col-

iseum Falls are about as small as waterfalls come, yet they are also about as pretty as they come. In fact, if you are traveling with young children you might choose to visit Bemis Brook and Coliseum falls and skip Arethusa Falls altogether. A short excursion to the two small waterfalls would be an excellent way to spark a child's interest in the woods and streams.

The Trail to the Falls

Driving up US 302 from Conway or Pinkham Notch, turn left onto the paved side road just past the sign marking the entrance into Crawford Notch State Park. If you are coming down the notch from the north, the turn is on your right about 0.5 mile beyond the Dry River Campground. (Campers staying at Dry River can easily reach Arethusa Falls in the early morning or late afternoon when it is much less crowded.) Park at the end of the short side road, below the railroad tracks. The white house above the tracks is privately owned, so keep out of the yard.

Alongside the Forest Service information board at the parking area an obvious trail can be seen leading into the woods. This is *not* the trail to take unless you want to reach the falls by hiking *up* the Frankenstein Cliff Trail on a 4.5-mile loop. The loop trip is quite beautiful, but most people prefer hiking *down* the imposing cliffs after visiting the falls.

Frankenstein Cliff, named for an eighteenth-century landscape artist, is the home of a peregrine falcon family. These swift avian predators can be recognized by their size (about that of a crow); their long, pointed wings; and their long, narrow tail. The cliffs are also a favorite haunt for another interesting species: winter ice climbers. In midwinter ice climbers may also be found picking their way up the blue-green mask of ice at Arethusa Falls itself.

The Arethusa Falls Trail enters the woods above the railroad tracks, to the left of the private yard. The trail shortly makes a right turn, ascends a small ridge, and then begins a steady climb along the north side wall of the Bemis Brook ravine. The path is well blazed and easy to follow after the initial turns have been negotiated, but irregular rocks and a maze of spruce roots farther along make for rough footing. For the first mile the trail follows an old logging road, with the brook out of sight below. When the trail does touch the brook, you will find small cascades and pools set in the smooth, flat slabs of exposed bedrock. These are excellent spots for a rest and a snack.

About 1.2 miles from the parking lot the trail crosses to the south bank of Bemis Brook. Avoid trying to perform a high-wire act on the thick log over the brook; its bare surface is too slick for safety. Instead, cross on the rocks and use the log for balance if necessary. Clambering up the roots and rocks beyond the crossing, you will begin to detect the rumble of the waterfall. In only 0.1 mile a sheet of shimmering silver appears as a backdrop to a tall spruce tree, and the trail emerges into a granite basin at the foot of the falls.

The hike up to Arethusa Falls is lengthened only slightly by taking the detour along Bemis Brook Trail, which forks off to the left 0.2 mile from the parking lot. This pretty side trail crosses over to the brook and follows its rise past charming Fawn Pool, Coliseum Falls, and Bemis Brook Falls, before climbing steeply to rejoin the main trail at about 0.7 mile.

From Arethusa Falls you can either retrace your steps back to the parking lot or continue into the woods on the north side of the basin onto the Arethusa–Ripley Falls Trail. The latter connects with Ripley Falls (2.1 miles north), after climbing over an intervening ridge, and descends to Willey House Station (see Chapter 24). By turning right onto the Frankenstein Cliff Trail after 1 mile, however, you can loop back to your car. After crossing the crest of the cliff, this trail descends steeply to US 302, where the Frankenstein Cutoff returns to the Arethusa parking lot. Sensible caution should be exercised on top of the cliff: one of the few waterfall-related fatalities in recent years occurred when a man slipped off Frankenstein Cliff in misty, wet weather. His party had been caught by darkness returning from a late afternoon visit to Arethusa Falls. (Note also that hiking on the old railroad tracks is strictly prohibited.)

Coliseum and Bemis Brook Falls

Coliseum Falls is located about 75 yards above Fawn Pool on the Bemis Brook Trail. Between the pool and the falls the brook slides in transparent sheets down a gently sloping ledge of brown, weath-

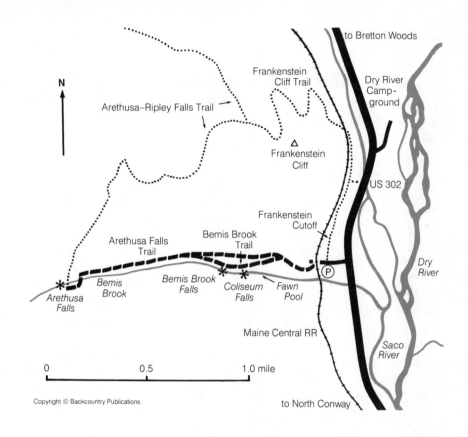

ered granite. You can approach the falls by the trail or by exploring up the streambed. Since the brook faces east here, the open ledges benefit from the morning sun, making Coliseum Falls an inviting place to enjoy the brook.

The falls consist of two short drops separated by a broad, flat slab. At each drop the rock is fractured horizontally and eroded in layers to form a series of short, regular steps. The lower drop, only 4 feet in height, has etched a wide horseshoe into the rock, ringing the curtain of water with layered platforms like the tiers of a miniature coliseum.

Above Coliseum Falls the trail angles away from the brook and climbs a bit before regaining the stream at an overlook atop a small crag beside Bemis Brook Falls. This picturesque waterfall consists of four short drops separated by terraces that are adorned with clear, shallow pools. Although not a very apt term for a waterfall, the word "delicious" comes to mind when I think of this tantalizing scene.

At Bemis Brook Falls the ravine is steeper and narrower than at Coliseum Falls, so it's not a good playground for little kids. But big kids can scramble down to the brook and explore the pools and the falls.

Arethusa Falls

Emerging from the woods at Arethusa Falls, you will be standing in a cool downdraft among angular boulders at the bottom of a small bedrock basin. Three sides of the basin are lined with spruce and birch. The fourth side, to the left, is a towering wall of pink-gray Osceola granite, draped with a wide veil of lacy rivulets. Depending on the water conditions, the falls can appear as an elaborate fountain tumbling playfully from ledge to ledge or as a thundering curtain surging over the wall in a single drop and filling the basin with chilly spray.

At the base of the falls the stream skips down slabs of scalloped bedrock, turns, and slides off into the woods below. There is no pool of any significance right at the falls. If you want to swim there are

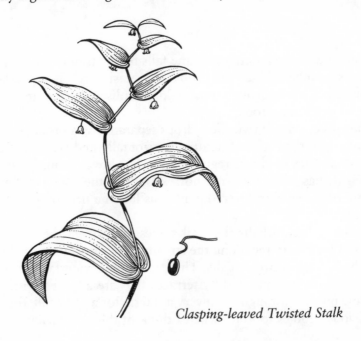

Clasping-leaved Twisted Stalk

good (but shaded) spots downstream, including one unusual tub pool lined with benches of horizontal rock strata.

Arethusa Falls is not made for scramblers any more than for swimmers. The bottom of the wall may look inviting to climb, but the rocks here are too steep and slippery to be safe. One young man who succumbed to the temptation in 1983 slipped and fell, resulting in severe head injuries. Less tragic, but equally to the point, the one and only dent in my camera was incurred while I was "testing" the rocks for this description! On a subsequent trip we saw three people slip on the rocks in a span of fifteen minutes. Fortunately no one was hurt. On the whole, though, scrambling is best confined to explorations farther downstream. One last word of warning: unguarded snacks may become chipmunk food!

Seen from below, Arethusa Falls does not appear as high as it is reputed to be, regardless of which estimate you accept. One way to appreciate its true size is to hike to the top by the badly eroded side path in the woods to the left. But the top of the waterfall is a very dangerous place, and farther upstream there is not much to see. So, in deference to the poor condition of the ascent path, it is best just to enjoy the superb view of the falls from below and leave the problem of gauging its height to the experts.

Historical Detour

According to Moses Sweetser's 1887 *Handbook for Travellers*:

> Arethusa Falls were discovered by Professor Tuckerman many years ago, but not visited by a dozen people since, and are well nigh forgotten. They were visited and measured by the Editor and Professor Huntington in September, 1875, and then (being nameless) received the provisional name of Arethusa Falls, in allusion to Shelley's lines. . . .

The professor here was Edward Tuckerman, a distinguished botanist after whom the great ravine on Mount Washington is named, and the allusion to Shelley refers to the poem "Arethusa," written by Percy Bysshe Shelley in 1820. The poem relates a story, from Greek mythology, of a beautiful nymph named Arethusa, a companion of Artemis. In a vain attempt to escape the amorous advances of the river god Alpheus, Arethusa was transformed into a fountain on the island of Ortygia. As described by Shelley:

> Arethusa arose
> From her couch of snows
> In the Acroceraunian mountains,—
> From cloud and from crag,
> With many a jag,
> Shepherding her bright fountains.
> She leapt down the rocks,
> With her rainbow locks,
> Streaming among the streams;
> Her steps paved with green
> The downward ravine
> Which slopes to the westward gleams;
> And gliding and springing,
> She went, ever singing,
> In murmurs as soft as sleep.
> the Earth seemed to love her,
> and Heaven smiled above her,
> and she lingered towards the deep. . . .

It is probably no coincidence that this very poem had been quoted by Thomas Starr King in his popular book on the "White Hills," published in 1859. King, however, used the poem to describe Silver Cascades, just up Crawford Notch, and he mentioned the waterfalls on Bemis Brook not at all.

Arethusa Falls is not mentioned in Lucy Crawford's *History of the White Mountains* either. This is curious, because for five decades Lucy's father-in-law, Abel Crawford—"the old Patriarch" of the Notch—resided at Mount Crawford House, only 3 miles south of the falls. Later, it was her brother-in-law, Nathaniel Davis, who forfeited Mount Crawford House and virtually all the real estate up to the head of Crawford Notch to Dr. Samuel Bemis, after whom the nearby brook and falls are named.

Bemis was a Boston dentist, an inveterate fisherman, and a pioneer tourist, if there can be such a creature. After visiting the notch every year from 1827 to 1840 he moved into the neighborhood permanently after foreclosing on a loan to Davis, who was the innkeeper at Mount Crawford House (and the pioneer of the Davis Path up Mount Washington). Despite having come by the inn as a financier, Bemis was widely beloved as a host, nature enthusiast, and local explorer. As a nature photographer, he was one of the first Americans to import a daguerreotype camera from Europe, where it had been invented in 1839. For his home Bemis built the stone house called Notchland, now the Notchland Inn.

Considering that Dr. Bemis and Abel Crawford were both living nearby when Professor Tuckerman discovered Arethusa Falls—indeed, Tuckerman stayed at Mount Crawford House—it is a mystery how the professor's tremendous discovery could have been "well-nigh forgotten" by the time the falls were christened!

Less of a mystery is how the surrounding virgin forests disappeared. In the late 1880s the whole area came under the control of timber interests. Just a mile south of Bemis Brook, Jones & Company established a large sawmill that grew into a substantial town called Carrigain. Beginning in 1892 a logging railroad into the Dry River basin was built through the very spot where you park your car to visit Arethusa Falls. Consequently, the highest waterfall in the White Mountains was still largely unknown to tourists when the state started acquiring property for the Crawford Notch State Park in 1912.

Finally, in the 1930s, the property around Arethusa Falls was acquired by the state, and thus preserved for Arethusa and her suitor:

. . .
At sunrise they leap
From their cradles steep
In the cave of the shelving hill;

At noontide they flow
Through the woods below
And the meadows of asphodel. . . .

CHAPTER 23

Dry River Falls

◆

Location
Deep in the Presidential–Dry River Wilderness, reached from US 302 in Crawford Notch.

Map
AMC Mount Washington Range Map: G-8.
DeLorme Trail Map: E-10.

Hiking Data
Distance, parking area to falls: 5.4 miles.
Altitude gain: 1600 feet (to altitude 2800 feet)
Difficulty: MODERATE, but long.

◆

Picture in your mind a walk along the Dry River into Oakes Gulf. Not very exciting? Unlike "Death Valley" or "Grand Canyon," the name "Dry River" doesn't exactly stoke the imagination. Neither does the view along US 302 by the trailhead. Passing through the southern reaches of Crawford Notch State Park, your attention will probably be drawn westward to the crags of Frankenstein Cliff, not to the wall of hardwoods on the east side of the road where the Dry River joins the Saco. Back in 1887 the Dry River basin didn't excite Moses Sweetser either: "There is but little of interest in this long glen . . . because the bottom and sides are so clothed with large trees as to hide the adjacent mountains."

Now think about hiking along the perilous Mount Washington River into the vast forests of the Presidential Wilderness to a thundering waterfall. Does that sound better? Welcome to Dry River Falls.

The Dry River—which was also called the Mount Washington River for many years—drains an enormous basin formed by the southern

Presidential ridge to the west, Mount Washington to the north, and the long Montalban Ridge to the east. At the head of the basin is Oakes Gulf, the most remote of the great glacial cirques of the Presidential range. The name "Dry" describes the river's bony appearance in Crawford Notch, which belies the formidable character of the watercourse.

The Dry River is actually longer than the Saco above the point of confluence, suggesting to some that the true source of the Saco lies up Oakes Gulf. Rain and snowmelt from the huge basin of the Dry River are funneled through a narrow constriction between the southern shoulder of Mount Webster and the northern flank of Stairs Mountain. This topography causes the water level to fluctuate dramatically in response to changes in the weather. These volatile moods make the Dry River a killer, as can be seen in the grim record of fatalities on Mount Washington posted at the AMC Trading Post in Pinkham Notch. At times the dull Dry River becomes the brash Mount Washington River: a Dr. Jekyll and Mr. Hyde of mountain streams. Fortunately the trail has been rerouted and a suspension bridge has been constructed to provide access to Dry River Falls from Crawford Notch without requiring visitors to risk fording the river during its violent Mr. Hyde phases—when the waterfall is especially impressive.

In 1974 the Dry River basin was incorporated into the 20,000-acre Presidential Range–Dry River Wilderness Area to protect its wild, natural beauty.

The Trail to the Falls

The hike to Dry River Falls from Crawford Notch is not particularly difficult, but it involves an 11-mile round trip. So this is one waterfall that is best suited for people who love to hike. In Crawford Notch, park on the gravel shoulder on either side of US 302, 2.6 miles south of the Willey House Site, or 0.2 mile north of the Dry River Campground. Watch for an inconspicuous trailhead sign on the east side of the road opposite Frankenstein Cliff. Because the Dry River Trail follows an old logging railroad route much of the way to the falls, long stretches are smooth and well graded. This is true of the first leg, a fast and easy 1-mile hike through a fine hardwood forest.

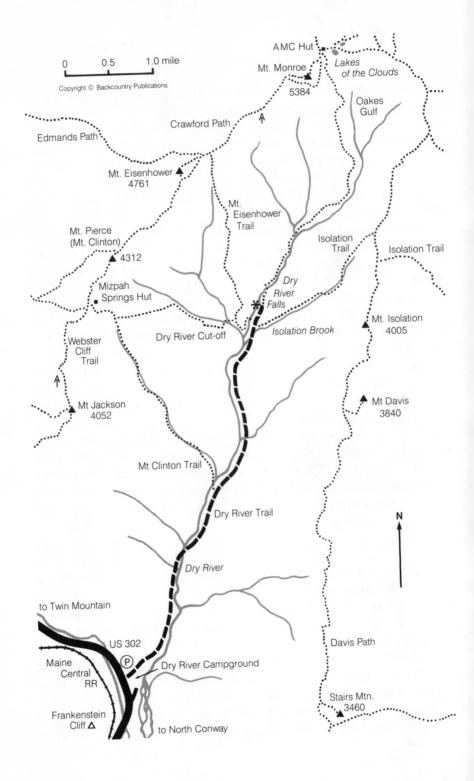

0   0.5   1.0 mile

Copyright © Backcountry Publications

AMC Hut

Mt. Monroe

Lakes
of the Clouds

5384

Oakes
Gulf

Crawford Path

Edmands Path

Mt. Eisenhower
4761

Mt.
Eisenhower
Trail

Isolation
Trail

Isolation Trail

Mt. Pierce
(Mt. Clinton)

4312

Dry
River
Falls

Mizpah
Springs Hut

Dry River Cut-off

Isolation Brook

Mt. Isolation
4005

Webster
Cliff
Trail

Mt Jackson
4052

Mt Davis
3840

Mt Clinton Trail

Dry River Trail

N

Dry River

to Twin Mountain

US 302

Maine
Central
RR

Dry River Campground

Davis Path

Frankenstein
Cliff △

to North Conway

Stairs Mtn.
3460

Where an old rail trestle once spanned the river, the trail turns to the left and surmounts a minor ridge. Just before this detour you can step down to the river from the trail and find a modest set of pools near the site of a former tent shelter. When the area was designated as wilderness, most tent shelters were removed, and the remaining shelters will soon be dismantled. Camping is now restricted to small groups applying low-impact backcountry camping techniques at sites at least 200 feet from the trail.

After climbing over the first ridge, the roller-coaster trail tackles a second, larger ridge. The path climbs steeply and then contours across the brow of the ravine wall, 200 feet above the river. Curving around the far end of this high platform, the trail passes the first and best panorama of the hike. Through a window framed in red spruce boughs you look across waves of overlapping ridges that sweep down from the mountaintops, like ribs protecting the heart of the wilderness. Here and there bristly spikes of white pine penetrate the matted canopy of tree crowns. Down the middle of the panorama winds the deep cleft of the Dry River.

The trail rapidly descends to cross the Dry River by the new suspension bridge at mile 1.7 (according to the AMC trail-guide; it seems farther, though). On the east bank now, the trail's ups and downs continue, though much more gently. As you pass into a transitional forest richly endowed with white birch trees, you can see that the ups are coming out ahead. In early summer the forest wildflowers are abundant here, while later in the summer you will find a splendid mushroom show along the trail.

After pulling temporarily away from the river the trail returns to a smooth stretch of the old railbed where you can find numerous opportunities for a riverside rest. Soon thereafter the Mount Clinton Trail branches off to the left (mile 3) to ford the Dry River and climb toward Mizpah Hut. At times the ford here may be impassable or unsafe. Remember: the Dry River is not just tricky; it has killed hikers trying to cross in high water.

The Dry River Trail continues along the east bank, ascending slowly but steadily for over 1 mile before making a sharp right turn. The trail then climbs eroded switchbacks to a junction with the Isolation Trail, just across Isolation Brook, at mile 5. Again, stay on the Dry River Trail, which contours around a narrow shoulder of land through an enchanting boreal forest. Its legions of spindly spruce and fir trees are bedecked with gray-green mosses and scaly lichens. A tenth of a mile on you will pass a clearing where the trees have been trimmed to provide a view up Oakes Gulf. This gulf is named for William Oakes, a pioneer of White Mountain botany, and one of the first people to explore the basin's steep headwalls and thick forests. Oakes also wrote what is regarded as the first popular guidebook to the region, *White Mountain Scenery*, which was published in 1848 only five days before his untimely death. (He drowned in Boston Harbor after falling overboard from a ferry.)

The Mount Eisenhower Trail comes in from the left at mile 5.2. This trail, too, fords the Dry River and may be impassable in high water. Beyond this last junction, the Dry River Trail becomes rough and narrow. It also badly needs a trim. Even when it is not raining, you may need rain gear to protect your clothes from foliage wet from earlier showers or heavy dew. Very soon a low, steady rumble can be heard in the ravine to the left. As the sound intensifies, watch for a very small hand-lettered sign tacked onto a birch tree, indicating that you have reached the short spur path down to Dry River Falls.

Beyond the falls the Dry River Trail continues climbing into Oakes Gulf, mounts the steep headwall beneath the sheer cliffs of Mount Monroe, and terminates at Lakes of the Clouds Hut. Altogether, a hike from US 302 to the Lakes hut (or vice versa) is just under 10 rugged miles. The Dry River must be crossed 0.25 mile above the

Eastern Hemlock

falls. The current is less formidable here than farther downstream, but caution is still advisable.

Rather than trekking in from US 302 you can also reach Dry River Falls from Mizpah Hut, a mere 2.7 miles away. The elevation change is no different, 1300 feet, except that you descend first. From the hut, follow the Mount Clinton Trail for 0.5 mile and turn onto the Dry River Cutoff, which descends eastward to the Mount Eisenhower Trail. There, turn right and descend to the Dry River, while hoping the river is low enough to be forded safely. Both going and returning! Once across the river the trail mounts the east bank and terminates at the Dry River Trail. The falls are less than 0.25 mile to the left.

The Falls

We hiked in to Dry River Falls one chilly (55 degrees), misty, drizzly day in mid-August after three nights of thunderstorms had ended a parching heat wave. Despite the preceding drought, these thunderstorms were enough to feed the Dry River to a fury. Dry River Falls mimicked the previous evening's thunder so loudly that we had to shout to be heard. From the waterfall heavy clouds of spray drifted down the ravine on powerful drafts, like ghosts of the Indian spirits that are said to haunt the gulf.

At Dry River Falls, the river's powerful current plunges more than 50 feet in three irregular steps down steeply inclined ledges of gray gneiss. The spur path from the main trail climbs down to the midsection of the primary drop, a turbulent plume of whitewater dashing 35 feet to a deep pool at the base of a narrow glen. The formation has been likened to Glen Ellis Falls (Chapter 20) on a smaller scale. But unlike Glen Ellis, the sides of this sheer ravine are shrouded with spruce, birch, and fir. The ambiance is quite wild, as befits a waterfall at the foot of Mount Isolation.

You can easily descend to the pool at the base of the glen or climb a trodden footpath to the top of a jagged crag on the shoulder of the headwall. This high perch provides a dizzying (and unprotected) bird's-eye view of the main falls and the winding ravine below, as well as a close-up view of the upper cascades. A quick scramble up the smoothed slabs above the crag takes you to a superb pothole pool fed by cascades 5 feet high. Although the waterfall itself is at its most spectacular when the river runs strong, the pool on the top deck is most inviting in sunny weather when the currents are less powerful and the water is not quite so cold.

A small knob just above the upper pool bears the scars of back-packers who evidently knew nothing about low-impact camping. The site is an excellent example of where and how *not* to camp in the wilderness.

Historical Detour

> The Indians believed in vast treasures of precious stones . . . suspended from big cliffs in the mountains. Then Darby Field [the first colonist to climb Mount Washington, in 1642] to the day of his death talked of dazzling diamonds and emeralds that blazed and flashed in the mountains. . . .
>
> *—Bisbee, 1938.*

The legend of the Great Carbuncle—variously reported as a lode of diamonds, emeralds, rubies, or gold—was a favorite fireside tale of the early White Mountain settlers. It is said that local Indians observed the treasure on many occasions and some had climbed the great mountain Agiochook seeking the Carbuncle, never to return.

Nathaniel Hawthorne heard the legend from Ethan Allen Crawford, on a visit to the mountains in 1832. Hawthorne's moralistic short story, "The Great Carbuncle," was very popular when published in 1835. Crawford, as a boy, had actually encountered a party of trampers who claimed to have found the treasure high on the steep headwall of the Dry River basin. They had been unable to reach the carbuncle without assistance, in part because they believed that the treasure was guarded by Indian spirits. Under the guidance of Abel Crawford (Ethan's father), the fortune-seekers headed back up the Dry River—accompanied this time by a minister who went along to ward off evil spirits. They set out anticipating "how rich they should be in coming home laden with gold" (Morse, 1978). But nothing was found, and the treasure was never seen again.

In truth, the earliest explorers, including Darby Field, hoped to find precious minerals in the White Mountains. Field even brought home a load of "diamonds" from his pioneering climb, only to find

Dry River

that the stones were merely quartz. Based on Field's report of seeing crystals, the White Mountains were often called the Crystal Hills.

The lower reaches of the Dry River basin—still called Cutt's Grant—were purchased from the state in 1810 by two Mainers, Thomas Cutt, of Saco, and Richard Conant, of Portland. They paid $340 for a grant of 7,680 acres of dense, unexplored forestland extending 6 miles up the river and 1 mile to each side. This land remained in the hands of the original families until it was acquired by the federal government in 1932 as part of the White Mountain National Forest.

Before the federal government got there, though, the vast stretches of virgin timber attracted the attention of the loggers who operated a large mill only a few miles down the notch. (See Chapter 22.) Francis Belcher (1980) relates that the landowners leased out timber rights to the Saco Valley Railroad in 1891. They restricted the lease to a period of not more than fifteen years, stipulated that no trees less than 8 inches in diameter could be cut, and limited the lease to only a single round of cutting. Needless to say, this was remarkably conservative forestry at the time.

A logging railroad was constructed up the Dry River valley to within 0.75 mile of the falls. It remained in operation only five years. As Belcher explains,

> This area was actually one of the most inaccessible of all the White Mountain locations to be logged by railroad. . . . [T]he maintenance costs of this lumber railroad line alone kept its owners on the narrow edge between failure and success at all times.

The topography of the Dry River basin forced the railway route to cross the river thirteen times, putting the ill-fated line at the mercy of the river's violent moods. By 1898 the track was dismantled, the lumberjacks were gone, and the forest had begun to recover from its limited encounter with the axe and saw. Perhaps the Indian spirits were hard at work once again protecting their mountain treasures.

CHAPTER 24

Ripley Falls

---◆---

Location
Willey House Station, in Crawford Notch.

Map
AMC Mount Washington Range Map: H-8.
DeLorme Trail Map: F-9.

Hiking Data
Distance, parking area to falls: 0.6 mile.
Altitude gain: 400 feet (to altitude 1800 feet).
   700 feet to Sparkling Cascade (altitude 2100 feet).
Difficulty: EASY.

---◆---

[A] more wild and beautiful waterfall than any hitherto seen on the western side of the mountains, was discovered on Mount Willey in September, 1858, by Mr. Ripley of North Conway, and Mr. Porter of New York. . . . Exploring the stream nearly a mile higher, other falls were discovered, each one deserving especial notice, and one or two of most rare beauty.

When Thomas Starr King wrote this announcement in 1859 he reported that Ripley and Porter had chosen the name "Sylvan-Glade Cataract" for the wild and beautiful waterfall. They christened the rare beauty above as "Sparkling Cascade." Both falls graced the channel of what was then known as "Cow Brook." King suggested that the lower falls be renamed in honor of Mr. Ripley, and he expressed hope that the brook could be renamed as a memorial to a tragic avalanche that had occurred nearby. These proposals took root, so today we can visit Ripley Falls on Avalanche Brook, rather than the Sylvan-Glade Cataract on Cow Brook.

Sparkling Cascade, meanwhile, effectively has vanished from view. Guidebooks in the early 1900s referred vaguely to "upper falls" on Avalanche Brook, and by 1940 trail descriptions had Ripley Falls standing alone. As recently as the early 1950s hikers could follow an old logging road up Avalanche Brook beyond Ripley Falls, but that route has since been reclaimed by the forest. (A park ranger we spoke to in 1988 knew of no upper falls, by any name.) To be sure, the upper falls—the merits of which King greatly exaggerated—never vanished from the mountainside. If a trail were ever restored, Sparkling Cascade might reappear on the roster of White Mountain waterfalls. Until then, however, the popular trip to Ripley Falls rests easily on its own laurels.

To complement the short hike to Ripley Falls, you might consider the nearby climb to *Kedron Flume*. The side trip to this interesting but unspectacular cascade is described briefly below.

The Trail to the Falls

The Arethusa-Ripley Falls Trail leads to both Arethusa and Ripley Falls, as the name suggests. (Chapter 22 described a more direct route to Arethusa Falls.) The trailhead is located at the end of a short side road off US 302 at the old Willey House station. A sign for Ripley Falls marks the turn, 1 mile south of the tourist information center at the Willey House Site, and 1.8 miles north of the Dry River Campground. If you see cars parked at the corner, don't conclude that the lot up the road has overflowed; these cars probably belong to hikers climbing the spectacular Webster Cliff Trail across the highway.

Starting behind the information sign at the top of the parking area, the trail crosses the railroad track and climbs through a stand of white birch. At the outset the Ethan Pond Trail coincides with the Arethusa-Ripley Falls Trail, so Appalachian Trail signs and white paint blazes mark the way. After only 0.1 mile the two trails diverge. The Ethan Pond Trail (and the white blazes) continues up the ridge, while the route to Ripley Falls, clearly posted, forks to the left and contours along the wall of the ravine. In rainy weather the trail crosses a few slippery spots that require caution, since the drop on the left

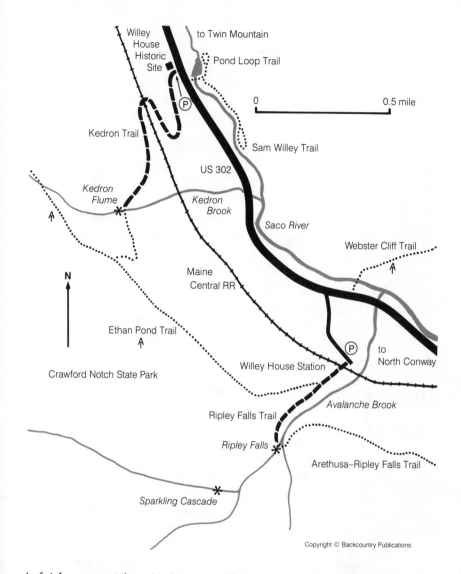

Willey House Historic Site

to Twin Mountain

Pond Loop Trail

P

0   0.5 mile

Kedron Trail

Sam Willey Trail

US 302

Kedron Flume

Kedron Brook

Saco River

Webster Cliff Trail

N

Maine Central RR

Ethan Pond Trail

Crawford Notch State Park

Willey House Station

P

to North Conway

Avalanche Brook

Ripley Falls Trail

Ripley Falls

Arethusa–Ripley Falls Trail

Sparkling Cascade

is fairly steep. After climbing gradually for less than 0.5 mile the trail abruptly turns left (watch the blue blazes) and descends to a narrow basin at the foot of Ripley Falls.

Here the trail crosses to the south bank of Avalanche Brook and ascends by switchbacks to the woods just above the falls. This section of trail is narrow and eroded, with exposed conifer roots that are slippery when wet. The smooth ledges at the top of the falls should be avoided when wet, since this is not a place where you would want to slip. In dry conditions, however, the ledges upstream from the head of Ripley Falls are fun to explore. From the top of the falls the trail itself turns generally south, climbs 800 feet to a ridge behind Frankenstein Cliff (mile 1.7), and traverses to Arethusa Falls (mile 2.7).

For the side trip to Kedron Flume, drive 1 mile north on US 302 to the Willey House Site. At the picnic area south of the gift shop you will find a sign marking the base of the Kedron Flume Trail. Incredibly, the sign indicates that the Flume is 0.5 mile away. This may have been accurate years ago when the trail shot straight up the steep mountain wall. Mercifully, switchbacks were added to the trail, doubling the distance, while making the climb much easier. After one long switchback the trail crosses the old Maine Central Railroad tracks. Above this you continue to gain elevation on shorter switchbacks and then contour toward the south. Shortly after the trail enters a zone of spruce and crosses a set of angular boulders, you reach Kedron Brook at the foot of the flume. Beyond this point the trail climbs steadily to intercept the Ethan Pond Trail, which connects to the Willey Range Trail and the summits on the west wall of Crawford Notch.

The Falls

At Ripley Falls, Avalanche Brook slips over a steeply inclined ledge 100 feet high. Compared to Arethusa Falls, its neighbor to the south, Ripley Falls is less precipitous and not quite as high. This makes it less dramatic, but no less beautiful. "Apples versus oranges," is how we heard it explained to inquiring tourists at one information booth, "and Ripley Falls is much easier to reach."

From the boulder-strewn basin at the foot of the falls you will see a long rippled ribbon of silvery water leaping and sliding down a steep bed of orange-gray granite. On overcast days the gray tones prevail, casting a cool and pensive mood over the waterfall basin. Sunny days accentuate the orange tones, displaying the falls in a warm, playful light that contrasts sharply with the bright green of the surrounding forest. This contrast highlights the outline of the granite bed, which is remarkably similar in shape to the state of New Hampshire!

A small, waist-deep pool lies at the foot of the cascade, enclosed

Ripley Falls in October

on the right by a vertical rock wall 20 feet high. With the falls facing east, the basin catches the summer sun from late morning through midday. A spell of sunny weather can warm the bright amber water to temperatures more tepid than usual for a mountain pool—near 60 degrees Fahrenheit. (In contrast, the water was only 36 degrees one chilly afternoon during foliage season.)

You can reach better swimming holes, however, by following the trail to the top of the falls. Just upstream you will find a series of small, delightful cascades and sunny, shallow pools scooped in the handsome bedrock. In his original description of Ripley Falls, King regarded these cascades as an integral part of the "singularly grand" formation.

The upper ledges are also the best place for exploring, especially considering that the steep granite wall of the waterfall itself is *not* a safe place on which to climb around. But above the main falls you can scramble quite a way up the smooth granite ledges with little difficulty. If you are lucky you might hear the lively piccolo trill of a winter wren from the thick brush above the streambed. There is a flavor of wildness about the place—a flavor that visitors should take care to preserve. Although exploring upstream can be great fun, it bears repeating that the ledges just above the brink of the falls can be slippery and dangerous and should be avoided in wet weather or high water.

At Kedron Flume, one brook north of Ripley Falls, Kedron Brook has hewn a shallow trench into a sloping granite ledge above the trail. Below the trail, the brook slips down a long chain of precipitous waterfalls. Unfortunately the brook tends to run low, so both the flume and the waterfall below are often unimpressive.

At the Ripley Falls turn-off from US 302, a road sign states that the hike to the falls takes only twenty minutes. An early AMC guide was more helpful in suggesting that it could take more than four hours "to visit and enjoy all the falls." Adding Kedron Flume to the itinerary, you can spend the best part of a full day enjoying the waterfalls in the vicinity.

Historical Detour

Two intriguing historical questions are posed by the place names Ripley Falls and Avalanche Brook. First, who was Mr. Ripley? And second, what avalanche?

Henry Wheelock Ripley was a friend and traveling companion to both Abel Crawford and Thomas Starr King. (Remember that King was the one who suggested naming the falls for Ripley.) Evidently addicted to the tonic of mountain air from an early age, Henry Ripley tramped the White Mountain trails for over fifty years, beginning at age seven. He is reported to have climbed Mount Washington eighty-five times (Hixson, 1980). In addition, it was Ripley who prepared the second edition of Lucy Crawford's *History of the White Mountains* for publication in 1883.

As recounted by his friend King, Ripley and Porter discovered the falls on Cow Brook after "an old fisherman" at Crawford House told of encountering some wonderful unknown cascades in that vicinity. Moses Sweetser, however, later wrote that Abel Crawford discovered the falls "while out on snowshoes, trapping sable," and that Ripley and Porter merely revisited and christened the falls in 1858. If these accounts seem contradictory, it might be noted that Abel Crawford was himself an old fisherman. Perhaps the Sylvan-Glade Cataract should have been renamed Crawford Falls instead.

The avalanche that King had in mind when proposing to rename Cow Brook was the 1826 Willey disaster—the most tragic catastrophe in the history of the White Mountains. It is also probably the most familiar story of the mountains, recounted time and again in book and ballad. The first detailed account, and still by far the best, appeared in Reverend Benjamin Willey's fascinating book, *Incidents in White Mountain History* (1856). Reverend Willey was motivated to write the book by the fact that he had been asked innumerable times to give his firsthand account of the story of his brother's doom.

In the autumn of 1825 Samuel Willey, Jr., son of one of Bartlett's early settlers, moved with his wife and five children into a small house deep in the trough of Crawford Notch. The house had been built before the turn of the century, but was occupied only intermittently. During winter of 1825–26 Willey began providing shelter and hospitality to teamsters working their way through the notch. Sometimes the winter winds were so severe, they say, that a man required help just to keep his hair on. The following spring the Willeys expanded their modest facility to provide better service for travelers.

After a June rain triggered small slides near his house, Willey grew apprehensive about his chosen location. He considered moving but decided that the risk of recurrence for such a rare event was slight, and so chose to stay. That summer, the topsoil was dried to an unusual depth by extremely hot and arid weather that lasted until after mid-August. Then came the rains. Light showers were followed by an extraordinary downpour on the night of August 29 that severely flooded both the Saco and the Ammonoosuc, and destroyed the turnpike.

The next morning, as the rivers subsided, Ethan Allen Crawford accompanied a traveler through the flood debris and down the storm-strewn notch from the north. Arriving at Willey House, they found the buildings undamaged, though totally surrounded by the massive tongues of an enormous landslide. As the only living creatures to be found were the family dog and two oxen, the men assumed the Willey family had escaped southward before the avalanche. Crawford returned home, while the traveler spent a night in the vacant house. He proceeded to Bartlett the next morning and learned that the Willey family had not been seen.

A search party was quickly dispatched to the scene of the devastating slide. From the swarms of flies the searchers—including Benjamin Willey himself—quickly found the bodies of Samuel Willey's wife and one hired hand. With some digging they also uncovered the bodies of Samuel Willey, two of his children, and another farmhand. The three other Willey children were never found.

Some say that when the family fled the house, presumably seeking high ground to escape the terrifying flood, their Bible was left open to the Eighteenth Psalm:

> In my distress I called upon the Lord, . . . Then the earth shook and trembled; the foundations also of the hills moved and were shaken, because he was wroth. . . . He made darkness his secret place; his pavilion around him were dark waters and thick clouds of the skies. . . . Then the channels of waters were seen, and the foundations of the world were discovered at thy rebuke, O Lord. . . . He sent from above, he took me, he drew me out of many waters. . . .
>
> —*King James Version*

The Willey house was reoccupied within a few years, and today the Crawford Notch visitor's center is located at the very site of the disaster, 1 mile north of the trailhead for Ripley Falls.

The Androscoggin
Watershed

◆

Screw Auger Falls

CHAPTER 25

Waterfalls of Grafton Notch

Step Falls / Screw Auger Falls

◆

Location
On ME 26, north of Newry, ME.

Map
AMC Carter-Mahoosuc Map, B13.

◆

Grafton Notch, at the northeastern tip of the Mahoosuc Range, is a splendid gallery of glacial earth art. Like other dramatic U-shaped valleys in the White Mountain region—such as Crawford Notch and Franconia Notch—this narrow mountain pass was molded and scoured by the grinding advances of the continental ice cap. Later, in retreat, the ice cap ornamented exposed surfaces of granite with the abrasive force of its gritty meltwaters. In the vicinity of Grafton Notch the glaciers left behind one stunning ornament on the Bear River at Screw Auger Falls, and a fascinating swath of sculpted granite on Wight Brook at Step Falls.

Although Step Falls and Screw Auger Falls highlight the waterfall trip to Grafton Notch, they are not the only waterfall exhibits in the gallery. Two neighboring formations, Mother Walker Falls and Cascade Brook, are also described briefly below.

Grafton Notch is a scenic delight in its own right, quite apart from its waterfalls. Precipitous cliffs rise 800 to 1000 feet on each side of Route 26, which traces the path of the glaciers through a gap between

Baldpate Mountain on the east and Old Speck Mountain on the west. North of the height-of-land the Swift Cambridge River flows to Umbagog Lake, a natural jewel at the head of the Androscoggin River. The Bear River runs south through the notch to join the Androscoggin at Newry. Thus Grafton Notch has the distinction of dividing two watersheds that serve the same river!

Grafton Notch State Park can be reached from Newry, ME, or from Errol, NH. The nearest camping facility is at Umbagog Lake, just across the state line in New Hampshire.

Step Falls

Hiking Data
Distance, parking area to top of falls: 0.6 mile.
Altitude gain: 300 feet (to altitude 1200 feet).
Difficulty: EASY.

If you are driving north from Newry, your first stop will be at Step Falls. This waterfall consists of an extensive series of cataracts and pools laced across a long bank of ledge on Wight Brook, which feeds into the Bear River about 0.5 mile below the southern boundary of Grafton Notch State Park. On approaching the notch you can see a set of cliffs, called Lightning Ledge, high on the mountain flank north of the road. Below these cliffs the ravine of Wight Brook can be discerned as a shallow groove in the Bear River escarpment, lined with dark conifer crowns.

Step Falls is located on a 24-acre preserve owned and managed by The Nature Conservancy, a quietly effective environmental organization that protects sensitive ecosystems and precious natural treasures through direct action: it buys the land, or it buys easements restricting future development. If you want to learn about The Nature Conservancy, a good place to start is the feature article on the organization in the December 1988 *National Geographic*.

Just before ME 26 crosses Wight Brook, 8 miles north of US 2, a grassy track on the right (north) runs to the Step Falls parking area. Neither the turn-off nor the parking area is marked. To confirm that you have taken the correct turn, look for a trail heading into a grove of spruce and balsam fir at the end of the parking area. You only have to walk a few yards along the trail to reach a large sign identifying the nature preserve. There is also a guest registration box here, with a limited stack of information brochures supplied by the Maine Chapter of The Nature Conservancy. According to the brochure the water volume in Wight Brook averages 6 cubic feet per second, but can swell nearly ninety-fold during the spring!

The path to Step Falls is very easy to follow as it ascends gradually through the shady forest. The only minor complication is that the path temporarily splits; the left-hand fork edges the rocky brook while the main path stays on the bank and heads directly to the falls. The forest changes to northern hardwoods as the path approaches the brook, where it emerges onto a pile of large boulders. Scramble onto the boulders for an introductory view of falls. From this vantage point, at the foot of the waterfall, you can see more than 100 yards of inclined ledges capped by an attractive cascade that fans over a granite bulge. But this is only the bottom half of the formation, and the most beautiful part is out of view above the bulge.

The path continues for 0.25 mile and nearly 200 vertical feet beside a chain of cataracts, passing sensational pools, smooth waterslides, small pothole bathtubs, and terrific scrambling ledges. In one radiant pool the deep, transparent waters glimmer with a cool tint of lemon-lime. At another spot a finger of current curls through a corkscrew slide into a bubbling trough tub. Best of all, the broad ledges face south and draw in the full warmth of the sun. Even the bedrock is fascinating. A blend of Devonian-period granites, the rock is interlaced with quartz bands and studded with mineral crystals, including garnet, mica, and tourmaline. The climb up Step Falls is also rewarded with fine views down the ravine and across the Bear River valley.

About halfway up the Step Falls trail you will notice a large pipe crossing the footpath. This pipe feeds water from a small dam above the falls (on private property) to a microhydroplant that generates electricity without marring the beauty of the falls.

The upper boundary of the preserve is just past a stand of red pine trees at the top of the falls, where a logging road approaches the brook. Avoid this logging road on your descent, because it is private property and not part of the preserve.

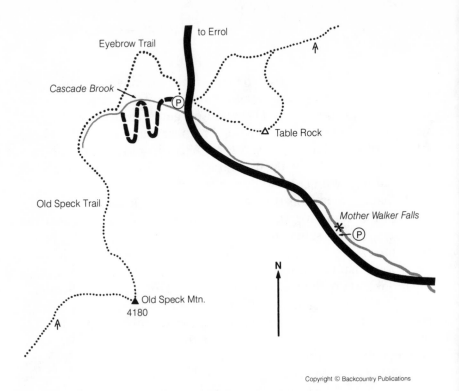

Screw Auger Falls

Hiking Data
Distance, parking area to falls: Roadside.
Altitude gain: zero (altitude 1100 feet).
Difficulty: EASY.

You can drag the family away from Step Falls by promising them another fascinating waterfall just up the road. The Screw Auger Falls parking lot is located on the south side of ME 26, 1 mile above the southern boundary of Grafton Notch State Park. At the parking area a line of picnic tables traces a sweeping bend in the Bear River, under the shade of a well-mixed roadside forest (bring a tree guide to practice identifications). To the west the blunt pyramid of Old Speck Mountain, cloaked in forest green, looms above the valley floor.

Downstream from the picnic area the Bear River slips quietly across a broad, sunny terrace of granite ledge and then plunges 20 feet into

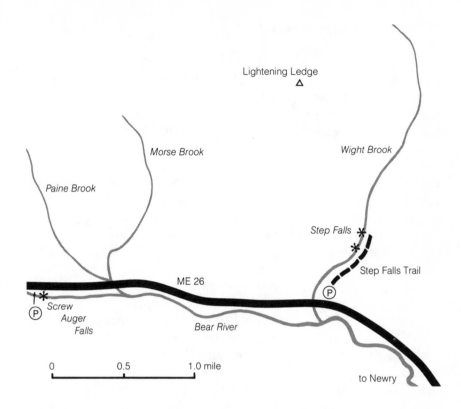

Lightening Ledge

Morse Brook

Wight Brook

Paine Brook

Step Falls

Step Falls Trail

ME 26

Screw
Auger
Falls

Bear River

0   0.5   1.0 mile

to Newry

the wildly contorted Screw Auger Gorge. Overall the river descends about 50 feet from the picnic area to the foot of the gorge, but what makes Screw Auger Falls extraordinary is its setting, not its size. The gorge is adorned with remnant arcs of giant potholes, scooped alcove shelves, and sharply undercut grottoes that usher the river through the slender defile.

This fancifully twisted granite masonry was crafted only ten to fifteen thousand years ago. As the ice cap slowly retreated, it blocked drainage to the north and created a temporary lake above the notch. For centuries—until further melting of the ice cap uncorked the reservoir—a torrent of highly erosive glacial outwash was discharged southward to scour the Bear River bedrock. These swirling currents carved out the Screw Auger Gorge.

The approach to the gorge from the east end of the parking lot is an easy stroll of only a few dozen yards. A well-maintained gravel footpath skirts the broad upper terrace and crosses to the rim of the gorge, where sturdy handrails provide secure views of Screw Auger

Falls and the marvelous rock formations. With minor difficulty it is possible to scramble down the side of the steep ravine below the gorge for a bottom-up view of the contorted chasm walls. In low water you can wade right up the river into the mouth of the formation, assuming the role of Jonah opposite nature's granite whale.

The best place for water play, however, is above the gorge, where the broad, sun-baked ledges furnish shallow pools with gentle waterfall curtains 4- to 8 feet high. These crystal-clear pools are safe enough for young children to splash and wade, and lovely enough for everyone to enjoy. After nature labored so long and hard to carve the fountains, how can anyone resist?

Neighboring Falls

The next stop is *Mother Walker Falls*. A short distance above Screw Auger Falls the road curves to the right, climbs straight toward the ramparts of Table Rock, and then dips slightly as it passes a paved pullout beside a chain-link fence on the right (northeast). A small sign announces that this is the parking area for Mother Walker Falls. Steps lead down to a walkway along the rim of a deep, wild ravine, strewn with granite blocks. From some vantage points you may see rapids, but nothing much resembles a waterfall, and there is no obvious path down to the river.

There is indeed a waterfall here, however. It consists of a narrow 9-foot spout that pours into a small horseshoe-shaped pool. The interesting part is that the waterfall is located inside a cave formed by an enormous flake that has split off from the bluff on the far side of the ravine. For this reason Mother Walker Falls can be difficult to find, and it is a bit disconcerting to contemplate that other huge chunks of rock will someday crash into the ravine. Not to spoil the thrill of the hunt, only two clues will be given here: (i) a rough path enters the ravine from upstream; and (ii) don't go during earthquakes or heavy thunder.

A second waterfall bonus, *Cascade Brook*, sounds more promising than it turns out to be. The brook is identified by name in descriptions of the Old Speck Trail—formerly the Cascade Brook Trail—but it was not deemed important enough to appear on either the USGS topographic map or the AMC map of the notch.

The starting point for the Old Speck Trail is a large parking lot near the height-of-land, 1.5 miles above Mother Walker Falls. In this lot we once found two severely vandalized automobiles that had been left out overnight by midweek hikers on the Appalachian Trail (of which the Old Speck Trail is a link). Regrettably, it is wise to check with local police before leaving a vehicle at a remote site like this for extended periods of time. A large red-lettered sign also warns DO NOT LEAVE VALUABLES IN VEHICLE. For the undaunted, the trail begins behind this warning sign.

Follow the white blazes, keeping left at the Eyebrow Trail fork. Two long switchbacks mount the wall of the notch, returning to the brook each time at feathery cascades on steep, irregular ledges. Above the cascades the trail continues to the summit of Old Speck Mountain, which, at 4180 feet, is Maine's third highest peak.

Surprisingly, the most dramatic waterfall in Grafton Notch is none of the above. Once, after a week of rain, we observed a spectacular 80-foot cascade plunging down the corner of a sheer bank of cliffs 0.1 mile south of the Old Speck Trail—with more water plumes leaping from higher ledges above. A rough, unmarked footpath led up a tongue of rockslide rubble to the base of this unnamed waterfall. It turns out that this dazzling cataract reverts to nothing more than wet rock for much of the season. After heavy rains, though, watch for the intermittent beauty above the forest floor on the west side of the notch just below the trails parking lot. If you can't see it from

Canada Mayflower

the roadside about 50 yards north of the trails parking lot, it probably isn't there.

Historical Detour

Traveling Route 26 between Newry and Errol, one sees little more than mountains and forests. This sums up much of the history of Grafton: mountains, forests, and a road. The best account of Grafton's history is a paper by Charles Fobes (1951), from which much of the following information is drawn.

Pioneer James Brown passed through Grafton Notch in 1830, when a blazed path was the only sign of development. Settling above the notch, Brown hewed a timber business out of the vast tracts of northern forest. He started by harvesting the towering white pines, and then proceeded to the spruce and fir. By 1838 Brown had built a mill, and dammed the Swift Cambridge River to control the water flow for the purpose of driving logs down to the Androscoggin River via Umbagog Lake. The community that grew up around the mill was incorporated as the town of Grafton in 1852. Small farms flourished and schools were built, but Grafton was a lumber town from start to finish. In the 1850s a competing sawmill was built right at the top of Screw Auger Falls. By one account, part of the spiraling gorge was blasted away by the lumbermen.

The town's population climbed to 110 in 1880, when demand for softwood pulp fueled a period of relative prosperity. It is said that Mother Walker Falls is named for one of the last homesteaders to arrive during the town's period of growth. After the best forest resources had been cut, the community began to shrink. By 1919, when its charter was repealed, the town of Grafton reported only one elderly inhabitant.

James Brown died in 1881, just as his company's timber operations were peaking. At about the same time another Brown was forming a timber company based in Berlin, NH. William Wentworth ("W. W.") Brown, formerly a shipbuilder from Down East, began aggressively acquiring forestlands and logging rights in the area. (A decade earlier, yet another family of Browns built a logging railroad out of Whitefield.) By the turn of the century the Brown Company of Berlin controlled most of the north-country timber on both sides of the New Hampshire–Maine state line. In 1919 the company acquired the forestlands in Grafton that had first been logged by James Brown. To this day much of Grafton remains in the hands of the Brown Company's modern embodiment, the James River Corporation.

Unlike many other timber companies, which desecrated the White Mountain forests around the turn of the century, the Brown Company was a forerunner of modern forest resource management (Holbrook, 1961) Influenced by Austin Cary, an innovative forester, the company began as early as 1895 to plan in terms of long-range tree harvests. This meant selective cutting and careful fire prevention. One indication: the observation tower on top of Old Speck Mountain was built for spotting forest fires long before the state park was created.

In addition to supporting 150 years of timber operations, Grafton has long been a lure for tourists. In his guide to the White Mountains (1887), Moses Sweetser became unusually tongue-tied writing about the notch. He described the scenery as being "of a high order of majesty and impressiveness." At that time Screw Auger Falls and Mother Walker Falls were among the prime attractions of western Maine. (Sweetser made no mention of Step Falls.) During the summer stage coaches served Grafton Notch three days per week from the railway station in Bethel. There was even a hotel in town—Captain Brown's.

CHAPTER 26

Moriah Brook

◆

Location
Reached from the Wild River Road, west of Route 113 via Hastings, ME.

Map
AMC Carter-Mahoosuc Map: F-11/12.
DeLorme WMNF Trail Map: C-14.

Hiking Data
Distance, parking area to:
  Moriah Gorge . . . . 1.4 miles.
  Upper Cascades . . . . 3.4 miles.
Altitude gain: 500 feet to the Gorge (altitude 1500 feet); 800 feet to Upper
  Cascades (altitude 1800 feet).
Difficulty: MODERATE.

◆

In Annex A you will find a master list of more than one hundred waterfalls. These are the generals and ranking officers of the army of White Mountain waterfalls. Missing, though, are the troops: the innumerable small cascades scattered along watercourses throughout the region. No names distinguish their identity, and no signs trumpet their presence. Yet it is the miniature falls that truly personify the spirit of the region's mountain streams. Unlike the other trips described in the book, this one highlights some of the waterfall foot soldiers.

On the "back" side of the Carter Range, nature echoes the great ravines of the eastern slopes of Mount Washington. One such echo is the ravine of Moriah Brook. Scooped between the brawny shoulders of Middle Carter Mountain and Mount Moriah, the ravine slopes more than 4 miles eastward to merge with the vast woodlands of the Wild River valley (formally Bean's Purchase, population, zero). Along its 3300-foot descent to the Wild River, Moriah Brook never drops in a single step much higher than a basketball hoop. Nonetheless, the brook bears a fascinating collection of small cascades, fine pothole pools, and an impressive gorge.

The Moriah Brook Trail provides access to these cascades from the Wild River Campground, which is located in the heart of Bean's Purchase. The campground has only eleven units, and no services or supplies are available nearer than Bethel or Gorham. Other than backpacking in from beyond the valley perimeter, the only access route to the campground is a 5-mile-long dirt road along the Wild River from ME 113, south of Gilead.

A larger (twenty-four unit) and less remote campground is located at Hastings, just across ME 113 from the Wild River turn-off. Hastings is the name of a vanished logging village that once occupied the site. Enormous quantities of Wild River timber were transported to large mills at Hastings by a logging railroad that penetrated a dozen miles up the valley. Today the Wild River Road follows the old railbed, and the Moriah Brook Trail climbs one of its spur lines.

The Trail to the Cascades

Driving into the Wild River Campground you will find the hikers' parking area straight ahead at the end of the road. The hike starts on the Wild River Trail, along the old railroad route. After 0.25 mile of easy walking, watch for a sign on the right marking the Moriah Brook Trail. This trail immediately descends to the Wild River and crosses on a wonderful suspension footbridge, which sways like a high cradle to the river's lullaby. As you enjoy the view from the bridge, watch for belted kingfishers swooping along the edge of the river.

On the west bank the Moriah Brook Trail turns left and heads upstream, merging temporarily with the Highwater Trail. The path passes through a dark grove of hemlocks and then enters a bright stand of white birch, where it curves to the right (northeast) and enters the wide mouth of the Moriah Brook ravine.

The Highwater Trail departs to the left at mile 0.7 from the parking area, while the Moriah Brook Trail continues in a beeline up a well-graded railbed, now scarred with gullies. After one large washout, the footing becomes rougher as the trail climbs a small rise and swings to the left. Here you have your first view of Moriah Brook, in a deep ravine below the trail. What you see is the outlet from Moriah Gorge, but the access points, described below, are still ahead. At mile 1.7 the trail reaches and crosses the brook just above the gorge. If you are hiking only to the first set of cascades, this is the end of the line.

Otherwise, cross to the south bank where the trail regains the easy gradient of the old railbed. Shortly you enter a zone of white birch trees. In the undergrowth young spruce and fir trees—the forest of the future—patiently await their day in the sun. The path soon pulls away from the brook, passes a large beaver marsh, fords some small side streams, and then climbs back to Moriah Brook at mile 3.1, crossing again to the north bank. This middle stretch of trail is in rather bad condition, with muddy washouts and encroaching brush.

For the next 0.3 mile the trail climbs more steeply and enters boreal forest just before reaching a knob of gray ledge that is bisected by a

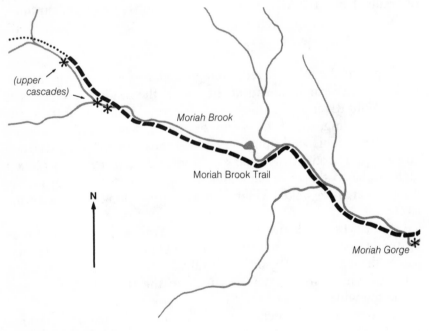

(upper cascades)

Moriah Brook

Moriah Brook Trail

N

Moriah Gorge

tumbling side stream. This very attractive landmark is a good terminus for the waterfall hike. The trail beyond climbs steadily to a col on the summit ridge between Mount Moriah and Imp Mountain. Other small cascades can be found higher up the brook, but the prettiest cascades lie off the side of the trail on the climb up to the gray knob. So have a snack and then turn to the enjoyable task of exploring the cascades.

The Gorge and the Cascades

Moriah Gorge is a rugged chasm over 100 yards long and yet barely 5 feet across at the neck. Constricted by high, sheer walls of the gorge, Moriah Brook accelerates down a series of abrupt steps separated by terraced pools. The lower shelves of the gorge are completely flooded by large pools, which preclude safe passage by anything other than trout, bugs, and small birds. The upper part of the gorge, however, provides more secure ground for scrambling,

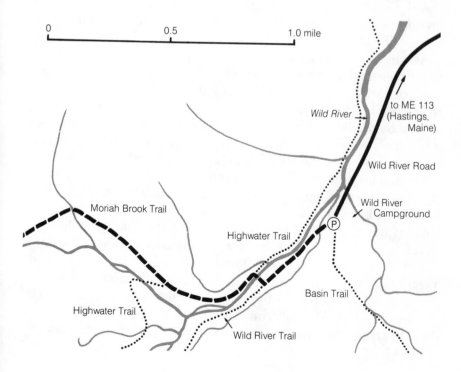

with good views of the formation. The prudent boundary for exploring is dictated by the level of the brook and common-sense caution. You won't want to risk being swept down the gorge by the swift currents.

You can climb down to the gorge two ways. First, from the point above the gorge where the trail crosses Moriah Brook you can scramble and wade down along the sloping ledges beside the top cataracts. This can be done in relative safety if the brook is not too high and if you are careful about slippery footing. Alternatively you can descend by a steep, dirty side path that turns off the trail about 50 feet below the brook crossing. This would be the best way down, except that there may still be a hive of bees guarding the final pitch!

Either approach brings you to the top of a large rectangular block of ledge 12 feet above a slender trench pool. At the head of this pool, a surging cascade spurts from a narrow side channel, ricochets off the opposite wall, and rushes down through the trench to the next cascade. And the next. And the next. And the next.

Although the gorge is a remarkable formation, the best water playgrounds are at the upper cascades. Only a few choice examples will be described here.

About 200 yards beyond the brook crossing at mile 3.1 the trail skirts the streambed beside a wonderful pool carved into a polished bank of banded gray gneiss. Quartz bands in the rock give the pool the appearance of an elegant designer spa. Below the designer pool, as we would call it, the brook tumbles down 30 feet of rapids through a portal of low bedrock walls, with horizontal fractures that resemble rough masonry. At the foot of the rapid is another fine pool.

But don't stop at the first set of pretty pools you see! Not far above the designer pool, the trail crosses a mud patch where a short log bridge has been placed to help with footing. Just beyond this mud patch watch for signs of foot traffic through the undergrowth in the direction of the brook, which here is hidden by the forest. Making your way to the brook, you will find an extraordinary pool beneath a set of sloping waterchutes spread across a 6-foot-high bedrock dike. A side stream entering on the far side of the channel spills over a similar collection of small chutes. Wedged between the brook and the side stream, the ledge has sprouted a water garden of wildflowers,

A triplet cascade on Moriah Brook

shrubs, and young trees. For later reference, let's call this spot the "Water Garden Cascades."

About 0.1 mile below the gray knob at the end of the hike, the trail passes another beautiful formation that might well be called the Triplet Cascade. From the trail only the near channel is visible, but when you climb out onto the open slabs of the streambed, you find three silver ribbons of water pouring through separate notches etched side by side in a broad wall of red-gray ledge. The largest of the triplets is about 10 feet high. Look for small, exquisite pothole tubs under the cascades. They are just the right size for a refreshingly chilly wilderness bath under the warm gaze of the noonday sun.

Historical Detour

> It is a child of the mountains; at times fierce, impetuous and shadowy, as the storms that howl around the bald heads of its parents, and bearing down everything in its path; then again, when subdued by long summer calms, murmuring gently in consonance with the breezy rustle of the trees. . . . An hour's time may swell it into a headlong torrent; an hour may reduce it to a brook that a child might ford without fear.
>
> —*Benjamin Willey, 1856*

Willey's moody "child of the mountains" was the Wild River. The unpredictable volatility of this river was appreciated even by the earliest settlers who arrived in Gilead, ME, around 1780. For over a century thereafter human activity made no permanent mark in the deep backcountry of the Wild River valley.

The eastern section of the Wild River valley, in Maine, was part of an 1807 grant to Josiah Batchelder of Boston. Although portions of the Batchelder grant up through Evans Notch were logged, the Wild River valley itself was still pristine wilderness in 1832 when Alpheus Bean bought the bulk of the remaining property from the state of New Hampshire. He paid $1,033 for 33,000 acres. Even after Bean's purchase, the Wild River woodlands were disturbed only by occasional forays for hunting and fishing, and intermittent logging for local use. The only inhabitant of the watershed before 1850 was a solitary fugitive slave who temporarily occupied a crude shack in the intervale at the mouth of Evans Brook. The fertile soil of this intervale, as well as its proximity to Gilead, lured the first Wild River homesteaders in 1852.

That same year the Atlantic & St. Lawrence Railroad was completed to Gorham, opening the region's timber resources to the voracious urban centers along the coast. A Saco lumber dealer, Joseph Hobson, acquired Bean's Purchase and began driving logs down the Wild River to the Gilead railhead. In 1860 he built a retaining dam near the present site of the Wild River Campground, to release water during the spring log drives. That same autumn, though, the dam was destroyed when the river's wild fury was unleashed by a heavy storm. Faced with the prospect of battling the unpredictable floods, Hobson's choice was to pull out. Round One to the river. Its prize was a thirty-year reprieve.

During the 1880s Major Gideon Hastings developed major timber operations up Evans Brook, and the village of Hastings began to flourish. The only camps up the Wild River valley at this time were for hunting. One Wild River visitor in 1885 was a youngster on his first hunting trip, whose name later became a symbol for outdoor sporting supplies: L. L. Bean.

In 1890, a second Hobson took up the challenge of taming the Wild River. This time it was Samuel Hobson who bought Bean's

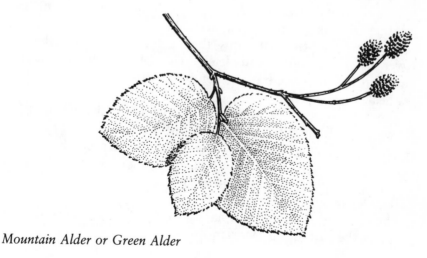

Mountain Alder or Green Alder

Purchase, for $100,000. After forming the Wild River Lumber Company in association with two timber barons from Island Pond, VT, he began building a logging railroad into the wilderness in 1891. The river responded with a huge freshet during a December thaw, destroying the new railroad bridges as well as other company structures.

This time the river's rage did not discourage the intruders. The bridges were rebuilt, and the railroad soon penetrated all the way to the end of the valley. One spur ran 2 miles into the Moriah Brook ravine to a camp just up the side stream above the "Water Garden Cascades." Moriah Gorge was spanned by a long trestle. After the ravine was logged clean, nearly 5000 acres of brush and slash along Moriah Brook went up in flames. In addition to fire, the Wild River Lumber Company was also plagued by spectacular train accidents, including one on the Moriah Brook spur. For a fascinating account of the wreck, complete with old photos, find a copy of D. B. Wight's *The Wild River Wilderness* (1971), on which much of the history recounted here is based.

In 1898 the lumber operations and the entire village of Hastings were sold to the Hastings Lumber Company. Under the new management disasters became commonplace. The first, in 1899, was a legendary train wreck in which an engine boiler exploded, shredding the locomotive and killing three men. Two years later the river brought down destructive floods, which were all the more severe due to loss of forest cover in the watershed. In the spring of 1903 devastating freshets recurred. That same May a severe fire burned out even the railroad ties. After this, the logging operations in the Wild River valley shut down completely. The "child of the mountains" had won Round Two, but not before incurring scars that have not yet healed completely.

The Wild River Road replaced the old railroad track in 1905. Between 1912 and 1918 the U.S. Forest Service acquired the entire watershed as part of the new White Mountain National Forest. The virgin wilderness that the state had sold for $1,000 plus change in 1832 was returned to public ownership as a ravaged landscape for $205,000—a single lifetime later.

The story, of course, has a happy ending. See for yourself when you visit the cascades of Moriah Brook.

CHAPTER 27

Giant Falls

◆

Location
Off the North Road in Shelburne.

Map
AMC Carter-Mahoosuc Map: D-11.
DeLorme Trail Map: A-15 (waterfall is off the map).

Hiking Data
Distance, parking area to top of falls: 1.9 miles.
Altitude gain to top of falls: 1100 feet (altitude 1900 feet).
Difficulty: MODERATE.

◆

In his reverent chronicle of nature's annual cycle, *Seasons at Eagle Pond*, Donald Hall calls springtime "the least of our seasons" in northern New England. His claim that spring, the mud season, "has built no constituency" is a common sentiment. Mud season is the time when proprietors shutter their inns and take a holiday, and the time when local townsfolk are most tempted by dreams of Caribbean islands. Only whitewater paddlers seem to welcome with good cheer the soggy months of melting snows and chilly rains.

Spring serves another devoted constituency, however: the waterfall buffs. The same conditions that thrill kayakers also transform the region's waterfalls into spectacles that summer visitors can hardly imagine. Many waterfalls and cascades are as different, spring from summer, as a gale from a breeze. Giant Falls, at the southern end of the Mahoosuc Range, is one of the region's finest spring specials. It is also one of the loftiest waterfalls in the White Mountains.

Giant Falls lies on Peabody Brook 800 vertical feet below the marshy outlet of Dream Lake, which occupies a shallow highland basin between Bald Cap Peak (2795 feet) and Mount Bald Cap (3065 feet). Most of the year the marshes of Dream Lake release a steady dribble of water, but in spring the runoff becomes a flood.

Over on the eastern side of the Bald Cap ridge, a sister waterfall called *Dryad Fall* is even higher and dryer than the Giant of Peabody Brook. In full flush Dryad Fall is a towering silver column over 400 feet high. So they say. On our two visits, in early July and mid-August, Dryad Fall was a mere trickle!

Both waterfalls can be reached in a single day trip by hiking across the flat-topped divide at Dream Lake. Keep in mind, however, that these waterfalls peak when the trails are at their mucky worst. In the depths of mud season the divide over to Dryad Fall becomes virtually impassable, and the trails are highly vulnerable to erosion. In the interests of conservation, wait until the footing dries up a bit before attempting this hike.

The Trail to the Falls

From the junction in Gorham where NH 16 turns south for Pinkham Notch, follow US 2 east through Shelburne. After passing through a lovely birch forest and skirting a lake formed by a dam on the Androscoggin River, you will reach a left turn onto North Road, 3.4 miles from Gorham. North Road crosses the Androscoggin atop the narrow dam, where you have a memorable view upriver to the northern Presidentials. After passing over the dam the North Road turns sharply to the east and soon dips to cross a bridge over Leadmine Brook (1 mile from US 2). Immediately beyond the bridge look for a small pullout on the left (north) shoulder of the road. No signs mark the pullout, but this is where to park for the hike to Giant Falls.

To reach the trailhead walk up the North Road another 0.25 mile. A pair of houses on the north side of the road—one with cobbled walls and one with shingled walls—mark the base of the Peabody Brook Trail. There may or may not be a trail sign here, but there will certainly be No Parking signs. Please respect the understandable desire of the residents for peace and privacy. It is worth noting that the hike past Giant Falls used to be a leg of the Appalachian Trail,

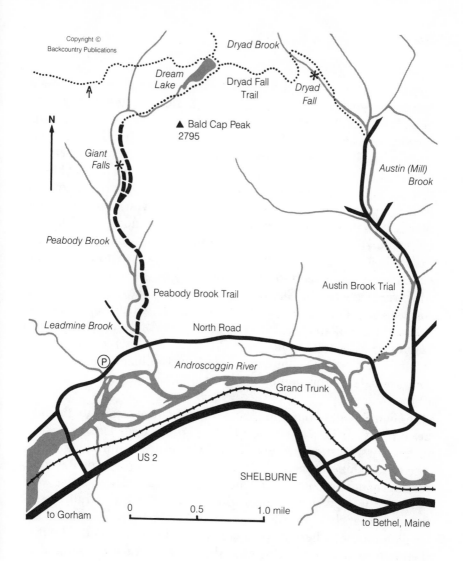

Dryad Brook

Dream
Lake

Dryad Fall
Trail

Dryad
Fall

N

▲ Bald Cap Peak
2795

Giant
Falls

Austin (Mill)
Brook

Peabody Brook

Peabody Brook Trail

Austin Brook Trial

Leadmine Brook

North Road

P

Androscoggin River

Grand Trunk

US 2

SHELBURNE

0   0.5   1.0 mile

to Gorham

to Bethel, Maine

but the AT had to be relocated because its heavy use created problems for the local property owners.

The Peabody Brook Trail starts out along an old grassy logging road between the two landmark houses. Bear right where the logging road forks at 0.1 mile, as indicated by a small brown trail sign. Pay no attention to the conspicuous red-diamond markers on the *left* fork; these are not meant for hikers, as we discovered when leading a group of grumbling Scouts on a fruitless excursion to see Giant Falls. The proper route is marked with blue blazes.

From the fork the trail fords Peabody Brook and turns upstream, entering a small reserve owned by the Society for the Protection of New Hampshire Forests. After 0.5 mile of gentle climbing through a grove of hemlocks the trail follows a logging road to the right (clearly marked), while another logging road forks off to the left and fords the brook. Shortly thereafter the trail turns left (mile 0.8 from the North Road). This turn, too, is clearly posted. After 0.1 mile of level walking through open hardwood forest you begin to ascend more earnestly past a wall of interesting crags. Another 0.25 mile of moderate climbing brings you to the spur path to the foot of Giant Falls. The 0.4-mile-long spur path becomes rough, narrow, and badly eroded as it descends into the ravine.

To reach the top of Giant Falls, continue up the main trail, which slabs up the steep eastern wall of the ravine. Watch for an inviting rock bench with an excellent view across the Androscoggin valley to Mount Moriah and the northern Presidentials. After approximately 0.5 mile of moderate climbing the trail levels off and approaches the brookside. From this point you can easily scramble down to the crest of the falls.

If Giant Falls is your sole destination, you can terminate the hike here. But there is more to see higher up the trail. Dream Lake is worth a visit just to see whether it lives up to its intriguing name. The upper trail climbs steadily along Peabody Brook for 0.4 mile, passing a nearly continuous succession of cascades that are very attractive in high water. When the brook divides, the trail crosses the main branch and turns right to climb a final 0.3 mile to the flat headland basin, where the brook is crossed one last time. The trail then makes a wide circle around the basin to reach the far end of Dream Lake and the Mahoosuc Trail (3.1 miles from the North Road). Unhappily, in high water the last mile of the trail can be extraordinarily wet and mucky. Part of the trail is a virtual streambed, part is a gooey marsh, and a few spots do a good imitation of quicksand. This is great territory for moose, bullfrogs, and white-throated sparrows, but not for hikers.

Your first view of Dream Lake comes almost immediately after you reach the headland basin. At this point, though, you see only a shallow marsh at the tip of the lake. The dreamiest views are around to the far (east) side. That is also where you find the Dryad Fall Trail (clearly marked). This horribly eroded trail descends eastward, following faded yellow blazes. After crossing tiny Dryad Brook, the trail turns to the right and drops steeply for more than 0.25 mile alongside Dryad Fall—or rather alongside the towering cut of ledge where the falls would be if there were enough water.

From the base of Dryad Fall the trail heads downstream 0.1 mile before crossing the brook and climbing out of the ravine. Watch carefully for the old yellow blazes so you don't miss the exit here. The trail then follows another badly eroded logging road down to the Austin Brook Trail, 2 miles from the North Road. The full loop up the Peabody Brook Trail, down the Dryad Fall Trail and out the Austin Brook Trail is nearly 9 miles long, including a 2.2-mile trek back along the North Road to the car.

It is possible to cut this distance down to just 5 miles if you can leave a car at the lower end of the Dryad Fall Trail. This is made possible by a passable dirt road that turns off the North Road 0.5 mile east of the Austin Brook Trail. The dirt road angles back to Austin Brook, whereupon it coincides with the Austin Brook Trail. The problem is avoiding wrong turns. Be sure to take the third right turn, which is marked by a tiny arrow sign. Also be double sure to park well off the road to leave room for any logging trucks that might rumble by.

The Falls

The Giant at Giant Falls appears in the form of a precipitous wall of ledge several hundred feet high, where a wide swath of tough mica schist cuts across the path of Peabody Brook. When nourished by melting snows or soaking rains, the brook rushes down from Dream Lake, surges through a narrow sluice on the cornice at the top of the wall, and dashes playfully down the dark gray facade of ledge in silvery ribbons of braided lace.

The very size of Giant Falls makes it hard to command a full view. The waterfall is a flirt, constantly hiding vital parts behind a veil of treetops or a steep outcrop of ledge. So, like the blind men investigating the elephant, we perceive only part of the waterfall from each point of contact. The initial contact is back along the North Road. From the edge of a pasture just west of the trailhead you can see a

Giant Falls in spring runoff

preview of the distant ribbon of falls adorning the tapered ravine of Peabody Brook.

A second vantage point is at the base of the falls. Following the spur path down into the ravine from the main trail, you will reach the brook at a very minor cascade. On one trip a friend ran ahead to see the falls, and found only this tiny cascade at the end of the path. He turned back, keenly disappointed. The trick is that you must scramble another 150 yards upstream to reach the main attraction. The path here ranges in quality from indistinct to nonexistent. Footing is tricky since the ravine is steep and the brookside is strewn with tumble-down boulders and slippery leaves. Fortunately, though, the high cover of hardwood trees keeps the basin floor relatively free of tangled scrub. The forest also creates a healthy environment for spring wildflowers, including fine crops of trillium and hobblebush.

There is nothing fancy about the design of Giant Falls: the plane of the stream and the adjacent woods simply tilt up steeply. The brook has hardly dented the bank of tough ledge, so no pool of any significance has been crafted at the foot of the falls, and no gorge has been carved into the mountainside to frame the scene. From the woods alongside the falls or from the angular boulders in the streambed you obtain intimate close-up views of the animated currents, but you can only catch a glimpse of the Giant's upper body.

To reach the top of the falls you have to return to the main trail and scramble down from above, as described earlier. The view from the top is the highlight of the trip. In addition to watching the current pour endlessly over the brink, you have an excellent view across the Androscoggin River valley. The fresh-scented conifer forest here is beautiful, too. It includes a stand of distinctive red pines. Far less common in the mountains than its majestic cousin, the white pine, the red pine is characterized by ruddy bark and tufts of extra-long double needles that flip up proudly at the tip of each bough. Above the falls the streambed is handsomely carved, because at this elevation the brook dashes across lime-silicate rock that is more easily eroded than the headwall schist. Consequently, the higher cascades can be very pretty, though dwarfed by the Giant in scale.

Historical Detour

Shelburne was chartered in 1769. One year later settlers began arriving to cultivate the fertile alluvial soils of the Androscoggin River valley. The biggest story in Shelburne's history was the Indian attack of 1781. Benjamin Willey (1856) provides a stirring narrative of this "outrage," drawing on an account written by one of the Indian's captives, a Revolutionary War veteran named Nathaniel Segar. By 1781 the French and Indian War was already a receding memory. Most surviving Indians had fled, defeated, to Canada, and frequent visits by these Indians to the colonial settlements were not considered a threat. On August 3, 1781, however, a band of six Indians went on a marauding spree along the Androscoggin River.

The Indians set upon Segar and two companions working in a field in Bethel, took the men captive, and plundered a house nearby. After killing a settler in Gilead, they led their captives to Shelburne, "now on the very outposts of the scattered frontier settlements." The group crossed the Androscoggin River to raid the house of Hope Austin, who just that April had battled five-foot snowdrifts to settle in Shelburne with his wife and three children. (Presumably, Austin Brook bears the family's name.) Finding Mr. Austin away, the Indians left his wife and children unharmed and proceeded to "the last house on the frontier," that of Captain Jonathan Rindge, another recent arrival. There they plundered the house, killed Peter Poor, an early settler, and seized a black farmhand named Plato.

Then the Indians turned north into "the unbroken wilderness." They compelled Segar to write on a piece of bark a warning that all the captives would be killed if they were pursued. Fearing further attacks on their homes some of the remaining settlers spent the night atop a steep mountain near Austin's homestead. Not far in the distance they could hear "the whoopings and shoutings" of the renegade band. From the geography, the Indians might well have been camped at Dream Lake.

After being driven to Canada, abused and half starved, the unfortunate captives were ransomed to British officers. Under Indian guard they were transported by canoe to Montreal, where they were interrogated and then imprisoned in a rat-infested jail for sixteen months. Segar later returned to the Androscoggin valley. In his own words, he lived to see the valley "rise from a howling wilderness into fruitful fields" (Willey, 1856).

Later in Shelburne's history, Giant Falls became a popular scenic attraction. This is not surprising considering that the old north road was well traveled even in the early nineteenth century, when a lead mine was discovered nearby. In 1859 Thomas Starr King exclaimed that "the rock and cascade pictures in the forests of Baldcap well reward the rambles of an hour or two." An article in an early issue of *Appalachia* (Volume II) described a path to Giant Falls that was cut in 1878, but King's description suggests that a route was known much earlier. The old AMC account describes Giant Falls as "truly magnificent cascades . . . after a heavy rain." And in the spring.

CHAPTER 28

Weetamoo Falls

◆────────────◆────────────

Location
In the Great Gulf Wilderness. Park at Great Gulf trailhead on NH 16, between Gorham and Pinkham Notch.

Map
AMC Mount Washington Range Map: F-9.
DeLorme Trail Map: C-10.

Hiking Data
Distance, parking area to falls: 5.6 miles.
Altitude gain: 2400 feet (to altitude 3700 feet).
Difficulty: STRENUOUS.

───────────────────◆───────────────────

Though Weetamoo Falls is considered by many to be the loveliest waterfall in the Great Gulf, the star attraction on this trip is the Great Gulf Trail itself. This rugged trail follows the West Branch of the Peabody River into the heart of the Great Gulf Wilderness, passing a succession of surging cascades, deep pools, and powerful rapids en route to Weetamoo Falls. As the trail penetrates farther into the Gulf the currents diminish in strength, but the cascades grow more numerous, and the mountain views more grand.

Like its cavernous neighbors to the south, Tuckerman and Huntington ravines, the Great Gulf was carved by local mountain glaciers before the great continental ice sheets arrived. The Gulf forms a huge dogleg basin with steep walls that drop more than 1500 feet from the shoulder of Mount Washington. Weetamoo Falls is the first major waterfall formed by the West Branch of the Peabody as it drains this huge basin—and therefore the last waterfall reached by hikers climbing upstream.

Most visitors to the Gulf's inner sanctum are backpackers hiking a long circuit up to the Presidential ridge. Serious trampers, though, can reach Weetamoo Falls as an invigorating day trip. The hike is most inviting during midsummer when the days are long, the black flies are on the wane, the more familiar trails are beset with crowds, and the Gulf's cold pools and cool conifer forests are especially refreshing.

If you are not enthusiastic about a strenuous hike, you can still enjoy the beautiful river scenery closer to the trailhead. Your trip can be as short as a 0.1-mile stroll to the footbridge spanning the Peabody River, or as severe as the 7.8-mile ascent of Mount Washington.

The Trail to the Falls

Darby Field, the first colonist to explore Agiochook (Mount Washington) in 1642, reported observing an extraordinary ravine to the north of the summit cone—an "almost umfathomable abyss," in the words of Benjamin Willey (1856). Not long after the first hiking trail was blazed to the summit of Mount Washington in 1819, Ethan Allen Crawford led a party astray in the clouds and wandered to "the edge of a great gulf." His simple description gradually displaced the earlier name, Gulf of Mexico. Not until 1881 was a path cut into the Gulf itself.

A large Forest Service sign announces the present trailhead parking lot on the west side of NH 16, roughly halfway between the Mount Washington Auto Road and Dolly Copp Campground. From the north end of the parking lot the Great Gulf Trail crosses a long suspension footbridge over the Peabody River, and then proceeds the entire length of the West Branch past Weetamoo Falls to Spaulding Lake. From the lake the trail ascends the towering headwall to the Gulfside Trail, 0.6 mile below the summit of Mount Washington.

For the first 2 miles the hike is quite gentle. At intersections with a cross-country-ski trail from Dolly Copp Campground hikers should stay on the well-trodden footpath. At several points you can descend easily to the river and find large pools, sunny ledges, and thundering rapids. Here are some of the most beautiful swimming holes in the region. But swimmers should bear in mind that even in midsummer

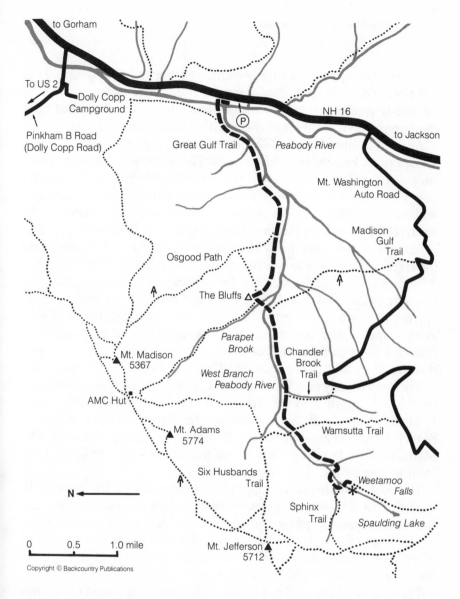

to Gorham

To US 2

Dolly Copp
Campground

Pinkham B Road
(Dolly Copp Road)

Great Gulf Trail

Peabody River

NH 16

to Jackson

Mt. Washington
Auto Road

Madison
Gulf
Trail

Osgood Path

The Bluffs

Parapet
Brook

Mt. Madison
5367

West Branch
Peabody River

Chandler
Brook
Trail

AMC Hut

Mt. Adams
5774

Wamsutta Trail

Six Husbands
Trail

Weetamoo
Falls

N

Sphinx
Trail

Spaulding Lake

Mt. Jefferson
5712

0   0.5   1.0 mile

Copyright © Backcountry Publications

this stretch of the Peabody is swept by strong currents, and the water
stays very cold.

At 1.7 miles the Osgood Trail diverges right to head up Mount
Madison, while the Great Gulf Trail stays by the river and enters the
Wilderness Area. Note that special camping restrictions apply in the
Wilderness Area. Camping groups must not exceed ten people, and
campsites should be located at least 200 feet from a trail or a wa-

tercourse. Also, no camping is permitted beyond the Sphinx Trail junction. You will pass spots along the trail where backpackers have obviously pitched tents, but using these sites is a violation of both the Forest Service rules and the spirit of wilderness camping.

About 0.3 mile into the Wilderness Area the trail passes a rocky set of rapids known as *Boulder Falls.* This inconsequential waterfall isn't much different from the other lovely rapids and small cascades that you see up and down the river, except that it has a name. To find Boulder Falls keep an eye out for evidence of an island in the river. The falls are on the far channel, out of sight from the trail.

About 0.6 mile into the Wilderness Area the trail veers away from the river and ascends to a prominent clearing called the Bluff. After 2.7 miles of hiking through the forest, beautiful though it may be, reaching the Bluff will feel like emerging from a tunnel into daylight. Surrounded by the tallest mountains in the Northeast, the Bluff provides a spectacular panoramic view. Rough, eroded paths descend from the Bluff to Parapet Brook deep in the ravine below, but there is no need to add to the erosion. The main trail itself drops to the brook immediately past the Bluff and crosses on a swaying suspension bridge. Here (mile 2.8) the Great Gulf Trail merges briefly with the Madison Gulf Trail. Soon, another footbridge crosses the West Branch of the Peabody above a darling set of small cascades. The Madison Gulf Trail branches off to the left, leaving the Great Gulf Trail to pursue the river into the Gulf.

The path now becomes rougher and steeper, and the river is diminished in size—though not in beauty. Indeed you continue encountering splendid pools and cascades, which are beset with great boulders and framed with dark forest. River formations that would be notable landmarks on other trails are simply nameless bends in the stream here.

The Chandler Brook Trail branches off from the Great Gulf Trail after a mile of hard hiking. Beyond this junction the main path climbs a steep shoulder and passes through a handsome stand of young balsam firs before reaching the intersection with the Wamsutta Trail and the Six Husbands Trail (mile 4.5). With luck you may spot the yellow cap of a black-backed woodpecker exploring the slide-damaged conifers.

The path then becomes rougher still. After mounting a slippery slab on a set of log steps, you will skirt a churning cascade that winds down a long, weathered ledge in a graceful arc. Almost immediately, you reach another fine waterfall: a bulging curtain of water is split by a narrow crag into a steep chute on one side and a 15-foot vertical drop on the other. From the trail only the left half of the lower falls can be seen, so you must scramble to the pool below to get a full view, with Mount Jefferson towering overhead.

After passing yet another waterfall—a broad white sheet spilling over fractured brown ledge—the path flattens out, crosses the streambed, and enters a marsh scattered with storm-strewn trees. The footing through the marsh is tricky. At mile 5.5 the Sphinx Trail cuts off to the right, after which the Great Gulf Trail crosses the river one last time. Only a short climb remains to Weetamoo Falls.

For those with time and energy, the trail beyond Weetamoo Falls ascends a long rockslide overgrown with dense scrub fir. The drudgery of climbing the scree is rewarded by the unforgettable pleasure of seeing Spaulding Lake (mile 6.4), a tranquil gem encircled by the awesome mountain wall.

The lake is named after John Spaulding, an avid White Mountain explorer whose trip into the Great Gulf in 1853 was one of the earliest on record. (The first recorded trip was in 1829, by Dr. J. W. Robbins, a botanist after whom no local landmarks are named.) In a book published two years after his exploration of the gulf, Spaulding described the set of cascades and falls he had found as "at least worth a trip from the Atlantic from all who would look with proud satisfaction upon nature in her sublimest mood."

The Falls

No trail sign signals that you have reached Weetamoo Falls; the spot is marked only by the enchanting geometry of the waterfall and the

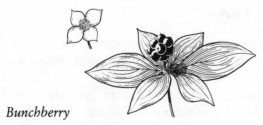

Bunchberry

Unnamed cascades along the Great Gulf Trail

foot pool. From the trail you see a vivid white curtain of water dancing laterally down the steps of a sloping ledge of ancient schist. The final tumbling step of the cascade sends ripples shimmering toward you across the clear pool. In subdued tones the gray-green waters reflect the rocks and mosses that line the pool, as well as the fir and the mountain birch that frame the scene. Just below, the river offers an encore in the form of another miniature waterfall, with its own sparkling pool.

Weetamoo Falls is not a place for scrambling on the ledge rock or sporting in the pool. The water is bitter cold, and the dense encroaching forest precludes exploration. A bit of rock-hopping is possible at the foot of the pool, but the cascades back down the trail are much better suited for recreation. At Weetamoo Falls you will have to settle for wilderness scenery of great beauty.

Historical Detour

> Child of the forest! Strong and free
> Slight-robed, with loosely flowing hair.

So John Greenleaf Whittier described Weetamoo in his narrative poem, "The Bridal of Pennacook." In this poem Weetamoo is presented as a lovely daughter of the great chief Passaconaway (see Chapter 18), and a romantic heroine who sacrificed her life in duty to her cold-hearted husband, Winnepurkit, sachem of Saugus.

More scholarly sources reveal that there was in fact an Indian queen by the name of Weetamoo and that Passaconaway did indeed marry off an ill-fated daughter to the sachem of Saugus, but Whittier was exercising artistic license in matching names. Perhaps he favored Weetamoo's lyrical name over Wanunchus, the bride's true name. He also found Winnepurkit more poetic than Montowampate, the Sachem's actual name.

The historical Weetamoo was a far more important figure than the bride of Pennacook, though her story is less romantic. She was a female chieftain of the Wampanoag tribe of what is now eastern Rhode Island and southeastern Massachusetts. Her first husband (of six, according to tradition) was Wamsutta, son of Massasoit, the great friend of the early Pilgrims. Wamsutta succeeded Massasoit as chief in 1662 but soon died. His brother Metacomet, who became known as King Philip, later led the Indians in a war with the colonists. In percentage of population killed, King Philip's War was the bloodiest in American history.

As one of King Philip's most ardent supporters, Weetamoo was pursued by the colonists' militia. She drowned crossing a river while fleeing on August 6, 1676, six days before King Philip himself was killed. Both Indian leaders suffered the fate of those guilty of treason—their heads were cut off and displayed on poles.

Both Weetamoos, the historical and the poetic, died by drowning. Whittier's queen met her fate when her canoe was swept over Amoskeag Falls on the Merrimack River (in what is now Manchester, NH):

> Down the white rapids like a sear leaf whirled,
> On the sharp rocks and piled-up ices hurled.
> Empty and broken, circled the canoe
> In the vexed pool below—but where was
>   Weetamoo?

CHAPTER 29

Waterfalls off Dolly Copp Road

Triple Falls
Coosauk and Hitchcock Falls

◆

Location
Dolly Copp Road (officially, the Pinkham B Road) is a rough shortcut route from NH 16 (at Dolly Copp Campground) to US 2 in Randolph.

Map
AMC Mount Washington Range E-9/10.
DeLorme Trail Map A-11/12.

◆

Dolly Copp Campground is by far the largest and most popular campground in the White Mountains. It has 176 sites interspersed through nearly a mile of forest on the west side of the Peabody River, 5 miles south of Gorham. From late May, when some campers may still be sporting skis, through the magic of the fall foliage in early October, the campground brims with visitors eager to explore the nearby mountain treasures.

The most popular waterfall attractions in the area are Glen Ellis Falls and Crystal Cascade, 6 miles south of the campground in Pinkham Notch (Chapter 20). Even nearer, though, are seven less well known but interesting waterfalls on the north slopes of Mount Madison and Mount Adams. Three of these—Triple Falls, Coosauk Fall, and Hitchcock Fall—are located off Dolly Copp Road (Pinkham B Road), a short but rough route across Pine Mountain Notch from

270

the campground. These three are the subject of the present chapter. Four more, reached easily from the Appalachia parking lot on US 2, are covered in the next chapter.

In character, the waterfalls off Dolly Copp Road are pretty woodland cataracts rather than grand mountain spectacles like their popular cousins in Pinkham Notch. By the same token they are uncrowded, unspoiled, and undeveloped—just right for a quiet side trip when you're in the neighborhood and have half a day to spare.

The falls can also be included in the itinerary for a hike up Mount Madison. The Pine Link Trail, near Triple Falls, starts at the height-of-land on Dolly Copp Road. By virtue of its elevated trailhead, Pine Link cuts 400 vertical feet off the summit climb compared to any other trail in the northern Presidentials. Coosauk and Hitchcock falls are also quite convenient for summiteers as they lie directly on the Howker Ridge Trail, a rough but rewarding route to Mount Madison.

All three of these waterfalls are fed by steep, narrow ravines that drain quickly after a rain. This means that the water flow can be quite low during dry weather. Also, all three falls have a northern exposure and heavy forest cover, diminishing the advantage of sunny skies. Consequently these waterfalls can be fairly dull during periods of "good" weather. During or after "bad" weather, however, you can take advantage of the ideal conditions and head for the falls!

Triple Falls

Hiking Data
Distance, parking area to falls: 0.2 mile.
Altitude gain: 200 feet (altitude 1700 feet).
Difficulty: EASY.

As the name suggests, Triple Falls is three for the price of one. A short walk up the Town Line Brook Trail takes you past Proteus Falls, Erebus Falls, and Evans Falls in quick succession. If you're tabulating waterfall visits, go ahead and count this as three falls; after all, they do have separate names.

The path to Triple Falls starts next to the bridge where Dolly Copp

Road crosses Town Line Brook, 1.5 miles from US 2 in Randolph and 2.5 miles from Dolly Copp Campground (0.8 mile north of the height-of-land). A small sign for Triple Falls on the upstream side of the road will confirm that you are at the right place. The only parking is on the narrow dirt shoulder of the road, which has room for just a few vehicles.

The path simply climbs along the east bank of Town Line Brook as far as the top of Evans Falls. From start to finish the distance is only 0.2 mile. Some stretches, though, are a bit steep. Small signs are posted on trees along the way to identify each of the triplets. The route is heavily shaded by a canopy of tall hardwoods and riverine hemlocks, which conspire with the topography of the falls to make photography very difficult.

At Proteus Falls, about 100 yards up from the road, the brook emerges from a damp, narrow gorge and drops 25 feet in three steep steps. The name of the waterfall comes from a sea god in Homer's *Odyssey* who changed form at will. The derivative term "protean"—meaning exceedingly variable—aptly describes the way the falls change character in response to the rains. The gorge above the falls is impressive, but its steep, wet walls restrict access and limit the scope for exploring around the falls.

A short climb brings you to the most striking of the three falls, named Erebus after the mysterious darkness through which souls passed on their descent to Hades in Greek mythology. At Erebus Falls the brook slides across a huge bedrock foot (use your imagination) and plunges 30 feet over the "toes" to gneiss slabs below. Here, again, in dry weather the water flow may be meager. And as with Proteus Falls, there is little scope for exploring the slick, steep ledges around the falls.

Evans Falls is just above Erebus. Unlike its myth-conjuring neighbors downstream, Evans Falls is a minor cascade with small, clear pools above and below. Although the least interesting of the Triple Falls, this is the best place to stop for a snack or a picnic before heading back to the car. The name presumably honors the nonmythological Captain John Evans, who worked on the first road through Pinkham Notch in 1774 and later commanded troops in the Androscoggin valley following Indian raids in 1781.

The Town Line Brook Trail simply climbs past the falls and back

Tiger Swallowtail and Orange Hawkweed

down again, but in earlier years it formed a link to Mount Madison. Past Evans Falls the trail proceeded up the streambed for another mile, rising 1200 vertical feet before veering toward the west and climbing to the Howker Ridge Trail. Hikers also used to follow Town Line Brook downstream to its junction with the Moose River, from which point they walked the railroad bed to Mineral Spring Station. If you are in the mood for exploring, these old overgrown routes offer interesting options to spice up an otherwise simple hike.

Coosauk and Hitchcock Falls

Hiking Data

Distance, parking area to:

Coosauk Fall . . . . 0.7 mile.

Hitchcock Fall . . . . 1.0 mile.

Altitude gain: 300 feet to Coosauk Fall (altitude 1600 feet), and 300 feet more to Hitchcock Fall (altitude 1900 feet).

Difficulty: MODERATE.

A large parking lot near the northern end of Dolly Copp Road, a few hundred yards south of US 2 in Randolph East, serves two trails: the Howker Ridge Trail and the Randolph Path. From the parking lot, don't be fooled by an orange arrow sign pointing into the woods a dozen yards up the railroad track. This sign is for snowmobiles, not hikers. Also don't be fooled by the Forest Service sign indicating

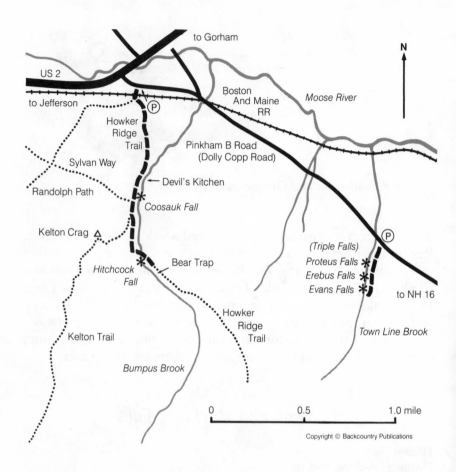

N

to Gorham

US 2

to Jefferson

Boston
And Maine
RR

Moose River

(P)

Howker
Ridge
Trail

Pinkham B Road
(Dolly Copp Road)

Sylvan Way

Devil's Kitchen

Randolph Path

Coosauk Fall

Kelton Crag △

(Triple Falls)

(P)

Proteus Falls

Hitchcock
Fall

Bear Trap

Erebus Falls

Evans Falls

to NH 16

Howker
Ridge
Trail

Town Line Brook

Kelton Trail

Bumpus Brook

0   0.5   1.0 mile

that Coosauk Fall is only 0.2 mile away. You won't reach the brook in 0.2 mile, let alone the waterfall.

The two hiking trails head together across the railroad track and immediately diverge. Take the Howker Ridge Trail, which arcs southeast to approach Bumpus Brook. (These unusual names commemorate early Randolph farmers.) This first leg of the trail is very gentle. Though poorly blazed in spots, the path is generally well trodden and easy to follow, as long as you keep an eye out for occasional turns. The hardwood forest here is privately owned and bears evidence of recent logging. Not until Coosauk Fall does the trail enter the national forest.

At Bumpus Brook the trail rises steadily but not steeply along the west rim of a small gorge. Very soon a sign by the trail points to Stairs Fall. According to the *AMC White Mountain Guide*, there should be a cascade on the far wall of the gorge where a side stream spills into Bumpus Brook, but we have seen nothing other than the Bumpus tumbling through the gorge below. For this reason Stairs Fall is excluded from the list of attractions for this waterfall trip. If it's there when you visit, so much the better!

Not far beyond elusive Stairs Fall a second sign calls to your attention the Devil's Kitchen. This ominous name refers to a fascinating stretch of gorge where the brook slides past shattered, undercut walls of heavily jointed Bickford granite. The trail continues along the rim of the gorge, passing a large snag that has been carved to Swiss cheese by diligent woodpeckers. Coosauk Fall is at the head of the gorge, only 0.1 mile above the Devil's Kitchen.

Coosauk Fall is available in standard and deluxe versions, depending on the weather. Normally, the waterfall consists of a series of waterslides, cascades, and small pools formed by Bumpus Brook as it descends into the Devil's Kitchen gorge. From the trailside there is only a limited view, framed by hemlock boughs. A rough path drops into the gorge to provide close-up views of the cascades and the large slabs of sloping granite in the streambed. The damp, angular rocks and the narrow gorge greatly limit the scope for exploring this intriguing formation.

In wet weather a deluxe version of Coosauk Fall is on display. On the far side of the gorge, above the cascades, a lovely water veil appears draped over the terraced wall of a shallow, mossy alcove. A side stream skips across the crest of the alcove and drops 15 feet in a fine spray, before making a final dash to join the Bumpus.

Just past Coosauk Fall the Sylvan Way trail enters from the right, providing a 1.2-mile link to the Appalachia parking lot (see Chapter 30). Shortly beyond this junction the Kelton Trail forks off to the right and climbs steeply to Kelton Crag, Dome Rock, and Salmacis Fall (1.6 miles away). You should stay to the left on the Howker Ridge Trail, which ascends the side wall of Bumpus Basin for 0.2 mile to Hitchcock Fall.

Approaching Hitchcock Fall, the trail enters a new environment. The forest opens up as the hardwood canopy thins out and spruce trees gain a foothold. The appearance of the rock is also distinctly different from what you saw 0.2 mile downstream. You have climbed to the transition forest and crossed into a zone of banded gneiss bedrock, which geologists call the lower Littleton formation. Because the rock here is tougher, the currents have not carved out a gorge. Instead, the brook now passes through an open ravine bestrewn with huge, weathered boulders. From a break in the wall at the head of the ravine, falling waters zigzag in and out among the ledges and boulders, streaking the rock mosaic with gleaming white ribbons that range in height from 2 to 12 feet.

Unlike other waterfalls you encounter on this trip, Hitchcock Fall is a scrambler's delight. The field of large, angular boulders nearly begs you to explore its nooks and crannies. Be quite careful, though, since the footing is very uneven; this is not a playground for small children.

After crossing the brook, the trail climbs switchbacks up the east wall of the ravine to an interesting rock pit called the "Bear Trap," just above the falls. Not far above is Blueberry Ledge, which speaks for itself. The trail then continues up the long Howker Ridge to Mount Madison. Back in Bumpus Basin, the Randolph Mountain Club guidebook, *Randolph Paths*, suggests, three more waterfalls await bushwhackers farther upstream. One is called *Muscanigra Fall* (translation: black fly!); the others are unnamed. There is no trail above Hitchcock Fall today, but until 1940 AMC trail maps showed a track up the west side of the brook to a small camp.

Historical Detour

It was around 1827 that Hayes Copp, of Stowe, ME, bought a parcel of land in the wilderness south of Gorham on which to homestead. He lived at first in a crude shelter, hunting, trapping and fishing to support himself while he readied the land for farming. In 1831, Hayes Copp took a bride. The lucky gal was Dolly Emery, a petite teenager from Bartlett. Dolly Copp returned with Hayes to his land, where they lived for fifty years. Though Hayes was there first, it was Dolly who became a White Mountain legend.

The Copps lived without neighbors for nineteen years, raising four children and living a life of virtual self-sufficiency. The family's backwoods mettle is illustrated by the story of how one son, Nathaniel,

Hitchcock Fall

lost his way while hunting deer in a bitter January blizzard in 1855. With the temperature at 30 below zero and no chance to build a fire, Nathaniel continued walking until he found a ravine he could follow back to civilization. He ended up 40 miles away in Gilead, ME. In the course of his wanderings he encountered and killed a deer, which his family recovered while searching for him the next day. So the drama ended with venison rather than tragedy.

In addition to raising her family and handling the household chores, Dolly began taking in travelers. Twenty-five cents a day covered bed and board and care for your horse. The Copp homestead became a haven for people passing through the notch, and for tourists who were lured by excellent views of the Imp Cliffs across the Peabody valley. Dolly herself gained repute for her attractive woolwork, her gritty self-sufficiency, and her habit of smoking a clay pipe.

Her lasting fame, though, was earned in 1881 when she gathered the family together to announce: ". . . fifty years is long enough to live with any man!" So Dolly and Hayes split up, he returning to his birthplace, and she moving in with her daughter in Auburn, ME.

As for the waterfalls, Coosauk was dubbed by William Peek, who helped build early trails in the Randolph area. The Hixsons, in their book *Place Names of the White Mountains*, claim that Peek thought the Abnaki Indian root *coos* meant "rough," and intended to have the falls called "rough place." Being a botanist rather than a linguist, however, he inadvertently chose an Abnaki word meaning "place of the pines"—of which there were none in the vicinity.

The Hixsons claim that Hitchcock Fall was named as a tribute to the renowned nineteenth-century White Mountain geologist, Professor Charles H. Hitchcock. Another possibility is that the falls were named after Colonel John R. Hitchcock, who had closer ties to the northern summit region. The colonel managed Gorham's premier hotel, the Alpine House, as well as the Tip Top House on the summit of Mount Washington and a summit lodge on Mount Moriah. He was also one of the founding directors of the Mount Washington Carriage Road Company.

Ironically, the two Hitchcocks were no strangers. Colonel Hitchcock, as proprietor, refused permission for Professor Hitchcock's research team to use the summit buildings on Mount Washington during the winter of 1869–70 to record meteorological observations. Instead two of the professor's associates—led by J. H. Huntington, after whom a precipitous ravine on Mount Washington was later named—endured a tempestuous winter atop Mount Moosilauke. The following year, the Cog Railway company granted permission for the professor's team to lodge in the new telegraph building on the summit of Mount Washington. Thus the first systematic observations of the arctic winter conditions on New England's highest peak were obtained in 1870–71. Professor Hitchcock's 1871 book, *Mt. Washington in Winter* (co-authored with Huntington), is a White Mountain epic.

Considering that his hardy researchers braved temperatures as low as 59 degrees below zero on Mount Washington, and winds stronger than any ever before recorded (over one hundred miles per hour), one would hope that Hitchcock Fall indeed honors the professor.

CHAPTER 30

Appalachia Waterfalls

◆

Location
US 2 in Randolph.

Map
AMC Mount Washington Range Map: E-9.
DeLorme Trail Map: A-11.

Hiking Data
Loop distance, parking area to:
Gordon Fall . . . . 0.2 mile.
Salroc Falls . . . . 0.5 mile.
Tama Fall . . . . 0.7 mile.
Cold Brook Fall . . . . 1.8 miles.
Return to car . . . . 2.6 miles.
Altitude gain:
400 feet to high point at Tama Fall (altitude 1700 feet).
Difficulty: EASY to Gordon Fall, and fairly easy for the rest of the loop.
(But optional grand tour: STRENUOUS).

◆

When the Boston and Maine Railroad opened its rail link from Whitefield to Berlin in 1892, the stop at Appalachia Station in Randolph
was a gateway to the Ravine House hotel, a mecca for White Mountain climbers. Ravine House served as a focal point for an expanding
web of footpaths up the daunting northern wall of the Presidentials.
Tourists were already flooding Mount Washington by carriage and
cog railway coach, but the northern peaks remained the exclusive
domain of hardy mountaineers.

Accounts of early ascents up Mount Adams and Mount Madison
described in detail the "exalted" summit views and the deplorable

weather of the summit ridge. Only in passing did they comment about the "many pleasing cascades" encountered in the rugged ravines above Appalachia. The nearby waterfalls were often visited, though, by genteel guests at Randolph's mountain inns, as well as by tourists lodging in Gorham or Jefferson. But for these visitors, too, the spectacular mountain scenery was the foremost attraction.

Over the ensuing century Randolph has undergone many changes. The grand hotels all burned down or were demolished, even as the web of footpaths expanded into a rather bewildering maze of mountain trails. The railroad shut down, and the old trackbed traded its boxcar traffic for a clientele of moose. Appalachia Station, sharing the fate of many a New Hampshire cornfield, was transformed into a parking lot—for hikers.

In one respect, though, little has changed: the grand summits of the northern Presidentials still command the attention of most visitors to Randolph. In fact, the waterfalls may be nearly deserted even when the Appalachia parking lot is overflowing with hikers' cars. This is not entirely surprising, because the summit ridge is truly dazzling, while the waterfalls are merely lovely. Yet nowhere else in the White Mountains does a single stop provide access to *so many* lovely, uncrowded falls!

This chapter describes an easy hike to four of these waterfalls— Gordon Fall, Salroc Falls, Tama Fall, and Cold Brook Fall—lying within a 1-mile radius of the parking area, though on two divergent trails. All four can be visited on a comfortable 2.6-mile loop. An alternative option is a strenuous 8.5-mile grand tour to Madison Spring Hut, which provides access to as many as a *dozen* waterfalls, plus a shot at two summits.

The Trail to the Falls

The Appalachia parking lot is located on the south side of US 2, about 2.5 miles east of Lowe's Store, and 1 mile west of the turnoff to Pinkham B Road (Dolly Copp Road). It is marked by a conspicuous "Trails Parking" sign.

A maze of trails branches out from the parking lot. For a hike to the summits, this maze poses no problem: take any path heading "up," or stick to a thoroughfare like Valley Way. The waterfall loop,

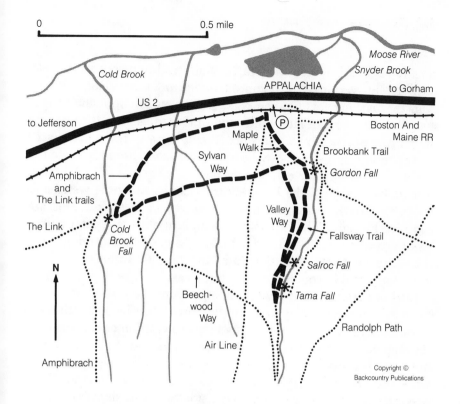

however, is unavoidably circuitous, so follow directions carefully, watch the trail signs, and ignore irrelevant trail junctions. If you want to construct your own itinerary, your best bet is to buy either the Randolph Mountain Club trail map (available at Lowe's Store), or the new 1:20,000 map of the Presidential Range by Bradford Washburn.

Since there are at least five ways to begin the waterfall loop, it is best to start with an outline of the basic plan of attack: (1) mosey over to Snyder Brook, which descends from Madison Spring to join the Moose River just east of Appalachia; (2) follow the brook upstream for 0.5 mile; (3) double back and cut over to Cold Brook, 0.5 mile west; (4) return to Appalachia. Only Leg 2 involves any significant uphill work, and even this is not at all steep. Now for details.

From the information board near the west end of the parking lot, take the Valley Way trail across the railroad tracks, through a power line cut, and into the woods. After entering the woods you will come quickly to a fork where the Maple Walk trail branches to the left. Take it. This very easy trail contours over to Gordon Fall, 0.3 mile from the parking lot. On the way, see if you can spot the "sugar shack" on the left. In late winter long tubes are strung through the woods to carry sap from the sugar maple trees to the sugar shack. There the sap simmers in large pans over a wood fire to become the world's best excuse for eating pancakes.

From Gordon Fall, the Fallsway trail climbs along the west bank of Snyder Brook, passing Salroc and Tama falls. All the falls are identified by signs. The only slight complication is that after Salroc Falls the trail merges briefly with Valley Way, before diverging again to swing past Tama Fall. You can also climb to Tama Fall on the Brookbank trail, a rougher route up the east bank of Snyder Brook. A third option, unless the water is high, is to forge straight up the streambed, barefoot, and detour to the formal trails when necessary.

The cascades and the old forests between Gordon and Tama falls make up the Snyder Brook Scenic Area. You can thank the AMC for preserving this wonderful brookside scenery. The club purchased the 36-acre tract in 1895, and turned the land over to the White Mountain National Forest in 1937. Aside from this slender corridor along Snyder Brook, nearly all of the forest on the waterfall loop is still privately owned.

Fallsway and Brookbank converge above Tama Fall and almost immediately terminate at a junction with Valley Way. To continue the loop, double back down Valley Way for 0.4 mile to Sylvan Way. This path contours east-west across the lower slopes between Cold Brook Fall and Coosauk Fall (Chapter 29), linking four major summit routes. Turn left (west) on Sylvan Way and follow this easy trail 0.7 mile to Cold Brook Fall. Take note that Cold Brook feeds into the town drinking water, so swimming, wading, and all other polluting activities are strictly prohibited at the waterfall.

Sylvan Way ends 100 yards below Cold Brook Fall, where it meets the combined Link/Amphibrach Trails. A right (east) turn here takes you back to Appalachia, finishing the loop. On this last leg, old logging roads can lure you into wrong turns, so keep an eye out for trail blazes.

If the loop walk just described sounds tame, you might consider a grueling grand tour to the Madison Springs Hut, with access to a dozen waterfalls and two summits. Briefly—it's a bit complicated—from Appalachia follow the Amphibrach Trail to the awesome King Ravine Trail. Take this to the Gulfside Trail, which leads to the hut. Start back down on Valley Way. After 1.0 mile, take the Lower Bruin Cutoff down to the Brookside Trail, which returns to Valley Way 0.3 mile above Tama Fall. From Tama Fall descend along Snyder Brook back to Appalachia. Or the other way around. Note, though, that climbing King Ravine is easier than descending.

This loop routes you directly past all four of lower falls, plus *Mossy Fall, Duck Fall,* and *Salmacis Fall.* In addition you can detour to: *Spur Brook Fall* (0.1 mile down Cliffway from Amphibrach); *Canyon Fall* (bushwhack 100 yards up Spur Brook from the King Ravine Trail just *below* its junction with Amphibrach); *Chandler Fall* (0.3 mile up the steep Spur Trail from Amphibrach); *Marian Fall* (0.1-mile bushwhack up Snyder Brook above Duck Fall); and *Thorndike Fall* (just above Marian). As a bonus you also have the option of scampering up to the summit of Mount Adams (0.7 mile from the Gulfside Trail) or Mount Madison (0.5 mile above Madison Hut).

It's a hard slog up those steep upper ravines, and the water volume tapers off the higher you climb. Consequently, the grand tour isn't worth the effort unless you're interested in the hike as much as the waterfalls.

The Falls

Gordon Fall is a small, charming cascade, where Snyder Brook tumbles 20 feet through a corridor of tall hemlock trees into a shallow, rocky pool. The pitch is moderate enough that one can scramble up the weathered slabs of ancient volcanic bedrock to the line of minor cascades, waterslides, and shallow crystal pools above the falls. The character of the falls is captured by its old name, Ripple Falls, (which appeared in an 1888 *History of Coos County*).

Gordon Fall is a special place to bring young children. It was here that we took our son to wade and splash when he was not yet three years old, so he would learn to delight in the spirit of brook and forest. Some small pools above the falls are embedded in smooth terraces for easy wading. Even in midsummer, however, the water is quite cold because of the northern exposure and the tall trees.

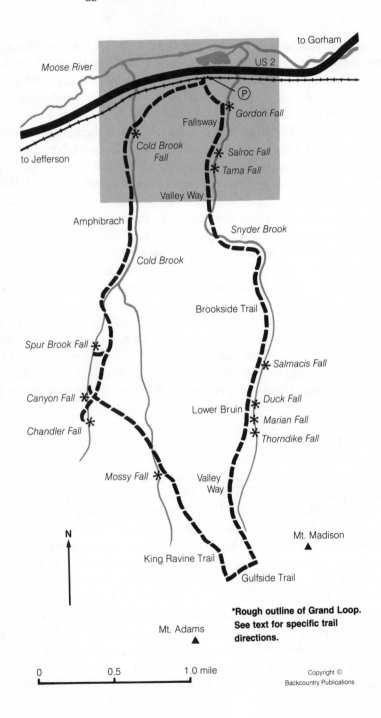

to Gorham

Moose River

US 2

(P)

* Gordon Fall

Fallsway

* Cold Brook Fall

* Salroc Fall

to Jefferson

* Tama Fall

Valley Way

Snyder Brook

Amphibrach

Cold Brook

Brookside Trail

Spur Brook Fall *

* Salmacis Fall

Canyon Fall *

* Duck Fall

Lower Bruin

* Marian Fall

Chandler Fall *

* Thorndike Fall

Mossy Fall *

Valley Way

N

Mt. Madison ▲

King Ravine Trail

Gulfside Trail

***Rough outline of Grand Loop.
See text for specific trail
directions.**

Mt. Adams ▲

0   0.5   1.0 mile

Note: The Gordon Fall here on Snyder Brook should not be confused with *Gordon Falls* on Gordon Pond Brook in North Woodstock. The latter is an interesting formation, but not interesting
enough to warrant the 7.4-mile round-trip hike required to reach it.

Salroc Fall lies about 500 yards farther up Snyder Brook. Here,
the waters cascade over a short flight of mossy steps and then slip
transparently down a 25-foot slide of pitched bedrock to a small,
tranquil crescent pool. Directly above you will see a second fine
waterslide and additional cascades. The two halves of the split composition are often referred to as Lower and Upper Salroc Falls. This
distinction reflects a lack of harmony that makes Salroc less absorbing
than its neighbors, despite its being higher and steeper than Gordon
Fall. Nonetheless Salroc is an interesting formation, and the adjacent
slides and cascades offer the best scrambling on the trip.

Tama Fall is the beauty queen of Snyder Brook. For the best view
climb down from the overlook to the edge of the shimmering pool
at the bottom of the glen. Across the pool, the brook has beveled a
broad channel into the bluff of heavily jointed granite. A fine curtain
of whitewater drapes over the steep, recessed crest of the bluff. Below
this the brook makes a shallow turn and slides down a sloped ledge
to the pool. The pattern is rather similar to that of Salroc Fall, but
here the patient artist has perfected the design.

With some caution, you can manage to cross the ledge to reach
the falls. The upper curtain of water makes an outstanding woodland
shower for crazies who have a high tolerance for cold. If you like
exploring, you should also investigate above the falls, where the
brook has sculpted fascinating waterslides and pools in the granite.

Despite the temptation to fritter away hours exploring Snyder
Brook, leave time for *Cold Brook Fall*. Though you can't play in the
water—because Cold Brook feeds the town water supply—some
observers consider this to be the "most spectacular" waterfall in
Randolph (RMC, 1977). During the era of the grand hotels this was
a favorite tourist stop.

Cold Brook Fall forms a wide ribbon of lacy whitewater that sluices
down a terraced wall into a rock-bound pool. The falls are about
30 feet high, with tree-topped cliffs to the left that rise half again as
high above the lime-green pool. Midway up this wall a thick dark
stripe can be seen, where a deep cave undercuts the uppermost bank

Tama Fall

of cliffs. The cave can be reached, with caution. Narrow fingers of carved rock at the base of the pool provide more accessible perches for admiring the picturesque glen. The immediate vicinity of the waterfall is protected today as a town reserve.

The granitic bedrock here, unlike that at the neighboring waterfalls, is formed from a dome of magma that invaded the region more than

400 million years ago. Not far above the falls Cold Brook exposes an even more ancient bedrock body of black Ammonoosuc volcanics, dating back half a billion years to an early period of intense volcanic activity.

As mentioned earlier, eight more waterfalls can be reached on the grand-tour loop up to Madison Hut. There is not space enough to describe each of these, but a few brief comments are in order. First, consider that Snyder Brook drops more than 3500 feet in 3-plus miles from Madison Hut to Tama Fall. The lower loop described here may be easy going, but the rest of the grand tour is an exhausting, sustained climb.

Second, some of the higher falls would be well worth a visit if less effort were required to reach them. Chandler Fall is especially elegant, and the ledges atop Salmacis Fall provide a wonderful, breezy spot for a picnic. Third, the narrow ravines grow more wild and fascinating the higher you go, even as the waterfalls thin out. Finally, the northern Presidential summits are indeed spectacular; this is a trip you may want to do over and over again, combining waterfall ravines with other superb paths such as the Air Line Trail or the Spur Trail.

Historical Detour

Whether you are heading for the waterfalls or the summits, you will be surrounded by homages to the mountaineers of the late nineteenth century who devoted so much effort to building the trails. The most explicit tribute is at Memorial Bridge, a sturdy stone and wood structure spanning Cold Brook 100 yards below Cold Brook Fall. The bridge was built in 1924 for a reason that is explained by a plaque embedded in stone nearby.

> Memorial to J. R. Edmands and E. B. Cook and those other pioneer pathmakers: Gordon. Lowe. King. Hunt. Watson. Peek. Sargent. Nowell. Everyman's work shall be made manifest.

Many of the place names hereabout also echo the spirit of the trailbuilders. Gordon Fall is named for James Gordon, a mountaineer from Gorham who guided Thomas Starr King on his excursions in Randolph. The three ridges drained by Snyder Brook and Cold Brook are likewise named for trail-builders: Gordon, Durand, and Nowell. Even Snyder Brook is alleged to be named after a dog owned by Charles Lowe, who cut the first path up Mount Adams in 1876. Until 1880 his route was operated as a toll path, perhaps a precursor of some future day when user fees may be introduced to help finance trail maintenance. Lowe was also one of the premier guides of the day, charging a then-princely fee of $3 per day.

Much of this early trail blazing was the work of public-spirited members of the Appalachian Mountain Club, which was founded in 1876. With Mount Washington already being served by the Cog Railway, the Carriage Road, and a handful of trails, energetic AMC members turned their attention initially to areas that were not yet easily accessible to the public. Their first projects included the completion of Lowe's path and the King Ravine Trail up Mount Adams in 1876. Two years later L. M. Watson blazed the first path up Snyder Brook. And in 1888, the AMC opened its first mountain hut at Madison Spring.

Not every Randolph place name commemorates a mountaineer. Indeed the name of the town itself honors a Virginia congressman, and later senator, who was a descendant of Pocahontas. Nor have Randolph citizens always been avid mountaineers. Thomas Starr King, who popularized the northern summits in his 1868 book, *The White Hills*, wrote about one old Randolph farmer who held the mountains in low esteem: "Blast 'em, I wish they was flat." King did not ask for his opinion of the waterfalls.

Annexes

Hawthorne Fall in May

Bedrock Geology
at Main Waterfalls and Cascades

Chapter	Waterfall	Bedrock	Map Code
1	Beaver Brook Cascades	Metagraywacke (Dlm)	WR
2	Bridal Veil Falls	Kinsman quartz monzonite (Dkqm) contact with Conway granite (Mzc)	FN
3	Silver Cascade	Littleton Formation, gray gneiss (Dllg)	CN
	Flume Cascade	Dllg	CN
	Gibbs Falls	Dllg	CN
	Beecher Cascade	Mzc	CN
	Pearl Cascade	Mzc	CN
4	Gem Pool	Littleton Formation, quartzite and schist (Dls)	MW
	the Gorge	Dls	MW
	the ledges	Dls	MW
	Upper Falls	Two-mica granite (Dgt, formerly Bickford granite)	MW
	Lower Falls	Mzc	MW
5	First Cascade	Littleton Formation, gneiss (Dlg)	MW
	Second Cascade	Dls	MW
6	Pond Brook Falls	Long Mountain granite (Lg)	P
7	Beaver Brook Falls	Waits River Formation (Dw)	DN
	Dixville Flume	Quartz monzonite (Qm)	DN
	Huntingdon's Cascade	Qm contact with Dixville Formation phyllite, schist, and quartzite (Od)	DN
8	Welton Falls	Dkqm	IGM
9	Cascade Brook	Norway quartz monzonite (Nqm)	MC
10	Georgiana Falls	Dkqm	FN
11	Avalanche Falls	Mzc	FN
	Liberty Gorge Cascade	Mzc	FN
	the Pool	Mzc	FN
12	the Basin	Mzc	WR
	Cascade Brook	Mzc	WR
	Kinsman Falls	Intrusive Dkqm breccia (Mzi)	WR
	Rocky Glen Falls	Dkqm	WR
13	Stairs Falls	Mzc	WR
	Swiftwater Falls	Mzc	WR
	Cloudland Falls	Kqm	WR
14	Franconia Falls	Mzc	WR
15	No. 13 Falls	Dkqm contact with Dlm	WR

Chapter	Waterfall	Bedrock	Map Code
16	Thoreau Falls	Mzc	CN
	Zealand Falls	Mzc	CN
17	Mad River Falls	Dlg	G
	Bickford Slides	Perry Mountain Formation, quartzite and schist (Spm) contact with Dtm	WR
18	Sabbaday Falls	Mzc, at diabase dike	MC
	Rocky Gorge	Dgt	WR
	Lower Falls	Porphyritic quartz syenite (Mzpqs)	WR
19	Jackson Falls	Mzpqs	WR
	Diana's Baths	Mzc	WR
20	Glen Ellis Falls	Rangeley Formation quartzite and schist (Sr)	WR
	Crystal Cascade	Volcanic vent metadiabase (V), with Boott member schists at base	MW
	Thompson Falls	Dlg	GQ
21	Nancy Cascades	Dllg	CN
22	Arethusa Falls	Mount Osceola granite (Mog)	CN
	Bemis Brook Falls	Black-cap granite (Bcg)	CN
	Coliseum Falls	Bcg	CN
23	Dry River Falls	Dllg	CN
24	Ripley Falls	Mog	CN
	Sparkling Cascade	Mog	CN
25	Screw Auger Falls	Biotite and hornblende-biotite quartz diorite to grandiorite and Dgt (Dqgt)	WIM
	Step Falls	Dqgt	WIM
26	Moriah Brook	Dlg crossed by bands of lime-silicate rock and biotite	G
27	Giant Falls	Boott member lime-silicate rock	G
28	Weetamoo Falls	Dls	MW
29	Triple Falls	Dlg	MW
	Coosauk Fall	Dgt	WR
	Hitchcock Fall	Dlg	MW
30	Gordon Fall	Ammonoosuc volcanics (Oam)	MW
	Salroc Fall	Dgt	MW
	Tama Fall	Dgt	MW
	Cold Brook Fall	Contact between Oam and Dgt	MW

Map Codes

WR   *Bedrock Geologic Map of the Wilderness and Roadless Areas of the*
          White Mountain National Forest, US Geological Survey (USGS), 1984.

FN   *Geologic Map of the Franconia Notch Quadrangle,* NH Department of
          Resources and Economic Development (NHDRED), 1935.

CN   *Geologic Map of the Crawford Notch Quadrangle,* NHDRED, 1977.

MW   *Geologic Map of the Mt. Washington Quadrangle,* NHDRED, 1979.

P   *Geologic Map of the Percy Quadrangle,* NHDRED, 1949

DN   *Geologic Map of the Dixville Notch Quadrangle,* NHDRED, 1963.

IGM   *Interim Geologic Map of New Hampshire,* NHDRED, 1986.

MC   *Geologic Map of the Mt. Chocorua Quadrangle,* NHDRED, 1938.

G   *Geologic Map of the Gorham Quadrangle,* NHDRED, 1975.

WIM   *Geologic Map of Western Interior Maine,* USGS, 1988.

Note: Information in the table is based on the various bedrock geology maps identified above. Bedrock identifications are not definitive. Some waterfalls are difficult to locate precisely on the relevant map because of the scale used. Other waterfalls occur in a well-defined bedrock zone, but have local irregularities that cannot be determined from the map. Also, some nomenclature changes from map to map, depending on the map's age. The table generally uses the nomenclature from the source map. Modifications have been made for consistency where confusion otherwise would arise from multiple labels for a single type of tock. The author thanks Professor Wallace A. Bothner of the Department of Earth Sciences, University of New Hampshire, for his assistance. Any inaccuracies, though, are fully my own responsibility.

Public Campgrounds and Mountain Huts

Facility	Capacity	Nearby Waterfall Trips by Chapter Number
White Mountain National Forest Campgrounds		
Campgrounds off Kancamagus Highway		
Big Rock—6 miles E of Lincoln	28 sites*	10, 11, 12, 13, 14, 18
Blackberry Crossing—6 miles W of Conway	20 sites*	18
Covered Bridge—6 miles W of Conway	49 sites	18
Hancock—4 miles E of Lincoln	56 sites*	10, 11, 12, 13, 14
Jigger Johnson—13 miles W of Conway	75 sites	14, 18
Passaconaway—15 miles W of Conway	33 sites	14, 18
White Ledge—NH 16, 5 miles S of Conway	28 sites	18, 19
Campgrounds between Franconia Notch and Crawford Notch		
Sugarloaf I—2 miles E of Twin Mountain	29 sites	3, 4, 16, 22, 23, 24
Sugarloaf II—Same as Sugarloaf I	33 sites*	3, 4, 16, 22, 23, 24
Zealand—Same as Sugarloaf campgrounds	11 sites*	3, 4, 16, 22, 23, 24
Campgrounds off I-93		
Campton—Exit 28, 2 miles on NH 49	58 sites	9
Campton Group Area—across from Campton Campground	16 sites* (3 for groups)	9
Russell Pond—Exit 31, 3 miles off Tripoli Road	87 sites	1, 9, 10, 11, 12, 13, 14
Waterville—Exit 28, 8 miles on NH 49	27 sites*	9
Wildwood—Exit 32, 7 miles W on NH 112	26 sites*	1, 2
Campgrounds in or near Maine portion of National Forest		
Basin—Route 113, 15 miles N of Fryeburg, ME	21 sites	17

Facility	Capacity	Nearby Waterfall Trips by Chapter Number
Cold River—same as Basin	14 sites*	17
Crocker Pond—ME 5, S of Bethel	7 sites*	25
Hastings—Route 113, 3 miles S of US 2	24 sites*	25, 26, 27
Wild River—Wild River Road, 5 miles SW of Hastings, ME	11 sites*	26
Campgrounds near Pinkham Notch		
Dolly Copp—6 miles S of Gorham on NH 16	176 sites	5, 19, 20, 27, 28, 29, 30
Barnes Field—Near Dolly Copp	11 group sites*	5, 19, 20, 27, 28, 29, 30
New Hampshire State Parks with Campgrounds		
Coleman—N of NH 26, 6 miles E of Colbrook	30 sites	7
Crawford Notch—US 302	30 sites	3, 4, 16, 21, 22, 23, 24
Franconia Notch—I-93	98 sites	2, 10, 11, 12, 13, 14
Moose Brook—N of US 2, just W of Gorham	42 sites	5, 20, 27, 28, 29, 30
Appalachian Mountain Club Huts (reservations required)		
Carter Notch Hut—between Carter Dome and Wildcat Mountain	40 guests*	20
Galehead Hut—W of South Twin Mountain	36 guests	15
Greenleaf Hut—Mount Lafayette	40 guests	12, 13
Lakes of the Clouds Hut—Mount Washington	90 guests	4, 23
Lonesome Lake Hut—Cannon Mountain	44 guests	12, 13
Madison Spring Hut—Mount Madison	50 guests	29, 30
Mizpah Hut—above Crawford Notch	60 guests	3, 23
Pinkham Notch Camp—NH 16, Pinkham Notch	100 + guests	19, 20, 28
Zealand Falls Hut—Zealand Notch	36 guests*	16

Notes:

*Open year-round without services; other campgrounds are open from before Memorial Day until after Labor Day, exact dates varying by site.

For additional information:
- On White Mountain National Forest campgrounds and recreation sites:
  White Mountain National Forest, P.O. Box 638, Laconia, NH 03247 Phone 1-603-528-8721.
- On New Hampshire State Park facilities:
  New Hampshire Division of Economic Development, P.O. Box 856, Concord, NH 03301. Phone 1-603-271-2666.
- On privately operated campgrounds:
  Office of Vacation Travel, P.O. Box 856, Concord, NH 03301.
- On AMC mountain huts:
  Hut Reservations, AMC Pinkham Notch Camp, P.O. Box 298, Gorham, NH 03581. Phone 1-603-466-2727 for reservations, or 1-603-466-2725 for information and weather.

Bibliography

1. Trail Guides and Histories

American Guide Series, *New Hampshire: A Guide to the Granite State.* Boston, Houghton Mifflin, 1938.

Anderson, John and Stearns Morse, *The Book of the White Mountains.* New York, Balch & Co., 1930.

Appalachian Mountain Club, *AMC White Mountain Guide*, twenty-fourth edition. Boston, 1987. Other editions used: 1922, 1931, 1940, 1952, 1976.

Appalachian Mountain Club, *Appalachia*, various issues.

Appalachian Mountain Club, *A.M.C. Field Guide to Mountain Wildflowers of New England.* Boston, 1977.

Beals, Charles Edward, Jr., *Passaconaway in the White Mountains.* Boston, Richard G. Badger, 1916.

Belcher, C. Francis, *Logging Railroads of the White Mountains.* Boston, AMC, 1980.

Bisbee, Ernest, *The White Mountain Scrap Book: Early Stories and Legends of the "Crystal Hills."* Lancaster, NH, Bisbee Press, 1939.

Brown, William Robinson, *Our Forest Heritage*, Concord, NH Historical Society, 1951.

Colby, Solon B., *Colby's Indian History.* Conway, Walker's Pond Press, 1975.

DeLorme Mapping Company, *The New Hampshire Atlas and Gazetteer.* Freeport, ME, DeLorme, 1987.

Doan, Daniel, *Fifty Hikes in the White Mountains*, 4th Ed. Woodstock, VT, Backcountry, 1990.

Doan, Daniel, *Fifty More Hikes in New Hampshire*, 3rd Ed. Woodstock, VT, Backcountry, 1991.

Drake, Samuel Adams, *The History of the White Mountains.* New York, Harper & Brothers, 1881.

Feller-Roth, Barbara (ed.), *Maine Geographic, Hiking*, Volume 2, Western Region. Freeport, ME, DeLorme, 1987.

Fobes, Charles B., "Grafton, Maine—A Human and Geographical Study," *Bulletin No. 42*, Technology Experiment Station, University of Maine, Orono, 1951.

Gabler, Ray, *New England White Water River Guide.* Boston, AMC, 1981.

Gibson, John, *Fifty Hikes in Southern Maine*. Woodstock, VT, Backcountry, 1989.

Gifford, William H., *Colebrook*. Colebrook, News and Sentinel, 1970.

Harrington, Karl P., *Walks and Climbs in the White Mountains*. New Haven, Yale University Press, 1926.

Hawthorne, Nathaniel, "The Great Carbuncle," "The Ambitious Guest," "The Great Stone Face," *The Complete Short Stories of Nathaniel Hawthorne*. Garden City, NY, Hanover House, 1959.

History of Coos County. Syracuse, W. A. Fergusson, 1888.

Hixson, Robert and Mary, *The Place Names of the White Mountains*. Camden, ME, Down East, 1980. [Note: the correct spelling of authors' surname is used here (at their request), but the book is listed in catalogues and indexes under "Hixon."]

Hodge, Frederick W. (ed.), *Handbook of American Indians*. New York, Rowman and Littlefield, 1971.

Holbrook, Stewart H., *Yankee Loggers*. New York, International Paper Company, 1961.

Hunt, Elmer, *New Hampshire Town Names*. Peterborough, Noone House, 1970.

King, Thomas Starr, *The White Hills: Their Legends, Landscape, and Poetry*. Boston, Crosby and Ainsworth, 1859.

Kostecke, Diane M. (ed.), *Franconia Notch: An In-Depth Guide*. Concord, SPNHF, 1975.

Lapham, Donald A., *Former White Mountain Hotels*. New York, Carlton Press, 1975.

Lehr, Frederic B., *Carroll, New Hampshire: The First Two Hundred Years*. Littleton, Courier, 1972.

McKnight, Kent H. and Vera B., *A Field Guide to Mushrooms of North America*. Boston, Houghton Mifflin, 1987.

Morse, Stearns (ed.), *Lucy Crawford's History of the White Mountains*. Boston, AMC, 1978.

Monegain, Bernie, *Natural Sites: A Guide to Maine's Natural Phenomena*. DeLorme Maine Geographic series, 1988.

Nutting, Wallace, *New Hampshire Beautiful*. Framingham, Old American, 1923.

Oakes, William, *Scenery of the White Mountains*. Boston, 1848. Reprinted by New Hampshire Publishing Company, Somersworth, 1970.

Pike, Robert E., *Tall Trees, Tough Men*. New York, W. W. Norton, 1967.

Pike, Robert E., *Spiked Boots*. St. Johnsbury, The Cowles Press, 1961.

Pinette, Richard E., *North Woods Echoes*. Colebrook, Liedl, 1986.

Poole, Ernest, *The Great White Hills of New Hampshire.* Doubleday, 1946.

Randolph Mountain Club, *Randolph Paths.* Randolph, RMC, 1977.

Reifsnyder, William E., *High Huts of the White Mountains.* Boston, AMC, 1979.

Spaulding, John Hubbard, *Historical Relics of the White Mountains.* Boston, Spaulding, 1855.

Speare, Mrs. Guy E., *New Hampshire Folk Tales.* Plymouth, NH, 1945 (revised edition).

Sweetser, M. F. (ed.), Ticknor's *The White Mountains: Handbook for Travellers.* Boston, Ticknor & Co., 1887.

Sweetser, M. F., *Chisholm's White-Mountain Guide-Book.* Portland, Chisholm Brothers, 1917.

Trail Map & Guide to the White Mountain National Forest, Freeport, ME, DeLorme, 1986.

Trigger, Bruce G. (ed.), *Handbook of North American Indians.* Washington, Smithsonian, 1978.

Vose, Arthur W., *The White Mountains: Heroes and Hamlets.* Barre, Barre Publishers, 1968.

Ward, Julius H., *The White Mountains.* New York, D. Appleton, 1890.

Waterman, Laura and Guy, *Backwoods Ethics.* Washington, Stone Wall Press, 1979.

Waterman, Laura and Guy, *Forest and Crag.* Boston, AMC, 1990.

Welch, Sarah N., *A History of Franconia.* Littleton, Courier, 1973.

Weygandt, Cornelius, *The White Hills.* New York, Henry Holt and Co., 1934.

Wight, D. B., *Wild River Wilderness.* Littleton, Courier, 1971.

Wikoff, Jerold, *The Upper Valley.* Chelsea, VT, Chelsea Green Publishing Co., 1985.

Willey, Benjamin G., *Incidents in White Mountain History.* Boston, Nathaniel Noyes, 1856.

2. Nature Guides

Billings, Marland P., et al., *The Geology of the Mt. Washington Quadrangle.* Concord, State of New Hampshire, 1979.

Chapman, Donald H., "New Hampshire's Landscape: How It Was Formed," *New Hampshire Profiles,* January, 1974, pp. 41–56.

Cobb, Boughton, *A Field Guide to the Ferns.* Boston, Houghton Mifflin, 1963.

Foley, Ernest, *Gold: How to Find and Pan Gold in New England.* Woodsville, NH, 1980.

Hall, Donald, *Seasons at Eagle Pond.* New York, Ticknor & Fields, 1987.

Henderson, Donald M., et al., *Geology of the Crawford Notch Quadrangle.* Concord, State of New Hampshire, 1977.

Jorgenson, Neil, *New England's Landscape.* Chester, CT, Globe Pequot Press, 1977.

Lawrence, Gale, *The Beginning Naturalist.* Shelburne, VT, The New England Press, 1979.

Marchand, Peter J., *North Woods.* Boston, Appalachian Mountain Club, 1987.

Morisawa, Marie, *Streams: Their Dynamics and Morphology.* New York, McGraw Hill, 1968.

Nyiri, Alan, *The White Mountains of New Hampshire.* Camden, Down East Books, 1987.

Petrides, George A., *A Field Guide to Trees and Shrubs.* Boston, Houghton Mifflin, 1988.

Press, Frank and Raymond Siever, *Earth.* San Francisco, W. H. Freeman, 1974.

Robbins, Chandler S., et al., *Birds of North America.* New York, Golden Press, 1983.

Sorrel, Charles A., *Rocks and Minerals.* New York, Golden Press, 1973.

Steele, Frederic L., *A Beginner's Guide: Trees and Shrubs of Northern New England.* Concord, Society for the Protection of New Hampshire Forests, 1971.

Steele, Frederic L., *At Timberline: A Nature Guide to the Mountains of the Northeast.* Boston, Appalachian Mountain Club, 1982.

Stokes, Donald and Lillian, *A Guide to Animal Tracking and Behavior.* Boston, Little, Brown, 1986.

Sutton, Ann and Myron, *Eastern Forests.* New York, Alfred A. Knopf, 1986.

Thompson, Betty Flanders, *The Changing Face of New England.* New York, Macmillan, 1958.

Van Diver, Bradford, B., *Roadside Geology of Vermont and New Hampshire.* Missoula, MT, Mountain Press, 1987.

Index and Master List
of White Mountain Waterfalls

NOTES:
- Waterfalls covered in book are indicated by appropriate page number.
- Details are provided only for waterfalls not covered in book.
- Hiking distances are one way.
- Altitude gain shows approximate net vertical change from start of hike to destination, excluding intermediate ups and downs.
- (U) = uncertain.

The Cataract
    Location: Frye Brook, near Andover, ME.
    Hiking Distance: 0.3 mile.
    Altitude Gain: 1000 feet to 1200 feet = 200 feet.
    Comment: On Frye Brook Trail, with The Churn and Flume.
Champney Falls, 174–182
Chandler Brook Cascades
    Location: Chandler Brook, up Great Gulf.
    Hiking Distance: 4.5 miles (via Great Gulf Trail).
    Altitude Gain: 1300 feet to 3800 feet = 2500 feet.
    Comment: Chandler Brook Trail cuts off Great Gulf Trail at 3.8 miles,
       and climbs to auto road.
Chandler Fall, 279–288
Chandler Gorge
    Location: Chandler Brook, North Chatham.
    Hiking Distance: 1.6 miles.
    Altitude Gain: 500 feet to 1100 feet = 600 feet.
    Comment: Side trip from south loop of Baldface circuit.
Chudacoff Falls
    Location: Peabody River, Pinkham Notch.
    Hiking Distance: 0.7 mile.
    Altitude Gain: 2000 feet to 2300 feet = 300 feet.
    Comment: Along George's Gorge Trail. No water in dry season.
The Churn
    Location: Frye Brook, Andover, ME.
    Hiking Distance: 0.2 mile.
    Altitude Gain: 1000 feet to 1200 feet = 200 feet.
    Comment: On Frye Brook Trail, with the Cataract and Flume.
Cloudland Falls, 131–137
Cold Brook Fall, 279–289
Coliseum Falls, 210–217
Coosauk Fall, 270–278
Crystal Cascade, 192–202
Crystal Falls
    Location: Phillips Brook, Stark.
    Hiking Distance: roadside.
    Altitude Gain: zero.
    Comment: In Crystal village.
Diana's Baths, 183–191
Dryad Fall, 255–262
Dry River Falls, 218–226

Kees Falls
  Location: Morrison Brook, Evans Notch.
  Hiking Distance: 1.6 miles.
  Altitude Gain: 900 feet to 1600 feet = 700 feet.
  Comment: 25-foot cataract on Caribou Trail. Other unnamed cascades
    above.
Livermore Falls
  Location: Pemigewasset River, near Plymouth.
  Hiking Distance: roadside.
  Altitude Gain: 600 feet to 500 feet = −100 feet.
  Comment: Old dam; popular swimming hole.
MacKeanon Falls
  Location: Dead Diamond River, Academy Grant.
  Hiking Distance: (U)
  Altitude Gain: (U)
  Comment: Small, remote. North of Wentworth Location on private
    timberland; public access discouraged.
Mill Brook Cascades (also called Rainbow Falls)
  Location: Mill Brook, West Thornton.
  Hiking Distance: 0.1 mile.
  Altitude Gain: zero.
  Comment: On private development, posted No Trespassing.
Mossy Glen
  Location: Carlton Brook, Randolph.
  Hiking Distance: 0.2 mile.
  Altitude Gain: 1300 feet to 1400 feet = 100 feet
  Comment: Small cascades, potholes. No swimming or bathing permit-
    ted.

Sculptured Rock
  Location: Cockermouth River, Groton.
  Hiking Distance: roadside.
  Altitude Gain: zero.
  Comment: Narrow gorge with fascinating pothole formations.
Shell Cascade
  Location: Hardy Brook, Waterville.
  Hiking Distance: 0.5 mile.
  Altitude Gain: 1250 feet to 1350 feet = 100 feet.
  Comment: Bushwack up Hardy Brook, across Mad River from NH 49, east of Waterville village.
Sylvan Cascade
  Location: Parapet Brook, Madison Gulf.
  Hiking Distance: 4.3 miles.
  Altitude Gain: 1350 feet to 3800 feet = 2450 feet.
  Comment: Take Great Gulf Trail to Madison Gulf Trail.
Triple Falls, North Chatham
  Location: north branch of Charles Brook.
  Hiking Distance: 2.2 miles
  Altitude Gain: 500 feet to 1800 feet = 1300 feet.
  Comment: Former spur loop north from Baldface Circle Trail below Eagle Crag.

Winneweta Falls
    Location: Miles Brook, Jackson.
    Hiking Distance: 1.0 mile.
    Altitude Gain: 1000 feet to 1200 feet = 200 feet.
    Comment: Off NH 16 north of Jackson village.

More from The Countryman Press and Backcountry Publications

Nature Guides and Country Living
Backyard Livestock: Raising Good Natural Food for Your Family, Revised
Backyard Sugarin'
Building Classic Salmon Flies
Camp and Trail Cooking Techniques: A Treasury of Skills and Recipes for All Outdoor Chefs
Earthmagic: Finding and Using Medicinal Herbs

Travel and General Interest
The Architecture of the Shakers
Covered Bridges of Vermont
Earth Ponds: The Country Pond Maker's Guide, Second Edition
The Other Islands of New York City
The **Explorer's Guide** series: Careful personal selections of the best attractions, lodging, dining, and places for kids. Editions for *Maine, New Hampshire, Vermont, Connecticut, Cape Cod, Rhode Island, Hudson Valley and Catskill Mountains,* and *Massachusetts*

Outdoor Guides
50 Hikes in the White Mountains
50 More Hikes in New Hampshire
25 Bicycle Tours in New Hampshire

Our books are available through bookstores, or they may be ordered directly from the publisher. For ordering information or for a complete catalog, please contact:

The Countryman Press
c/o W.W. Norton & Company, Inc.
800 Keystone Industrial Park
Scranton, PA 18512
http://web.wwnorton.com

under SHIFTING glass

under SHIFTING glass

NICKY SINGER

chronicle books · san francisco

First published in the United States in 2013 by Chronicle Books LLC.

First published in Great Britain in 2011 by HarperCollins Children's Books under the title
The Flask. HarperCollins Children's Books is a division of HarperCollins Publishers Ltd.

Library of Congress Cataloging-in-Publication Data

Singer, Nicky, 1956–
Under shifting glass / by Nicky Singer.
p. cm.
Summary: Jess is grieving for her beloved aunt, and when she finds a mysterious flask hidden in
an antique bureau that belonged to Aunt Edie on the same day that her conjoined twin brothers are
born, she begins to believe that the flask is magic and that their survival depends on it.
ISBN 978-1-4521-0921-3 (alk. paper)
1. Conjoined twins—Juvenile fiction. 2. Antiques—Juvenile fiction. 3. Brothers and sisters—
Juvenile fiction. 4. Bereavement—Juvenile fiction. [1. Conjoined twins—Fiction. 2. Twins—
Fiction. 3. Antiques—Fiction. 4. Brothers and sisters—Fiction.
5. Grief—Fiction.] I. Title.
PZ7.S61728Un 2013
813.54—dc23
2012004942

Book and North American type design by Alison Impey.
Typeset in Bulmer.

Manufactured in China.
3 5 7 9 10 8 6 4 2

Chronicle Books LLC
680 Second Street, San Francisco, California 94107

www.chroniclebooks.com/teen

For my daughter, Molly,
who taught me everything I needed
to know to write this book, and

who is teaching me still

1

I find the flask the day the twins are born, so I think of these things as joined, as the twins are joined.

The flask is in the desk, though it is hidden at first, just as the desk itself is hidden, shrouded inside the word *bureau*— which is what my gran calls this lump of furniture that arrives in my room. I hate the desk. I hate the bureau. It is a solid, everyday reminder that my Aunt Edie is dead.

Aunt Edie isn't—wasn't—my real aunt, she was my great-aunt, so of course she must have been old.

"Ancient," says my friend Zoe. "Over sixty."

Old and small and wrinkled, with skin as dry as paper.

No.

Her bright blue eyes gone milky with age.

No. No!

My Aunt Edie blazed.

At the back of her yard there is a rock garden in which she grew those tiny flowers that keep themselves closed up tight, refusing to unfurl until the sun comes out. They could be closed up for hours, for days, and then suddenly burst into life, showing their dark little hearts and their delicate white petals with the vivid pink tips. That's what I sometimes thought about Aunt Edie and me. That I was the plant all curled up and she was the blazing sun. That she, and only she, could open up my secret heart.

A week after her death, I find myself standing by that rock garden, staring at the bare earth.

"Looking for the mesembryanthemums?" says Si. Si's my stepfather and he's good with long words.

I say nothing.

"They're annuals, those flowers, the ones you used to like. Don't think she had the chance to plant any this year."

I say nothing.

"What're you thinking, Jess?"

Si is good with questions. He's good with answers. He's good at talking. He's been talking in my life since I was two.

"About the music," I say.

I'm thinking about Aunt Edie and the piano in her drawing room. About how her tiny hands used to fly over the keys and the room fill with the sound of her music and her laughter. I'm thinking about the very first time she lifted me onto the stool to sit beside her as she played. I must have been about three years old. There was no music on the stand in front of her; she played, as she always did, from memory, or she just made stuff up. But I didn't know that then. I thought the music was in her hands. I thought music flowed out of people's fingers.

"Come on, Jess, your turn now!"

And that very first day, she put my hands next to hers. My hands on the keys of the piano, the keys to a new universe. And, of course, I can't have made a tune. I must have crashed and banged, but that's not how I remember it. I remember that she could make my fingers flow with music, too. I remember my dark little heart opening out.

After that I couldn't climb onto that stool fast enough. Every time I went to her house, I would pull her to the piano and she would lift me, laughing. When I sat on that stool, nothing else in the world existed. Just me and Edie and the music. Time passed and my legs got longer. I didn't need to be lifted onto the stool. And still we played. Hidden little me—unfurling.

"Where shall we go, Jess?" she'd ask. "What's your song today?"

My song.

Our song.

I thought it would last forever.

Then she was dead. It was Gran who found her. Gran and Aunt Edie were sisters. They had keys to each other's houses, had lived next door to each other for the best part of forever. In the fence that separates their gardens there is a little gate. During daylight hours, summer and winter, they kept their back doors open, and you never knew, if you called on them, in whose house you'd find them. So they were joined, too.

All sorts of things I'd thought of as separate before the twins were born turn out to be joined.

2

The whole family gathers at the memorial home for the funeral. The hearse is late. My cousin Alistair, who is only five, keeps asking when Aunt Edie is going to arrive. Finally, the hearse turns up with the great brass-handled coffin.

"But where's Aunt Edie?" persists Alistair.

The grown-ups hush him, but I know what he means. You're invited to Aunt Edie's for tea and there she is with a plate of pimento cheese sandwiches. You're invited to her funeral, why wouldn't she be there, too? Aunt Edie at the memorial home with a plate of pimento cheese sandwiches.

Besides, as I know (and Alistair obviously knows), you can't put the sun in a box.

After the service there is a party at Gran's that Si calls a *wake*. I don't ask about the word *wake* but Si, with his Best

Explaining Voice, tells me anyway. The Old English root of the word, which means *being awake*, he says, changed in late medieval times to *wacu*. He pronounces this like *wacko*. It means *watching over someone*, he tells me. People used to sit up overnight, apparently, with dead bodies, watching.

I wacu the wacko people at the wacu. There are some I don't know and no one else seems to know them either, as they are standing in a corner by themselves. Mom is sitting on the window seat, weighed down by the coming birth. I listen to her hiccup; she can barely breathe because of the two babies pressed together inside her. She asks me to take some sandwiches to the newcomers. There's one plate of sandwiches, so I take that. The strangers—two men and a woman—don't notice me at first because they are deep in conversation. They're talking about Aunt Edie's money and about who is going to get it, as she doesn't have any children of her own and therefore no grandchildren.

"Sandwich?" I say.

"Oh—and who do we have here?" says the woman, as though I just morphed into a three-year-old.

"Jessica," I say. No one calls me Jessica unless they're angry with me. But I don't like this woman with her hard face and very pink lipstick and I don't want her to call me Jess, which is what the people I love call me.

"And what's in the sandwiches, Jessica?"

"Pimento cheese."

"Oh—not for me, thanks."

"It was Aunt Edie's favorite," I say.

"Why don't you have one then, Jessica?" the woman says.

I have three. I stand there munching them in front of those strangers, even though I'm not in the least hungry. When I've finished I say, "Aunt Edie left everything to Gran."

Si told me that, too.

Si doesn't believe in keeping things from children.

3

Later Gran says, "I want to give you something, Jess; something of Edie's." She pauses. "Edie would have wanted that. What would you like, Jess?"

I do not say *the desk*.

I certainly do not say *the bureau*.

I say, "The piano."

This cannot be a surprise to my grandmother, but her hand flies to her mouth as if, instead of saying *the piano*, I'd said *the moon*.

"I don't know," says Gran from behind her hand. "I don't know about that. I mean, I'll have to talk it over with your mom. And Si."

Mom says, "You already have a piano, Jess."

This is true and not true. There is a piano in our house, an old upright, offered—free of charge—to anyone who cared to remove it when the Tinkerbell Nursery closed when I was about six. I'd jumped at the chance of a piano—any piano. But the keys of the Tinkerbell piano had been hit for too long by too many small fingers with no music in them at all. The felt of the piano's hammers is worn and the C above middle C always sticks and the top A doesn't sound at all, no matter what the piano tuner does.

Aunt Edie's piano has a full set of working keys. Aunt Edie's piano keeps its pitch even though it's only tuned once a year. Aunt Edie's piano holds all the songs we ever made together.

It's also a concert grand.

Si says, "This is a small house, Jess."

This is also true and not true. The house is small, but the garage is huge.

Si says, "You can't keep a piano in a garage, Jessica."

And you can't. Not when the garage is filled up with bits and pieces for your stepfather's Morris Traveller 1000. And the Traveller itself. And the *donor* cars he keeps for spare parts.

"What about the bureau?" says Gran.

"Bureau?" I say.

"Desk," says Si. "A desk's a great idea. A girl your age can't be doing her homework at the kitchen table forever."

"It belonged to my father, Jess," says Gran. "Your great-grandfather."

But I never met my great-grandfather. I don't care about him, and I don't care about his desk.

But it still arrives.

That's when I learn you don't always get what you want in life; you get what you're given.

Which is how it is for the twins.

4

It is as if the desk has landed from space. My room is small, and it has small and mainly modern things in it. A single bed with a white wooden headboard and a white duvet stitched with yellow daisies; a chrome-and-glass computer station; a mirror in a silver frame; a slim chest of drawers. And a small(ish) space, where they put the desk.

Two men puff and heave it up the stairs. They are narrow stairs. The men bang it into the doorjamb getting it into the room and then they plonk it down in the space and push it hard against the wall.

"Don't make them like they used to," says the sweatier of the two men. "Thank the Lord."

The desk—the bureau—is made of dark wood. It has four drawers with heavy brass locks and heavy brass handles, which make me think of Aunt Edie's coffin. The desk bit is a flap. You pull out two runners, either side of the top drawer, and fold the desk down to rest on them. One of the runners, the one on the left, is wobbly, and if you're not careful, it just falls out on the floor. Or your foot.

Si comes for an inspection. "I could probably fix that runner," he says. "Or you could just be careful. It's not difficult. Look."

I look.

"Marvelous," Si says, testing the flap. "You can do your homework and then—voilà!—fold it all away."

"I hate it," I say.

"It's a desk," says Si. "Nobody hates a desk."

5

The desk squats in my room. I don't touch it, I don't put anything in it, I don't even look at it more than I can help, but it certainly looks at me; it scowls and glowers and mocks me.

Here I am, it says. *Just what you wanted, right? A bureau.*

I turn my back on that bureau. But it still stares at me— stares and stares out of the mirror.

I turn the mirror to face the wall.

Some weeks later, I hear Mom puffing up the stairs. She puffs more than the delivery men, because of carrying the weight of the babies curled together inside her. And also the weight of the worry they are causing.

"Jess," she says, stopping by my door.

"Yes?"

"Jess—I wish you could have had the piano, too."

And that makes me want to cry, the way things do when you think nobody understands but actually they do.

6

The next day my friend Zoe comes over.

Zoe is a dancer. She doesn't have the body of a dancer; she's not slim and poised. In fact she's quite big: big-boned and, increasingly, curvy. But when she dances, you think it is what she was born to do. I love watching Zoe dance. When Zoe dances, she's like me with the piano—nothing else exists, she loses herself in it.

Otherwise, we're not really very alike at all. She's loud and I'm quiet. She's funny and I'm not. And she likes boys. Mom says that's because, even though we're in the same grade at school, she's nearly twelve months older than me, and that makes a difference. Mom says it's also to do with the fact that she's the youngest child in their family.

Soon I will not be the youngest child in our family.

I will no longer be an only child.

Si says, "Girls grow up too fast these days."

And I don't ask him what he means by this or whether he'd prefer Zoe (I've a feeling he doesn't like Zoe that much) to go back to wearing a romper, because this will only start A Discussion.

I have other friends, of course—Em, Alice—but it's Zoe I see most often, not least because she lives at the bottom of our cul-de-sac, so she just waltzes up and knocks on our door.

Like today.

Then she pounds up the stairs and bursts into my room. Sometimes I think I'll ask her if it's possible for her to come into a room so quietly no one would notice her, which is something I'm quite good at. But I'm not sure she'd understand the task, which is another reason I like her.

"Hi, hi, hi. Hi!" says Zoe. She wheels about, or tries to, which is when she comes face to face with the desk.

"What," she says, "is that?!"

"It's a bureau," I say.

"A what?"

"A bureau."

"But what's it doing here?"

"It belonged to my Aunt Edie."

"It's hideous," she says. "And ancient."

Ancient is one of her favorite words. Anything more than two weeks old is ancient as far as Zoe is concerned.

"It's George the Third," I say. Si again.

"Hideous, ancient, and *pre-owned*. Who'd want something that already belonged to some George whatever?" she says.

I'm going to explain that George Whatever didn't own this piece of furniture, that he just happened to be on the throne of England when it was made, but that would turn me into Si, so I don't.

"Hideous, ancient, pre-owned, and bashed up," she continues.

Bashed up?

I actually take a look at the desk. It's not bashed up. And the wood isn't as dark as I'd thought, either; in fact it's a pale honey color and the grain is quite clear, so even though it's more than two hundred and fifty years old, you can still imagine the tree from which it was originally cut. There are dents in the surface, of course, and scratches, too, but it doesn't look bashed up, just as though it has lived a little: lived and survived.

"It's not bashed up," I say.

"What?"

"And it's not hideous. Look at the locks," I say. "Look at the handles."

The locks and the handles are also not as I'd thought. They're not heavy, not funereal; in fact they're quite delicate. Around the keyholes are beautiful little curls of brass in the shape of leaves, and even the little brass-headed nails that hold the handles in place are carefully banged in to look like part of the pattern.

"Hideous, ancient, pre-owned, and IN THE WAY," says Zoe. She pirouettes. "I mean, how is a person supposed to dance in this room anymore?"

Then she sees the mirror turned against the wall.

"And what's this?" she says. "Are you having a bad face day?"

She hangs the mirror the correct way around and checks to see if she has any pimples, which of course she doesn't. Even when she gets to be a teenager I doubt she'll have pimples. Things like that don't happen to Zoe.

"I'm sorry about the dancing, Zo," I say. "But I really like this bureau. In fact," I add, experimenting, "I think I love it."

"Huh?" says Zoe, who's still searching for pimples.

Sometimes I think Zoe is a mirror. I look into her to find out who I really am.

7

As soon as Zoe leaves (flamboyant twirl and a shout of *Bye-eee* as she flies down the stairs), I take my chair and sit at the desk.

I never saw Aunt Edie at this desk, as I saw her so often at the piano. But she must have sat here, I realize. Sat writing letters, private things—not things you do when you have guests in the house. I pull out the runners (and Si is right about this, it isn't difficult at all) and lay down the lid.

Inside it is like a little castle. In the middle, there is a small arched doorway, the door itself hinged between two tiny carved wooden pillars. On either side of the door are stepped shelves and cubbyholes of different sizes, to store envelopes or paper, I suppose. There are also four drawers: two wide, shallow ones next to the pillars, and at either edge of the desk two narrower, longer ones. The desktop itself slides away if you pull a little leather tab. Underneath is a cavernous little underdrawer.

"That's where they would have kept the inkwells," says Si in passing.

I can see dark stains that could have been ink. People writing at this desk long before Aunt Edie. I imagine a quill pen scratching out a love letter. And suddenly those faraway people who sat at this desk, family or strangers, they don't seem so faraway at all. They seem joined to me by the desk and all the things that have been written and thought here. And then I think about Edie herself, and how maybe she loved this desk. Sun-bright Edie, maybe coming here to be quiet, to be still, to unfurl her own dark heart.

Then I know I want to claim this desk after all.

8

But I still don't put anything in the desk. Not until the morning my mother is to deliver the babies. This is going to be a long day, a difficult day. "We'll need to keep busy," Gran says, "you and me."

Gran has agreed to stay in the house with me so that Si can be in the operating room with Mom.

"It's an elective Cesarean, Jess," says Si. "The surgery itself is quite safe."

They have to go in the night before, as Mom is first on the list. Si stands in the hall holding Mom's suitcase.

"Don't worry, Jess," Mom says, and stretches out her arms for me. But I can't get close, because of the babies. "I'll bring them home safe," she whispers into my hair. "I will."

"Time to go," says Si.

I lie awake a long time that night. Keeping vigil. Watching. I imagine Mom being awake. And Si. And probably the babies too, waiting.

In the morning I skip breakfast.

"You're growing," says Gran. "You have to eat."

But I can't.

I go to my room and start on the desk. I have decided that I will put in some homework stuff, but also some private things. In one of the cubbyholes I lodge my English dictionary, my French dictionary, my class reader. I pay attention to the height of the books, their color, shuffling them about until I am sure that I have the correct book (the stubby French dictionary), in the middle. In the inkwell space, I put pens, pencils, glue, sticky tape, and my panda eraser with the eyes fallen off.

Then I move on to more precious things. Behind the little arched door, I put ScatCat. He's a threadbare gray, his fur worn thin from having slept in my arms every night for the first four years of my life. His jet-black eyes are deep and full of memories. I think I'd still be sleeping with him if Spike hadn't arrived. More about Spike later.

To keep Scat company, I add the family of green glass cats made, as I watched, by a glassmaker one summer vacation. Then I add a bracelet that Zoe made for me (braided strands of pink and purple thread) and also one made by another good friend—Em—(purple and green) when we were in fourth grade. I once suggested we make a friendship bracelet for the three of us, winding Zoe's colors and Em's and mine (purple and blue) all together. Zoe laughed at me. She said friendship bracelets could only be exchanged one-to-one. That's what Best Friends meant, Zoe said. Didn't I understand about Best Friends? I close the little arched door.

Next I select my father's ivory slide rule. Not Si's slide rule, but one that belonged to my real father. Gran thrust it into my hand one day.

"Here," she said, quite roughly. "Your father had this when he was about your age. You should have it now."

"What is it?" I asked.

"A slide rule, of course."

I must have looked puzzled.

"It was how people did math," said Gran. "Before calculators."

Before calculators sounded a bit like *Before the Ark*. It made my father seem further away, not nearer. Or it did until I held the slide rule. Carefully crafted in wood, overlaid with ivory ("I know we shouldn't really trade ivory," said Gran, "but this elephant has been dead a long, long while"), it's bigger and deeper than a normal ruler, with a closely fitting sliding section in the middle slightly broader than a pencil. Along all its edges, carved numbers are inked in black.

"It originally belonged to your grandfather. Passed down," Gran said. She paused. "Useless now, I suppose. It's useless, isn't it?"

Gran talks to me quite often about my father, although only when we are alone. Normally it makes me uncomfortable, not because I'm not interested, but because she always seems to require a response from me and I'm never quite sure what that response should be. And the more she looks at me, the more she wants, the less I seem to be able to give. Though I think she believes that, if she talks about him enough, I'll remember him. It will unlock memories of my own. But I was only nine months old when he died and I remember nothing.

But the slide rule is different. It's the first thing I've ever held in my hands that he held in his.

"It's not useless," I say. "I like it. Thank you."

And all the roughness falls away from her.

I'm thinking all this as I select a drawer for my father's ivory slide rule. Right or left? I choose the right, slip it in. Then I change my mind.

I just change my mind.

I open the left drawer and transfer the slide rule. But it won't go, it won't fit. I push at it, feel the weight of its resistance. I push harder; the drawers are an equal pair, so what fits in one has to fit in the other.

Only it doesn't.

I pull out the right-hand drawer. It runs the full depth of the desk, plenty long enough for the slide rule. I pull out the left-hand drawer. It is less than half the length of its twin. Yet it isn't broken. It is as perfectly formed as on the day it was made.

Which is why I put my hand into the dark, secret space that lies behind that drawer.

And find the flask.

9

My heart gives a little thump. I've no idea, this first time, what I'm touching, except that it is cold and rounded and about the size of my hand. As I draw it out into the light, I feel how neatly its hard, shallow curves fit into my palm.

I call it a flask, but perhaps it is really a bottle, a flattish, rounded glass bottle with a cork. It is very plain, very ordinary, and yet it is like nothing I've ever seen before. The glass is clear—and not clear. There are bubbles in it, like seeds, or tiny silver fish, swimming. And the surface has strange whorls, like fingerprints or the shapes of contour lines on a map where there are mountains. I think I should be able to see inside, but I can't, quite, because the glass seems to shift and change depending on how the light falls on it: now milky as a pearl; now flashing a million iridescent colors.

I sit and gaze at it for a long while, turning it over and over in my hands, watching its restless colors and patterns. It is a beautiful thing. I wonder how it came into being and who made it. It can't have been made by machine; it is too special, too individual. I remember the glassmaker who made my green cats and I imagine a similar man in a leather apron blowing life down a long tube into this glass, putting his own breath into it, lung to lung, pleased when the little vessel expanded. And then, as I keep looking, the contours don't look like contours anymore but ribs, and the bowl of glass a tiny rib cage.

I have these thoughts because of the babies. Everything in the last nine months has been about the babies. They get into and under everything. They aren't even born and they can make you frightened, they can make Mom cry, they can make me see things that aren't there under shifting glass. Because, all of a sudden, I think I can see something beneath the surface of the glass after all.

Something and nothing.

I do make things up. Si says, "You are certainly not a scientist, Jessica. Scientists look at the evidence and then they come to a view." But it's not just Si, it's Gran and even Mom. They say I make things up. I see things that aren't there. And hear them sometimes, too. Like now, beneath the glass, through the glass.

Some movement, a blink, a sigh. A song. Some sadness.

The sensation of life, of a rib cage, breathing.

"Jessica!" That's a shout, a real-world shout. Gran is shouting. "Jessica, Jess!"

I jolt out of myself. "What?"

"The phone, Jess."

Gran is standing at the bottom of the stairs, the phone in her hand.

It has come. The message. She knows. She knows about the babies.

I abandon everything, fly down the stairs, rip the phone from her.

"Yes?"

It is Si.

"Jess," he says. "Jess."

"Yes!"

"They're alive. They're alive, Jess." His voice doesn't sound like his normal voice, it sounds floating. I conjure his face. His eyes are full of stars.

I know I'm supposed to say something, but I don't know what.

"Isn't it wonderful?" says Gran.

"And they both have a heart," says Si. "Two hearts, Jess. One heart each."

Then I find something to say.

"Omphalopagus," I say.

10

Omphalopagus is the technical term for babies joined at the lower chest. These type of babies never share a heart, so I don't know why Si is so surprised. After all, it was Si who did the research, hours and hours of it online. Si who taught me the word, made me pronounce it back to him. *Omphalo*—umbilicus. *Pagus*—fastened, fixed. Fixed at the navel. The twins umbilically joined to each other and to Mom and right back through history to the Greeks who coined the word in the first place.

Me and the joins.

Si and the statistics.

Si's endless statistics. Seventy percent of conjoined twins are girls. Thirty-nine percent are stillborn. Thirty-four percent don't make it through the first day of life.

Si's eyes, shining.

"Can you give me back to Gran now, Jess?" says Si.

As I hand over the phone, I remember the night of Mom's nineteen-week scan. I'd come down for a raid on the cereal cupboard. Si and Mom were talking in the sitting room, hushed, serious talk.

"They're gifts of God," I heard Mom say.

I stood at the door of the kitchen, waiting for Si to put Mom right about that. I waited for him to tell Mom what he'd told me earlier that afternoon that, despite a great deal of mystical mumbo jumbo talked about conjoined twins down the ages, they are actually just biological lapses, slips of nature. Embryos that begin to divide into identical twins, but never complete the process, or split embryos that somehow fuse back together again. A small error, a malfunction, nothing to be surprised about, considering the cellular complexity of a human being.

I wait for him to say this. But he doesn't.

"They're miracles," Mom says. "Our miracles. And I don't care what anyone says. They're here to stay."

And Si doesn't go on to mention the thirty-nine percent of conjoined twins who don't make it through the birth canal, or the thirty-four percent who die on day one.

He just takes her in his arms and lets her bury her head in his chest. I see them joined there. Head to chest.

11

I've only been gone from my bedroom a matter of minutes, but it feels like a lifetime. Even the room doesn't look the way it did before. It's bigger, brighter, there is sunlight splashing through the window.

"The babies," I shout. "They're alive!" I jump on the bed and throw myself into a wild version of a tribal dance Zoe once taught me. Then I catch sight of myself in the mirror and stop. Immediately.

I also see, in the mirror, the flask. It has fallen over, it's lying on its side on the desk.

No. No!

I scoot off the bed.

Please don't be cracked, please don't be broken.

The flask has only just entered my life and yet, I realize suddenly, I feel very powerfully about it. *Connected*, even. I find myself lurching forward, grabbing for it. But it isn't my beautiful, breathing flask; it is just a bottle. Something you might dig up in any old backyard. It isn't broken, but it might as well be, because the colors are gone and so are the patterns. No, that's not true; there are whorls on the surface of the glass still, but they aren't moving anymore, and the bubbles, my little seed fish, they aren't swimming. And there is nothing—*nothing*—inside.

I feel a kind of fury, as though somebody has given me something very precious and then just snatched it away again. I realize I already had plans for that flask. I was going to remove the cork and . . .

The cork—where is the cork?

It isn't in the bottle. I scan the desk. It isn't on the desk. But how can it be anywhere but in the bottle or on the desk? Did I imagine a cork? No, I saw it: a hard, discolored thing, lodged in the throat of the flask. I look into the empty bottle, as if the cork might just miraculously appear. But it doesn't. The smell of the bottle is of cold and dust. There can't have been anything in that bottle.

And yet there was.

There was something crouched inside that glass, waiting.

No, not crouched; that makes it sound like an animal. And the thing didn't have that sort of form, it was just something moving, stirring. Then I see it, the cork. Look! There on the floor. It's not close to the flask, not just fallen out and lying on the desk, but a full yard away. Maybe more. To carry the cork that far, something big, something powerful, must have come out of the flask, burst from it.

So where is that thing now?

12

It's on the windowsill.

What I thought was a patch of sunlight isn't sunlight at all. It's bright like sunlight, but it doesn't fall right, doesn't cast the right shadows. Light coming through a window-pane starts at the sun and travels for millions of miles in dead straight lines. You learn that in fifth grade. Light from the sun is not curved, or lit from inside, or suddenly irides-cent as a soap bubble or milky as a pearl. It doesn't expand and pulse and move. It doesn't breathe. Whatever is on the windowsill, it isn't light from the sun.

I go toward it. It would be a lie to say I'm not frightened. I am frightened, terrified even, but I'm also drawn. I can't help myself. I remember my old math teacher, Mr. Brand, breaking off from equations one day and going to stand at the window where there was a slanted sunbeam. He cupped his hands in the beam and looked at the light he held—and didn't hold.

"You can't have it," he said. "You can't ever have it."

And all of the class laughed at him. Except me. I knew what he meant because I've tried to capture sunbeams, too.

And now I want the thing on the windowsill, because it is strange and beautiful and I don't want to lose it again. I don't want to feel what I felt when I saw that the flask was empty, which is sick and hollow, my stomach clutching just like in the moment when Mom told me Aunt Edie was dead.

So I move very slowly and quietly, as though the thing is an animal after all and might flee in fear. And it does seem to be vibrating—or trembling, I can't tell which—as though it is aware of me, watching me, though something without eyes cannot watch.

"It's all right," I find myself saying. "It's all right. I won't hurt you."

I won't hurt it! What about it hurting me?

My room's not big, as I've said, but it takes an age to cross. I am just a hand-stretch away from the pearly, pulsing light when there is a sudden whoosh, like a wind got up from nowhere, and I feel a rush and panic, but I don't know if it is my rush and panic or that of the thing that seems to whip and curl past my head and pour itself back into the flask.

Back into the flask!

Quick as a flash, I put my thumb over the opening and I hold it down tight as I scrabble in the desk for my sticky tape. I pull at the tape, bite some off, jam it over the open throat of the flask, and then wind it again and again around the neck so the thing cannot escape.

I have it captured.

Captured!

Then I feel like one of those boys you read about in books who pull the wings off flies: violent, cruel. But here's the question: If you had something in your bedroom that flew and breathed and didn't obey the laws of science, would you want it at liberty?

That's what I thought.

13

When my heart calms down, I feel I owe the flask (or the thing inside it) an explanation. I think I should tell the truth, about the fear as well as the excitement. But I don't know who or what I'm dealing with, so I also feel I shouldn't give too much away. I should be cautious. Si's always saying that *A man of science proceeds with care.* Or, *If you're going to mix chemicals, Jess, put your goggles on.*

I'm not sure what sort of goggles I need to deal with the thing in the flask, but I think the least I can try is an apology.

"I'm sorry about the sticky tape," I say.

I'm not really expecting a reply and I don't get one, but the movement inside the flask does seem to become a little less frantic, so I have the feeling the thing is listening.

"I guess you must have been in that flask a long time," I say next.

Where does that remark come from? From the cold and the dust I smelled in the bottle? Or from some storybook knowledge of things in bottles, genies in lamps? What am I imagining, that the thing is some trapped spirit cursed to remain in the flask for a thousand years until—until what? Until Jessica Walton arrives with her father's ill-fitting slide rule? They say (correction: Si says) if you put a sane person in a lunatic asylum for any length of time they become as mad as the inmates. Me? I'm talking to a thing in a flask.

I'm calling it *you*.

The word *you* implies that the thing I'm talking to is alive. I mean, you don't say *you* to a box of tissues, do you? Or to a hairbrush or a necklace or a cell phone? So I am making a definite assumption about the thing being alive. Mr. Pug, our biology teacher, says that only things that carry out all seven of the life processes can be said to be alive. Pug calls all seven life processes Mrs. Nerg.

M—for movement   N—for nutrition
R—for reproduction   E—for excretion
S—for sensitivity   R—for respiration
                            G—for growth

I look at the thing in the flask. Movement—no doubt about that. Reproduction—I'm not sure I want to think about that right now. Sensitivity—definitely. It's sensitive to me, I'm sensitive to it. Nutrition—does the thing eat? Unlikely. It doesn't have a mouth. But then plants eat and they don't have mouths. Excretion—not important. If you don't eat you don't need to excrete. Respiration—yes, it breathes, doesn't it? And it has to get energy from somewhere or it couldn't move—and it certainly moves. Growth—yes again; I think I can imagine it growing.

To be alive, Pug says, you have to be able to carry out all seven of the processes. Not two, or five, or one. All seven.

I think Pug may have missed out on some of his training. This thing is definitely alive.

"Who are you?" I say. "What are you?"

The thing does not respond.

I retreat a bit. "I think you'll be safer in the flask for a while," I say.

I mean, of course, that I'll feel safer if the thing is in the flask. I've heard adults do this. They tell you something they want by making it sound useful to you, like, *You'll be much warmer in your coat, won't you?*

"Because," I add, "I have to go to the hospital in a minute. Gran's taking me to the hospital."

No reply.

"To see the babies."

No reply.

"So I'm just going to pop you (*you*) back in the desk for a bit."

No reply.

"Okay?"

"You see, I noticed how you rushed back in the flask yourself, so it must be your home, I guess. Am I right?"

No reply.

"My name's Jess, by the way."

Some little silver seed fish, swimming.

"How do you do that? How do you make the fish swim?"

No reply.

"It's beautiful."

No reply.

"So just wait, okay?"

No reply.

"Promise?"

Very gently, I place the flask back into the dark space behind the left-hand drawer in the desk.

"See you later," I say as I leave the room.

14

Our local hospital is too small to deal with cases like the twins', so we have to go to the city. It's a long drive.

"Your Mom will be very tired. You know that, don't you?" Gran says.

She makes it sound like we shouldn't be going, but I know why we we're going. In case the twins belong in the thirty-four percent who die on day one.

The Intensive Care Baby Unit is in the high-rise part of the hospital, on the fifteenth floor. We come out of the elevator facing a message telling us we are *In the Zone* and to make sure we scrub ourselves with the Hygienic Hand Rub. The doors to the unit are locked and we have to buzz to be let in.

Si hears us as we check in at the nurses' station and comes out to greet us.

"Angela," he says to Gran and then, "Jess." And he puts his hand out to touch me, which he doesn't usually. I look at his eyes. They aren't sparkling, but they are smiling. "Come on in."

There are four incubators in the room and five nurses. Two of the nurses are wearing flimsy pink disposable aprons and throwing things into bins. There's an air of serious hush, broken only by the steady blip of ventilators. Beside each cot is a screen with wavy lines of electronic blue, green, and yellow. I don't know what they measure, but they're the sort of machines you see in movies that go into a single flat line when people die. Mom is not sitting or standing, but lying on a bed. They must have wheeled her in on that bed, and parked her next to the twins. She doesn't look up immediately when we come into the room; all her focus, all her attention, is on my brothers.

Brothers.

All through the pregnancy, Mom's been calling them my brothers. *When the twins are born, when your brothers are born....* But, I realize, standing in the hospital Intensive Care Baby Unit, that they are not my brothers. Not full brothers, anyway. We share a mother, but not a father, so they are my half-brothers. But half-brothers sounds as if they're only half here or as if they don't quite belong. And that's scary. Or maybe it's actually me who doesn't quite belong anymore, as though a chunk of what I thought of as family has somehow slid away. And that's even scarier.

So I'm going to call them brothers—my *brothers.*

Mom looks up, shifts herself up on her pillows a little when she sees me, although I can tell it hurts her.

"Jess . . . come here, sweetie."

I come and she puts her arms right around me, even though it's difficult leaning from the bed.

"Look." She nods toward the incubator. "Here they are. Here they are at last."

They lie facing each other, little white knitted hats on their heads, hands entwined. Yes, they're holding hands. Fast asleep and tucked in under a single white blanket, they look innocent. Normal.

"Aren't they beautiful?" says Mom.

"Yes," I say. And it's true, too, though there is something frail about them, two little birds who can't fly and are lucky to have fallen together in such a nest.

"You were a beautiful baby, too, Jess."

She is making it ordinary, but it isn't ordinary. Somewhere beneath that blanket, my brothers are joined together and I want to see that join. At least I do now, although for months the idea of the join has been making me feel queasy.

There, I've said it.

The truth is, when Mom first told me she was pregnant I felt all rushing and hot. Not about the join, which we didn't know about then, or even about them being twins. No, I felt rushing and hot about her being pregnant at all. I can't really explain it except to say I didn't want people looking at my mother, I didn't want them watching her swelling up with Si's baby. It seemed to be making something very private go very public. And I didn't like myself for the way I felt, so when it turned out to be twins, and conjoined twins at that, I hid myself in the join. I made this the secret. I didn't want people to know about the join (I told Zoe, I told Em), because of all the mumbo jumbo talked about such twins across the centuries. I didn't tell them that I wasn't so sure about the babies myself, that the idea of the join actually made me feel sick to my stomach. I kept very quiet about that.

Am I a bad person?

A nurse is hovering and sees the babies stir.

"Do you want to hold them, Mom?" the nurse says as if my mother is her mother.

"Yes," says Mom.

Si helps Mom into a comfortable sitting position while the nurse unhitches one side of the incubator and adjusts some tubes. Then he stands protectively as the nurse puts a broad arm under both babies and draws them out. Si never takes his eyes off the babies. There is something fierce in his gaze and something soft, too, which I've never seen before.

"There now," says the nurse as she gives the babies to Mom. They are in Mom's arms, but they are still facing each other, of course. The nurse has been careful to keep the blanket round the babies as she lifts them and she's careful now to tuck it in.

One of the babies makes a little yelping noise. Mom puts a finger to the baby's lips and he appears to suck.

"They're doing very well," says Mom, and then she loosens the blanket.

The babies are naked, naked except for oversize diapers that seem to go from their knees to their waists—where the join begins. Mom leaves the blanket open quite deliberately. Gran turns her head away, but I look. I look long and hard, as Mom means me to do.

The babies' skin is a kind of brick color, as if their blood is very close to the surface, and it is also dry and wrinkled, as if they are very old rather than very young. Aunt Edie again. But the skin where they join is smooth and actually rather beautiful, like the webs between your fingers. It makes me feel like crying.

Very gently, Mom strokes the place where her children join, and then she draws the blanket back around them.

I realize then I don't know what the babies are named.

"Richie," says Mom, "after Si's father. And Clem, after mine."

15

It seems to be enough for Mom. She lies back and closes her
eyes and the nurse comes and takes the babies away again. I
think Si would like to lift them himself, but he doesn't dare.
Maybe he feels they are too fragile, that he'd hurt them.

Mom seems to have gone into an almost immediate sleep,
and just for a moment, I feel we might all be just some dream
of hers—me and Si and Gran and the babies, all rather
unlikely conjurings of her exhausted brain. And then, as I
watch her chest rise and fall, I think about the flask and that
seems like an even deeper dream. I had planned to tell Mom
about the flask, how I found it in the desk and how it was
full of something unearthly, something beautiful and scary
at the same time, and how I captured it, because I feel fierce
and soft toward it, just like Si does toward the twins, but

that I also feel bad because, as Mr. Brand says, you can't catch things that are supposed to be wild and free and...

"I think we ought to go now," says Gran.

"Mom..." I say.

"Shh," says Si. "She needs to rest."

16

By the time we get back home, it is almost dark.

"Who's that?" Gran asks as we turn into our driveway.

It's Zoe, of course, knocking at our front door. She turns as she hears the car pull up. I roll down my window.

"Want to come to the park?" she asks.

Zoe and I often go to the park at dusk. It's one of our little rituals. We swing on the swings after all the little kids have gone home. We swing and talk. Or Zoe dances. She dances around the swan on its large metal spring. She dances along the wooden logs that are held up by chains. She back-flips off the slide. When she's tired, which isn't often, we lie together on our backs in the half-moon swing and look at the sky. Or I look at the sky, anyway. She looks upward, but what she sees I don't know, because people can look in the same place but not see the same things, can't they?

"Bit late for the park," says Gran.

But I want to go to the park because I want some private time with Zoe. I want to tell her how beautiful my brothers are, after all; I want to take time, sharing all the details of those little birds and the web of their join. I want to look in her eyes, see myself reflected in the mirror of her, the big sister of two baby boys.

"Please," I say to Gran. "Just for half an hour."

I also want to tell Zoe about the flask.

"Well," says Gran. She looks at her watch. "Oh, all right then. Just while I make dinner."

"Thanks, Gran," I say, and I actually lean over and give her a kiss.

Zoe doesn't know we've just come from the hospital and I don't tell her. I want to be lying in the half-moon when I tell her about the babies. I want her to be the first to know, as she was about the join. A special moment, shared. Luckily, as we head down the cul-de-sac, she's already chatting to me, telling me about her sister's boyfriend and his new car and how her mother won't let the boyfriend drive Zoe around but doesn't mind him driving her sister around, which is ridiculous and . . .

And soon we're at the park and Paddy and Sam are there, too, with a soccer ball and two sweaters to mark a goal. Paddy isn't Paddy's real name; his real name is Maxim, but he doesn't look like a Maxim so everyone calls him Paddy. He has a big, round, smiling face and he bounces through life like a beach ball. Happy and full of air. Or, at least, that's what I think. Zoe thinks he's massively handsome and has an Outstanding Sense of Humor. It's Paddy, in fact, who Zoe has her eyes on.

I'm desperate to skirt behind the chestnut tree so we can get to the playground unseen, but Zoe is heading straight for the boys.

"Zoe..." I start urgently, clutching at her jacket.

But she's already pulling away, calling. "Hi! Hi! Hi, Paddy. Hi, Sam."

So there I am, trailing behind her.

The boys look up.

"Hey," Sam says. Sam wears slouchy pants and likes to think he's cool. "How's it going?"

"Great," says Zoe.

"We were just going to the swings," I say quickly.

"Well, in a sec," says Zoe.

Paddy looks at Zoe and then he looks at me. "Did the babies arrive yet?" he asks.

And there's a moment where I could just say no. I could just say no, and then we could walk away, and I could tell Zoe like I planned to as we lay in the half-moon swing.

"Well, did they?"

"Yes," I say.

"What?" shrieks Zoe.

"They arrived." I think I say it because I don't want to deny them anymore, these baby birds who are my brothers. I need them to be around me. Solid.

"Why didn't you tell me?" shrieks Zoe.

Why didn't you ask?

"Oh, right," says Sam, whose interests are pretty much confined to sports and his computer.

"And?" asks Paddy.

"And they're beautiful," I say. "Boys. Two boys."

"They're all right, then?" says Zoe. "They're both all right?"

"They've got eight legs," says Paddy.

"What?" says Sam.

"That's what my nana said," Paddy continues. "They could have eight legs."

"Mumbo jumbo," I say, and I shoot a look at Zoe. "They have four legs."

"Four!" exclaims Paddy.

"Yes," I say. "Two each. Like normal people."

"Oh—normal!" Paddy laughs.

Zoe's shrugging. Zoe's making out that whatever Paddy's saying, it's nothing to do with her.

"What are you talking about?" Sam asks.

"Jess's brothers," says Paddy. "They're not just any old twins. They're Siamese."

Sam is doing knee-ups with the soccer ball. "Siamese?" he says.

"Conjoined." I hear my voice going up. I hear myself about to shout. "The correct term is *conjoined twins*. And as for normal, they *are* normal. Considering the cellular complexity of the average human being, that is." *Shut up, Si.* "They're as normal as me. Or you. If you call that normal."

Paddy ignores *normal*. "Point is," he says, "they're joined down the chest."

Sam drops the ball. He drops his jaw. His mouth hangs open. "Man," he says. "Joined down the chest? Wow. Like, you mean, face to face? Like they're facing each other all the time? Jeez."

"If I was stuck onto my brother," says Paddy, going to retrieve the ball, "if he was the first thing I saw when I woke up and the last thing I saw before I went to sleep, that would kill me."

"More likely kill your brother, being stuck to you," I say. Then I round on Zoe. "Come on," I say. "We're going."

But Zoe's feet seem planted in the ground.

"In the old days," says Paddy, "they put Siamese twins in the circus. People paid to see them."

"Conjoined!" I shout.

"You could do that," Paddy continues. "You could bring your brothers in next semester and charge a dollar a time to look at them."

"They might not even last that long," I say. Or maybe I don't say it. Maybe it's the silent thing shouting in my head. *They might not even last that long.*

Paddy's big face is shining with excitement. "I'd pay," he says. "I'd pay to look. Wouldn't you, Sam?"

"Yeah," says Sam.

"You could have a different rate depending on whether it was just a look or a touch," Paddy continues.

"Shut up," I say.

"A dollar for a look, two dollars for a good look, and five dollars for a touch."

"I said SHUT UP."

"We could call it JFS—Jess's Freak Show."

And now everything that's been silent and bottled up comes frothing and boiling over at last and I go right up to him because I'm going to hit him in his stupid, shining face. I draw back my fist and I lash out as hard and fast as I can, but he just catches my wrist.

"Hey," he says. "Hey. What's up with you? It was only a joke. Can't you take a joke now?"

"I hate you!" I scream.

But it's actually Zoe I hate.

17

I turn and march away from the park. Of course, Zoe follows me.

"Jess," she says. "Jess, Jess, Jess!" And now it's her turn to clutch me by the sleeve. "Come on!"

I stop. I wheel around. "Come on *what*, exactly?"

"I never told him," she says. "I didn't."

"Oh, right; he just made it up, did he? Thought it up out of his own stupid little brain?"

"I didn't tell him, Jess, I promise, I swear."

I stare at her. Her eyes are all lit up bright, but not like a mirror. I can't see myself in them, in her. "Then who did?"

"I don't know," Zoe exclaims. "Maybe your mom told his mom and she told Paddy."

"Oh, yeah, right."

"Or Em. You didn't tell just me, did you? You pretended you did, but you didn't. You told Em, too. So maybe it was Em who told Paddy."

Very clever. And hurtful, because it's true. I did tell Em, actually, and I did pretend to Zoe that she was the only one who knew. Why did I do that? Because Zoe can be jealous, probably. She can go crazy just like she did about the friendship bracelet thing in fourth grade. But Em's away on vacation. Em isn't here to defend herself. "Why would Em tell Paddy? She doesn't even like Paddy. No one likes Paddy." I pause. "Except you."

"I still didn't tell him, Jess. I mean—why would I?"

And I can't say it. I can't say, *Because I think you're beginning to like him more than you like me*, because that sounds totally pathetic. So I say, "For a laugh. So you could both have a laugh behind my back about my so-not-normal brothers."

"Jess, you're way out of line. I didn't tell him. I didn't!"

"So why did you let him say all that stuff—all that eight-leg circus-freak stuff?"

"That's just mumbo jumbo, Jess. Like you said yourself. You said people would say stuff like that. How's that my fault?"

"You could have spoken up—you could have said something. Anything."

Now she's silent, biting her lip.

"But you just stood there." I ram it home. "You let him say all of it and you just stood there."

I start walking again now, turning my back on her and walking, walking.

She runs after me again, but I shake her off.

"I didn't know I had to say anything. Anyway, you were saying stuff," Zoe remarks to my back. "And what does it matter? They're born now. They're okay."

It matters because she promised, because I trusted her. And I need to go on trusting her. Because of the flask. "Who says they're okay?" I say.

"What?"

"The babies—who says they're okay?"

"You did!" says Zoe. "You said it!"

"I said they were beautiful. I didn't say they were okay."

"Well—are they okay?"

I say nothing.

"Well, are they?"

"I'm not telling you," I say. "I'm not telling you anything ever again."

18

I don't say a single thing over dinner. And if Gran notices, she doesn't mention it. She probably thinks it's to do with the babies. And she's right. Everything's to do with the babies these days.

Except the flask.

I delay going up to bed, partly because I'm no good at sleeping when I'm angry, and partly because I expect to see little bits of sticky tape on the floor. I mean, something that can blow a cork from a bottle can burst through sticky tape, right?

Wrong.

There is no sticky tape on the floor. The desk is still closed, the drawer inside still shut. I reach my hand in and feel the cold, rounded form of the flask.

"I'm back," I say, sliding my fingers up the throat of the bottle, just to check the sticky tape is really still in place.

It is.

So I draw the flask out into the light. It is blue. Really blue—like a summer sky. Like happiness. Whatever I expected, it wasn't this.

I just stand and stare, trying to work out whether it is the glass or the thing inside that is blue. But I can't separate the two. Nor can I understand why—despite Zoe and Paddy and the park and the mumbo jumbo—just holding it makes me fizz with joy, as though I am holding a tiny, perfect other universe.

"You're extraordinary," I say. "You know that?"

No reply.

But then what would a universe reply? And I remember Si showing me pictures taken by the Hubble Telescope, pillars of dust 57 trillion miles high and some nebula thing called the Eye of God because that's what it looked like, some astonishingly beautiful giant eye. And Si was busy explaining about gas and cusp knots and interstellar collisions, and I was just thinking it was all too much and too beautiful to look at even in a newspaper. And here is something even more extraordinary in the palm of my hand.

I don't want to put the flask back in the dark drawer; I want to keep it close by me. So I take it to my bed and lay it on my pillow as I undress. I don't know how long the blue will last, the blue and the bright happiness inside me. And it's not just the thing about Zoe (why couldn't it have been my mom talking to Paddy's mom?), it's also the first time, I realize, I've felt really happy since we knew about the babies. The babies have shadowed everything for months, the worry of them. Would they be born alive, and if so, would they be able to survive? And now this glowing blue seems to have the power to push the gloom away. Or maybe it's just that I've seen the babies. Seen them alive with their bright little bird faces.

I get into bed, thinking sleep will come with the sweetest of dreams.

19

But sleep doesn't come.

Not quickly.

Not at all.

My mind will not be quiet; it refuses to listen to my happy heart. The flask is tucked beneath my pillow, but my thoughts still toss about the park (of course my mom didn't talk to Paddy's mom—why would she?). Eventually, my restless anxiety pokes its way under my brothers' sheet at the hospital.

Richie and Clem.

I'm glad the babies have names; it makes them seem less vulnerable somehow, as though they really are here to stay, have personalities of their own, a right to exist. *Richie* seems a slightly bigger name to me than *Clem*, just as Richie himself, I realize as I picture them again in my mind, is the bigger twin. Not by much, of course, but if one twin could be said to be clinging to the other, then it is Clem who is clinging to Richie. Clem who, if there is to be trouble, is the weaker one.

Thirty-four percent of conjoined twins don't make it through the first twenty-four hours.

Clem's a strange name, a strange word. It sounds to me like *clam*. Clem the closed-up clam, clinging.

I turn over.

And over.

I feel bad characterizing Clem like this, as though naming him as weaker makes him weaker still. They are both strong, I tell myself.

Strong enough to get through this dangerous night. Their first on earth.

I put my hand under my pillow, reaching for the flask, as if blue were something you could feel or touch.

Then my thoughts return to Zoe: Em would never betray a secret and I haven't once seen her talking to Paddy. It's Zoe who's always talking to Paddy. Though I can't check, can't be sure, because Em's away on vacation for pretty much the whole Easter break. But it must have been Zoe, confiding in Paddy. Making the join of the twins the butt of

Paddy's Outstanding Sense of Humor, which he clearly gets from his nana and her eight legs and . . . And my thoughts find the twins, sleeping together, breathing together, the little sheet rising and falling around them. And as they breathe, the flask seems to breathe, too, inhaling and exhaling beneath my hand. A tiny rib cage. And then things begin to get muddled and I hear a moan of the sort people make when they're dreaming and they want to wake up and they can't. And I don't know if I am really awake, or just dreaming that I am awake, but I do hear the moan get louder, becoming more of a wail, and suddenly I'm sitting bolt upright in bed, my heart pounding.

It makes me gasp, how fast my heart is pounding. It's deeply dark, the middle of the night. So I must have slept after all, slept for a long while. I try to calm myself, try to remember the blue, the overwhelming happiness. But all I hear is the wail, only it isn't a wail anymore, it's a howl. Something dark and inhuman is howling from beneath my pillow.

I stumble and fling myself out of that bed. Fear makes many shapes, but this thing has only one shape, the shape of the flask. The same thing that splashed light on my window-sill and held a universe of brilliant blue is now pulsing black wolf howls into my night, into my head.

Stop, stop, stop! I want to shout, to scream, but the words are stuck in my throat.

There is nothing for it but to reach through the dark, reach under the pillow. I am afraid the flask will be soft under my hand, like a heart, but it is hard and cold, holding its glass shape. I want to smash it. If I smash it, the noise will stop. It will have to stop.

I pick up the flask, intending to fling it against the wall, but that's when the howl goes higher and also softer, not so much wolf as wolf cub, and there is suddenly something so terrible and so sad about the noise that I just pull the flask to my chest and hold it there. Then I rock with it, like you'd rock with a baby who was crying and you had nothing to give but the warmth of your own flesh.

Which is when Gran comes into the room.

"Jess?" she says. "Jess, can't you sleep either?"

"No," I cry. "No!"

The spill of light from the hall turns my bedroom bright and ordinary.

"I thought I heard you," Gran says.

"Heard me?"

"Walking about."

"Water," I say. "I need some water."

"You look half-frozen," she replies. "I'll get the water. Come on, now, get back to bed. It's after two o'clock."

Gratefully, I get back into bed. Under the covers, I look at the flask. It is not a heart, not a rib cage; it isn't pulsing. There is nothing black about it, but nothing blue either. It is calm and hard and glassy, colorless.

As Gran returns with the water, I slip the flask back beneath the pillow.

"He told you they could die on their first night, didn't he?" Gran says.

"Who?" I say, as though I don't quite understand her. Though of course I do.

"Si. He told you the babies could die, didn't he?"

I shrug.

"He has no business saying things like that." She sits down hard on the edge of the bed. "No business at all."

"He only mentioned the statistics . . ." I begin.

"Statistics," says Gran, "are bosh."

And I know this. I've heard it all my life.

Statistics are bosh.

Statistics are bosh.

Gran says it like a mantra, her own little song.

This is something else Si has told me about. Something

he's explained. Si explains everything; Gran explains nothing. You just have to guess what Gran means; you have to look around her corners. "Your grandmother," said Si, "has never trusted statistics since your father died of something people don't normally die of. Hiatal hernia. A million-to-one chance, that's what the doctors told her. So now she doesn't believe in the numbers game."

I should never have mentioned statistics.

"Anyway," Gran continues, "you saw your brothers. Saw them with your own eyes. They're going to be fine. Do you hear me?"

I hear her.

"So you're not to worry. Right?"

She comes to tuck me in like I'm some baby myself. As she fusses about me, I realize that I will always be her baby in a way that my brothers will not. Si is the twins' father, but not mine. So Gran has no blood relationship with the twins. Gran and the babies—they aren't joined at all.

In the last chink of light, before Gran shuts my door, I check the flask. In its whorls, its worlds, there are a couple of bright seed fish swimming.

After that, I sleep.

20

The following morning, the phone rings at 7:36. Nobody calls our house that early.

I arrive in the kitchen to hear Gran say, "Yes, of course I'll tell her, Si."

She puts down the phone. I wait for her to give me the news.

"Morning, Jess," she says. "Breakfast's up." From the oven she takes a steaming plate of bacon and eggs. The smell of it makes me want to retch.

"What did he say?" I ask. "What's happened?"

"Your mom's fine," says Gran.

"And the babies?"

"They're fine, too." But there is something too bright and too quick about the way she says it.

I look at her. "What?"

"What what?" she repeats.

"What did Si say? What did he want you to tell me?"

Gran wipes her hands on her apron. "Your stepfather," she says, "wanted you to know that your mother and your brothers are fine."

I stare at her and I keep on staring. I want the truth.

"Clem..." Gran says finally, lips pressed tight.

"Yes?"

"He took a little dip in the night...but he's absolutely fine now."

A little dip.

I can't imagine Si using these words. Si would use precise medical terms.

"What kind of 'dip'?"

"Oh, I don't know, Jessica. Nobody said it would be smooth sailing. The important thing is that he's okay now."

"And when exactly?" I ask.

"When what?" says Gran.

"When did Clem take this dip?"

"Does it matter?"

I think of that great sobbing howl.

"Yes. It does matter."

"Look, Jess, I know things have been difficult in this house over the last few months. And I know you didn't sleep very well last night. So I'm going to ignore your tone of voice. But you have to trust me and Si and the doctors. And you have to eat your breakfast."

I sit down. I try my bacon, toy with my eggs. In the right-hand pocket of my jeans I can feel the weight of the flask. Calm this morning, colorless. But opalescent on the day the twins were born, its cork bursting from its throat, and then black and howling the night that Clem took *a dip.*

"Do you ever think," I ask Gran, "that things are more..." I want to use the word *joined*, the word that's been stuck in my head for weeks, but I choose to say *connected.* "Do you think things are more connected than they might appear?"

Gran is eating toast. "I'm not sure I understand you, Jess."

"That there are more things on earth than can be explained by—well, science?"

"Are we talking God?" asks Gran.

"No!" Actually, I think we're talking Si; I'm talking about whether there is more in the universe than can be explained by my stepfather.

"Ghosts?" she hazards.

Ghosts. That makes a patter in my heart. When did the flask come into my life? After Aunt Edie died. And where did it come from? Aunt Edie's desk. Ghosts are spirits without bodies. Like the thing in the flask. And they arrive after people die. . . .

"Jessica?"

"No, no!" I don't want a ghost. A ghost is scary.

Scarier than the howls?

Besides—a ghost doesn't make any sense. Not the ghost of Aunt Edie. I'd know that ghost, surely. And it—she— would know me. We'd chat, wouldn't we? *Hi, Jess, it's me, Aunt Edie, just came to see how you were getting on with your piano playing.* And in any case, ghosts don't exist, do they? Pug and his Mrs. Nerg wouldn't have anything to do with ghosts. Si wouldn't have anything to do with ghosts. But is a ghost any more extraordinary than a disembodied something connected to the twins?

My mind is going round in circles. I blame Zoe. If Zoe and I were on speaking terms I wouldn't be having to share all this with Gran.

"What do you mean, then?" Gran asks.

"I was just thinking . . . last night—I couldn't sleep, you couldn't sleep, and Clem—he wasn't well. Maybe we some-how . . . sensed that?"

"Nice idea," says Gran. "But a bit far-fetched. It's just worry, I'm afraid. Keeps people awake all the time." She gets up to reboil the kettle. "And knowing too much. Sometimes the less you know, the better."

I say nothing. I don't like the dig at Si. *He told you the babies could die, didn't he? Sometimes the less you know the better.* I'm allowed to have a dig at him, but she isn't. Why is that?

"You've always been a sensitive child, Jessica," Gran continues. "Sometimes that's a good thing." She pauses. "And sometimes it's a curse."

"A curse?"

"You imagine things that simply aren't there."

"Last night," I say, suddenly angry, "there was a howl, a terrible, terrible sobbing howl. Didn't you hear it?"

"Jess, love, it was a difficult night. You were tossing and turning. I know—I peeked in on you. I think you must have been dreaming."

Dreaming?

I never actually *saw* the flask go black, did I? I never saw it pulse. When I did look at it, when light finally spilled into the room, it was just glassy, colorless, ordinary.

Though it had been blue. Fizz-heart, sky-happy blue. I definitely saw that.

And I saw

the cork on the floor

and

the light that didn't travel in straight lines

and

the opalescence

and

the breathing and the flying

and

the little seed fish swimming

and...

"And that's before we get to your overactive imagination," Gran says. "Don't forget—you are the girl who invented Spike."

21

We don't go to the hospital. Mom says the twins have to have tests.

"Plenty of cleaning to do at my house," says Gran.

She means Aunt Edie's house.

"That'll take our minds off things."

Her mind, maybe.

In the car on the way over, I don't answer my phone when it rings. Gran doesn't like me answering the phone when we're in the middle of a conversation (though, as it happens, we're not in the middle of a conversation) because she says it's rude. But that's not the reason I don't take my calls. I don't take them because they are all from Zoe. By the time we arrive I have four missed calls and a text: *sry. SRY cll me. xx.*

Besides, I need to think about Spike. Spike is small and blond and he never brushes his hair, so it's always wild and knotted. He comes with me everywhere, or at least he used to. He arrived when I grew out of ScatCat, sometimes smiling and full of jokes, sometimes irritating and demanding. He'd hide when I wanted to speak to him or shout right at the moment I tried to ride my bike without training wheels. He'd knock my juice over. But at night he was always calm, and came to bed with me, lay his head on the pillow beside mine. Only he never slept. He spent the whole night watching over me.

I'm here, Jess, right here.

Wacu. To be awake.

I'll never leave you.

To watch over.

I love you, Jess.

As Gran pulls up in her driveway, I realize I haven't been in her house since the day of the funeral. And I haven't been in the house next door—Aunt Edie's house— since Aunt Edie was there to open the door to me.

On Gran's porch is a blue-and-white china umbrella stand that used to be on Aunt Edie's porch. It makes my stomach lurch.

I love you, Jess.

"You'll never guess what I found," says Gran, leading me straight past the umbrella stand that is in the wrong place and into the dining room. "Look."

On the dining room table is a stack of Aunt Edie's photo albums, the sort that have real old-fashioned photos in them, ones on glossy paper, not the flimsy pixelated ones you print off the computer.

She points at a picture of me at about four, pushing an empty swing. Beneath the photo, there is a scrap of paper on which is written, in Aunt Edie's loopy handwriting, *Jess and Spike.*

"Do you remember?"

Yes. Forever. I often pushed Spike on the swing. Spike liked the rhythm; it soothed him.

"For three whole years, you wouldn't go anywhere without him," says Gran. "Jessica Walton and her imaginary friend, Spike." She laughs. "And the sandwiches you got Edie to make for him! Every time you had a plate, he had to have one, too."

Then I remember something else. Aunt Edie made plates and plates of sandwiches for Spike—pimento cheese sandwiches, which were Spike's favorite. But Gran, she never gave Spike food. Not one sandwich in three years.

The place where I join with Aunt Edie burns.

22

Gran and Aunt Edie's gardens are both shaped like witches' hats, wide close to the house and then narrowing to not much more than a compost pile where they back onto the park. The boundary between the two begins as a fence, making it quite clear which piece of land belongs to whom, but seventy feet farther on there is just an increasingly tangled hedge where plants and boundary seem to twine together without end or beginning.

That makes me think of the twins and the web of their join and how they are both clearly separate and yet, beneath it all, they must tangle, too.

The gate, which has a latch but no lock, is about a third of the way along, by Gran's eucalyptus tree. I know it is a eucalyptus because Aunt Edie would sometimes crush a leaf in her hand as we passed.

"Smell this, Jess."

The smell was pungent, fragrant, oily.

"That's *my* tree," Gran might say, in a tone that wasn't quite joking. "And I'll thank you two to respect it."

"It's only a leaf," Aunt Edie would retort. "Just one leaf."

They did bicker sometimes, Gran and Aunt Edie. Two increasingly old ladies: one who'd lost her husband early, one who'd never married. Sisters whose lives had joined along this boundary for more than ten years.

Another pair of siblings joined.

I really hadn't thought about that before, but I think about it now, as Gran presses down on the latch and the gate swings open as it has so many times before.

Aunt Edie's house is to be sold. The gate will have to be locked, a bolt on Gran's side, a bolt on the side of the new neighbors. Gran will never go through that gate again. I will never go through it again. It makes me want to unlatch the gate and run back and forth a thousand times.

It also makes me want to ask Gran how she is, how she's feeling. Gran who has no husband and no son and now no sister. All her joins, her connections, broken. But I don't know how to open that conversation.

Gran shuts the gate behind her and puts a bony arm around my shoulder. And then, as if she can read my mind, she says, "I feel so lucky to have you, Jess."

23

Gran opens the door of the glass lean-to (which Aunt Edie called the Sun Room) and we go in. The house smells damp and forgotten, as if it has been unlived in for years, not just for a couple of months.

I go straight into the drawing room, which is where the piano is. The room runs the length of the house, and the piano is in the bay window to the front and the sofas around the fireplace to the rear. Only there aren't any sofas anymore. All the large items of furniture have gone, leaving a rolled-up carpet, a few piles of books, and Aunt Edie's ancient...

Ancient... there's Zoe again, nagging in my ear.

...ancient TV. The piano, alone at the far end of the room, looks abandoned, cheerless. Its lid is down. Down! Aunt Edie's piano lid was never down.

"Who's going to have it?" I blurt out. "Who's getting Aunt Edie's piano? Where's it going?"

"It's not going anywhere," says Gran quickly. "Well, only next door."

"You're going to have it?" I must sound astonished.

"It's not that surprising," says Gran.

"But you don't play!"

"Ah, but you do. So instead of going to Aunt Edie's to play, you can come to my house, can't you?"

And I should be glad, I should be grateful. The piano won't be sold, won't to go into some stranger's house. It will be just next door; I can play it any time I want. Any time I visit. But I still feel like someone threw a blanket over my head, hot and suffocated.

"Of course I'll have to make some space in my drawing room," says Gran. "Move things around, sell a few more bits and pieces at auction. But it'll be worth it, Jess, to have you coming to play."

I can't meet her eyes, so I turn my back, go over to the piano, lift the lid, and try a chord. Still in perfect tune.

"Are you pleased?" Gran asks.

"I love this piano," I say. This at least is true.

"Oh, and one more thing. Look." Gran scrabbles beside the pile of books. "I found this."

It's a stack of music books—Bach, Beethoven, Chopin, Mozart.

"Bit beyond you at the moment, probably," Gran says. "But practice makes perfect. You'll be needing to come over to my house a lot."

24

Gran hands me the stack and goes off to *sort the vases*. I hear her clattering about in the kitchen.

Music.

Aunt Edie and I never read music. Notes have always filled me with fear. There, I've said it. Right from the beginning, they swam in front of my eyes. I never knew what lines they sat on, or why. I didn't understand the spaces or the clefs or the time signatures.

"She doesn't seem to be making much progress," my mother reported.

Nor was I making much progress with reading. I was—I am—dyslexic, but nobody knew it then. Except perhaps Aunt Edie. Despite the fact she'd never even heard the word *dyslexic*, she just *knew*.

"Her music's all here," said Aunt Edie, tapping her ears. "Where it should be. And also here." She tapped her heart.

It was Aunt Edie who suggested I give up learning with a conventional teacher and start learning the Suzuki way. She even managed to convince Si on the subject. The founder of the Suzuki method, Aunt Edie told him, observed how effortlessly Japanese children learned their mother tongue. No one taught them their letters; they just listened to words and repeated them, like every other child in the world. A child could learn music the same way, said Shinichi Suzuki, by using his or her ears, by listening and then repeating. *If a child hears fine music from the day of his birth and learns to play it himself*, the master said, *he develops sensitivity, discipline, and endurance. He gets a beautiful heart.*

So finding a slew of music books belonging to Aunt Edie feels like a betrayal. Which is stupid, because of course I know Aunt Edie could read music—even I can read some now—but I just don't want these books right now. I throw them on the floor. Concertos and sonatas and sonatinas skid about on the carpetless boards.

Then I sit down to play.

I play something very simple, a song we used to call "Spring Garden."

"This is the grass growing," Aunt Edie would say. "And this, this is a cherry tree bursting into bloom. And these are the birds. Can you hear the birds, Jess?"

I didn't cry when they told me Aunt Edie was dead. I didn't cry at the funeral or at the wake. But when I hear those birds singing again, I sob my heart out.

25

After a while I stop playing and blow my nose. Then I think I should pick up the music books because Gran has never been very good with messiness. There is the Beethoven, the Bach, the Mozart, the Chopin, and a single sheet of paper. At first I think it's blank, because it's upside down, face to the floor. I am just about to slip it back inside *Chopin's Preludes* when I see that it is music, too. A handwritten song, or a composition anyway, tiny little blue ink notes jumping about on neatly ruled (if fading) blue ink staves. The piece doesn't have a title, but in the top left-hand corner there is a dedication. In Aunt Edie's distinctive, loopy handwriting it says: *For Rob.*

This is even more of a shock to me than the books of music. Aunt Edie—writing a song down, committing it to paper? Aunt Edie, who could remember every note of a piece, but who also liked to change things, experiment, improvise according to her mood—or mine?

And worse than this: Rob.

Who is Rob that Aunt Edie should dedicate a song to him? Something flashes hot across my heart.

Jealousy.

Aunt Edie and I made many songs together, but she never dedicated one to me. Never wrote it, fixed it down, put my name in blue at the top. *For Jess.*

I put the music on the piano stand, sit myself down, stare at the notes. I need to hear this piece, need to know what Aunt Edie has written to this Rob I've never heard of. I'm a good player, I really am, but I have to count the lines and spaces, try to find where the first ink dot lands. It makes me cross to look at all of Aunt Edie's notes arranged in front of me like some locked-up treasure chest to which I do not have the key.

What level are you on? That's what they always ask at school. And: *Did you get a merit, or a distinction, or just a pass?* Zoe's always doing dance exams, always getting distinctions. And even Em and Alice, who both do singing, get the odd merit or two. With Suzuki you don't do exams. And anyway—who cares? Who cares! I've never wanted a piece of paper with some official stamp to say how good or bad I am. I've just wanted to be able to listen and then play the way Aunt Edie played. But today is different. Today I want to be able to sight-read, to recognize every note on the stave, be able to lift my hands to the keys and make immediate sense of the fading dots. What if they fade right away before my eyes? What if I never find out what Aunt Edie wrote to Rob? *For* Rob.

I try again. I find the first note. I check to see if there are any sharps or flats. I look for the rhythm. Minims or quavers? Notes with dots or notes without? Gradually I assemble a chord, and then another, and something in the baseline, too, a sad, rocking sound. Then I think I hear something, catch something, like a melody coming by on the air, a haunting, hunted sound. And it's suddenly as if I can hear much more than I can play, a whole tune singing itself out loud. I stop playing and start listening and there it is, just as Aunt Edie always said it would be, a song in my ears, in my heart.

And also in my pocket.

The flask is singing. A song even sadder and stranger than the wolf lament of the previous night—and bigger, too. Much bigger—a huge song. Something that makes me feel that this is how God would have sung if, when he called the world into being, when he made the stars and the seas and the land and the lions, when he crafted each spark of sky, each drop of water, each blade of grass, and every single hair in the lion's mane, he also knew that, one day, the stars would burn out, the seas dry up, and the land and the lions die.

I draw out the flask, oh so slowly, because it feels unholy to disturb this song.

You know how it is sometimes when you see someone crying and you know you can't comfort them? That even if you put your arm around them, it won't make any difference, they just have to cry until they're finished with it? That's how the song is making me feel.

I stand the flask on the piano. Its heart is swirling, gray and purple, the color of storm clouds and bruises. Gently, I unwind the sticky tape from the throat of the glass, not to hear the song better—I could hear it if I were on the other side of the world—but just because I think the song, the flask, needs to be free.

Then, of course, my hands begin to find the notes. I can just lay my hands on the piano and feel the music flow out of my fingers. I can play the sadness, play the stars and the seas and the land and the lions.

"How do you know that tune?" Gran is suddenly in the doorway, statue-still, face like she's seen a ghost.

My hands falter, they fall from the notes. The spell breaks.

"Where did you get that music?"

"Found it," I say. "With the other music. Aunt Edie's music."

"I haven't heard that since . . ." Her voice dies away.

"Since what?" I ask. "Since when?"

She unlocks, comes across the room, her footsteps hollow on the bare floorboards. "Never you mind," she says.

"But it's such beautiful music."

"Beautiful!" she exclaims. She stops in front of the stand and stares at the faded notes.

"And sad," I say, "really sad. Who's Rob, Gran?"

Gran says nothing.

"It says *For Rob*," I repeat.

"Does it." And Gran takes the sheet of music and she folds it—no, she crushes up that paper and puts it in her pocket. "And what," she adds suddenly and just to change the subject, "is that?"

26

It's the flask.

But it isn't swirling with storm clouds and bruises; it's just its quiet, colorless self.

"It's a bottle," I say.

"Where did you get it from?" Gran asks.

"Just found it."

"You seem to be finding a lot of things, Jess."

"It was in the desk. Aunt Edie's desk."

"I thought I cleared that bureau," says Gran, and then I see her hand lift and the bottle becomes my precious flask and I know I don't want her to touch it. I like my gran, I really do, but I just don't want her to touch Aunt Edie's flask.

My flask.

"No," I cry.

But just before Gran's fingers reach the glass, there's that whoosh again, that wind out of nowhere, and into the air comes whatever it is that lies in the flask. The living, breathing thing, whirling and trembling. I hear it, so Gran must hear it, too. Only she doesn't, so her fingers keep reaching, they close around the neck of the bottle.

And the whooshing breath, that big-as-a-storm-wind, tiny-as-a-baby's-snuffle breath, it comes eddying and circling toward me, and I stretch out my hands and suddenly it's between my palms. I can feel it beating there, like a trapped butterfly.

And for two seconds, or maybe two hundred years, I hold myself like a sheet of glass, terrified that, with a single movement, I could crush that breath forever, though some other part of me feels that, for all its trembling, that beating is the strongest thing in the world.

27

Finally, Gran puts down the bottle. "The things my sister kept," she says.

At once the butterfly breath flies and curls itself back inside the flask.

I look at Gran's face. She has seen nothing, heard nothing. How is it possible for people to see and hear nothing?

"Well, enough time-wasting," Gran says and smiles, as though we were both having the most ordinary of days. "Come on, we've got jobs to do."

I slip the flask back inside my pocket and Gran sets me to work. I dry the vases she's washed; sort the good tools from the broken ones in Aunt Edie's shed; help her lift things, like the old coal bucket, that are too heavy for her alone. And actually it feels good to be doing some helpful, simple things. Although maybe the joy is to do with the flask because I'm no longer afraid that, without a cork, without sticky tape, the butterfly breath will fly away.

Because it chose me, didn't it?

It sheltered under my hand.

28

It's about four o'clock before we set off for home.

I have another text from Zoe. She reminds me that tomorrow is the day we're going—with Paddy—to the Buddhist Center for our vacation project on Places of Worship. Will I just text her back to say I haven't forgotten?

We are going with Paddy because Zoe was in charge of the arrangements and she deliberately arranged the visit on a day she knew Em and Alice were both going to be away and Paddy wasn't. Zoe told me this was just an oversight, but I didn't believe it then and I don't believe it now.

I don't text her back. This is what my mother, who is a very gentle person, calls *holding a grudge.*

"Si called," says Gran in the car. "He's coming back tonight. Check I'm feeding you properly."

As Gran plans to sleep in her own house that night, I wonder why it is that she's driving me home, why Si hasn't come to collect me. I think Gran wonders this, too, when we pull into our driveway to find the garage doors open and Si on his back underneath the Morris Traveller 1000.

"Oh, for goodness' sake," Gran says as she pulls up.

Hearing us arrive, Si slides out from underneath the car. He is lying on a little dolly, a wooden platform on casters that he made himself.

He looks like a daddy longlegs, too thin and sprawly for the platform. He's tall, Si, and bony, and has springy, sandy-colored hair. I'm not particularly tall for my age, but I'm also a bit bony and have that same sandy-colored hair. We also both have grayish eyes.

Don't you and your dad look alike! Lots of people have said that to me. I don't tell them Si's my stepfather; it just causes complications. In fact there have been many times when I've pretended that Si is my father. It makes things easier, like at school, when they ask you to write stuff about your family. What does your father do for a living? *My father's a mechanic.* Actually Si is not a mechanic, but he might as well be, the amount of time he spends on this car.

He has been working on his "little moggie" pretty much the whole time he's been in my life. Him and the oily cardboard and the spare parts and the wrenches and the tinkering. *Tinkering*. That's what Mom calls it, though she says it lovingly.

"You'd think he could leave it alone for one day," says Gran. "With everything that's going on."

"Hello, Angela," says Si, as she gets out of the car. Then he swivels around to face me. "Hi, Jess. How's tricks?"

The dolly on which he swivels is my fault. If I had been the stepchild he wanted, it would have been Si lying—dollyless—under the car tinkering and me lying beside him. Me being interested in exhausts, radiators, crankshafts, and timing chains, and me wriggling out to fetch whatever bolt or socket wrench he had forgotten, so he could keep lying there, hour after hour. And it's not that I haven't tried to be interested, I have. I just never quite got the point of Roger the Wreck. Yes, that's what he calls it—Roger the Wreck. Because when he bought it, it wasn't really a car at all, more a sort of heap of junk. But over the years he's lovingly put it all back together again. He's screwed and bolted and joined and greased it into some sort of whole, bursting with the pride of it.

"Fit like a glove, don't they, Jess? The new doors."

But actually there's still a gale-force draft around those doors, and the word *new* would not pass a lie detector. There is nothing new about this car. All its components, the wood frame, the chrome trims, the headlights, they all come from the other cars, the "donor" cars, which squat in our garage. Other heaps of junk he raids to make Roger run. Roger who occasionally roars into life sounding, Mom says, like a wartime Spitfire.

I was nine when Si made himself the little dolly on casters, nine when he finally admitted to himself that, as a mechanic's assistant, I was a failure. That if he forgot the socket wrench (the heavy one from the toolbox marked *war issue*) he would have to crawl out from under the car and get it himself. The dolly made things easier— he could just roll in and out—but whenever I see it, I can't help feeling his sense of disappointment.

"How are the babies?" asks Gran pointedly, as though a real man would not be tinkering under a car when his new-born babies are lying tangled up in a hospital crib.

"Heart ultrasound. EKG. CT scans. Blood work. Even skin tests—mouths and noses checked for bacteria and fungi and..." He suddenly pauses. "They're fighting," he says. "They're giving it everything they've got."

And his eyes go fierce and starry again, not like the Si I know, and do you know what? That red hotness flashes across my chest a second time in one day. And I imagine how it would be if the twins come home and lie under the

Morris Traveller 1000 and pass their father (their *father*) the war-issue socket wrench. And because there are two of them, one could always be under the car and the other hopping around for the wrench, so they'd never have to leave him and he wouldn't be disappointed ever again. And, of course, I know I'm being ridiculous. I'm being totally unfair to these two babies, who might not even make it to being grown-up enough to get under a car, and in any case, just because they're boys it doesn't mean they'll be any more interested than me in oil and grease and coveralls but, but...would he really have wanted them if I'd been good enough? If there'd never been a dolly?

And then it hits me. I've separated them, haven't I? I've put a knife down their join and I've put one twin under the car and the other hopping around for wrenches. And of course there's been talk in our house about separation. But it's so risky, so delicate, that even Si hasn't talked so very loudly about it. And here I am, just dividing them willy-nilly, sticking the knife in. Statistic: Since 1950, seventy percent of separations result in one live twin.

One.

Just one.

"I don't suppose you've thought about dinner?" Gran says.

"Take-out?" hazards Si.

Gran rolls her eyes, as though this is the most ludicrous thing she's ever heard, and then marches into the house to *rustle something up*.

Which leaves me just standing there.

Si looks up. "All right, Jess?" he says and then, with an expert kick of his left heel, he disappears under the car.

29

Si would have preferred take-out, I would have preferred take-out, but we get rice and frozen vegetables and leftover (Zoe would say *pre-owned*) chicken. Instead of discussing the babies, we talk, or rather Gran talks, about adventures with vases and coal buckets and garden sheds. I say nothing and Si doesn't say much either.

"Hope it hasn't been too dull for you," Si says, as Gran's car finally pulls out of the driveway.

"Gran told me about Clem's little dip," I jump in straight-away with this, because part of me fears that Si will disappear under the car again. Or back to the hospital. Or just disappear, plain and simple.

"Hmm?" says Si.

"Dip—in the night."

"Oh. The murmur. Clem has a VSD, a ventricular septal defect—what they used to call a hole in the heart. So there was a bit of a dip in his breathing last night. Monitor went off. But lots of kids have holes like these, apparently—and they can often spontaneously resolve. So we're not worrying too much about that at the moment."

"What time did the monitor go off?"

"I don't know—somewhere round two o'clock, I think. Why?"

You look frozen, Jess. Come on now, back to bed, it's after two o'clock.

"Are there explanations for everything, Si?" I ask then.

"You mean real ones, scientific ones?"

When I was about five, someone apparently asked me, in Mom's hearing, what "Si" was short for. And I didn't reply *Simon*, I replied *Science*. That became a family joke for a while, though I never found it very funny.

"Yes," I say, even though it's not really what I mean at all.

"There are explanations for everything we've been clever enough to work out so far," Si says. "But there's still a whole lot of stuff we don't really understand. Which is why people still believe in God."

God again.

"Or gods," he goes on.

I prepare myself for his Best Explaining Voice, though I only have myself to blame.

"Take Helios," Si says. "The Greek sun god who was supposed to drag his four-horsed chariot across the sky each morning and with it the rising sun. Each night, the ancients believed he, rather conveniently, traveled back to the east in a golden cup ready to ride across the sky the following day. That story lasted pretty much until we discovered that actually it's Earth's rotation that causes night and day. After that, Helios was out of a job."

This is quite interesting, and it's also not nearly as involved as Si's usual explanations, so I think he must be tired. In fact, when I really look at him, he seems exhausted. So I hurry up, and I tell him about waking up at the exact moment that Clem's heart was murmuring.

"Gran said it was just worry . . ." I start.

"Reasonable enough," says Si. "Though you'd also have to consider simple coincidence."

I consider it. If the flask is in some way connected to the twins, then how can it also be connected to this Rob person, or at least to the song Aunt Edie wrote for him? So maybe the howling and the waking up was just coincidence. But then again, coincidences don't normally crush your heart up.

"Coincidence is a perfectly rational explanation," says Si. "Not everything happens for a reason, you know."

My face must not be liking this answer, because he goes on. "Trouble is, human beings seem to be wired to believe just the opposite. We find it difficult to accept that things can be random. That stuff just happens."

Stuff, I suppose, like Aunt Edie writing a really important song to someone I've never heard of. Just some random piece of nothing. And I'm about to ask Si who this nothing, random Rob is, when I realize there is no way Si will know because Si and Edie—they're not even part of the same family.

So instead I say, "I don't think everything does come down to science."

"What?" says Si.

"I mean," I say, keeping calm enough to choose my example with care, "I mean, when you're in a car, just driving along, and suddenly you *feel* there's someone looking at you and you turn around, and there in the next car, there is—there's someone staring at you. That's not science, is it?"

"Sixth sense," says Si. "That's what that is." He smiles. "Which is just another way of saying we can't explain it *yet*. Bit like Helios. Maybe in a hundred or two hundred years' time—then we'll have an explanation for car staring as well."

It's his smile, his smug smile, that makes me take out the flask and put it on the kitchen table.

"What would you say," I ask and it all comes out in a rush, "if I told you that, when Clem's heart was murmuring, this old bottle started pulsing, started howling, like some wolf, crying and howling and pushing black, black stuff into my bedroom and it wasn't a dream, it really wasn't. And what if I told you that the flask can sing as well, that it can sing something bigger than God, bigger than planets, and—"

"Jess, Jess, steady." He puts his big, bony arm around my shoulder. Then he says he's sorry.

"Sorry?"

"We've all been taken up, haven't we, with the twins."

"It's not that!"

And I'm probably furious because I shouldn't be talking to him about this sort of stuff. I should be talking to Zoe, my beautiful, dancing, mirror-image friend Zoe. Only I've pushed her away, haven't I? I'm busy hating her and pushing her away when I've never needed her more than I do now. So it's all my fault that I'm alone with Si and a flask that doesn't make any sense.

Si picks up the flask.

I wait for the whoosh, the breath, and the butterfly beating under my hands. But nothing happens. The bottle, the flask, is still.

He turns it around in his hands.

"It's a beautiful thing," he says. "Eighteenth-century. Whiskey flask, if I'm not mistaken. They're called pumpkin-seed flasks, I think, because of their shape."

He is giving it a name, he's describing it, making it just some stupid historical object.

"You don't understand!" I shout.

"I'm a parent," says Si. "That's my job."

"You're not *my* parent," I shout.

I have never said this to Si before.

Ever.

Si moves a little closer. "Jess," he says. "Jess, it's all right."

But it isn't.

30

The following morning, Paddy's mother's car pulls up in our driveway at 10:30. Paddy's sitting in the front and Zoe's in the back.

"Our big day at the Buddhist Center with Onion Bhaji," announces Paddy.

"Not Onion Bhaji," says Mrs. Paddy. "Lalitavajri." Mrs. Paddy has a name of her own—Sarah, I think—but everyone calls her Mrs. Paddy because she just looks like a bigger, smilier version of Paddy himself. That big, round, cheerful beach-ball face.

I look at Paddy. He's grinning. I don't think he remembers anything that happened in the park. I don't think he remembers that I would have liked to beat him to death.

Zoe does remember. There's something flickering and anxious about her.

"In you get," says Mrs. Paddy.

I get in. I'm carrying my clipboard and my Places of Worship questionnaire.

"Hi, Jess," says Zoe.

I look out the window.

"As it's Easter," Mom said before she went into the hospital, "I don't know why you can't visit a Christian place of worship."

"It's to broaden our minds," I told her.

"Going to a Christian church would probably broaden most of you kids' minds," Si remarked.

The truth, which I didn't tell them, is that we could have chosen a church or a temple or a mosque, for that matter. We probably would have chosen a church if Em or Alice had been part of our group. But, thanks to Zoe and the issue of the vacation dates, they got paired with Jack and we got Paddy.

"I vote for Buddhism," Paddy said. "Father Neville knows a big fat zero about Buddhism, so I reckon we'll be on safe ground whatever we write."

"How're things with the babies, Jess?" Mrs. Paddy asks as we head out of the cul-de-sac.

"Fine," I say.

"And your mom?"

"Fine."

"Well, give her my very best, won't you?"

I say I will and then Mrs. Paddy leaves the subject alone. Sometimes you have to be grateful for adults.

Zoe then asks Paddy if he's seen some new movie and it turns out he has, and she stops being anxious and flickering and starts one of those conversations that go: "Oh, my gosh, wasn't it amazing when..." Or: "Yeah, but did you see— wow, I mean..." And they're completely involved in the excitement of it all and I'm still staring out the window. Which is, of course, entirely my own fault.

"You haven't seen the movie yet, Jess?" says Mrs. Paddy, picking up on my silence.

And I know the *yet* is just to let me off the hook, to make it clear that I'm not really some excluded saddo, it's just that I haven't seen the movie *yet*.

"No," I say. "Not yet."

"Bit too much going on at your house, probably," says Mrs. Paddy kindly.

Bit too much going on in my mind.

About a million years later we arrive at the Buddhist Center.

"Do you know what this building used to be?" Mrs. Paddy asks as we pull up.

"No," I say. Paddy and Zoe are still on the movie.

"A shoe factory," says Mrs. Paddy.

We tip out onto the street.

"I'll be back for you in an hour," says Mrs. Paddy.

The double doors to the center open onto a small porch with hooks for coats and racks for shoes. Beyond this the ground floor is divided into an open-plan office, a library, a tiny kitchen, and a reception area with comfy chairs and cushions and rugs that looks like someone's sitting room. We all hesitate long enough on the porch for someone to ask us our business and suggest we remove our shoes.

"We've come to see," Paddy pauses, "Lalitavajri."

"Ah, that's me." A small, smiling woman with oceans of curly orange hair rises from one of the comfy chairs. "You must be Maxim."

Paddy nods. "And this is Zoe, and Jess."

"Welcome," says Lalitavajri. "You're all very welcome." Her orange curls bob as she talks. "Shall we go to the Shrine Room, then?"

We follow her up three flights of stairs, passing a number of small rooms and closed doors, so the Shrine Room is a surprise. It runs the full length of the building, a spacious, airy room with a huge skylight beyond which frothy white clouds scud across the sky. At the far end of the room, where the altar would be in a church, there's a golden screen painted with the image of the Buddha, and arranged simply on the floor in front of him are some candles and vases of flowers. The flowers don't look store-bought, but like they've been cut from people's gardens. There are a couple of branches, heavy with pink cherry blossoms; a few hyacinths in a jelly jar; and a vase with some tall bell-shaped flowers I don't know the name of. There are also three bendy stems of eucalyptus.

Yes, eucalyptus.

Si would probably say it's just a coincidence that some of the fragrant, oily leaves Aunt Edie pressed for me to smell are here in this room where I've come only because Zoe wanted to do the project with Paddy and Paddy thinks our Religious Studies teacher is a goon, but it doesn't feel that way to me. It feels that this room is welcoming me.

And then I think a bit more about coincidences. Was it a coincidence that instead of getting Aunt Edie's piano, I got the bureau—and inside the bureau was the flask? And was it a coincidence that I found that flask? Or was that to do with my real father, whose slide rule wouldn't fit? And was it a coincidence that Gran gave me that slide rule in the first place? How far back can you trace these so-called coincidences? All the things that might have happened but didn't because you made this choice, not that one. All the coincidences that have led me into this room with the eucalyptus. And then I wish I'd brought the flask with me, instead of leaving it behind in my bedroom, thinking that this project was just some homework thing and not part of my real life. Maybe the flask would have had something to say about the eucalyptus.

"Now," says Lalitavajri, "how do you want to do this?"

"We've got a questionnaire," says Paddy, waving it as though it's a map of the entire known universe.

Lalitavajri sits down on a mat beside a golden gong and invites us to sit beside her.

"Fire away," she says.

"What drew you personally to Buddhism?" reads Paddy solemnly.

"Ah, that's easy," says Lalitavajri. "A world where kindness and generosity have the highest value."

And straightaway I feel bad, because here I am sitting cross-legged in this beautiful Shrine Room and a large part of me is still holding a grudge against Zoe. And

Paddy, for that matter. And Si, who calls himself my father, but is actually only the babies' father. And the babies themselves, for being so dangerously muddled up together. And, actually, against myself. I'm holding a grudge against myself for being so stupid and never letting go, and . . .

"And what for you is the most important belief in Buddhism?" asks Zoe.

"That we can change," says Lalitavajri. "That each one of us can be the most compassionate person we can be."

This hits me like a thrown stone. Or maybe it's not Lalitavajri's words but Zoe's glance that hits me. I'm not looking at Zoe, but she's looking at me. She's giving me one of those totally nonscientific stares, which bangs right into the heart of things.

The heart of me.

"Now," says Lalitavajri, "do you want to know about the statues?"

According to Paddy's list, we do. Also on his list are *puja*, gongs, and drums.

"And what's that?" asks Paddy.

"Incense," says Lalitavajri. "We use incense because it smells beautiful and, most importantly, it blows in all directions—like a smile. If you smile at someone they feel happy, and then they smile at someone else. Incense passes on like this."

Paddy smirks, but Lalitavajri smiles and Zoe smiles back. Quite a shy smile for someone so big and so bold and really—now I'm looking at her—so beautiful. I don't know if I'm smiling, but I hope I am.

"How do you think your shrine reflects the Buddhist faith?" reads Paddy.

"Can I ask you first how the Shrine Room strikes you?" Lalitavajri asks.

"Well, it's kind of big," says Paddy. "And empty, you know, compared with a church."

"And peaceful," I say. I'm still looking at Zoe. "Somewhere you can think."

And now Zoe feels my look and she lifts her eyes to me, all hesitant and hopeful at the same time.

"I like that," says Lalitavajri. "Western life is so busy we need a space to be peaceful. Buddhists choose for their shrines whatever's beautiful and makes them happy."

My gaze moves. It finds the eucalyptus branches and, therefore, Aunt Edie.

"Is that what the flowers are for?" I ask. "Beauty?"

"Yes," says Lalitavajri. "And they also symbolize impermanence. Nothing lives forever. All things die."

Aunt Edie again.

And also Zoe. My friendship with her. Am I going to let that die?

No.

Never.

"What do Buddhists believe happens after you die?" I ask.

Paddy looks confused. This question is not on our sheet.

"We believe in rebirth," says Lalitavajri. "After you die, you go into a state of life between life, which we call *bardo*, like night is the bardo between two days, or a dream is a bardo between two wakings."

"A join?" I say. "Do you mean a join?"

"I'm not sure about that," says Lalitavajri. "But your body falls away and your consciousness remains."

"And what happens to that consciousness?"

"It remains until it is attracted to a man and a woman having sex," says Lalitavajri, "then it goes into the soul and enters the baby."

At the word *sex* Paddy sniggers.

But Lalitavajri just goes on: "This is why babies arrive with personalities already formed."

And I'm still thinking about the bardo that (whatever Lalitavajri says) does sound like a Buddhist version of a join, and about the knotted threads of friendship and about how a consciousness might remain, when Paddy says, "Do you mean souls hang about, you know, like ghosts, they haunt you?"

"Not haunt, no. Although Buddhism does stretch the Western idea of the rational. Like some Buddhists have claimed to be able to walk through walls."

"Walk through walls!"

"I don't disbelieve this," says Lalitavajri. "Just as you can have déjà vu about someone coming into a room and then they come into a room."

Or you can have someone look at you and feel that look.

"Ghosts and the supernatural," Lalitavajri continues, "are much more real for people in the East."

And for me. And for the flask.

Paddy is scribbling in his notebook.

"Well, is that it?" asks Lalitavajri.

"Yes," says Zoe. "Thanks. Except—what does your name mean, Lalitavajri?"

"When you're ordained, you are given a new name by the person who ordains you," says Lalitavajri. "You don't know your name until this moment. You are named either for things you have achieved or for the potential seen in you.

Lalita means *she who plays* and *vajri* means *diamond thunderbolt*. The diamond thunderbolt represents reality, the truth, and unstoppable energy."

"Wow," says Paddy, looking up from his notes. "So if I was a Buddhist I could get called Supreme Striker, or something?"

"Well, maybe not something so . . ." Lalitavajri pauses, ". . . specific."

"You could be called Paddy, though," says Zoe and laughs. But she's not laughing at him, she's just laughing because everything suddenly feels relaxed, easy.

"Sorry?" says Lalitavajri.

"They call me Paddy," says Paddy. "Because..." He looks at Zoe. "Why do people call me Paddy?"

And Zoe laughs some more and Paddy grins in his Happy-to-Be-the-Center-of-Attention way, and I feel a strange warmth wash through me, which takes in, without judgment, Zoe and Paddy and Aunt Edie and the supernatural and ghosts and souls.

"Well, I need to prepare now," says Lalitavajri. "I have to lead a meditation in a minute. Although you'd be welcome to stay if you'd like. A meditation would give you a very good idea of Buddhist practice."

Paddy's face suggests that the last thing in the world he'd like to do is stay for a Buddhist meditation.

"No," he says. "Thanks. I think my mom will be back for us any minute now."

"Well, another time," says Lalitavajri. "I'm here every Tuesday if you want to change your mind."

And I think, yes. I'm going to come back here.

And I'm going to bring the flask.

31

"Well?" asks Mrs. Paddy. "How was it?"

"Buddhism," says Paddy, "is mental."

"Mental?" repeats Mrs. Paddy.

Paddy consults his notes. "'Buddhists,'" he reads, "'claim to be able to walk through walls.' 'I don't disbelieve this.' That's what she said, Onion Bhaji: 'I don't disbelieve this.'"

Mrs. Paddy laughs. "Bit like Christians, then."

"What?" says Paddy.

"Well," says Mrs. Paddy, "Christians believe that, three days after being crucified, a man rose to life again."

"That's different," says Paddy.

"Is it?" says Mrs. Paddy.

"Course," replies Paddy. "Christianity's true."

"Oh," says Mrs. Paddy. "Says who?"

"Father Neville!" says Paddy, like he's just played the Ace of Spades.

Mrs. Paddy keeps quiet.

"Anyway, it's not just the walls stuff," continues Paddy. "There's plenty of other weird stuff in Buddhism."

"Such as?"

"Such as after you die, your soul hangs about until, until..."

"Until?"

"Until a man and a woman have sex," adds Zoe helpfully.

Paddy sniggers and Zoe beams, as if the joke is all hers.

"And then," Paddy adds, "your soul goes into the baby, which means..."

"Everyone gets a pre-owned soul," concludes Zoe.

Then they both laugh and things seem to be going back to the way they were with the conversation about movies.

"Isn't that horrible?" says Paddy. "I mean, having someone else's soul inside you. How creepy is that?"

"But if it was in you," I say, maybe just because I'm beginning to wish I was back in the Shrine Room, where all things seemed possible, "it wouldn't be someone else's, it'd be yours."

"It would still be pre-owned," says Zoe.

Pre-owned is clearly going to take over from *ancient* as Zoe's new favorite word.

"Pre-owned," considers Mrs. Paddy.

"You know, like in an Xbox game or a DVD that used to belong to someone else."

"Oh," says Mrs. Paddy, "you mean secondhand."

"Pre-owned," repeats Zoe. "Disgusting. Yuck, yuck, yuck."

"Hang on," says Mrs. Paddy. "We're all a bit second-hand—*pre-owned*—if you think about it."

"What?" says Paddy.

"What?" says Zoe.

"Well, genetics," says Mrs. Paddy. "Like you have your dad's eye color, Maxim, and my face shape and your grandad's laugh, and you don't think of that as disgusting, do you?"

Paddy looks like, all of a sudden, he's not quite so sure about this.

"So why would it seem so strange," Mrs. Paddy adds, "to share a soul with someone?"

I look at Mrs. Paddy, trying to work out whether she believes what she's saying or is just doing what Si calls Playing Devil's Advocate, which is saying stuff you don't believe just for the sake of A Discussion. I decide she's being truthful.

"Well, it might not even be the soul of someone in your family," says Paddy. "I mean, you might get the soul of an ant."

Paddy having the soul of an ant could explain a lot of things.

"I didn't know Buddhism did the animal thing," says Mrs. Paddy. "Are you sure about that?"

"Or what if it was the ants who were having sex?" says Zoe (and I'm hoping *sex* isn't going to become her new word). "I mean, that would be even worse. You'd end up inside the ant."

"On the other hand," says Paddy, "you'd probably be so much cleverer than all the other ants, you'd be Ant Emperor and then you could marshal the forces of ants worldwide and take over the universe."

"Who says souls are clever?" says Mrs. Paddy.

"What?" says Paddy.

"What?" says Zoe.

"Well, souls can be many things," says Mrs. Paddy, "but I'm not sure clever is one of them."

I'm beginning to change my mind about Mrs. Paddy. Other than Si (who's a life-form that would probably baffle even Pug), most adults I know talk about Nothing in Particular. They can talk about Nothing in Particular for hours on end: homework, washing dishes, taxes, the education system, lawnmowers, lost keys, and the grocery list, and here is Mrs. Paddy, who I've always thought of as simply a larger version of Paddy, actually being interesting. Thoughtful, even. I'm not sure I should be calling her Mrs. Paddy anymore. I think I should be calling her Sarah, because even if it turns out that she has a pre-owned soul, I think she definitely has a brain all her own.

"What do you mean?" I ask her.

"Well, you hear of 'old souls,' don't you?" says Sarah. "Sometimes people look into the eyes of babies and say, 'Well, here's an old soul,' as though that baby has some sort of wisdom they couldn't possibly have unless they'd been around once or twice before. But 'clever' souls—I don't know."

"What's the difference between being clever and being wise?" asks Paddy.

"Quite a lot," says Sarah.

32

When we get back to the house, it's Gran who opens the door. Si has obviously returned to the hospital. Gran invites Sarah in for tea and that leaves me with Zoe—but also with Paddy. I wish Paddy would just Go Away, I wish he'd disappear in a Puff of Smoke. It's so difficult to think around someone who treats the whole universe as a joke. And I need to do some thinking and I need to check in with Zoe, to see how we are.

I also need to be with the flask.

But Zoe's already bounding up the stairs to my bedroom and Paddy's following her, and I'm following both of them.

Why am I always following people?

It's Zoe, of course, who's first into the room.

"Wow," she says. "Will you look at that!"

We look.

As I managed to get up and leave the house this morning without opening the curtains, there is nothing in my room but darkness.

Nothing, that is, but the flask.

The flask is sitting on my computer table, swirling clouds and clouds of fluorescent green.

And Zoe is looking straight at it.

Zoe can see the flask—she can see inside it!

"Jeez," says Paddy. "That's amazing!"

And Paddy—Paddy can see inside it, too.

Paddy!

I feel something thrill up my spine. I am not alone. I am not alone! They can see it. I am not going mad. I am not the only person in the universe who can see beyond science, beyond Si, just…beyond. And, all at once, I love Zoe! I even love Paddy.

"What on earth is it?" Paddy is advancing into the room, making for the green swirl of the flask.

Zoe moves, too, she's almost dancing toward the glow. But I remain where I am, stuck in the doorway, because suddenly I think there's something wrong, something unholy about the flask and its color. It's not making me feel good, not like the fizz-heart blue. It's coming to me slowly, oh so slowly, across the room. I'm fighting to think exactly what it is that's wrong and then I get it: Until now the flask has only held natural colors—the iridescence of pearls, the blue of the sky, the gray of storm clouds, the purple of bruises, the black of night. This green is alien, lurid, electric.

Paddy arrives at the computer table. He stretches out his hand.

"Wait," I cry.

But he's already lifting the flask, holding it in his hands.

"Oh, you're joking," he exclaims.

At desk level are the four flashing, fluorescent green lights of my Internet router. In his hands is a colorless flask.

"It's just a stupid old bottle," he says.

"Give it to me," says Zoe.

He gives it to her, all interest gone. She places it down in front of the router again, watches the clouds gather and swirl, the green computer lights refracted through the uneven contours of the glass. Then she picks the flask up, puts it down again, just to check.

"Oh," she says, equally disappointed. "Just for a moment I thought we might all have walked through a wall, actually found something special, a genie in a bottle. Wouldn't that have been something?"

"Me," I say. I've begun to unlock. I'm going across that room faster than light. "Give it to me!"

"Calm down," says Paddy, sensing my urgency. "It's not going anywhere."

But it is going somewhere. In fact, it's already gone. I know even before I lay my hands on the bottle: The flask is empty. The butterfly breath has gone.

33

I snatch the flask from Zoe's hands, stare down its glass throat, just like I did when I couldn't believe the cork was missing.

"There's nothing in there," says Paddy, as though I'm a total imbecile. "It was just the lights. The lights of the computer."

"But what if it had been for real?" says Zoe. "Imagine that. Our very own genie. We could have asked for whatever we wanted."

"Correction," says Paddy, "*I* could have asked for whatever I wanted. I was the one that touched it first, you know, as in me: master, you: slave."

"Not *me* slave," says Zoe. "*Genie* slave."

"No," I roar. "Not a slave. Not now, not ever. The biggest, freest, most extraordinary being in the universe."

"What?" says Paddy.

"What?" says Zoe.

"In this bottle, in this flask. Big as a storm wind, tiny as a baby's breath. It was here!"

Zoe and Paddy exchange glances.

They think I've lost it.

Paddy puts his head to one side. "Jess," he says solemnly, "did you bang your head when you stepped through one of those Buddhist walls?"

And Zoe laughs.

She *laughs*.

"Tell you what," adds Paddy, "why don't we shed some light on this sad little scene?" He opens the curtains.

And there it is, there on the windowsill, like some curled, pearly cat.

"Look," I shriek, spilling over with happiness. "Look!"

They look.

"Oh," says Paddy. "I see."

He sees!

He leans forward, putting his hand straight through the pearly cat, and knocks on the windowpane.

"Sam," he yells. "Look, it's Sam!"

Zoe joins him at the window. The pearly cat has reformed, close to the glass, but away from Paddy's huge, clumsy hands. Zoe will see it. Surely Zoe will see it?

She looks straight at the pulsing light, straight through it, out over the rooftops, down the street, and toward the rising mound of the park.

"And Alice," she says. "That's Alice with him, isn't it?"

"Yeah," says Paddy. "Come on—what are we waiting for?"

Paddy isn't waiting for much. He takes off down the stairs and Zoe would be with him, with hardly a backward glance, only I grab her elbow.

"Wait!" I cry.

"Huh?"

"Don't go," I say.

"Why?"

I mean to say, *There's so much I need to share with you.* And, *Please, because it's scary having to deal with this all by myself.*

What I actually say is "Don't go. Don't go with him."

"With Paddy?"

"Yes. No. I mean it, please." And I give her one of those looks that, between friends, don't usually need words. The look that says simply: *Be there for me.*

"You're not making sense," says Zoe.

"Wait," I say again, unwilling to let go of her arm in case she just runs straight out of my life, but needing to get something from the bureau. I scrabble behind the arched door flanked by the two wooden pillars. "Look."

She looks. I'm showing her the braided bracelet of pink and purple she made for me in fourth grade.

"So?" she says.

"Best friends," I say. "That's what you said. When I wanted to wind Em in, when I wanted to make a bracelet for all three of us. 'Don't you understand about best friends?' That's what you said."

"I was nine," says Zoe, incredulous. "Ten, max. What are you talking about?"

"Zoe!" yells Paddy from the front door.

"Look, either come or don't," says Zoe. "I don't care one way or the other. But don't get all serious on me. Since when were we joined at the hip?"

34

I stand stunned. Loneliness never felt this big or close before. If it wasn't for the relief of getting rid of Paddy, I'd cry.

"Are you okay?" I finally manage to ask the iridescent breath on the windowsill.

No reply.

"I'm sorry about, you know, Paddy's hand."

No reply.

"He's got stupidly big hands. Should really be a goalie, not a striker." I'm making light of it, but it doesn't feel light.

"Why do you go there?" I ask then. "To the windowsill?"

No reply.

"You're not a, you know, consciousness, are you?"

In the Shrine Room the concept of a consciousness sounded quite reasonable, ordinary even. In my bedroom it sounds ridiculous.

"Or a soul," I try. "An old soul. Like Mrs. Paddy said?"

No reply.

Sometimes I think I made up not just Spike, but half of the universe. The half that doesn't fit.

You're not making sense. You're not making sense.

I go to the window myself. I look out. Paddy and Zoe are already halfway down the street.

On the windowsill, the butterfly breath continues to pulse quietly.

"Are you looking for something? Well, I know you can't *look*, exactly . . ." Do I know that? What I mean is, I can't explain how something without eyes can look, but then I can't explain déjà vu, or the car staring thing, or . . .

The breath seems quite calm, but I feel that it must keep going to the windowsill for a reason.

Not everything happens for a reason.

Shut up, Si.

Perhaps what I'm really saying is that if it were me with my nose pressed up against the glass, then I'd be looking out, wouldn't I? I'd be searching for something. Trapped behind glass (the glass of the flask, the glass of the window-pane), I'd be all full of longing.

"What is it you want?" I ask. "What are you looking for?"

No reply.

"Or is it who? Who are you looking for? Is it Rob?"

No reply.

"Who is Rob, anyhow?"

No reply.

"If I knew what you wanted," I hear myself say, "I'd find it. I'd give it."

The light trembles. No, it shimmers, all of the colors inside it increasing in intensity.

Part of me wants to touch each of those shimmering pearly colors, the vivid threads of blues and greens, the opalescent pinks and whites. Touch them not with some fat fist, but just with the lightest of fingertips, to give some reassurance, to say: *I am here. I am with you*—as Spike was for me. Though this urge to touch also feels intrusive, like touching the join between my brothers. So I put my hands together, cup them, like Mr. Brand did when he tried to catch a sunbeam. Only I'm not trying to catch anymore. I'm trying to offer, like you do with a gift or a prayer.

And then it comes to me, the light: It touches me, it settles not beneath my hands, but in them. Like my hands are a nest.

35

Perhaps the breath lies in my cupped hands for just a few seconds, or maybe it's a minute, or five minutes, or even an hour. I can't say; I lose track of time. Nothing seems to matter very much anymore, and I have a sense of peace and happiness and of being full up, but not like when you've eaten too much, just in the way of being complete, of not needing to worry or search for anything anymore.

Then, of course, there is a whoosh and a whistle and the breath flies back, as it always does, to the flask. But I am still in a slightly dreamlike state and my mind washes around until it finds something on which it can settle, and that thing is names.

Lalitavajri.

Supreme Striker.

Zoe.

Jess.

Jessica.

Even though this has been my name since I was born, I've never thought about it before and I don't know what it means, so I take myself to the computer and do some Googling. The first site I try says *Jessica* means *wealthy*, which doesn't feel like me at all. But what was I expecting? What name would be right for me? *She who is alone? She who never quite seems to fit? She who makes stuff up?* Next I Google *Zoe. Zoe* is apparently Greek for *life*, and that sounds like a much stronger, more interesting name than mine. But then I suppose Zoe *is* life; she's just brimming with it, which is why I love her.

Yes, despite everything, I love her.

I move on to Richie and Clem. I can't help myself. *Richie* is the Scottish form of *Richard* and means *ruler of power*, whereas *Clem* comes from *Clement*, meaning *merciful, gentle*. Clem, my gentle little clam.

Then I realize what all this name stuff is actually about. The breath. Because when I look down at the pearly, pulsing thing, I think it should have a name. I think I shouldn't be calling it *Thing* or *It*, or even *The Breath*, because it's too big and important for that. And if Lalitavajri can have a name made up for her, why can't I make one up for my breath?

No, not *my* breath. *The* breath—the biggest and smallest thing in the world.

What should you call such a breath?

And I want to call it (or is it actually him? Or her?) *Storm*, but that's too violent, doesn't describe the lounging on the windowsill, the tender nesting. So I think of *Snuffle*, and that's too small and far too like a kitten, and I begin to think this naming stuff isn't as easy as you think and no wonder my parents stopped at Jess.

Then the word *bardo* pushes itself into my mind and I start some more Googling, and I get a heap of stuff I don't understand like *simplex physics* (which doesn't seem so simplex to me) and *octonionic space-time* (which Si would probably understand perfectly) and also a big wiki article on the Six Bardos and other *intermediate or liminal states*.

Liminal.

What about that as a name? It doesn't sound like a boy's name or a girl's name. And that's good. Because, if we're talking bardos, my beautiful butterfly breath seems like a bardo between genders: not exactly a girl, but not a boy either. Something that could be both, perhaps—or neither. On the negative side, Liminal sounds a bit like a lemon. But it means *threshold* (Si would be proud of my research), and that's what I think my breath is: on the threshold of something, though I don't know what.

"How would Liminal be?" I ask the flask. "You know, as a name?"

No reply. Not even the slightest twitch or swirl or glint of a fishtail.

And I'm just about to justify my choice, start being persuasive, when I remember how I felt when Si took the flask in his hands and declared it to be an eighteenth-century whiskey bottle, a pumpkinseed flask. How he tried to tack it down, see around all its corners, know what it was, only he didn't know at all.

And I think, maybe I'm just trying to do the same thing. I'm trying to know something that perhaps can't be known. And what this flask and its inhabitant need more than anything else is just some space, some peace and quiet to be whatever—whoever—it is. Free from people like me trying to tape up its throat or slap a name on its ever-changing colors.

Which is, I realize suddenly, not unlike the way I sometimes feel myself.

That sometimes I'm small and sometimes I contain mountains.

How do you put a name on that?

36

Gran calls up the stairs to say she just has to pop to the store and will I be all right alone for a moment?

I call back *yes* although, of course, I will not be alone.

As soon as I hear the front door close, I take the flask downstairs and set it on the piano. Another thing I hate about the Tinkerbell piano, other than the fact that it has two nonworking notes, is that it stands in the hall. Yes, the hall. I think a piano should be in a room where you can go in and close the door, where you can be all lost in that piano for a while, with nobody coming and going and nobody interrupting and nobody hearing anything you play until you're ready to play it to them.

Si, who understands many things, does not understand this.

Si says, "This space in the hall, it's a perfect piano-sized space. What are you complaining about?"

I'm complaining about them listening in. Them hearing me struggle to express whatever's going on in my heart, here in the hall. Which is why I often play when people are out. Like now.

I've been making up songs since I was about six.

"They just flow out of her," says Mom.

But actually they don't. They come very quietly and from somewhere far away and deep, and often I don't quite hear them right at first. I have to be very quiet and still and strain to listen. Sometimes there's just a note or two, sometimes a chord, and the words, if there are words, they don't come until the tune has almost finished itself. Because it's only when the song is almost complete that I begin to know what it might be about.

Today the song, which has been whispering to me for a couple of days now, comes in small and fragile. I want to say to it, *Be brave, I'm listening for you, I'll find you*, but sometimes it doesn't work like that. Sometimes a song has to find its own bravery.

I don't know how long I sit at the piano, listening, and letting my hands wander gently, carefully over the keys. Then I hear a phrase I recognize, and I can put my fingers and my mind straight on it. But it's only when I play it out loud that I hear what it is. It's a hair from the lion's mane in Aunt Edie's song "For Rob." It's the smallest, tiniest thread and probably nobody would recognize it but me—but there it is, right inside this new song. I listen even harder, expecting perhaps to hear other notes from "For Rob"—a spark of sky, a blade of grass—but I don't. Instead there's something else coming, something broader, richer, happier than anything in "For Rob," and then I think perhaps it's some blossom from the cherry trees in Aunt Edie's "Spring Garden." Only I can't quite catch it, and the more I reach for it, the more it pulls away. I want to bring the two things together, the sadness of "For Rob" and the other happier thing; I want to make them fit, find their harmonies. But the harder I try, the more the music resists me. The song says, *Do not summon me now, Jess, you do not know who I am.* So I go quiet and patient again, start listening, whisper back to the song: *I'll wait.*

I'll wait as long as it takes.

"Oh, good girl, Jess," Gran bustles through the front door with a bag of groceries in each hand. "I meant to tell you to get on with your practice."

Practice.

I get up and shut the lid of the piano.

37

In the evening, Mom calls. Her voice from the hospital sounds stretched thin.

"Are you all right, Jess?"

"I'm fine."

Si must have told my mother about her strange daughter and the singing flask. Can that conversation really have only been last night? It seems like a million years ago.

"I know it must be difficult for you . . ."

"It's fine, Mom. I'm fine."

"Sure?"

"I'm sure."

"You know I love you?"

"Yes."

"And Si loves you, too."

Do I know that?

"He really does."

I say nothing.

"I'm sorry I can't come home," says Mom. "Not yet, anyway."

"It's okay. I'm fine. How are the babies?"

She lets out a little sigh. "We had some results today. Some of the tests came back."

"Yes?"

"They share a liver, Jess. Separate hearts, but only one liver." She pauses. "Do you know what that means?"

"Yes," I say. Because Si has told me. The more organs the twins share, the more difficult any separation is. "Why can't they stay together?" I burst out then. "Why can't they?"

"I don't know," Mom says. "I don't know anything anymore."

And then, very softly, she begins to cry.

38

Si has barely been home since I informed him he was not my parent, and when he does finally appear, he goes straight into the garage and gets out Roger the Wreck's dolly.

"I have to fix the timing chain," he announces.

It's the timing chain that drives the camshaft that, in turn, opens the valves that let the fuel mixture in and the exhaust out. I know this because, for nearly a year, Si's been talking about the function and importance of a timing chain and how this particular one could break at any time on account of The Rattle.

"Hear that rattle, Jess?"

Actually, no. Mainly because this boneshaker of a car makes so many bangs and clatters and rattles that distinguishing The Rattle from any number of other rattles is beyond me.

"It's a very distinctive sound," says Si. "Like a bike chain slopping."

And the faster the car goes, the louder the rattle.

Apparently.

Anyway, here we are on Good Friday, and Si is all cover-alled up with his tools laid out beside him.

"I have to fix it today," says Si.

For a whole year he hasn't fixed it.

Why now?

And then I have a totally nonscientific, nonrational thought about the timing chain. Maybe that's why it's called a timing chain, because the timing is crucial. Si has to fix the chain today, otherwise … otherwise …

Otherwise what?

The monsters will get us.

Have you ever played the Sidewalk Crack Game? Zoe and I used to play it all the time. *If we step on a single crack in the sidewalk on the way to the park, the monsters will get us.* At five, Zoe and I knew every crack between the cul-de-sac and the swings. We never stepped on a single one, and that's how we kept safe.

I decide the broken timing chain is a crack. If we can mend it today, Si and I, then the monsters won't come. They won't get me, and more importantly, they won't get the twins.

"Do you need some help?" I ask Si.

He stands quite still then and looks me straight in the eye and I hold his gaze. Si could win an Olympic medal for talking, but he doesn't talk now. Which makes me want to say I'm sorry about the parent thing, but I don't know how to, so I just go to the back of the garage and find a pair of blue coveralls. As I roll up the sleeves and the legs, I remember how this man, who is not my father, used to lift me onto his shoulders at the end of a walk too long for my toddler legs. I remember how he was never impatient with me when, with Mom already waiting in the car, I cried for him to take me back into the house so I could check on Spike. And—speaking of monsters—I remember how he would make sure to close the door of my closet at night because he knew I feared the things that lurked there in the dark. I return to Si looking like the Michelin Man. I still don't say anything to him, but he speaks to me.

"Thank you, Jess," he says. "Thank you very much. I could really use some help today."

And he smiles one of those smiles like incense.

"First up, the radiator," says Si.

He begins by loosening the radiator hoses, talking as he goes, explaining what he's doing, and I'd forgotten this about his maintenance work, how very instructive it is, as though he's passing on wisdom that will, one day, allow me to construct an entire engine from scrap metal and memory alone.

I help him lift out the radiator.

"Now for the crank pulley bolts," he says. "Pass me the wrench."

And I do. Like some junior doctor in an operating room.

Which, of course, makes me think about the twins. Though, in fact, I'm never not thinking about the twins.

"Mom told me," I say, "what the tests said. That they share a liver."

"Yes," says Si. "Not great news."

"So what do the doctors say now?" I ask. "About the operation?"

"Depends which one you ask," says Si, as he puts metal to metal and turns. "At the last count there were about twenty-two of them."

"Twenty-two!"

"Four surgeons, four anesthesiologists . . . Can you pass me that hammer?" I pass him the little copper mallet and he begins a soft tap-tap-tapping. "Remember, always go gently on a crank pulley," he says, tap-tap-tapping. "Although they won't all be in the operating room at once. They have to work in shifts. Ah, here we go." The crank pulley comes out. "Now for the timing chain cover. Ratchet, please, and socket."

There are about twenty small tubular attachments in the socket tray. "What size?" I ask.

"Nine-sixteenths should do it, I reckon."

I pass him the right socket and he screws it onto the ratchet head.

"But when are they going to do it?" I ask. "The operation?"

"Not for a few months still," says Si. His arm is deep inside the car engine. "It's safer for the babies if they can grow a bit first. Hmm. I think I'm going to have to go at this from underneath."

I get out the jack for him and wheel it under a jack point.

"Haven't forgotten everything, then, have you?" says Si. And he's pleased with me, and right now I like him being pleased with me.

He cranks the car up and then goes to fetch the dolly.

And with the dolly come the twins, of course, one underneath the car and one hopping about for a wrench.

"And what," I say, "what are their..." Only I can't finish the sentence.

"Chances?" says Si. "Good. Basically good, I think. But no one's really prepared to stick their neck out. There are so many different factors to be taken into consideration."

He slips himself under the car and I go with him, elbowing my way along the oily cardboard so I'm lying right beside him. Almost as close, I think, as Clem is to Richie. But not quite.

"If it was just their livers that were joined, that would be one thing. But it's also the lower sternum and the ribs and some part of the abdominal cavity and..." He pauses to fit the socket head over the lowest bolt.

"But the heart, they don't share a heart," I say. I hadn't realized I'd been hanging on to this fact. "That's the main thing, isn't it?"

"Well, apparently there may be a small joining of the pericardium, after all." He begins to turn the wrench. "That's the covering of the heart. And Clem's VSD doesn't help, and..." He spins the ratchet. "Ow! Ow! Jeez!" A stream of curses follows.

Instead of catching the bolt, he's caught his knuckles.

He kicks himself out from under the car, still cursing, and I scuttle out behind him.

His knuckles are bleeding and I don't like the blood, not because my stepfather is hurting, but because the blood came when he was speaking about Clem and that brings the monsters closer. I mean, why did it have to be Clem, the weaker twin, the one who *dips*—why did it have to be Clem's name all spilled and spattered with blood?

"Half-inch," says Si, sucking at his fist. "Should have used a half-inch, not a nine-sixteenth. Idiot."

I need to do something to help. "Want me to get you a Band-Aid?"

"Yes—over there." He nods at a cabinet at the other end of the garage, beneath the Morris Authorized Dealer sign and a bunch of red onions. "Top drawer, I think."

I find an old box with a random selection of different-sized Band-Aids and help him patch himself up. Mom would have made him wash his hands first.

"First rule of mechanics—check your socket size. Right. Let's try again."

I hand him a half-inch socket and we resume positions underneath the car. This time the bolts come away easily.

He removes the timing chain cover and then slides out again.

"We'll do the timing marks from up top," he says. "They need to be lined up and the crank has to be at TDC," he says. "Do you remember TDC?"

"Top Dead Center," I say.

"That's my girl!" he says.

His girl.

He works in silence for a while, but his mind, not unlike mine, remains with the twins, because then he says, "There'll be a rehearsal operation first."

"What?"

"A rehearsal. When they go through everything. Who's going to do what on the day. So, unlike us, they don't end up with the wrong-sized socket."

"But what if they do end up with something wrong?"

He pauses. "They won't. That's exactly the point of the rehearsal." He smiles, but this time it's a little tight. "Come on, now—chain tensioner."

He fiddles with something I can't see and the timing chain comes free. It looks like nothing much; it looks like a slightly bigger version of a bicycle chain. Yet it can rattle and break and make the engine fail. The car remains all mixed up with Clem.

"Now all we have to do," Si says, holding the new chain, "is fit this little beauty and redo everything in reverse order."

But it doesn't happen quite that way, because when he's fitted the new chain and checked the timing marks again and refitted the tensioner, he has to turn the crankshaft two revolutions, and when he does that one of the chain teeth jumps and the timing marks are out of alignment.

"Typical!" he says. He looks at his watch. "Maybe we should break," he says. "Get some lunch."

"No," I say, "we have to finish it. Get the job done. Now."

"Since when did you become chief mechanic?" he says, but he's smiling as he starts all over again.

I wonder then what will happen with the babies if something goes wrong, because an operation is not like a car, and the doctors won't be able to just start it all over again, will they?

Eventually Si gets the cover back on and checks and seals the new gasket so it doesn't leak oil. Then he reassembles the radiator. It's late, late into the afternoon now.

"Now for the moment of truth," Si says, and he starts the engine.

The car coughs and spits and rattles and then roars to life.

"Fantastic," he says. "Listen."

I listen.

"Not a peep," he says, face beaming.

So we won this one, I think, despite the blood on Clem. We've kept the monsters at bay.

Si turns the engine off, gets out, and pats the car's hood. "My perfect, perfect little moggie."

39

I think about perfect.

I think about this Morris Traveller 1000, Si's little moggie, which still rattles and bangs and splutters, but is—according to its loving owner—perfect.

I think about the flask, which is slightly lopsided, the glass of one of its shoulders slightly thicker than the other. I actually go upstairs and hold it in my hand. The little seed fish (which aren't swimming today) are actually blemishes, bubbles in the glass that shouldn't really be there, mistakes in the glassmaking process. These imperfections are also the beautiful part of the flask. They are what shimmer and shine as the flask breathes, lives.

Then I think about my brothers lying together in their cot. They are not perfect; they are not even *normal*, according to Paddy.

They're not any old twins. They're Siamese.

In the old days, before medicine could make people perfect, conjoined twins stayed the way they were born. Like Chang and Eng. Si showed me pictures of them online. Born in Thailand (or Siam, as it was then) in 1811, Chang and Eng were joined down the chest in just the same way as Richie and Clem. They began life in the circus, just like Paddy said, being exhibited as "curiosities" all over the world. But soon they left, bought a plantation, ran their own businesses, got married to sisters, and had twenty-one children between them. They were happy and lived until they were seventy-two.

No one tried to separate Chang and Eng. They were allowed to stay together.

Then I wonder—what's more perfect? Two little boys separated, or two little boys joined? And I try to imagine a world where everyone is born conjoined and only once every thousand, thousand births, do separate human beings arrive. Then I watch conjoined people bending over the separate cots and gasping. And, all at once, a team of twenty-two doctors (in eleven pairs of two) arrives to sew those little babies together again, so nobody will ever know they were born apart. And when the doctors have done their work and it's all gone all right, I hear the relatives heave sighs of relief and say, "What perfect little boys."

40

While I'm on perfect, I think about Zoe. I haven't spoken to her since I discovered her name means *life*, since she shouted over her shoulder, *Since when were we joined at the hip?*

And she hasn't spoken to me either.

This friend I made in kindergarten. This person who bounds up my stairs and into my life and with whom I've been as close as Richie is to Clem.

I decide to call her. I decide to tell her about her beautiful life-giving name.

"Hello," I say brightly.

"Hi," she says, but she sounds suspicious, like I'm just about to to get all serious on her again.

So what I actually say is "They share more organs than we thought." It just sort of falls out of me, so maybe I was always going to say this.

"What?" says Zoe.

"The twins. They share ribs and a bit of their lower sternum and their abdominal cavity and a bit of pericardium, which is the heart. Their heart."

"Oh," says Zoe.

"And also their liver. They only have one liver."

"Urgh," she says. "That's gross."

Gross.

I hang up.

She calls back.

"Look," she says, "I didn't mean gross, like . . . *gross.*"

"What did you mean?"

"I meant, you know . . . Nothing against your brothers or anything. And I don't have a problem with internal organs, but *livers.* I mean, nobody wants to talk about stuff like that, do they?"

I do. I have to, otherwise it all just sits like a heavy red stone in my brain.

"Since 1950," I say to my friend Zoe, "seventy-five percent of separations result in one live twin." This isn't one of Si's statistics. It's one I found myself. Online.

"Seventy-five percent?" queries Zoe, as if she's trying to do the math.

"Yes," I say. "Or, to put it another way, seventy-five percent of the time, when they separate people who've been"—I pause—"so close . . . one twin dies."

"Oh," she says.

"So who do you think it'll be?" I ask.

"Jess . . ." she begins. "*Jess* . . ."

"Who?" I say.

"Do we have to—"

"Who?" I interrupt. "Which one?"

"Neither—probably neither. Jess—what's gotten into you?"

"You have to say: Richie or Clem."

Zoe or Jess?

"Why are you asking me this stuff?"

I have a vision: me on my cell phone, Zoe on hers. No wire between us, but joined nonetheless, joined by some powerful but invisible signal, and if I press the red button on my phone, that signal will just snap off, snap away.

I press the red button.

There should be silence. So how come I hear the rip of a surgeon's knife?

41

The following day we go to the hospital.

"We're going to bring your mom home," says Si.

"And the babies?"

"No, not the babies. Not yet. And Mom only for the afternoon. Apparently I can't be trusted to bring in the right change of clothes."

In my pocket I have the flask. It has been quiet and almost colorless every day since I tried to paste the name *Liminal* onto it. But I'm aware of the breath, its quiet ins and outs. Sometimes I think I even hear it when I'm sleeping. Which is impossible.

Only, recently, I've begun to believe that nothing is impossible.

Si turns the radio on and we don't talk much and eventually we arrive at the hospital and ascend fifteen floors in the elevator.

In the Intensive Care Baby Unit, Mom is not on a bed anymore; she's sitting in a chair beside the babies. I've been doing a lot of worrying about the babies, but maybe not enough about Mom. She looks drained and thin.

"Here you are," she says, and she gets up to greet me. "Missed you." She gives me a hug and I think I can feel her bones.

"Here's your big sister, boys," she says to the babies.

I look into the incubator and I expect to see that the twins have grown, because babies do grow fast, everyone says so. *My, how they've grown!* But my brothers still look tiny, their heads still not filling their tiny knitted hats. I pay particular attention to Clem—is he really smaller than his brother? I don't know, maybe not, but his little hand is on Richie's shoulder, so it still looks like he's holding on.

Both babies are asleep, facing each other, their little mouths occasionally munching at precisely the same moment, as if they are having exactly the same eating dream. And then I wonder about their dreams. Do they share dreams, or do they have separate ones?

"Happy dreams," I whisper down at them. "Have happy dreams." And they munch and their eyelids flicker, too, and I suddenly feel overwhelmed with love for them.

It seems no time at all before a nurse comes to wheel them away for yet more tests.

"They'll have done so many tests by the time they get out of here," jokes Si, "they'll be able to go straight to college."

The nurse laughs, but Mom doesn't. She just watches the babies leave as if somebody were wheeling away her life.

"Come on, now," says Si. "Let's make the most of the time."

He takes Mom's suitcase and her hand and helps her into the elevator.

When we get down to ground level and the doors swish open to the outside world, Mom seems to stumble a little, blink in the daylight.

"Are you all right?" says Si. "Are you sure you want to make the journey? I mean, for such a short time?"

"Sure," says Mom. She nods at me. "I have to see my other baby, don't I?"

Si helps her into the car and we begin the journey home.

"It's amazing," says Mom.

"What?" asks Si.

"The world," says Mom, as if she's been gone from it for a hundred years. "It's so bright. And big." She pauses. "And busy." Then she turns around and looks at me. "And you, Jess, even you've changed."

"Have I?"

"Yes—you've grown up a bit, I think."

And I don't know if she means *grown up—mature*, or *grown up—taller* or even just *grown up compared with the tiny, tiny twins*, and I don't have time to think about this because Si butts in with: "Jess helped me with Roger the Wreck yesterday. We did the timing chain."

"The timing chain!" Mom exclaims. "So you've finally done it? Turned Roger the Wreck into, well, just Roger?"

"Well," says Si, slightly taken aback. "There's always more one can do on a moggie."

Mom laughs and touches him very lightly on the back of the neck.

And, just for a moment, everything feels all right.

42

Si asks Mom what she wants to do with her few hours at home.

"I want to eat fresh vegetables," says Mom, "and go to church."

There are very few vegetables served in the hospital, apparently, and only frozen ones. Mom wants to eat fresh zucchini and fresh onions and fresh tomatoes and fresh mushrooms.

"And green beans," says Mom. "I could kill for some green beans."

So Si says he will drop her at the church and go on a vegetable hunt.

"Will you come with me, Jess?" Mom asks.

Mom doesn't go to church so much for the the services, but for the candles. When we're on vacation, she goes into every church we pass. She lights candles in memory of my father, and I light them, too.

"Yes," I say. "Of course."

Si drops us at St. Nicholas' Church, which is a small flint building with a square tower.

"Do you know what day it is?" she asks as we enter.

"Saturday," I say.

"Holy Saturday," she says. "The day between Good Friday and Easter Sunday. The day of Christ's entombment."

"A bardo, then," I say.

"Huh?" says Mom, but she's not really listening.

We're whispering, even though there is no one in this quiet place but us. The last time I was in this church was at Christmas, when it blazed with light and golden angels and dark holly, and statues of the Holy Family stood in real straw. Now the church is stripped; there are no flowers, the altar is bare, the cross covered in a black cloth.

Mom takes a seat at the back of the church, as though she hasn't quite got the energy to go to the front yet, and I sit beside her. She takes a kneeler and sinks down, head in her hands. I don't know what she's praying about, but I can imagine.

I don't take a kneeler. I just sit on the hard wooden pew and look at the dense gloom in the church. I wish it were

Easter Sunday, I wish someone would just roll back the rock like they did in front of Jesus' tomb and everything would be light and bright again forever.

But maybe nothing's forever.

Zoe.

She's not forever; she's moving on, moving away from me. And if she isn't going all of her own accord, then I'm pushing her, aren't I? I'm just putting the knife in and hanging up the phone to show her I don't care, which just shows how much I do care. Can't she see that?

Then I get cross with myself for sitting in a church and thinking about Zoe when my brothers are probably dying. How can Zoe be as important as the twins? I mean, our relationship, Zoe's and mine, it's hardly life or death, is it?

But that's how it sometimes feels to me.

In fact, more than this. It feels that my join with Zoe, which, okay, didn't start at birth, but was certainly there by the time we were both four, that join sometimes gets all muddled up in my head with the web that joins my brothers. As though what happens between me and Zoe will affect what happens to Richie and Clem.

Yeah, right.

Mom picks herself up from her prayer and pushes the kneeler back under the pew.

"The Anglo-Saxons believed," she says, "that life is just the flight of a sparrow through a great lighted hall, that we come from the dark and will return to the dark."

I don't know what this means and I don't ask her, because she looks so sad and I know that she's been to her place when kneeling, just as I've been to mine, and it's probably a private place.

We go together and then toward the front of the church where there's a candle rack, four rows of little black metal dishes with black metal candle spikes in the middle, and a locked box for donations. There are normally one or two pale, thin candles burning here, but today there are none and Mom hesitates, as though maybe we shouldn't be lighting candles here on Holy Saturday, maybe we should wait until the Easter light comes in on Sunday.

But she won't be here on Easter Sunday. And there are candles waiting beneath the rack, so she takes three and puts money in the box.

Three candles. She has never taken three candles before.

"First," she says, "for your father."

I hold the candle and she strikes the match.

"For Jeremy," she says as the wick catches.

"For Dad," I say, and I push the thin wax end onto the

spike. You mustn't push too hard; the candles are so thin that if you do, they can split and fall.

There's a moment's silence between us and then she says she wants to light candles for the babies. And part of me wants to stop her. I want to say, *We can't light a candle for Dad, who's dead, and for the babies, who...*

Mom interrupts my thought. "I'll do one for Richie. Will you do Clem's?"

Which brings me the monsters.

Because sometimes, when you light one candle from another, one of the flames gutters, it dies.

"Yes," I say, "I'll do it."

The Sidewalk Crack Game.

Mom holds Richie's candle. I hold Clem's. If either of the flames gutters...

I light mine first, from Dad's, and I do it very, very carefully and the flame leaps up. It burns strong and bright, and I let out the breath I've been holding and push the candle end very gently onto the spike.

Clem lives.

Then Mom takes Richie's candle and lights it from Clem's and it doesn't take immediately, so she pushes down a little harder and there's a sudden fizz and when she takes the candle away, Richie's candle is lit and Clem's is extinguished.

Clem's candle is dead.

Clem again. Why Clem? The monsters laugh, just like they did in the garage when Clem got all spattered with Si's blood.

I hear myself gasp, but Mom just says, "Oh, shoot. Let's try that again."

She places Richie's candle on the rack and relights Clem's from Dad's. It burns brightly, innocently.

"There," she says. "God bless and look after them all."

But I don't think he will.

All of a sudden, I don't think He Gives a Damn.

43

When we get back home, Mom organizes clean clothes for herself and Si makes some sort of stew with the vegetables. By the time we sit down to eat it's about 3 P.M.

I sit at the table, but even though it's late, I'm not hungry—and it's not the fact that it's a plate of vegetables. I like vegetables just fine. It's about what happened in the church; it's about playing the Sidewalk Crack Game and losing.

"I'm not hungry," I say.

"Eat," says Si.

So I do. It feels like a kind of giving-in. Afterward, while Mom and I do the dishes, Si drives off to get more gas for the return journey to the hospital.

Mom has been home less than three hours and soon she will be gone again, who knows for how long.

"Mom . . ." I say.

"Yes, Jess?"

"Do you know anyone in Aunt Edie's life named Rob?"

"Rob?" says Mom. "Rob who?"

So I tell her about Aunt Edie's song "For Rob."

"Must have been someone really important," I say.

"How do you know that?"

"Because of the music. Because of what she wrote."

Mom pauses. "No, sorry, doesn't mean anything to me. Why don't you ask Gran?"

And I say I will, but I won't, of course, because whatever Gran knows, she's not telling.

There's a silence and then Mom says, "Do you want to know why I really came home today, Jess?"

"Vegetables?" I offer.

Mom laughs. "Of course not. And not for church or the clothes either. I came home to see you."

"I know. You said."

"Did I?" She looks at me quizzically.

"At the hospital."

"Yes. I suppose I did. But no one but you would have noticed, Jess. You're a really special person, you know that?"

I shrug.

"And sensitive. And sometimes . . ."

I wait.

"Sometimes I'm a bit like that, too. I can tell what people are saying when they're not saying things."

This would be a muddle in anyone else's mouth, but I know exactly what Mom means.

"What am I not saying?" I ask.

Mom puts her head to one side. "You tell me."

So many things. Where to begin? The flask, the worry about the babies, the Sidewalk Crack Game, the monsters coming closer. Zoe.

Zoe.

Zoe.

"Zoe," I say.

"Go on," says Mom.

Then I think maybe Si hasn't gone to get gas (why couldn't he get gas on the journey back?). I think he's gone to give Mom and me Some Space.

"I don't think Zoe likes me anymore."

"Oh? And why do you say that?"

I don't tell her it might be because I shouted at her about livers and hung up the phone on her, deliberately cutting the cord between us. I say, "I think she'd rather be with Paddy."

Mom takes my hand and I let her. "People can like more than one person at a time, you know," she says. "Like just because I have two more children now doesn't mean I love you any less, Jess. Not at all."

Ha. I bet she's glad she's had an opportunity to work that into the conversation. Still—it's nice to hear. It gives me the same sort of feeling I had when I was tiny and had a fever and she put a cool hand on my forehead.

"Human beings," she continues, "they—we—have an infinite capacity for love."

"But Zoe," I begin again, "she used to come here all the time. Come over. Bound straight in. Barely knocked. You'd have thought she lived here. And now," I pause lamely, "she doesn't."

Mom takes a breath and I prepare myself for Something Adult.

"Jess," she says, "you and Zoe may just be growing apart. You've known her since you were in kindergarten. When people get older, they find different parts of themselves. What used to be a good fit might not be such a good fit as you grow up, develop your interests. Find out who you really are." She pauses. "And that's okay, Jess."

"It's not okay," I say solidly.

"I don't mean it doesn't hurt. It can leave a hole—"

A hole?

"—but in that space," continues Mom, "new things can come, new friends."

But I don't want any new friends. I want only Zoe, my mirror image, my better, bolder other half. And suddenly Zoe seems to me like Richie, she seems zesty big. And I'm the smaller, weaker twin; I'm Clem, clinging to her for dear life.

"Why do they have to cut them apart?" I exclaim then. "Why can't they just let the twins stay together forever and ever?"

Mom raises an eyebrow. "Maybe they'll have a better life apart."

"They won't," I cry.

Mom still has my hands in hers. Very gently she begins to stroke my fingers. "Maybe together..." she says, "maybe together..." she repeats, "they might just...suffocate each other."

44

This is what usually happens on my Easter Sunday: In the morning, Mom makes me an Easter basket. The basket always contains one large hollow chocolate egg, numerous tiny, loose, sugar-coated speckled ones, a couple of chocolate ducks in golden foil, and—sometimes—a box of flat little bunnies eating flat chocolate carrots. Mom puts all the goodies into a plastic bag and then hides them: They might be buried in the ironing pile, hung behind a coat in the front hall, or locked in the Christmas trunk.

"She's a bit old for an Easter basket, isn't she?" Si said last year.

And the previous year.

And the year before that.

But the basket still comes. Except this year Si has driven Mom back to the hospital, so there is no basket. Plonked in the middle of the kitchen table is an oversized chocolate rabbit. Not hidden at all.

"Happy Easter," Gran says.

In the afternoon of an Easter Sunday, at four o'clock precisely, Zoe always comes. She even knocks on the door, so I actually have to open it for her.

"Surprise," she says.

Only it isn't, because she's come every year since her mom brought her when she was four. She brings what she brought that first-ever time—a Cadbury Creme Egg—and she says what she said that first-ever time: *I gots it for you special.* And I say *Special smeschal* (I don't really know why I say that) and then, in return, I give her a Kinder Egg with the orange-and-white foil wrapping and the little plastic toy inside and she says *Special smeschal*, and then we hug and laugh and eat the chocolate and make the stupid toy (it's usually a tank), but of course it isn't about the chocolate or the toy and we both know that.

I start clockwatching at 3 P.M. The second hand of the kitchen clock ticks impossibly slowly. Every minute takes approximately two weeks. I listen for the sound of footsteps (running, bounding, enthusiastic footsteps) in the cul-de-sac. There aren't any, but I tell myself that's because it's early, three-quarters of an hour early, half an hour early, ten minutes early.

I don't go to look out the window, not even at four o'clock. Not at 4:05. Or 4:10. Or 4:15. At 4:20 I accept that it's over. Our friendship. It really is. And it doesn't matter how long I sit stubbornly watching the clock (I'm still there at 5:30), it won't make any difference.

I can feel the Kinder Egg in my pocket going all hot and sweaty, probably because I keep touching it, I keep squishing at it, to check it's still there, to check I've kept my part of the bargain. By six o'clock the egg is mainly mush.

Gran watches me watching the clock.

"What's going on?" she says.

"Zoe didn't come," I say.

"It's Easter," says Gran. "Why would she?"

"She always comes on Easter Sunday."

"Probably got family visiting," says Gran. "Or gone out somewhere. Maybe she'll come later."

But she won't. I know she won't. The only time her family ever went away for Easter she told me, told me weeks in advance.

"You could always call her," says Gran.

But I'd just hear the rip of the surgeon's knife again.

45

When I wake the following day, there is a light frost on the windowpane and everything in the world seems colder. There is no news from the hospital.

"No news is good news," says Gran.

There is no news from Zoe.

Which is not good news.

The breath is on the windowsill, looking out.

"What do you want? What are you waiting for?"

No reply.

Everything seems suspended, waiting.

"Haven't you got anything to do?" asks Gran.

"Yes," I say. "I have."

I go to the local shop and buy a new Kinder Egg. The sight of the orange-and-white foil brings a lump to my throat. Why is it always Zoe's responsibility to come to my house? Overnight, I have reexamined my friendship. I have noticed that, for years and years, Zoe has been the visitor and I have been the visited.

Why?

Am I some queen who sits in state to receive her? Or is it just that she's so full of life—so full of *Zoe*—that she's made all the running, and I've just stood by, watching? Waiting? What's wrong with me? Friendship is a two-way street—or it should be. I have decided that I will go to Zoe's house and give her my small gift.

The car is in the driveway; Zoe's family is home. I go up to the front door, press the bell, and listen to the two-tone ring.

Ding-dong.

Like my heart.

Ding-dong. Ding-dong. Ding-dong.

Someone comes to the door. I see the shadow on the other side of the glass as whoever it is pauses to peek through the peephole. I half-hope it's Zoe's mother, who'll greet me with a smile.

It isn't Zoe's mother. It's Zoe.

"Hi," she says, not aggressive, but not really friendly either, somewhere between wary and neutral. It makes me feel confused, as if whatever I say isn't going to be the right thing. So I say nothing.

"You all right?" she says. She keeps the door not quite open enough for me to come in. So, of course, I don't go in. I stand in my big silence. If it were her at my door, she'd just bound in.

"Happy Easter," I say at last. It doesn't sound that happy, but it doesn't sound ironic either.

"Sorry about yesterday . . ." she begins.

"Doesn't matter at all," I say, far too fast. "I'm sorry about the phone thing."

"Hmm," she says.

I go on standing.

"I was going to come around yesterday," she adds, "only . . ." She trails off.

"Doesn't matter," I say again, as if that will make it more true. "We were busy, too." I try a little smile.

She shrugs, embarrassed.

"Zoe?"

"Yes?"

I'm getting an idea; it's coming in very sudden and important. "I want you to do something, do something for me. Will you, Zoe? Please." I hear a certain desperation in my voice.

"What?" she says, curious but flat.

"I want to go to the Buddhist Center again," I tell her. "I want to go there with you."

"Huh?"

"Do a meditation like Lalitavajri offered."

"Why?"

Because things melt away in that Shrine Room, I think. Because it's a place where you seem to be able to say things without words, where there are smiles like incense, where my friend Zoe looked at me with hope and longing and I swore never to let that friendship die.

"Please, Zoe," I say.

"Well..."

"It's Tuesday. It's every Tuesday. That's what Lalitavajri said. Tomorrow. Come with me, Zoe."

"Sorry," says Zoe. "I can't."

Can't or won't?

"I'm busy." She shrugs.

I shouldn't push it, I should leave it right there, but I plow on through the humiliation. "Oh—doing something nice?"

"Movies. We're going to a movie. It's all figured out."

And I don't ask her who the *we* is because I already know. Her.

And Paddy.

"Right. Okay, see you some other time, then."

When I arrive home, I realize the Kinder Egg is still in my pocket. As for the hole Mom talked about—it's now a chasm.

46

In the night I dream about the Shrine Room. Across the golden belly of the Buddha there are little seed fish. When the Buddha breathes, the seed fish swim. I wake with a stubborn golden hope inside me. At least I still have the flask.

I take it out.

"I promised you, didn't I?"

No reply.

Bit like Zoe.

To Gran I say, "We have to go back to the Buddhist Center. You know, for the project. Zo's...um, having her hair cut first, so she'll meet us there. Can you take me at eleven-thirty?"

Gran huffs and puffs, but since it's for schoolwork, she has to agree. I make sure we arrive early.

"Zoe will be here in a sec. You can leave me, it's fine."

So Gran leaves me.

As I put my shoes on the rack in the hall and head up alone to the top floor, I wonder what I really hope to find here.

I want the Shrine Room to be just as I remember it, but it isn't. The previously spacious, empty floor is laid with neat rows of maroon mats, each with two small puffy blue cushions, a few with people sitting on them. Through the skylight there's no blue sky, no scudding clouds, only a uniform gray coldness. In front of the Buddha there is no eucalyptus. There are other flowers, but I wanted there to be eucalyptus and there isn't.

I hesitate, and that's when Lalitavajri, who is rearranging some candles, turns and sees me. At once she stops what she's doing and comes toward me.

"It's Jess, isn't it?" she says.

"Yes." I feel surprisingly shy.

"Have you come alone?"

"No," I say, because the flask is snug in my pocket. And then, seeing her scan the room, I realize what I've said, so I add, "You're here."

She smiles. "You're a very thoughtful person, aren't you, Jess?"

I'm surprised at this. I'm always surprised when people notice me.

Then she tells me to take a mat and make myself comfortable and not to worry that it's my first time. I see how other people are sitting or kneeling on the little blue cushions and I kneel like they do.

Then, keeping very still (and I wonder suddenly if Zoe could be this still), I cup my hands in front of me. I make a little nest in case the breath wants to be with me in this place.

"You'll be safe here," I whisper.

Lalitavajri goes to sit at the front of the room beside a golden bowl with a golden hammer. A few minutes later the whole room is full, maybe twenty or thirty people silently coming to rest on their cushions.

Lalitavajri welcomes us all and then, in a soft, slow voice, she asks us all to be aware of our bodies, to feel the weight of them from the ground up.

"Imagine," she says, "awareness filling your body, like soft, warm light, penetrating your bones, your muscles."

Already my eyes are closed. I've shut them instinctively. I just want to be all wrapped up alone with these words that seem like spells.

"Listen to the breath, the rising and the falling."

And I do listen to my breath and I feel the movement of my rib cage, just as Lalitavajri says. And then, in my hands, I suddenly feel it there, too. The fluttering of a butterfly wing.

It has come.

"Imagine where your heart is. Make a space around your heart."

But I think there's a space around my heart already.

"The *metta bhavana*," Lalitavajri is saying now, "for those of you who are new today, is about universal loving-kindness. And loving-kindness starts with ourselves. To love others, we must first love ourselves. So I ask you to wish yourself well. Say, 'May I care for myself?'"

This feels strange to me, and slightly selfish, so I can't quite say the words even inside the quietness of my head.

"Now think of a close friend," continues Lalitavajri. "Wish them well, hope for their happiness."

I wish she'd said not *friend* but *relative*, because I want to wish the babies well, I want them to have all the love in the world. But she said *friend*, so it's Zoe who comes into my mind, Zoe dancing in the park and lying in the half-moon swing with me and looking at the sky. Only Zoe will probably never come with me to the park again.

So I haven't chosen anyone before Lalitavajri goes on. "Now, keeping yourself relaxed and open, hearing your own breath, turn your attention to a difficult person, an enemy."

And just before I tell myself I have no enemies, Zoe's face comes again. Zoe telling Paddy mumbo jumbo about the twins, Zoe shutting me out in the car, Zoe saying, *Since when were we joined at the hip?* Zoe failing to come to my house on Easter Sunday with a Creme Egg. Zoe going to the movies. With Paddy.

"And noticing any resistance," says Lalitavajri, "and not judging it, imagine this person well and happy."

I notice the resistance. I notice that my bones aren't made of light anymore. They're made of glass.

And I want to wish Zoe well, but right now I just can't.

Can't.

Can't.

I'm too busy.

"Now," says Lalitavajri, "move your *metta*, your loving-kindness, outward. Let it take in everyone in this room and everyone in this town, everyone in this country, all those awake and all those asleep..."

And I see where she's going with this and I want to follow, I want to expand outward and embrace the whole world with my calm, warm bones of light. But if your bones are made of glass, you can't do that. You're all hard and fragile and have no give in you at all.

"Let your loving-kindness," says Lalitavajri, "flow over all those on islands and all those on continents, all those babies being born and and all those people dying..."

But nothing flows out of me except this one thought: Why has Lalitavajri yoked together these babies and these dead people? And why is she talking about babies and death at the precise moment when I'm thinking about the death of my friendship with Zoe? As if she knows something, if she knows what I know, that they're interconnected, that if one dies the other dies. Make her stop talking about babies and death!

Only then I think maybe it's me who's joining everything so bitterly together, me sitting here all crunched up with my mouthful of glass.

And I realize there's no space around my heart anymore. It's all gone very tight. Just like my hands. My hands are clenching so tight there is no nest anymore.

I've crushed it, crushed it to nothing.

So what's happened to the breath?

47

It's back in the flask. It looks weak, feeble. My mind was so full of hate I didn't notice how I'd squeezed it out, and now it lies shivering and defeated at the bottom of the glass. It reminds me of the candle in the church, how the flame guttered just before it died.

So I know something bad's happened even before Gran's car arrives. Before I see her face—gray and panicked.

"It's Clem," I say, as I climb into the front seat beside her. "It's Clem, isn't it?"

"How do you know?" she says. "How can you know that?"

"Your face," I lie.

"He's taken another—dip," Gran says.

She makes no attempt to stall, to hide things. So it must be worse than I thought. It must be terrible.

"What does it mean?" I can hear my voice, all high and tight.

"They have to bring the surgery forward."

"To when?"

"Tomorrow."

"Tomorrow!"

"Yes."

"But what about the rehearsal, the practice operation, where...?" Where they learn how not to pick the wrong socket wrench.

"There won't be time for that," says Gran.

48

Of course, I blame myself, for all that absence of *metta*. What if I'd loved everyone, loved Zoe, kept myself warm and open? It wouldn't have happened, would it? It's all my fault.

"I'm sorry," I say to the flask. The gray sky outside my room makes it feel darker than ever. "I'm really sorry."

No reply.

"Why don't you scream at me? Yell?"

Silence.

"Why don't you howl? What happened to your big black howls?"

I'd prefer the black howls, horrible as they were. Anything would be better than this shivering, dying, guttering, nearly ended flame.

I remember how I held the howling black flask close to my body and how I rocked and gave it warmth and it seemed to make a difference. I hold the flask close again, glass to skin. It makes no difference at all.

It just feels cold.

I feel cold.

Really cold.

How can you have a cold flame?

Because the flame is dying.

"Do you think Rob would want you to behave like this?" I shout at the flask.

No reply.

"And who is Rob, anyway?"

No reply.

Everything is colder. I don't know if it's my head, my heart, or the weather.

I find myself at the piano. What happened to my new song with the lion thread? I haven't heard a single note of it for days. Maybe I haven't been listening right, or maybe everything that's been going on with the babies and Zoe and the hate has blocked my ears.

I put my hands on the keys, but my fingers are frozen. There is no more music in them than there is in my head.

You cannot force a song; it comes when it's ready. Surely I, of all people, know that?

I shut the lid of the piano.

One long night before the twins' operation.

How will I be able to sleep?

"Here," says Gran. "I've made you some warm milk."

I watch the hot drink going cold, just like everything else.

"Get into bed," says Gran.

I get into bed holding the flask. I think maybe I shouldn't take my eyes off it for a second. But then there's never anything new to see, only the cold, hopeless, guttering thing.

"Why don't you make the seed fish swim?" I cry. "Just one. For me. So I know you're still there. So I know Clem's still there. Please. Please!"

No reply.

No reply!

"I hate you, hate you, hate you."

But actually it's me I hate. Because no matter how many times I go over it in my head, try to convince myself that it could just be a *coincidence*, that this new dip has nothing to do with me the way the first howling dip had nothing to do with me, I can't let myself off the hook. I'd never heard of the word *metta* before this afternoon, but now it seems the only thing that matters. Loving-kindness. I mean, if you have a fight with a friend, you think it's just to do with the two of you, don't you? But what if (I'm thinking this looking at the guttering flame), when any one of us is angry or hurt, then the whole sum of human happiness goes down? What then? If we're all connected, all in this together (which is, I think, what Lalitavajri was saying), then how we behave every minute of every day—that must matter, too.

This is a late-night conversation I'm having with myself, and I know I'm tired and I might not be thinking too straight, but the bottom line is this: To help Clem, I feel I have to do something about the way things are with me and Zoe.

Right Now.

Then I remember that I did try—I went to her house, right? And she brushed me off. No, no, she just said she was busy and...

Think *metta*. Think loving-kindness. Try again. Never give up.

An idea comes to me. I get out of bed, pull my robe around me, and because I'm still shivering, add my duvet and go to sit at the desk.

The bureau.

The place where Aunt Edie sat to write her private letters, letters from her secret heart. I fold down the desk lid and find some paper and a black ballpoint pen. Letters, I think, are not like texts—*sry. SRY cll me*—which can be brushed aside like flies. They're more than that, deeper. You can say things in a letter that sometimes you can't say face-to-face.

But what should I say?

Dear Zoe, I write.

Dear, dear, dearest Zoe.

Please feel free to go to a movie with anyone you like. Not that you need my permission. You don't, of course. You're a free agent, you just do whatever you want, with whoever you want, whenever you want....

I break off. I'm laying it on too thick, making it sound as if she's doing all the taking and I'm doing all the giving. I crumple the paper up, start again.

Dear Zoe,

You're wonderful. You're amazing. I love everything about you. I even loved when you were four and wore that stupid shirt with the pink rose on it. Wore it over your sweater! I thought that was so funny. Did I ever tell you that I asked my mom for a shirt with a rose on it? And she bought me one. Though I only ever wore mine under my sweater....

I stop again. *I don't care whether you come or not. Just don't get serious with me.* This is serious, isn't it? This is pressure, too. This says: You have to love me as much as I love you; you have to remember how frail I am compared to you; you need to protect me. Pressure, pressure, pressure. Heavy, heavy, heavy. Sad, sad, sad. Did Aunt Edie have this trouble with her letters? I crumple up the second piece of paper.

Dear Zoe, I begin for the third time. Beside me on the desk, the flame in the flask is still guttering.

I'm sorry. Sometimes my heart's all messy. Sometimes I say the wrong things. Want the wrong things.

Forgive me?

Love you.

Jess.

Then I add some kisses.

xxxxxxxxx

I notice how the kisses look like a daisy chain and think that maybe this is the right letter to send, or at least a good-enough letter, so I fold it in three and tape it down (as I don't have any envelopes) and write her name bold on the front.

ZOE.

Life.

I look at the flask again. Still guttering. I wrote the letter to change things with the flask and it hasn't. But it has changed something in me.

I feel lighter, more positive.

I rearrange the duvet from clothing to bedcover and climb into bed.

In the morning I will put this letter in Zoe's mailbox. I won't ring the doorbell, I won't make a big deal about it, she'll just find it when she finds it. I am calmer now, the way you are when you stop shouting and begin to do something about a problem. I hold the flask close for a moment.

"You'll be all right," I whisper. "You'll see. I'll find a way. You'll be all right."

Then I sleep.

49

I wake with a start, a muscle in my leg spasming. I kick out, knock the flask (which is somehow still in my hands), grab it back, look. No change. The flame fluttering—weak and low.

Then I wonder how, in the dark of night, I can see the flask so clearly. Which is when I realize it's not dark at all. My room is full of a strange white light. It's also very quiet, like someone threw a blanket over the whole world.

I get up. As I peel back the duvet, I feel goose bumps flash up my arm. By the time I get to the window, I'm hugging myself, arms clasped tight, for warmth, for security. Then through the crack in the curtains I see it.

It's snowing.

The huge hush is four or five inches of snow. I unclasp my arms and open the curtains wide. The sight is astonishing. Snow—on Easter! The world I see from my window is not the one I went to bed with. The snow covers everything, cars and houses and trees, so that the view is just one landscape of white—everything joined—yes, everything joined up together, because of the snow.

"Is this it? The next part of the journey?"

No reply.

I'm going to go out in the snow, though it's deep in the middle of the night. I can't not be part of this world where white earth meets white sky. I dress as quickly and as quietly as I can, tuck the flask and the letter into my pocket, and tiptoe downstairs.

I'm glad that I'm so practiced with cracks and creaks and floorboards; waking Gran is not part of my plan. I take gloves and a scarf from the chest in the hall and my coat and boots from the closet. What to do about a house key? There are keys in the kitchen, but the kitchen is directly under Gran's bedroom. I decide just to leave the door unlocked.

Then I step out into the joined-up world.

The sky is white-blue, in some places completely white, as white as the earth, which is why it's so bright, why there seems to be hardly any darkness at all. The snow itself has eased. It is very light now, just a few flurries, though it must have been snowing really heavily for hours.

The hush is extraordinary. Nothing seems to be moving except for me, so I hear every sound I make as though it is amplified a thousand times. The crunch of my own footsteps in the deep new snow and the in-out of my breath that crystallizes in a small cloud of warmth in front of my cold mouth.

I see how deep my feet go, maybe it's not four or five inches, maybe it's only three or four, but seeing my footprints where there are no others makes them seem significant. The map of my journey.

All along the cul-de-sac are streetlights that look very orange against the white, white snow. It's only a matter of moments before I arrive at Zoe's house, me the midnight mailman. I think of her tucked in bed knowing nothing about what's going on in this bright new world—but she will know. I watch my prints come up to her door. Her mailbox is low, so I have to kneel to push the letter in.

As I stand up again, I imagine her coming (bounding) downstairs in the morning, all excited about the snow, picking up the envelope, reading what I've written, and just smiling, smiling at the world, at the words, at me. She has such a wonderful smile.

I trot happily back down her path, thinking how even my footprints have joined me to her, my house to hers.

I don't go home. I have a second mission. I'm so wrapped up in my head that I almost fail to notice there's someone else out in this night. Several doors down from Zoe's there's a young guy I don't recognize heaping snow outside his garage, shaping it into something, molding it. I don't want him to see me, I don't want him to stop me, or chat, or ask me where I'm going, because I realize I don't really want anyone in this world but me. I want it all for myself for a little while longer.

But he's too absorbed to notice anything. His head (like mine) is right inside whatever he is doing outside the garage in our joined-up cul-de-sac. So he lets me be and I let him be as I walk on, on toward the park.

The streetlights stop here, so it is a little darker, but not much. I pass some kind of large electrical junction box, which I must have passed a million times before and never noticed. I notice it now because, in the huge hush, it hums.

The park is a winter wonderland, better than any Christmas card I've ever seen, the trees dark shapes beneath their glittering coats of white, the odd winter pansy, yellow and purple, pushing its velvety head through the blanket of snow. I feel full of joy, as though I could run and laugh, but I don't. I keep very quiet and still, at one with the landscape.

I pass the playground, looking at the ledges of snow on the swings and slide, and on the half-moon swing where Zoe and I have talked so many times, and on again to the bowling green, where the old men and the old women come out in the summer and play together with whispers and the soft clack of balls. The path to the bowling green is lit, though I've never noticed these lamps before. They are not oval-shaped, like the streetlights, but round like little yellow globes, like little worlds all their own.

Why have I chosen the bowling green?

Because it's gated off. Because the bench I have in mind is screened from the rest of the park. It is not a place you just pass; you have to choose to go there, go deliberately.

I open the gate. *No Dogs*, it says. *No Games*.

I go straight to the bench and sweep all the snow from the left end of the bench toward the middle. I hear a rustling, which surprises me, so I look up at the plant that screens the bowling green from the road, which turns out to be a palm tree. Or maybe not a palm tree (because how can there be a palm tree here?), but certainly a tree with long, spiky fronds that looks as if it belongs in a warmer climate. The wind is rustling through the spikes, shivering them.

Next I sweep all the snow from the right-hand side of the bench toward the middle. Now I have two mounds of snow, very little mounds, but the babies are very little, too, so it doesn't matter. The piles seem to be leaning toward each other. I start sculpting little arms and little hands, and bring the mounds closer together so the space between the two gets smaller and smaller and then, all at once, there is no space between the mounds. The babies are joined.

Then I start on the heads, only there really isn't quite enough snow, so I have to pick up some from the green itself, and I forget that there is a ditch all around the bowling area, and I nearly fall, but I don't, and that feels good. I take only as much snow as fits into my cupped hands.

I begin with Richie's head, because Richie always seems to come first, and I take time to make his head strong and stable. Then I cup my hands once again and I take snow for Clem. I don't intend to use less snow for him, but when I join the ball of snow to his chest it seems as if his head is smaller than Richie's. It is also not as stable. I press it in around the neck, but still the head wobbles, leans, seems to want to rest against his brother. I try to separate the heads.

Joined chest, separate heads.

But Clem resists me. He wants to lean against his brother. He's only happy, only stable when their heads are touching, kissing. I think, fleetingly, how it would be if my head were leaning on Zoe's shoulder, if she were supporting me.

So I let Clem be, let Richie support him.

Clem's choice.

How many other choices does my little brother have right now?

Then I stand back, look at the snow babies clinging there together, and finally pull the flask from my pocket. What am I expecting? A sign, I guess. I'm hoping that the little flame will be just slightly stronger, slightly brighter. What I'm not expecting is what I find: a globe of shining white. The surface of the glass is dense but sparkling, like a frosted windowpane and inside... oh, inside. How can I describe it? It's lit and fluttering and it looks like there are strips of paper floating there, thin pale strips, the color paper would be if you cut it from moonlight. It's ghostly and beautiful and it makes me happier than I can say, because I know where it belongs. It belongs at the heart of the snow babies.

So I put it there, lean it just where the babies join, so that they can share. As the flask shimmers between them, I half-expect it to act like a real heart, and for the babies to get up off the bench and walk and dance and fly like they did in *The Snowman*, a movie Zoe and I used to watch when we were five.

They don't, of course. It's just my heart lifting, because I've finally made a difference. Writing the letter, building the snow babies, one or the other, both, I don't know. But instead of destroying something, crushing something up, as I did in the Shrine Room, I've begun to build, to create, to add to the sum of human happiness.

"Is that it?"

No reply.

Then, as I gaze, the flask tips slightly, responding to some unevenness in my packing of the snow, probably, but it comes to rest more on Clem's side, just under his arms, as though he were reaching for the flask, wanting it nearer. In this night of messages, what can this be but a message?

"You want Clem? Clem wants you?"

No reply.

"Then I'll take you. I'll take you to the hospital. After the operation—yes?"

After the operation. What if there is no *after the operation*?

What if, because there's no time for the rehearsal operation, they choose the wrong socket wrench and Clem doesn't make it—he dies on the operating table?

This is a night for bravery, but suddenly I don't feel at all brave. I feel the monsters begin to crowd around again.

So I hedge my bets. I can't stop myself, I play the Sidewalk Crack Game one final time.

To date, the monsters and I are running even. Si and I won (just) with the timing chain. The monsters won in the church. This will be the decider.

"Winner takes all," I say. "Yes?"

No reply.

Not from the flask.

Not from the monsters.

"If the snow babies still exist when the operation starts tomorrow morning, then everything will be all right."

The operation is scheduled for 8 A.M. I don't know what the time is now (the bowling green clock says 3:30, but it's been saying that ever since I arrived). Whatever time it is, the snow babies only have to last about four or five hours, and it's cold and there's no one in the park, and anyway they're hidden and even the early sledders won't come here because the bowling green area is so flat and…surely I can win this one? For sure—right?

"If the snow babies exist when the operation starts," I repeat, "Richie will live. Clem will live. Both of them. They'll both survive." Then, like chucking salt over your shoulder for good luck, I add, "As will my friendship with Zoe."

Out in the moonlight, where the white sky touches the white earth, dreams feel real.

50

The wet of the snow has penetrated my gloves and my fingers are freezing. I didn't notice this before, but I'm noticing it now, just as I'm noticing how the white-blue sky has gone slightly rose-colored and gray. Maybe it's dawn already. Only three hours for the snow babies to last. I listen for the birds, but I don't hear any. Maybe the birds are hiding. Maybe the hush has gotten them, too. There aren't even any cars. There's just me and my breathing again and a sudden desire to be home, to be tucked up in bed.

I feel exhausted.

I say good-bye to the babies, tuck the flask back in my pocket, and follow my own prints out of the park, messing them up slightly by the entrance to the bowling green, as if I could disguise my going there.

As I enter the cul-de-sac, I see that my neighbor, the other night sculptor, has mounded his snow into a huge snow mermaid, a beautiful woman who seems to be compacted together, carved out of ice. I stop to admire her. The boy (or guy) is no longer there, but he's signed his name on the sculpture, as if it were a work of art: Bruno Teisler, it says. And I wonder briefly about this Bruno Teisler who lives in my cul-de-sac who I've never seen before, and then I pass on by, stopping only to glance up at Zoe's window before arriving at my own house.

The porch light is on. The door is not quietly closed. It's wide open. And in that open doorway, coat and gloves on, is Gran.

51

"Where on earth have you been? Just what do you think you're doing? Don't you think I've enough to be worrying about without this, you selfish, selfish child?"

These are just some of the things Gran says, or rather she shouts. She is shouting so loudly I think the whole street, the whole world, will hear her. There will never be hush again.

"And you're shivering. Look at you! LOOK AT YOU! And wet. You're wet. Jess, you'll be sick. You'll be really sick. You know that?"

I don't know anything. I just feel tired and silent.

"Well, what have you got to say for yourself?"

Then she scoops me up and hugs me tighter than I've ever been hugged before, and just for once, I don't mind being all scrunched up against her.

She brings me in and strips me down and makes me drink hot cocoa (I am shivering even with my hands around the warm mug). And she never stops talking and still I don't say anything.

"How could you?" she repeats, over and over. "How could you? You know about your father, don't you?"

And of course I know, but it doesn't stop her telling me again anyway.

"He went out," Gran says. "Went out in the snow when he was six. Not at night, of course. Not at night. Even he wasn't that stupid. No, in the day. He was supposed to be in the garden, playing. Children do play in the snow. For hours. And I was getting on with something in the house, like you do, and suddenly it was six o'clock. So I called for him. Called and called, only he didn't answer. So I went out. And that's when I found him. Lying flat out in the snow. Flat on his back. I thought he was dead. But he was just asleep. Asleep. How could anyone—ANYONE—just fall asleep in the snow? I'll never understand that as long as I live. Never."

There are tears in her eyes.

"And that's why he always had such a weak chest. He was a sickly boy after that. And I always wondered, when he died so young, I always wondered: If I'd looked out that afternoon, if I'd seen him, if I'd stopped him..."

I've heard this story many times and it always ends here, with the blame. But now, for the first time, I wonder, too. I wonder why my father lay down in the snow to sleep. It can't have been because he was tired. There are many more comfortable places to sleep than the snow. So maybe, like me, he was trying things out, experimenting, playing a Sidewalk Crack Game all of his own. If I lie down in this snow and no one finds me, then . . .

The monsters won't get me.

I so wish I could know that game and the boy who played it. The boy who grew up to be my father. Perhaps he would have things to teach me about monsters. And then, suddenly, I experience the loss of my father as a physical thing, an emptiness somewhere deep inside me. And I want to fill that hole with the sound of his voice; I want to hear my father's voice. I could listen to him for a lifetime.

But there's only Gran talking.

52

When Gran finally finishes, she fusses me into bed.

"And don't think you're going out anywhere tomorrow!" is her parting shot. As she closes the door, I reach into my pocket.

The flask is still white, though not quite as sparkling, not on the surface, anyhow. But inside, among the floating paper strips of moonlight, there's something new, a thread of yellow. Or gold, pale gold, like a hair from the mane of a lion, or the brightness of a smile. It throws a filament of light to the white swirling surface, where a single seed fish swims.

"Thank you," I whisper. "Thank you, thank you, thank you."

I lie down and sleep. I dream that I am lying in the snow next to my father and we keep each other warm.

53

I wake to find the flask still in my hand. I must not have let it go all night. The glass has taken heat from my body so it's warm, too, its surface not frosted anymore but transparent. I can clearly see the strips of moonlight, the threads of gold, and, yes, the seed fish; the single seed fish is still swimming.

The snow babies must have made it through the night!

So the real babies will make it through the operation.

Clem will live!

Richie will live!

Zoe will smile on the world and on me!

I pull my alarm clock close. It's ten o'clock already. The babies will have been in the operating room for two hours. I charge downstairs in my robe and arrive in the kitchen just as the phone rings. I get to it before Gran.

It's Si.

"They're okay?" I cry. "Aren't they? Richie's okay and Clem's okay and it's all going fine, even though there hasn't been a rehearsal operation. Right?"

"Not exactly," says Si.

"What?"

"The operation. It's been delayed."

A sudden chill. "Why?"

"The snow. Half the team haven't managed to get in. One of the doctors is marooned somewhere way out of town. Dug his car out, but the roads are impassable."

"But they're going to do it later?" I say. "As soon as every-one's there?"

"No," says Si. "They're going to delay it. They have to have everyone and they have to start on time. Can't start late and work through the night. It's a long, long process, Jess."

"But what about Clem?" I burst out.

"He's stabilized, much to everyone's astonishment. Didn't I say that? That's the good news, Jess."

Of course he has, because of the building, because of not destroying, but . . . but . . .

"When's it going to be—the operation—when's it going to be?"

"Tomorrow," says Si. "We hope."

"The snow babies!" I cry.

"What?" says Si.

"The snow babies have to last another twenty-four hours!"

"What are you talking about?" says Si.

54

I'm talking about marching straight to the park and standing over the snow babies with Si's large socket wrench. If anyone comes within a foot of them . . .

But what if they just melt? What if the God that let Clem's candle gutter in the church just parts the clouds and the sun comes out? What then? I rush to the window. No sign of a thaw. On our garden table the snow is still piled four inches deep at least. And it's cold, bitingly cold. Even Gran, who likes to tell you that she was a War Baby, and War Babies know about hardship, is standing next to the stove with a gas ring lit to provide the warmth that the heater seems to be struggling to achieve.

I go straight upstairs and get dressed so fast I forget the flask. I don't put on my shoes because I'm going to be wearing boots, and I'm down to the porch in less than two minutes.

But so is Gran.

"And what exactly do you think you're doing?"

"I'm going out." I just have to be there, with the snow babies. That's all there is to it. I will defend them to the death.

To the life.

"Have you gone crazy?"

Yes. I think so.

"Did you listen to anything I said last night?"

Yes. All of it.

"You will be ill. You are ill."

"I am not ill."

"You will be ill if you don't stay in today. You need to rest."

"I don't need to rest. I can't rest."

"Besides," says Gran, "you haven't had breakfast."

I don't take on the breakfast issue. I just say, "No one stays in when it snows, Gran. Everyone goes out. They play."

"You played last night," says Gran grimly. And then she takes the large brass key that fits the bottom lock on our front door, the deadbolt, and slots it in. She turns her wrist with something like triumph.

She is locking me in.

She is locking me into my own house.

"You can't do that," I say.

"Can't I?" she replies, and she drops the key in the pocket of her apron.

There's only one thing to do—I'll have to make a run for it. I don't have time for a jacket, I don't have time for boots, or a scarf, or a hat, or gloves. I just run, in my socks, down the hall and through the kitchen and I unlock the back door (which does not have a deadbolt) and I tear out into the garden—nearly stopping immediately as my feet land in the freezing wet snow—and around the side of the house and into the street.

"No!" shouts Gran.

But she isn't even close to being behind me.

55

Running isn't exactly an option, what with the thick wet of the snow and the surprisingly hard and uneven sidewalk below, but I'm still moving fast. As fast as I can. At the bottom of the cul-de-sac I pass the ice mermaid. Her proud, beautiful head and carved ice eyes watch me pass. She is intact, so the snow babies must be, too.

I'm glad for my jeans and my shirt and thick fleece hoodie, but my feet are already in pain and so are my hands. The wind is managing to find the gap around my throat and send icy blasts down my chest, but I just stumble on, not caring. At least the speed is helping, the stumble-running is warming my core, that space around my heart.

I pass the electrical junction box at the edge of the park. It's still humming, though you can hardly hear it over the shouts and yells and laughter coming from the park. The park is full of brightly colored people shrieking as they speed down slopes on sleds and tin trays and flattened cardboard boxes. There are mothers and fathers and tiny children all muffled up and dogs barking. One little gray dog has a series of tiny snowballs attached to all four paws which he's trying, in vain, to bite off. I think I recognize some people from school at the top of the hill by the chestnut tree, though everyone is twice their normal size in ski jackets and snow boots. Closer to me, in the playground, a child is eating snow from a swing and being reprimanded.

It's all so very ordinary.

Most people are busy with what they are doing, but some turn as I pass and one child even points, maybe because I'm stumble-running still, maybe because I don't look dressed for the snow.

Soon I'm at the bowling green. I can no longer feel my feet. I think they have joined some other body. Or maybe they've become part of the frozen earth; they certainly don't seem to be mine anymore. My head takes no responsibility for them. Or for my hands.

The gate of the bowling green is wide open. *No Dogs. No Games.*

It doesn't say anything about the Sidewalk Crack Game.

There are four dogs in the area and a huge snowball fight in progress, right at the center of which is beach-ball-grinning Paddy. Sam is with him, and Alice. And also Em. Em is back.

Do I care?

No. I don't care about Em or Alice. I don't even care about Zoe, who now I see is crouching, face to the ground, gathering snow. Whether Zoe's smiling, whether she's read the letter—it all seems totally unimportant. The only thing that matters now is the babies. Protecting them.

You can't see the bench from the gate, so I know nothing until I turn in and pass the shivering palm tree.

There they are: Snow Richie, Snow Clem, just as I left them.

No, not just as I left them. They are slightly more slumped, slightly closer together, their little heads gone crystalline.

I will sit with them all day if I have to.

All night. All day again. As long as it takes.

"Jess, is that you? Jess. Jess!" Em is coming over. "Yay—Jess!"

"Hey, what's with the footwear, Jess?" Paddy is coming, too.

"Bombs away," shouts Zoe. Now she's looking up, standing up, and she is smiling, widely, broadly. Grinning like a lunatic. She lobs a snowball at Paddy, which catches him right on the side of his head.

"Hey!" he yells. He's less than an arm's length away from me, and to retaliate, I think he's just going to bend down and scoop snow from beneath his feet. But he doesn't. He's in a rush so he just leans forward and grabs Clem's already neatly balled head.

"No!" I scream.

But he's already done it. He's taken Clem's head and he's lobbing it at Zoe. It flies through the air, but his aim is wide and he misses her.

Zoe does her tribal victory dance. She's stamping and yelling and whistling and GRINNING.

"No! No! NO!" I cry.

"What is up with you?" says Paddy.

I could hit him, push him, kill him, put the whole force of my body between him and what remains of the babies. But I do nothing. I just stand there, completely unable to move, staring at headless Clem and also the join. The join—the babies are still joined. Maybe that's enough. Could that be enough? It's my game, my Sidewalk Crack Game; it wouldn't be changing the rules to say, *It's the join that matters, if the join survives, then . . .*

"Bombs away," shouts Zoe again. And it's coming at me this time, a huge white ball of snow flying through the air alongside Zoe's ecstatic GRIN. I observe myself stepping aside; I do it instinctively, so as not to be hit.

So the biggest snowball in the world makes a perfect arc over the bowling green and lands smack between the babies, right on the join.

Splitting them asunder.

56

I don't know why or how I move after that. There is no
part of my body I can feel, my bones are solid ice, yet I'm
moving.

I brought it on myself, didn't I? The death of Clem, of
Zoe and me, of everything I've ever wanted. If I were looking for a message—what could be clearer? Headless Clem.
Smashed-up join. If I believe in pictures and symbols and
things without words, what more is there to say?

"Jess?" Someone is behind me. It isn't Em or Alice or
Paddy. They're all still screeching in the park. "Jess. Jess!"
It's Zoe. Screeching Zoe.

Her voice is just one of many because no one's laughing
anymore. All the mothers and all the fathers and all the
children are screeching, they're screaming, wailing, crying,

their noise like fingernails down a chalkboard in my ears, because there can never be any happiness.

Not now.

Not ever.

"Jess!"

"Leave me alone."

But she doesn't.

Haven't we played this scene before? Jessica Walton fleeing the park pursued by her friend Zoe? And it doesn't end well. It ends with Jess screaming: *I'll never tell you anything ever again.* Only this time Zoe's still coming.

"It's over. It's all over. Can you see that? I've lost, you've lost, the babies have lost—"

"Lost what?"

"Everything."

The snow mermaid is still outside Bruno Teisler's garage. It remains proud, beautiful, and intact. I punch that mermaid's head off.

"Jess?" It's difficult to hear Zoe's voice above the screeching, but I do hear it. It's full of horror. And fear. "What's gotten into you?"

"Go away, Zoe. Forget it. Forget everything I wrote in that letter. It's over. Finished."

Zoe does not go away. "What letter?" she says.

"The one I wrote last night, and put in your mailbox last night."

"So what if I came out my back door this morning?"

"Did you come out your back door?"

"Why are we even having this conversation? Jess—"

"Just Go Away!"

But she's still right by me when I arrive at my own back door. I expect to see the towering figure of Gran, but there is no Gran. Gran must be wandering the park, the streets. Gran must be saying to every passing stranger: *Have you seen my granddaughter? She's lost. Lost. You must have seen her, she went out without shoes, without boots. Have you seen her? Have you seen her lying in the snow?*

I go into the house and Zoe follows.

"Jess, please, tell me, just tell me."

Zoe is back in my house.

"Whatever it is," Zoe says, "we can work it out."

We.

We can work it out.

"Look, okay, I know I haven't exactly been, well, oh, Jess . . . you know what? You scare me. You're so wrapped up in yourself right now. I can't reach you anymore. I don't know who you are anymore, Jess. Are you hearing me? Jess!"

I'm hearing her and the other noises, the screeching ones, they're getting a little quieter. She's come. She didn't get the letter and she's come. Anyway.

I stop running.

She puts out her hand, touches me on the shoulder.

"Jeez," she says, "you are so cold."

She slips off her boots and her jacket and pushes me through to the kitchen.

"How can anyone be that cold?"

I stand there and suddenly, like Roger the Wreck, I just rattle. My teeth rattle, my bones rattle, my mind rattles, and shivers go up and down my body in continuous waves.

"You've got to get warm," Zoe says, and she tries to hold my hands in hers, but even the faint difference in temperature (Zoe's hands are not warm, but they're warmer than mine) makes me cry out with pain.

"Get those clothes off," says Zoe. "Get those stupid socks off."

But I can't bend and my fingers won't work.

She makes me lie down, right there on the kitchen floor, and she pulls at all the wet clothes and still I shiver.

"Rug," she says. "You need a rug. Where's a rug? No, bed. You'd be better off in bed. Or a bath. Yes, that's it. You should go in the bath."

I don't resist. I just let her push me up the stairs and I sit on the bathroom stool while she runs the water. I notice I still have my underwear on, but that seems wet through, too.

"Take it off," she says, nodding at my underwear, and when I just continue to sit there, she comes to help me.

And then I'm naked.

Which is okay.

With Zoe.

"Get in."

I try my toe in the water and shriek with pain.

"What is it?"

"Too hot."

She puts her hand in the water, stirs it about. "It's not that hot. It's fine." But she puts some more cold in anyway. "Maybe your body . . ." She doesn't finish the sentence.

And then I get in. Then I lie in the warmish water and let my body thaw.

Tears well out of my eyes.

"Don't cry," says Zoe. "Why are you crying?"

And I don't know if it's the warmth of the water or the warmth of *we*, or whether it's just my body giving up, giving in.

"I don't know," I say.

She sloshes some water over my stomach. "It's not about Easter, is it?" she says. "Or Paddy. It's not about any of that stupid stuff, is it?"

I look right into her mirror eyes.

"Did you like going to the movie with him?"

"With who?"

"Paddy."

"When did I go to a movie with Paddy?"

"Yesterday. When you couldn't come with me—to the Buddhist Center."

"Who said I went with Paddy? I went with my cousin— Savvy. I went with my family."

The water is lap-lap-lapping around my body. Or slap-slap-slapping. Stupid, stupid, stupid Jess. Jumping to conclusions—that's what Si calls it. Sensible people, says Si, do not jump to conclusions.

"Though I don't see why I shouldn't go with Paddy. Not if I want to."

"No. You're right," I say. "You're right, Zoe. I mean, a person can like two people at the same time, right? Like just because I love Clem, doesn't mean I have nothing left over for Richie, does it?"

"Huh?" Zoe stares at me. "I'm not sure where love comes into this. Not with me and Paddy, anyway. I mean, he's funny, he's good to have around, but... well, if I wanted to go to see a movie, I'd probably rather go with you."

"With me?"

"Yes, with you, stupid."

Water slaps around me.

"And just for the record," continues Zoe, "I didn't tell Paddy about the babies being joined either. Alice did that."

The water slaps some more. "Alice?" stupid Jess repeats.

"Yes, Alice. You told Em and Em told Alice."

How to Be Your Own Worst Enemy. Zoe is right, I've been so wrapped up inside my own head I've forgotten that other people exist, that they have lives and thoughts of their own. I've blamed Zoe and hated her and all along it was just me. Jumping to conclusions. Making stuff up. They've always said that about me. I just make stuff up.

I think I'm sobbing now. "I'm so sorry, Zoe."

"Well, don't be. And stop that crying, too. You have to stop, Jess. And you have to tell me what this is really all about. Please."

She hands me some toilet paper on which to blow my nose. And after I've done that, I tell her.

I tell Zoe everything.

57

It pours out of me like I'm some waterfall that just fell over a beautiful rock. I'm rushing and rushing to tell Zoe about the color of the skin where the babies join and how I felt when I saw it that first-ever time, and about the operation being moved up and the light in the flask guttering and about the snow babies and the Sidewalk Crack Monsters, and how if the snow babies ceased to exist before the operation, then both boys would die.

Will die.

Temporarily, I keep back the bit about how I also chucked our friendship over my shoulder like salt, for good luck.

Zoe doesn't laugh once, not once.

"That's all right, then," she says.

"What?"

"If it's about still existing—did you say *still exist* or *not melt* or *not be destroyed*?"

And I look at her hard, to see if she's just humoring me. But no, there's something intense and piercing in her eyes, as if she really wants to be in the same crazy space as me, because she knows how important it is to me.

"I don't understand," I say. "What are you getting at?"

"Just tell me," Zoe orders. She fumbles in her pocket and brings out her phone. "*Exist* or *not melt*?"

"I said they had to exist," I say.

"Well, they do," says Zoe. She flicks her phone to the camera. "Look."

I lean out of the bath. The heat is making the screen hazy. "Look," Zoe repeats, flicking through some pictures. There's a winter wonderland panorama of the whole park, a picture of a pink scarf tied around a pole, a shot of Paddy sledding with Sam on a tray, a close-up of a giant snowball ("Alice and I made that," she says), and then, finally, there are the snow babies on their bench, their little heads nestling against each other.

"I don't believe it," I say.

"Believe it," says Zoe. "They exist. I captured them." She pauses. "And do you want to know why I took the picture? Because when I first saw them, they reminded me of me and you. You know, when we were about four or five and we used to . . ."

". . . snuggle up on a sofa together," I say.

"Yes, and watch . . ."

"*The Snowman*," we say together.

I want the moment to last forever, but there's something else I have a pounding need to know. I start scrambling out of the bath.

"Where are you going?"

I grab for a towel and run down the hall. Zoe trails after me.

"Where are you going now?"

In my room, on my bedside table, is the flask.

I'm stumble-running all over again, stretching out my warm—trembling—hands. I clutch the flask close, and look and look. Through the transparent whorls of glass the colors shine. The threads of yellowy gold, deeper now, more intense, intertwined, curled together into this light, bright mist. And there's a seed fish swimming. No. No! Two seed fish swimming—there they are, sparking the air.

"Two!" I shout. "Look, Zoe, two!"

"Two? Two what?"

"So you're right, you must be right. You've done it. They're going to live. They're going to be all right. The babies. Both of them. Oh, thank you, thank you, thank you, Zoe. Thank you forever!"

I fling my arms around her, feel my head rest a moment on her shoulder, my chest flush with hers, and, because I am smaller than her and all curled up, my heart beats against hers.

"Thank me," says Zoe, "or that bottle?"

Which is when I realize that there's something I've left out.

"It's a flask," I say, and I pull away a little.

"Yes," says Zoe, "I remember. *Big as a storm wind, tiny as a baby's breath*. Right?"

"Yes."

She raises an eyebrow, but I've started now and I have to go on and I want to go on. I want to share with Zoe the most difficult thing of all.

"This bottle, this flask . . ." I begin.

"Yes?"

"It isn't empty." I'm still afraid; I'm afraid of saying it out loud. "It contains something."

"What?"

"Well, I don't really know. I know it has something to do with Clem, because when Clem's not well, the flask howls." I tell her about the pulsing blackness. "Or it goes very dim and defeated. It gutters." I tell her about the flattened flame.

"But that could have to do with me, because sometimes, I think, if I'm bad, the flask suffers."

"Suffers?"

"Yes."

"But you're never bad," says Zoe simply. "You haven't got a bad bone in your body."

"Huh?" That would be something to think about, but I don't have time because I need to get to Rob. "It's also got to do with this person—Rob. In fact, the flask can sing, a song called 'For Rob,' which is really beautiful, but sad at the same time. It makes you want to cry, hard as rain, beautiful as a rainbow."

"You're really losing me now," says Zoe.

I can see how ridiculous it all sounds. Especially Rob and his song. Rob, who I still don't know anything about, except that he's got something to do with Aunt Edie. And I haven't even got to the fizz-heart blue and the strips of paper moonlight yet.

"I'm not explaining this very well," I say.

But Zoe is, for once, all patience, and I know how difficult it must be for her so I try harder.

"You remember," I say, "when we were at the Buddhist Center and Lalitavajri talked about consciousnesses and how they have to wait around and . . . well, sometimes I think that the thing in this flask is, um, like that." I finish lamely.

"What?" says Zoe. "You mean—a soul?"

And so it's her who finally says it, lays it like a jewel between us.

"Yes," I say, relieved. "A soul. One that maybe hasn't found its place yet."

"You mean it missed its sex slot?"

Trust Zoe to mention that. "Sort of. Or one that just got left behind. Lost."

"A lost soul," says Zoe, and she's still not laughing.

There's a silence.

If I'm crazy, she's crazy, too, now.

"Zoe," I say, "will you tell me something truthfully?"

"Of course."

I put the flask in her hands. "Tell me what you see."

Zoe turns the flask over. And over. Just like I did the first time I held it.

"Well," she says carefully, "I see a bottle, a flask, which is very beautiful, really, with little silvery lines and whorls and stuff in the glass that looks like little seeds."

"Or fish," I say.

"Yes, or fish."

"And are they swimming? Are two of those seed fish swimming?"

"Swimming?" says Zoe. "No, I don't think so."

"What about inside?"

"Inside," says Zoe, "it's sort of misty, but bright, too."

"And is that misty-bright something ordinary—or not?"

"Well," she says again, "I think it's just the light, the way the light plays through the glass."

"You don't see colors?"

Zoe looks up at me. "What colors?"

"Yellow? Gold?"

"No, not really." Zoe pauses. "But you do, don't you?"

"Yes."

"Same as you heard the howls and Rob's song."

"Yes."

Another silence.

"Am I crazy, Zoe?"

Zoe puts the flask down very carefully, and then she turns to me and puts her hands on my shoulders. "I think you're extraordinary," she says.

"That's not the answer to the question."

"I think it is. I think maybe some people have, I don't know, thinner skins than other people. Feel things differently.

I think you're one of those people. Like you and music. You feel it differently from everyone else."

"No, I don't," I protest. "You feel just the same about dance."

"No, I don't, actually," says Zoe. "I dance to other people's tunes. You—you sing stuff that comes right from deep inside you."

"Does that mean I can spot a soul when I see one?"

"Not necessarily. But you are open to possibilities. I don't know about this Rob, or how the flask tells you when stuff is wrong with Clem. I don't know anything about that. But I believe you."

She believes me.

"And I think you should believe yourself. Trust your instinct. That's all. I can't really say any more."

But she has said enough.

I hug her tighter than I ever did over any Cadbury Creme Egg. This time, she hugs me back. So there we are in my bedroom—totally separate, yet joined.

58

We are so involved in our conversation that we do not hear the front door open, and we are still hugging when there are footsteps on the stairs. So we hear nothing until the bedroom door opens, and standing in the doorway, still in her coat, is Gran. She is not towering, she is not angry, in fact, she just looks old and frail and exhausted.

"I'm sorry," I say immediately. "I'm really sorry, Gran."

And she doesn't shout. Not at all. She just presses her lips tight together, as if she's trying to hold in some emotion and her eyes squeeze up, and despite the outdoor coat, a big shudder goes through the whole of her body.

And then I go over to her, one hand holding the towel around me, one hand around her neck.

And she kisses the top of my head.

Kisses me.

There's a long moment of silence and I feel (but cannot see) her looking out over my head and finally noticing Zoe.

"Hello, Mrs. Walton," says Zoe.

"Hello, Zoe," says Gran.

"Zoe helped me," I say. "It was Zoe who got me home, got me warm."

Gran looks at Zoe and then at me and she nods. "Thank you, Zoe," says Gran. "Thank you very much." Then she adds, "Why don't you put on a robe, Jess, while I make us some tea and toast. Would you like toast, Zoe?"

And it's the robe that takes me by surprise. Gran is not a robe person. More particularly, she is not in favor of people eating breakfast in their robe. She calls it *lazy*. Gran thinks people who are going to make something of their lives get dressed in the morning.

Gran escorts Zoe out of the room and I slip on my pj's, robe, and slippers. In the pocket of the robe, I put the flask.

Then I go downstairs and we all sit around the kitchen table and the mugs of tea steam and I eat four slices of hot buttered toast.

Eventually Zoe says thank you and that she needs to be getting home, or her mom will worry (at this Gran flashes me a not-quite-so-benign look), and then she turns to me.

"Bye, Jess," she says.

"Bye," I say, "my best friend in the whole universe."

Zoe smiles.

When she's gone, I expect Gran to turn around and ask me to explain myself. But she doesn't. On top of that, she allows me to stay in my robe all day and all evening.

I think I love my gran.

59

The next day it's as if the snow never existed. I look out the window and I am astonished. The whole world has turned green and the sun is out. The sun is shining brilliantly.

I go downstairs (dressed) to see Gran staring out the kitchen window.

"It's an omen," she says.

And I nod, because neither of us has to say the word *operation*, it just hangs in the air of the house. I imagine the babies being wheeled down the long corridor toward the operating room, Mom and Si walking close behind, holding hands, joined. I see the anesthesiologists checking charts and flicking syringes and Mom and Si just looking at the babies' faces as though it could be the last time.

Which is what you would feel if you didn't know how brightly the flask is shining this morning.

"How can it all have just gone?" I ask Gran about the snowless world.

"I've only seen it once before like this," says Gran. "When I was a little girl, about the same age as you. Only that time it was only one day. It snowed in the night, really heavy snow, and in the morning we went out sledding with a sled my father made himself, and then, by the afternoon of the same day, there was nothing left at all. It was like a dream."

Gran opens the back door. "Feel it," she says. "Feel how warm it is."

And I go and stand outside and feel the sun on my face and that reminds me of the mesembryanthemums in Aunt Edie's garden and how their faces opened to the sun, and I feel something open in me, too.

"Shall we go out?" I say to Gran. "Before breakfast?"

There is no *before breakfast* in Gran's life. Nothing can be achieved *before breakfast*.

"Yes," says Gran. "Let's."

We put on jackets, but we could almost have gone out in T-shirts. We walk down the cul-de-sac and take great gulps of air.

"It smells of…" I begin.

"...of summer," Gran finishes.

"What is that smell?"

"I don't know," says Gran, sniffing again. "I'd like to say it's flowers. But it isn't. It's just...a kind of warmth."

"A promise," I say.

"A promise?"

"That summer will come. That after the winter, summer will come."

In my pocket, the flask that was so cold is warm to the touch.

"I'm not sure you can smell a promise," says Gran.

But I think you can.

We pass the garage where Bruno Teisler built the ice mermaid. Not a single crystal of snow remains. Which is strange, too, because isn't it the compacted snow that usually remains? The giant snowballs, the thick trunks of snowmen? They sit solid for days, no matter how green the grass around them. The lack of any trace of the mermaid makes me feel slightly (but only slightly) better about knocking her head off.

We're not aiming for the park, we haven't discussed where we're going, but Gran and I arrive there anyway.

Some trees are blossoming, not the heavy pink cherry kind, but the lighter, paler sort.

"Apple," says Gran. "It's apple."

And I look through the blossoms up into the sky, which is a very pale blue with high, wispy clouds.

But it's not the sky or the blossoms that's so extraordinary, it's the tiny shoots of green on almost every tree and bush and plant in the park. They look to me suddenly like tiny green flames, as if the whole park will soon combust in a great conflagration of green.

"Look at the flower buds," says Gran.

And I hadn't noticed those.

Tight buds on the rosebushes, their delicate pinks masked with a kind of brown papery exterior petal.

"And this is choisya, I think," says Gran, bending down to examine a dark green bush dense with teeny white buds. "It will smell amazing in a few weeks."

The whole park is pulsing with the promise of new life.

Then we see the butterfly.

"It's a red admiral," I say, "isn't it?"

Gran nods and I concentrate on its bright colors and its delicate, delicate beating wings.

"How could it survive?" I ask Gran. "How could it survive the snow?"

"I don't know," she says. "Maybe it didn't. Maybe it came out of its chrysalis just this morning."

I don't know if this is true, but I want it to be true. I want this beautiful creature to have been born today, liberated today, come into the world today. This day of my brothers' operation.

Beating wing.

Beating heart.

I watch it flutter from bush to bush, looking for some place of welcome, an open flower, then flutter on, searching wider, trying harder. And then it just lifts into the air, where I watch it, outlined against the sky.

Then I have the strangest sense that I, too, am fluttering, growing, promising. That I'm totally myself, Jessica Walton, but that I'm also a leaf unfurling, a rosebud waiting to bloom, a cloud scudding across the sky, a butterfly on the wing. That I belong to myself, but also to the whole world; that I'm part of it, every cell of mine indivisible from every other cell in the universe. It only lasts a moment, this feeling, but it pierces me with happiness and with hope.

"Gran?" I say.

"Yes, Jess?"

"Can we go to Aunt Edie's house?"

"Why?" asks Gran.

"I want to play the piano."

60

She takes me to Aunt Edie's in the afternoon.

"Might as well," she says. The sun is still shining, but Gran's mood has darkened. She's thinking, but not saying, that this is the most dangerous time for the twins, Phase Four, when the team of surgeons will divide their single liver.

"We can't discount the possibility of hemorrhage." That's what the doctors say. That's what they fear. In her dark afternoon, Gran is afraid.

I am not afraid.

The flask is green.

Not lurid, electric green as it was when it stood in front of the green buttons of my Internet router, but the bold, gorgeous green of nature. It came in, a flame at a time, with the tiny shoots of new life on the trees in the park. It pushed itself through the misty white and gold, like young blades of grass. All through the day the green has come, promising pulsing spring. Now there is nothing left of white and gold, the flask is just one whole globe of green.

We don't go through the little garden gate; we park in Gran's driveway and approach Aunt Edie's door from the road.

"I've got the piano men coming next week," Gran says. "This will be the last time you can play the piano in Edie's house."

And previously that would have chilled me, but it doesn't today, because today is full of hope and glory.

I go straight to Aunt Edie's front room. I hope Gran won't follow me and she doesn't. Maybe she knows I need to be alone now.

I set the shining green world of the flask on top of the piano.

"Now," I say. "It's now, isn't it?"

I can hear the notes, of course I can, they began to come when we walked in the park. They pushed into my mind along with the blades of grass.

I lay my hand on the hair from the lion's mane, and around it a chord builds, quite easily, fluently, as though it could never be or have been any chord but the one that finds itself under my fingers. It makes me think of Aunt

Edie and how music flowed out of her hands. Alongside the lion are other notes from "For Rob," but they don't make you want to cry, they are not a lament. It's the same music, but not the same music at all, it's a mirror reflection: stronger, more powerful. I realize then where this song is heading, what the mirror is: All the minor chords of "For Rob" have parallels in the major keys. If I can stretch my hands and my mind, then I will find this jubilant thing, this thing that has been just out of my reach for so long.

"It's what you showed me in the park?" I say to the flask. "Yes?"

This possibility, this song that says that God's creation cannot fail. Everything counts: the tiniest trill of the sweetest bird to the loudest, most crashing crescendo wave. They all have their part to play in the whole beautiful pattern and rhythm of life. Only I still can't hear it all. There's something missing.

"What is it? Tell me! You must know this song. You sang it first."

The flask glows and glows.

But the ending will not come. It makes me feel like I'm suspended on the edge of a cliff—I could fall, I could fly, fall, fly...

The door opens.

Someone comes in.

It's not Gran.

It's no one I know. In fact, it's three people I don't know.

Three people in Aunt Edie's house who I haven't heard coming because I've been all wrapped up in the music.

I fall. Or at least my hands do—off the piano.

There's a man in a sharp suit with a fat tie and scrubbed-clean face who looks startled, and a young couple, at least I think they're a couple, because of the way they're standing, so close they're almost joined, barely a kiss apart.

"That was nice," says the woman, nodding at the piano. "Really nice."

Nice. This song of creation.

Nice.

But she means it kindly, I see that. She's got warm brown eyes.

The fat-tie man taps at his clipboard. "I wasn't expecting anyone," he says, "to be in."

Then I see what the woman is carrying. A sheet of paper with a picture of Aunt Edie's house on it, and below the picture, details of all of Aunt Edie's rooms, the precise measurements, a layout of the first floor, a layout of the second floor. And a price.

Aunt Edie's house is for sale and here is the real estate agent and a couple who might come into this house and repaint the walls (well, actually, they need repainting), and fill the rooms with their own furniture, and maybe have a baby here. A baby of their own.

"You're her granddaughter," says Fat Tie. "Is that right? Mrs. Walton's granddaughter?"

I say nothing.

"Nice room," says the man, beginning to explore, to look out of Aunt Edie's bay window. "Spacious."

The woman hasn't moved. "Don't let us disturb you," she says again. "You just go right on playing."

But, of course, I can't.

The man comes up behind the woman and slides his hand around her waist. "Your piano would fit here," he says. "Wouldn't it?"

"Yes," she says.

And then Fat Tie says, "Of course, the conservatory is a huge asset to the house," and he takes them through the Sun Room and out into the garden.

I want to start the song again, but I can't. There is only one way back into the house, and it's through this room. Even if Fat Tie takes the couple right to the end of the witch's hat garden where the compost pile is, and even if they stop off on the way back to inspect the gate to Gran's garden or observe how her eucalyptus tree leans over the joint fence, they will not be gone very long. They will be back, disturbing my song again.

I pick the flask up off the piano and hold it in my hands. It's green and quiet.

"But you don't mind, do you?"

No reply.

"You could have sung and you didn't. Yes?"

No reply.

"So when? If not now? When?"

No reply.

I put the flask back on the piano. I will have to wait again. Listen. Be patient.

"A song always chooses its own time. Yes?"

I can hear voices from the garden. I haven't thought about people coming to buy Aunt Edie's house before. I've blocked them out, not wanting anyone to tread in the sacred places that were Edie's. Edie's and mine.

But if someone has to buy this house, I suddenly hope that it will be this young couple with their near-kiss join and their hopes and their piano. Or her piano, anyway.

Soon enough they're back.

Fat Tie is all for pushing them quickly through the room, but the woman hovers, comes close to the piano, looks at me, looks at the flask.

"That's a very beautiful object," she says. "I like the way it seems to," she pauses, "capture the light."

"Capture the light?" I repeat.

Can she see it? Can this total stranger see it?

"Yes," she says. "It's very unusual, isn't it?" She smiles. "Like your playing," she adds. "Did you make up that piece yourself?"

"Sort of," I say.

She nods. "If we buy this house," she says, "I will always remember you. You—and your music."

Then I'm pierced again with a hope and a happiness, which lasts right up until the evening.

When Si calls.

61

Although we have been waiting for the call all day, we still both jump when the phone rings. Gran nods at me to pick up, as if some part of her cannot bear to know what we have waited so long to know.

"Jess?" Si is bleary with exhaustion. "They're back in the ward, Jess."

They're back in the ward.

They are.

They.

"They're back in the ward," I shout at Gran. "Both of them are back in the ward! Told you. Told you, told you, told you!"

Gran lifts her hand to chest, crosses herself.

Si is silent. Si is not joining in the jubilation.

"What?" I say.

"Richie's good. Richie's doing really well." He pauses.

"And Clem?"

"The next twenty-four hours," says Si, "they're going to be critical for Clem."

"But he's going to be fine," I say. In my pocket is the flask. It's still a brilliant, gorgeous green. I've checked every five minutes since we returned from Gran's. I check again. "He's going to be fine."

"I wish I had your confidence," says Si quietly. "Now, can I talk to Gran?"

I hand over the phone and Gran listens and listens and says nothing. After what seems like a lifetime, she finally speaks. "Tomorrow, then," she says. "We'll come early. We'll be there as soon as we can."

62

"What?" I say to Gran. "What?"

"Clem," she says.

"I know Clem," I exclaim. "But what?"

"The operation went really well, better than they expected. No hitches at all."

"So?"

"So they can't explain it. Why Clem isn't doing better than he is."

I can't explain it either. The snow babies exist. The flask is green, both seed fishes are swimming. Both of them.

I call Zoe. "Can you come over?"

"It's late," she says. "Really late."

"I know."

Zoe comes over.

"This is a bit late," says Gran.

"It's important," Zoe and I say together, not a breath between our words.

"It may be . . ." begins Gran. "But people have to sleep."

"I'm not sure I'll be sleeping tonight," I say. "Will you?"

Gran lets Zoe in.

We go to my room. I put the flask on the desk.

"What do you see?" I ask.

"Not much, I'm afraid," she says.

"But does it look the same, the same as it did before?"

"Brighter, possibly. With a tinge of something."

"Tinge of what?"

"Color?"

"Green," I say. "It's green." I tell her about my day, about the park and the green and the song and how everything has to be okay, only it isn't.

"He's critical," I tell Zoe.

"Have they said that?"

"Yes. As good as."

Zoe picks up the flask.

"Pity it can't talk," she says. "Then it could tell us what to do." As she turns the flask over in her hands, her fingers seem to tremble, or else she's just clumsy, and the flask falls—it falls out of her grip.

"No!" I cry.

But of course, the flask doesn't fall far. It's only an inch or so to the desk, so it simply skids a little, knocks into one of the wooden pillars that stand on either side of the arch that houses ScatCat and the friendship bracelets.

The pillar wobbles.

"Oh—I'm so sorry," Zoe says, grasping the perfectly strong flask and righting it again.

"Did you see that?" I ask.

"Of course I did. It was me who dropped it," she says.

"No," I say. "The pillar."

"What?"

I stretch out my hand and touch it. It moves again.

"Loose piece of wood?" says Zoe.

But I know it isn't, and actually she knows it isn't, too. At least, it is a loose piece of wood, but it wobbles not as if it's broken, but sturdily, as if there's a purpose to its wobbling. My heart gives a little thump, just as it did when I discovered the too-short drawer that hid the flask. I put my hand up to the curved wooden surface of the column and I pull. I expect it to give way immediately, but it doesn't.

"Let me try," Zoe says. She jigs with her fingers, pushes her nails, which are longer than mine and painted a vivid red, into the gap between the pillar and the surrounding surfaces. And there's the answer: It's not just the pillar that's loose, but the apparently solid piece of mounting behind.

"You do it," she says suddenly.

Is she afraid? Beautiful, bold Zoe?

My smaller, quieter hands get to work. I readjust my grip and pull. This time, pillar and mounting come straight out, revealing themselves as the front end of a small, perfectly crafted compartment about an inch wide and eight inches deep. The sort of place you might hide a document or a letter. *Thrum, thrum, thrum* goes my heart. And from the look on Zoe's face, so does hers.

But the slim wooden box is empty. I turn it upside down and tap it on the bottom, just to make sure. There's nothing in it at all, not even an old button or a pin.

"Oh," says Zoe, somewhere between disappointed and relieved.

I'm already turning my attention to the second pillar. Of the desk's two "matching" drawers, only one actually concealed a secret space, so I shouldn't expect the second pillar to move. . . .

But it does.

It wobbles just like its twin.

Its twin.

A little pair of pillars. Joined.

"Oh, oh," says Zoe again.

I pull out the second pillar. It conceals an identical one-by-eight-inch secret space. Only this box isn't empty.

"What is it?" says Zoe.

"Don't know."

Thrum. Thrum. Thrum.

It contains an envelope.

I shake it out onto the desk and it lands facedown, so I have to turn it over to read the writing.

For Rob, it says.

Am I surprised? No, I am not surprised. Nothing surprises me anymore. Especially when it's part of a pattern. You think things end, but they don't; they begin all over again. Like summer follows winter or night follows day.

"Don't open it," says Zoe.

"I have to." The loopy black writing is Aunt Edie's. "It's from my aunt."

"From her, but not to you," remarks Zoe.

"It's not sealed." And it isn't. It's one of those old-fashioned envelopes you have to lick. "If Aunt Edie didn't want anyone looking in this envelope, she could have sealed it. But she didn't."

"Even so," says Zoe.

"Look," I say. "It was you who said, 'Pity it can't talk.' Well, maybe the flask just did."

"Okay," says Zoe. "Do it."

She's talking like the envelope is an unexploded bomb. And it is, in a way, or so I find when I tip its contents out.

There's just one sheet of pale cream paper without an address.

My darling, darling boy, it begins.

"Read it aloud," says Zoe.

So I do.

My darling, darling boy,

You will never read this—one of a lifetime of things you'll never do—so I don't really know why I'm writing it. Except I have to talk to someone and the only one I want to talk to right now is you.

It's been only four hours since they took you out of my arms. They didn't want me to hold you at all, they said it would be "easier" that way. Easier not to hold my own son?

You just looked asleep, a baby snuggled in some blankets, napping. You fooled me with your beautiful face and your perfect little lips. You'd wake at any moment, I thought, wake and open your eyes and look at me.

That's why I couldn't leave you alone in the cot, even when I had to go to the bathroom. I couldn't bear the thought of you waking alone, waking when I wasn't there.

When they came to take you away, I didn't cry. I didn't scream, not out loud, anyway. I just thought, as the little white shawl of you disappeared through the door: I should have unwrapped you. Why didn't I unwrap you? I never saw you naked, never held you skin to skin. Never saw your feet.

And now I'm back home, sitting at my ordinary desk, writing with my ordinary pen. Writing to you. But perhaps you already know that. Because now I'm not so sure you've gone after all. I can still feel you, so close. I can feel the breath you never took on my cheek. So do you know what I think, darling boy? I think one day you'll wake after all. And when that day comes, I'm going to be right beside you still.

Until then, my darling boy, keep safe.

Love you forever.

I pause. I can barely say the last word.

"What?" says Zoe.

"*Mommy*," I read.

63

I'm wrong about not being surprised anymore. My head is
zinging with surprise. I see (as if she were in the room) Aunt
Edie holding her dead child in her arms. Because that's
what it means, doesn't it? That Aunt Edie had a son, Rob, a
baby who was born dead.

"That's so sad," Zoe says, all ghostly quiet.

"Yes," I say, zinging. "And no."

"No?"

"Well, yes—of course *yes*." The very idea of Aunt Edie
holding her dead child is enough to tear my heart out. "Sad
then—but not now." I pause. "Don't you see?"

"What? See what?"

I hold up the shimmering green flask. "This. What this
could actually be?"

"A soul, you said a soul...oh, my gosh," Zoe says.

"*I can still feel you so close.* That's what she said. All those years ago."

"No."

"Yes," I say. "It has to be."

"But what's that...that thing got to do with Clem?"

"Everything. Remember when I was out in the park, when I put the flask between the snow babies? You remember? And it sort of slipped, or Clem took it, under his arm. And it looked like the flask *belonged* somehow, and I thought that Clem was saying something, or the flask was saying something..."

"What? Saying what?"

"Zoe—if you were a soul, a lost soul, the soul of a little boy who died, what would you want?"

"A body." Zoe's whispering. "I'd want a body."

"Yes. Of course. Which is why it must have kept coming back to the bottle, to a thing that looks a little like a rib cage, to the only place of safety it could probably find. But inside this hard, hard glass, you'd never give up looking, would you?" I think of all the times the breath sat on the windowsill, looking out. "You'd be wanting, yearning...searching for your real other half, your perfect match..."

"...your twin," says Zoe.

"Yes." We hold each other's gaze a moment. "And Clem," I go on. "Think about Clem." My mind is rushing again. "Why do you think nothing's making any difference? The doctors, the medicine? *It all went so well.* That's what Gran said. So the doctors can't understand why Clem isn't doing better than he is."

"Because he has something missing, too."

"Yes. It has to be. Richie always had more of everything. He was—he is—the bigger twin. He didn't have the damaged heart. He had a greater share of the liver. . . ."

"And now they're separated," Zoe says. "You think Richie has the greater share of their joint soul?"

"Yes. Or all of it, maybe. What if Richie has all that life force pounding in him and little Clem has nothing?"

"Which is why he's fading. . . ."

"Yes. Exactly. Because it's not just a body that makes us alive, is it? Whatever Pug says about Mrs. Nerg. We're not just blood and bones." I hold up the shining flask. "We're something more."

I come to a breathless pause.

"You have to get to the hospital," says Zoe. "You have to go right now."

I run into the hallway, where Gran is making preparations for bed.

"We have to go to the hospital," I shout at her. "We have to go now."

"Don't be ridiculous," says Gran. "It's nearly eleven o'clock."

"No, you don't understand. We have to go now."

"We're going tomorrow, first thing. That's time enough."

"It isn't. He won't last that long."

"I don't know what you're talking about."

I hold up the flask. I'm talking about holding the hope of Clem's life in the palm of my hands.

"You should be going now," Gran says to Zoe.

Which is when the phone rings.

It's Si.

Si says we need to get to the hospital right now.

64

Zoe hugs me tight. "Good luck," she whispers.

But I don't think luck will have anything to do with it.

The journey to the hospital passes in a blur. A blur of colors. I cannot take my eyes from the flask; it swirls and changes continually. The closer we get to the hospital, the more definite the new colors become. Peach, apricot, a flutter of pink. As we enter the hospital parking lot, there isn't a single thread of green left. Not one. I don't know what it means, but the new colors are strong and warm, and in that my courage holds.

We arrive, ascend the fifteen floors, and buzz to get access. A nurse greets us, avoids eye contact, and leads us to a different ward in the Intensive Care Baby Unit. I see Richie at once. There are a million wires going in and out of him, and arranged around him, overhanging him, are machines that hum and beep and flash. The bandages, which cover most of his tiny chest, disappear beneath his huge diaper. His fragility shocks me: If Richie is like this, then Clem . . .

Clem.

Where is Clem?

Clem is not lying beside his brother in the cot.

He is not lying in an adjacent cot.

Clem is not there at all.

Without Clem beside him, Richie does not look whole; he looks like a ghost of himself.

"Poor little thing," says Gran in a whisper. "Oh, you poor little thing."

"Where's Clem?" I ask the nurse in a voice far too loud for this hushed and beeping place. "Where's my other brother?"

We cannot be too late. We cannot.

"This way," says the nurse, and we follow her through the ward to a side room.

Mom is sitting in a chair and Si is sitting on the edge of the bed beside her. Mom has Clem all bundled up in white in her arms. He's not hooked up to any machines and there's not a single tube or wire going in or out of him. This should be good news, but from Mom's face, I know it isn't. Mom isn't crying, but it looks as if she has been. It looks as if she has been crying all night.

The only part of Clem that isn't swaddled is his head. I'm close enough now to see his skin. It's not the right color—it's a pale and slightly sweaty gray. Gran asks some question without moving her lips and Si shakes his head. But I already know why they've taken the wires out of Clem and put him in Mom's arms.

They've put him there to die.

The hush in the room is suffocating, heavier than snow. The only thing holding Clem to the earth is his mother's love. Mom is holding that gray body as I imagine Aunt Edie once held Rob. Holding him so close that you would have to kill her before she let go of him. And Si is so close to Mom he's part of it, too; Mom is holding Clem and Si is holding Mom. They're all wrapped up there together in defiance of the whole world.

I take out the flask.

I don't know what I expect to happen; I haven't got that far. But this is what happens: nothing.

Nothing at all.

I wait and I wait and I wait and there's still nothing. No matter how I turn or hold or offer or clutch the flask.

I feel hopeless, sick, foolish.

Please, I say, I beg. *Please.*

No reply.

No reply at all.

It's as if death has taken our breath away and filled the room with stillness and silence and we're all just waiting and waiting for the terrible thing we know must come.

For minutes and minutes, there's nothing in this room but death, unless it's grief. That's one thing you can hear: grief, crying for itself like it did in "For Rob." I can hear all the notes and twists of it, sobbing and sobbing for the little boy who was never to grow up, whose life ended almost before it began. Edie's Rob. My Clem.

It's as if, somewhere very close, Aunt Edie is still playing the tune, her tune, "For Rob," and weeping.

"No," I cry out. "No!"

Or maybe I don't cry out, because nobody hushes me, nobody does or says a thing. We're all in the same space and not in the same space. All locked together and apart. So I don't know, when the tune begins to change, whether it's me who's singing, or someone—something—else. Knowing what's inside and what's outside my head—I've never been very good at that.

But the "For Rob" tune is changing; the minor chords, they're shifting slightly, just as they did in Aunt Edie's front room. It's coming, I think, it's coming, the creation song, only it isn't notes; it's more like a breath, or one of those very gentle summer breezes that carry sounds from somewhere so far away you think you must be imagining it.

The breeze blows across Clem's forehead. There isn't much hair sticking out from under his white cap, but what there is quivers, one or two sandy strands of hair suddenly lifting, and, despite the harsh hospital strip light above, sparking gold.

Hair of the lion.

My heart lifts, but Clem doesn't react at all.

Clem is still a closed-up little clam.

The breeze increases in intensity, blowing not just on Clem, but up my arms, raising goosebumps. Behind Mom the curtains begin to buffet and the sounds, such as they are, come closer. Get louder. More major, less sad. Gran said you can't smell a promise, so I don't suppose you can hear hopes and dreams. But that's what I think I'm hearing: hopes, dreams, and the sudden whisper of a woman.

Rob, Rob, I'm here.

She isn't here; my aunt isn't here. I'm not that stupid. But the hopes and dreams are. The hopes and dreams of anyone who brings new life to earth.

Which are my mother's dreams, too, as she hangs on, refusing to let go. Not now. Not ever.

Love can do that, I guess.

The song changes again, deepens and broadens, but it's nothing I could ever play, nothing I could ever sing. No wonder I couldn't put my hands on it in Aunt Edie's house. It's way, way beyond anything I've ever heard before. Huge and strange and beautiful. I don't really know how to describe it, except to say this is how I think the earth would sound if you could hear dawn breaking or the roots of a giant redwood searching the soil for water, or the petals of a mesembryanthemum unfurling to welcome the sun.

Wake. Wake, my darling boy.

The words come on the breeze, tiny as a baby's snuffle, big as a storm wind. I cannot tell now which is stronger, the wind or the song, but the curtain behind Mom is flapping furiously. She moves her arm around Clem, perhaps to protect him, and that lets his head move, so he seems suddenly to be facing right into the wind. And all at once, he doesn't look so gray anymore; there's a more natural glow to his skin, there's a peachy color, a flutter of pink.

Of course—how could I not have known? Guessed?

I have to touch him, just to make sure. I have to feel what I can see, I have to touch the life that's coming back into his cheeks. So I reach and touch and all the noise subsides. The wind and the song both end the moment he opens his eyes.

He looks straight up at me.

And, of course, he's just a baby and babies can't focus, so actually he's not looking at me at all, he's looking through me, past me, to whatever lies beyond.

Then his little blanket lifts, as though he's taken a huge gulp of air and his rib cage has to rise as he breathes.

And breathes.

And breathes.

We all stare at Clem's chest, at its rise and fall. Rise and fall. And no one says a thing.

Except my stepfather.

Si, the Man of Science, says, "Oh my God."

65

Afterward, we talk about what happened in that room.

Mom says, "It was a miracle. I told you those babies were miracles, didn't I? Right from the beginning, I knew. God's graciousness, his gifts to us."

Gran says, "I heard angels. Did anyone else hear that? It was like a choir, celestial music; I can't really describe it, voices far away and yet terribly near, and so beautiful, it just made me want to cry."

And Si says, at first, "There was a strange sound in the room, not singing, I didn't hear singing, more like wind in trees, on the coast, where there's also the sea. And that curtain flapping madly as though there were some storm outside when there wasn't."

"A miracle," repeats Mom.

Si looks at her. "We have to be careful," he says. "We're not out of the woods yet."

Mom looks at him. "Did you ever wonder why the babies chose to be born at Easter? At the time of spring and rebirth and Jesus?"

Si says, "Maybe it was a mass hallucination."

"Stop," says Mom. "Just stop."

And actually, he does. He stops.

It's not until I return home that anyone thinks to ask me what I saw or felt.

"What happened?" says Zoe. "What happened, what happened, what happened?"

"I heard the universe," I say, "whispering."

Zoe says, "No surprise there, then."

It's wonderful to be able to tell her everything, every little detail. When I finish, she says, "You know that letter you wrote? The one you left on the doormat, about how your heart's all messy?"

"Yes?"

"Well, it isn't. And you know what?"

"What?"

"Being your friend. It's just..." Zoe pauses, "...amazing."

66

Of course, the flask is empty. Though not empty in the sense of lonely or miserable, it's just empty in the sense of not being full. It remains iridescent, cool to the touch, beautiful. Not at all everyday—the flask could never be that.

I wonder what I should do with this marvelous empty flask?

I don't know, so it sits on my windowsill like a piece of unfinished business. Also unfinished is the business of Aunt Edie's letter—and Gran. I want to talk to Gran about Rob. I want to know everything there is to know about the little boy who gave his life's breath to my brother.

"So why don't you just ask her?" says Zoe.

So simple. So Zoe.

I remember the look on Gran's face when she came into Aunt Edie's sitting room when I was playing "For Rob." That look, I now realize, was pain.

"I don't think I could," I say.

"Why?"

"I think it would hurt her."

"Why?" says Zoe again. "I mean, it didn't happen to her."

"I can't explain. I just feel, I feel I ought to...protect Gran."

"Your gran's an *adult*," Zoe says. She puts a big stress on *adult* as though if you were an adult, you'd be beyond hurt. It's the first time I've ever really thought about adults hurting.

We leave it alone, then, Zoe and I, but the letter doesn't leave me alone. It bangs around in my head. It's like it was with the twins: Even when I'm not thinking about it I am thinking about it. About him. Rob. Aunt Edie's Rob. I mean, I didn't even know she was married.

I carry the letter around like I used to carry the flask. In my pocket. It bangs around in there.

Bang, bang, bang.

It's there when I come down for breakfast, or go to the park, or sleep. It's there when Gran drives me home from yet another visit to the hospital.

We're not out of the woods yet. That's what Si said, and it's true, though the doctors are surprised, in fact the doctors are amazed, at the progress the twins are making. Especially Clem.

The drive back is rainswept, the windshield wipers going so hard the outside world seems a blur and the inside world, the one that includes just Gran and me, appears very small and close. There's a box of Kleenex on the dashboard of the car, but when I want to blow my nose, I reach inside my pocket (the one that has the letter in it) and pull out an old tissue. With it comes the letter; I have it half in my hand and half not, so it spins a little and falls into my lap, the right way up. You can see the writing.

"What's that?" says Gran.

"A letter." Did I deliberately pull the letter into my lap? There doesn't seem to be anything up my nose that needs blowing.

"I can see it's a letter," says Gran.

"From Aunt Edie," I say. "To her son."

Gran nearly swerves into a stop sign.

"What did you say?" asks Gran.

But I know she's heard. "I found it." I say. "In the bureau."

We are passing a turnout; Gran brakes sharply and in we go. She yanks up the hand brake and turns off the car engine. Rain cascades down the windshield.

"Give it to me."

She takes the letter. I know it by heart, so I don't need to see the words to hear every one of them in my mind as Gran reads.

When she finishes, Gran doesn't say a word; she just takes a tissue out of the box on the dashboard.

"I never even knew Aunt Edie was married," I begin.

Gran does blow her nose. "She wasn't. That was part of the problem."

"Problem?"

"Well, not *problem*. Look, it all happened a very long time ago and I'm sorry you found that letter. Such things are often best forgotten."

"I bet Aunt Edie never forgot," I say quietly.

"No," Gran says at length. "A mother doesn't forget a dead child."

It occurs to me she isn't thinking about Rob now, but about her own dead child, my father.

"What happened to him?" I ask. "To Rob?"

"He was stillborn. That's all. It happens. We never really got a good explanation."

I can't help this random thought: If Si were telling this story, he'd know the details, he'd have done the statistics.

"We were pregnant together, Edie and me. A time of joy, despite everything." There's something softer in Gran's voice now, and further away, as though she's no longer sitting in a car in a turnout in the pouring rain. "Edie just shone."

"She always shone," I say.

But Gran isn't listening to me.

"The man concerned, he was a musician, of course, a jazzman on tour, and he just flew right on back to wherever he came from. But Edie didn't care—in fact, to be fair, I'm not even sure she told him. Edie only cared about the baby. Thought it might be her last chance." Gran pauses. "The babies were due within a week of each other. Rob on the nineteenth and your father on the twenty-fifth. Though your father was late, of course. . . . Anyway, they would have been cousins, your father and Edie's Rob."

I imagine Gran holding newborn Dad in her arms and Edie holding an empty blanket. It makes my throat go tight.

"It must have been horrible," I say. "For Aunt Edie."

"And a blessing," says Gran sharply. "In a way. Those weren't the days for having a child out of wedlock. And who knows how she would have coped financially. She was in cloud-cuckoo-land, really."

I don't know anything about in or out of wedlock, or finances, or cloud-cuckoo-land, but I do know how I felt when Clem was gray and still. "Horrible," I whisper.

Gran clicks her tongue against her teeth. "Well, you're right, of course. It was horrible for her. Especially seeing me and your father. And I never really understood that until..." She trails off.

"Until Dad died," I say.

"Yes," says Gran. "And even though your dad was hardly a baby, he was a grown man with a child of his own, but... well, I felt it then. The hole that a child leaves."

"She wrote that song, didn't she, in memory of him? 'For Rob.'"

"Yes, she played it day after day, month after month. Drove us all mad with it. Drove me mad with it. I thought she needed to move on."

"It's strange," I say, and this, I realize, is partly what's been bothering me. "I always think of her as such a happy person."

"Well, she was, or was again—particularly after you were born."

"Me?"

"Yes, you." And she starts the engine again. "You changed everything."

There seems to be something more to say, but Gran doesn't say it. She just drives hard and fast and in silence until she comes to the intersection where you go right for her house and straight for ours. She turns right.

"There's another letter," she says, "that you have to read, Jess."

67

As she unlocks her front door, Gran starts telling me that
she would have given me the letter sooner, only there's been
so much to do and the letter got muddled up with all sorts of
other documents she'd cleaned out from the bureau and...

And she leads me to her desk. The letter is not in sight.
In fact, it's in a blue file inside a green file in the very back
compartment of a deep file drawer. I would call it hidden.

"Here you are," says Gran, and she thrusts it into my hand.

For Jess, it says.

The writing is loopy blue, loopy blue ink.

For Jess.

My heart does a somersault.

This envelope is long, white, and businesslike, one of the
self-seal types where you can lift up the flap and then seal it

down again to make it look as if you haven't read what's inside. And that's what I think has happened: Gran has read this letter already. But I can't really complain, because I looked in *For Rob*, didn't I?

I pause long enough to wonder whether the contents of this letter addressed to me bang, bang, banged in Gran's brain like the contents of Rob's letter banged in mine.

"Go on," says Gran, impatient now. "Read it."

So I do, though it's difficult to see the writing because my hands are trembling.

My dear Jess, it says.

My dear Jess,

If you are reading this, then I will be gone. But not quite gone, I hope. I hope when you go to the piano you will think of me sometimes.

It's impossible, really, for me to express the joy you've given me, ever since you were a tiny child. Ever since that first time I lifted you onto the piano stool beside me. I don't suppose you remember that day, do you? Well, most children that age crash and bang, but you put your tiny fingers down really carefully. You listened to every note you played. And every note I played, too. I don't know how old you were then, not much more than three or four, I think. But I knew instantly. It was like looking in a mirror. You, too, I thought, are a maker of songs.

*I don't know what you think, Jess, but I think there are
connections between people. You aren't my child, you aren't
my grandchild, but there's some bone of my bone that is your
bone, too. Blood of my blood. I couldn't love you more if you'd
sprung from my own body, my own soul.*

*Over the years you've given me so many gifts. I'd like to
give you one in return. I want you to have my piano. I want
you to play and play, so when I'm up in heaven (if they let me
in!) I can look down and say, "There's my Jess." And they'll
all say, "She plays better than the angels, doesn't she?"*

With a very big kiss from your aunt,
Edie

I read this letter once, I read it twice, and I don't want to
take my eyes off the paper because I can feel Gran looking at
me, I can feel her staring me down, because she wants to
know—as she always does—what my reaction is. I feel her
all needy because Aunt Edie has said what we tried so hard
never to say—bang, bang, bang—that we were always pieces
of each other. That we belonged.

Like Rob and Clem.

And I can see how this sits with Gran. It sits like me trying
to make a friendship bracelet for Zoe that also included Em.

Don't you understand best friends?

Don't you understand that a great-aunt cannot be as close as a gran? Nowhere near as close?

And that's why, I guess, when Gran asked me what I wanted to have of Aunt Edie's and I said *the piano*, her hand flew to her face as if I'd said *the moon*.

Bang, bang, bang.

But I know something about this feeling, a jealousy that stirs something deep, like when you think your best friend prefers beach-ball Paddy to you, or like when you read two simple words.

For Rob.

Or perhaps *For Jess.*

I look up from the letter.

"Aunt Edie wants me to have the piano," I say.

"Yes," says Gran, and waits.

And waits.

"Only our house isn't big enough, is it?" I say.

"No," says Gran, "it isn't." Her out breath is audible. "So you'll still need to come over to my house a lot, won't you?"

And I say, "Yes."

68

A week later, Si is back at work, I am back at school, and Mom is home more often. It's not exactly normal—the babies are still in the hospital—but it's more normal than it has been.

On Saturday Si says, "Do you want to come out with me for a ride in Roger?"

The only difference between going out in an ordinary car and going out in Roger the Wreck is the noise. And the running commentary from Si on the wheezes and coughs and the perfectly fitting doors. And the fact that you don't really go anywhere. You just drive. Or he does. He just drives around.

"No, thanks," I say.

"It'll be the last time," Si says.

"What?"

"I'm going to sell Roger."

I get in the car.

I smell the familiar odors of leather and oil, polished wood, polished chrome, cold, and dust. Si pulls out the choke and the engine spits to life. As we pull out of the driveway and into the road, I expect him to mention how quiet the engine is now that the timing chain's been fixed. But he doesn't. He doesn't say anything at all. He drives down the cul-de-sac and turns left and I don't ask where we're going because it doesn't matter. We roar up a hill to the screeching sound of the fan and we decelerate to the fut-fut noise of the exhaust and still Si says nothing.

So it's me who speaks first. "Are you going to get another car?" I ask. "Now that Roger's running . . . so perfectly?" I imagine a new car, a new wreck, just a bit of trim and half an engine in the garage and me being twenty-one by the time it's all fixed.

"No," says Si. "No one could replace Roger." He pats the walnut dashboard. "This little moggie. He's my first and last."

"Your last?"

"Don't look so surprised."

But I am surprised. I'm stunned. That would be like me shutting the lid on the piano and saying, *That's the last time I'll ever play that*, and expecting other people to believe me. Expecting to believe myself. And I realize I've never thought of this before, how this car is Si's piano, the place where he goes to be totally himself.

"But what are you going to . . ." I'm struggling for words, ". . . tinker with?"

Si laughs. "I think I'll be tinkering with the babies quite a bit. Or at least they'll be tinkering with me."

The image of him spending his special moggie time with the babies makes me feel okay for him; even more, it makes me feel warm inside.

"And—if I get any time left over from that," Si continues, "which I'm not expecting, I might start a vegetable garden."

"A vegetable garden!" I imagine it. Si digging in the ground—having first read a gardening manual cover to cover. Si planting carrots in not-completely-straight lines. Si checking charts and adjusting the watering and the feed. The carrots growing into knobbly specimens of randomly different sizes. Si saying, *Look at these utterly perfect carrots.*

Then I feel warm about Si himself. My stepfather.

"Have you told Mom?" I ask.

"What—about the babies or the vegetable garden?"

"About giving up the car."

"Yes, of course. In fact, it was partly her idea. See, the house is very small, as you know. But the garage..."

"Is huge," I say.

"Exactly. So we thought we'd convert it. Knock a window in the side, French doors, carpet. Make it into a playroom."

"A playroom?"

"Yes, for the boys."

And I know he's saying something he's never said before, never even dared to think. He's saying the babies are going to come home. That they have a future, that they are going to grow big enough to need a playroom.

There's a gale-force wind coming through Roger's perfectly fitting doors and it's blowing at Si's hair, and he's smiling and smiling.

"That's wonderful," I say.

And it is.

So how come my insides twist with jealousy?

Again.

69

The babies don't come home, not for weeks. Which is just as well, because that's how long it takes to clear the garage. The oily cardboard is folded up and thrown away, old tire rims and engine parts that look like saucepans are advertised, wrenches are systematized, the old toolbox is put under the stairs, and the Morris Authorized Dealer plaque with its picture of a red bull walking on black water is nailed up on the kitchen wall.

"Hang on," says Mom, "I don't remember saying that my kitchen was the new garage."

They almost have an argument about it, which actually I'm glad about because, for months and months, no one's had the courage or the energy to have an argument, so that makes things more normal, too.

When you can almost see the garage walls again, men come and knock out a window and other men come with doors and sheets of glass. Concrete is laid and plaster skimmed.

And all the time, I look at the space. I look at just how much space there is in that playroom.

Zoe looks, too. "Awesome," she says, doing a cartwheel and a couple of backflips. "Perfect dance studio."

"Or grand piano space," I say.

Of course I've told her the grand piano story.

"So why don't you ask?" says Zoe. "Why don't you mention it?"

So simple. So Zoe.

I say nothing. It's all very clear to me now. Gran lost her only son. She doesn't want to lose her only grandchild. With the house getting busier, with the twins taking up so much of Mom and Si's time, what space will be left for old Gran? She needs me to have a reason to visit her, to be clamoring to visit.

"I'm not like you, Zoe. I'm not as good at saying things as you are."

Mom chooses green for the carpet. "Green's a very restful color," she says. And then the walls go Linen White, which is actually a kind of cream. And finally, the weekend before the babies are due to come home, it's finished.

Si stands in the space and Mom stands in the space and I stand in the space.

"It's a beautiful room," says Mom. "I can just see them playing here."

I imagine the boys running up and down, maybe playing soccer with a squashy patchwork ball.

"Yes," says Si. "And I can see you playing here, too, Jess."

"What?"

"I can see you—"

"*We* can see you," says Mom.

"Playing here," they say together.

There's a rumble in the driveway, as if the biggest moggie in the world were reversing over the gravel. Outside the French doors is a moving van. "Surprise," says Mom.

I can't help my hand flying to my mouth, like my mouth was a little moon.

Because, of course, it is a surprise and yet I know at once what it is.

Two men get out of the van and press some buttons and the back door scrolls and clatters upward. Revealed, brass feet first, is the grand piano.

Aunt Edie's beautiful, beautiful grand piano.

Its lid is down and it's all tied up to keep it secure.

"Gran told us," says Mom, "about Aunt Edie's letter."

And suddenly Gran is here, too, parking in the cul-de-sac. She must have followed the moving van, so as to be here at this moment when the men are throwing the blankets off the piano and preparing the dolly.

It's hardly any time at all before they swivel the piano and prepare it to come down the ramp, as though it were earth's most majestic creature emerging from Noah's Ark after the Flood.

They have to put boards on the gravel to stop the piano from sinking in, and they have to put boards up to the French doors, too. Everyone is talking at once.

The men are saying (through puffs and heaves), "A little to the left, Rod. I said *left*." And, "Mind that window, Dan. *Dan!*" And it reminds me of the time when the men puffed upstairs with the desk. A time that seems both yesterday and a million years ago.

Mom says, "Gosh, it looks a little larger now that it's actually here," and Si says, "Of course, it will need retuning; I'm not sure pianos like being moved that much," and Gran says, "Edie got one sent out to India once."

I say nothing at all; I just watch this huge, shining piano coming into my home.

Aunt Edie's piano.

My piano.

Gran says, "Are you pleased?" She grabs me by the arm. "Are you pleased?"

"It's a gift," I say.

"Yes," says Gran flatly. "From Edie."

"And also from you."

"Me?"

"Yes." Because I know what it's cost her. "Thank you so much, Gran." Hugging her, I realize I'm about half an inch taller than her and will probably get taller still. "Do you know what this means?"

"What?" she says.

"If you want to hear me play now, you'll have to come over to my house."

"You think?" she says.

"Yes. And since I'll be playing a lot, you'll have to come over a lot, won't you?"

I might be wrong, but I think there's a tear in those tough, dry eyes.

70

It's a school day when the twins finally come home.

"Can I come and see them?" says Zoe. "Can I, can I, can I?"

Of course I say *yes*, although Zoe, being Zoe, would have bounded in anyway.

The space in the hall that used to be the perfect place for the Tinkerbell upright piano is now perfect for a double stroller. All the equipment in our house is double, including the Moses baskets on their double rocker in the playroom.

"When they get bigger," says Mom, greeting me, greeting Zoe, "they'll have a basket each, although they'll rock together. You see how one push moves both baskets? But for now..."

For now, the babies are small enough still to be side by side, lying together on a floaty blue mattress surrounded by floaty white blankets. They look like they dropped straight from heaven and are still clutching little bits of sky and cloud.

Zoe looks in the basket. Both boys are fast asleep, their lips wobbling with dreams. "Oh," she exclaims. "Oh, look at them. They're so cute, so gorgeous, so . . . scrunchy."

"Scrunchy?"

"Yumptious. Yummy. I could eat them up."

"You could?" I peer in the basket. I try to see my brothers as Zoe sees them, and for the first time, they don't fill me with fear. There they are in their basket, quite ordinary.

"Yes," I say, "they're adorable."

"Couple of pests," says Mom. "That's what they are. You don't have to get up in the night for them." But she's smiling like she has just invented the universe.

"Can I come and see them often?" says Zoe.

"Of course," says Mom.

"I'll help them play with blocks."

Mom laughs. "Not for a bit."

"And I'll dance for them, too. And in a few years, when you and Si and Jess want to go out, I could babysit them."

"We'll see," says Mom.

I like the fact that Zoe has my brothers in her future; it helps me believe they really are here to stay. I'm glad she sees me in her future, too, the two of us together. Friends. The idea that I was all for hating her, refusing to speak to her, chopping her out of my life—that all seems very strange to me now. But then perhaps you can't really love a person unless you can hate them, too, as the flip side of the same coin. I mean, nobody hates an acquaintance, do they? You have to feel powerfully about someone to be able to hate them.

"When are they going to wake up?" says Zoe.

"Not for a bit," says Mom. "They've only just gone down."

"Oh," says Zoe, full of disappointment.

"You'll have to come back another time."

"Can I?" says Zoe. "Can I come back tomorrow and the day after that and the day after that?"

"You'll get bored," says Mom.

"No, I won't."

She will, of course, but Mom just smiles, and I smile, too.

When Zoe leaves, Mom and I sit quietly in the playroom with the sleeping babies. The late-afternoon sun pours through the French doors. After a while Mom says, "What are you thinking, Jess?"

As it happens, I'm thinking two things simultaneously. I'm thinking how Em will come and visit the babies, and Alice, too, and maybe even Paddy. And then the visiting will stop, and we'll know they really are here to stay. Clem. Richie. Nothing remarkable.

I'm also thinking about love and hate. How I hated Si when he said he was my parent and he wasn't, and how I loved him when he fixed the timing chain so the babies wouldn't die, and so maybe it is right that you can't love someone without being able to hate them, too. I try to explain the hate thing to Mom.

"Only with you," I tell Mom, "it doesn't work, because I've never hated you."

Mom laughs that very gentle, beautiful laugh of hers.

"Plenty of time yet," she says. "You probably just need to get a little older."

"But I don't want to hate you!"

"And I don't want you to hate me. The point is only that you have the option; you can. You can feel safe to." She pauses. "Sometimes when a child loses a parent, arguing with the only parent they have left feels dangerous."

"So you mean if I had a fight with you, I'd be acting brave?"

"Yes. Exactly."

"I'll think about it," I say.

"But then you're brave anyway," says Mom. "Brave and very special. But I think I've said that before."

"Not about brave," I say.

Mom smiles. "Speaking of which, it all looks fine with Zoe now."

"Yes. Closer than we were before, I think."

"That's how it goes," says Mom. "It's only when you're on the point of losing something—someone—that you really know what you've got."

"That's not what you said last time."

"Oh?"

"You said we might be growing out of each other."

"I offered it as a possibility, that's all. That it's okay to move on sometimes."

"And also okay to stay together. To make it work."

"Yes, of course."

"You know what, Mom?"

"What?"

"Sometimes I think, Zoe and me, we might grow old together, use our walkers together. Live next door to each other, maybe, like Gran and Aunt Edie."

"So long as you don't bicker like they did."

"Well, maybe we will."

"Yes," says Mom. "Maybe you will."

The front door opens. Si is home, but I haven't finished with this conversation yet.

"What's a soul, Mom?" I ask, not quite out of the blue.

"Mmm?" says Mom. She's listening to Si, the noise he makes in the hall with his keys and the drawer. "Sole fish, sole shoe, soul as in not-body?"

"Soul as in not-body."

"Well, your spirit, I guess. Your essential spirit." Mom looks in her sons' basket. "The color with which your life burns."

Iridescent pearl and fizz-heart summer-sky blue and moonlit white and lion-mane gold and new-shoot green and fluttering pink and even howling black.

"Is that what you meant?" asks Mom.

I don't have a chance to reply before Si comes in.

He's obviously overheard us talking because (as he looks in at the twins and gives Mom a peck on the cheek) he says, "Not what the Romans would have said. *Anima*—that's the word they had for the soul. Not so much color as wind or breath. Did you know that?"

"No," says Mom.

"I did," I say. *Strong as a storm wind, tiny as a baby's breath.*

"Oh," says Si. "That school of yours must be doing a better job than I thought."

71

Si goes upstairs to change out of his suit. I keep looking at the babies, expecting them to wake up.

"Babies always sleep longer than you think," says Mom. "Sleep, eat, poop, sleep. That's pretty much it for babies."

"But I want them to be awake," I say. "I want to play a song for them."

"Well, play away. They'll hear it in their dreams. Your Aunt Edie always said that—people respond to music even when they're asleep."

"I never heard Aunt Edie say that."

"You weren't the only person Edie spoke to, you know, Jess." Mom gets up. "Guess I'd better start thinking about making some food for the rest of us."

As she heads for the kitchen, I draw the rocking Moses baskets closer to the piano. I want to be able to see the babies' faces as I play.

"This is 'Spring Garden,'" I announce. "One of Aunt Edie's favorite pieces. This is the grass growing. Can you hear the grass, Richie? And this part's the cherry trees, bursting into bloom. Can you hear the blossoms? And the birds, singing in the tree? Can you hear the birds, Clem? Are you dreaming of birds?"

I lean over the baskets. Clem is not dreaming anything. Richie is still fast asleep, but his brother is awake. Clem is wide awake.

"Oh, Clem, do you like it? Do you?"

No reply.

Kind of like the flask.

"I'll teach you. I'll teach you everything I know. Everything Aunt Edie taught me. Would you like that?"

No reply.

But he's listening, he's listening to the music and also to the sound of my voice.

"You'll be good," I say. "You'll be a brilliant player, you know that?"

No reply. He's staring at the ceiling.

"Better than me, I reckon, because of your beautiful soul. You owe that to Rob, you know, Edie's Rob. You were really lucky there, Clem."

A little munching sound of his lips.

"You're scrunchy, Clem. You really are. Why don't you talk back?"

Clem scrunches and munches.

"I love you," I hear myself say before I realize that Mom is standing in the doorway.

"Has he woken up?" she asks.

How does Mom know that?

"I think he's going to be a better player than me," I say. "Clem. Better at the piano. Better at songs."

"Oh, I don't know about that," says Mom.

But I do. I know it like Mom knows that Clem has woken up even though she wasn't in the room and he never made a sound. I imagine all the family standing around Clem when he's nine or ten, or thirteen or fourteen. I imagine them saying, *Where did all this boy's music come from?*

And Si saying, "It can't have been from my family."

And Mom saying, "Nor mine, for that matter."

And me saying, "It came from Aunt Edie."

And both of them laughing and saying that although Edie was my aunt, she wasn't Clem's aunt; she's only related through my father, so it can't be that.

Which is where they're going to be wrong.

"Maybe it was you," Mom might add. "Maybe it's you who helped Clem get where he is."

And that will be wrong, too—but not entirely.

72

Aunt Edie's house is sold.

"To the couple you met," says Gran. "The ones who looked around the house the day of the twins' operation."

"I'm glad," I say. "I liked them."

"Yes," says Gran. "So did I. She's pregnant, apparently, so there'll be a baby in the house soon."

"And she plays the piano," I say.

"Oh, how do you know that?"

"She talked about it, or her husband did."

If we buy this house I will always remember you—and your music.

"Do you want to go over there one more time?" asks Gran. "Say good-bye to the house and all that?"

"No," I say, maybe too fast. "Thank you." Without Edie, without the piano, the house is, well, it's like the flask. Empty.

"Fair enough," says Gran.

"There is one thing I would like, though," I say. "Since I'm here."

"What's that, Jess?"

"A sprig of eucalyptus."

Gran doesn't ask why I want a sprig from her eucalyptus tree; she just goes to the kitchen drawer and gets out her pruning shears.

"Come on, then."

We go to the gate between the houses, which is bolted shut, and stand by the eucalyptus tree.

"Do you want to do it yourself?" Gran asks.

"Yes, please."

"Remember to cut it at an angle, and just above a leaf stem. It's better for the plant that way."

I cut a small piece, only five or six leaves long.

"That's not much," says Gran.

"It's enough," I say.

"I think I'll take some, too," says Gran, and she cuts herself a number of small silvery branches and adds some orange trumpet daffodils from the border.

She offers me daffodils, too, but I say no.

"Sure?"

"Sure."

"Suit yourself."

She arranges her flowers and then soaks some paper towels in water to wrap around my single eucalyptus stem.

"That should keep it moist till you get back home."

"Thanks, Gran."

"Do you know what *eucalyptus* means, Jess?"

"I didn't know it meant anything."

"Most plants are supposed to have some sort of properties. Eucalyptus is usually associated with protection. And healing."

When I get my little piece of healing home, Mom says, "Do you need a vase for that, Jess?"

But I've already got one.

Because this is what I have decided to make of my marvelous empty flask. I fill the flask from the tap in the bathroom, and when the water gets up to the neck, there's a sudden rush of bubbles, so, just for a moment, it looks like there are little seed fish. Swimming.

I don't know how or why, but the bubbles keep on coming long after I put in the eucalyptus stem. Some of them rise to the surface of the water and burst, but others, millions of others, cling to the inside of the glass like stars in a tiny galaxy. I stand the flask on my bedroom windowsill, put it in the exact spot where the breath used to sit, and wait. Late-spring sunshine slants in perfectly straight lines through the windowpane, but the mountainous whorls and the impurities of the glass—and the bubbles—tease and refract that light so my little flask shines and shimmers, just like I hoped it would.

And of course my stem of eucalyptus will die, because everything that lives dies. I have learned that. When that happens, I'll go out into the garden or into the woods behind the park and I'll find something new: a leaf, a blade of grass, a bluebell, a nettle, maybe. In summer, I might ask Mom for a rose. A pink rosebud with brown papery petals on the outside. Because every day things are made anew; I've learned that, too. The vase will hold all of these treasures, and every time one falls away, another will rise.

So there will be a rhythm to the flowers and a rhythm to my remembering. And when Clem's old enough, maybe I'll tell him about Rob and the flask and how there are always things in the universe bigger than your understanding.

But then again, when I look in his fizz-heart blue eyes, I think he may know that already.

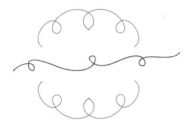

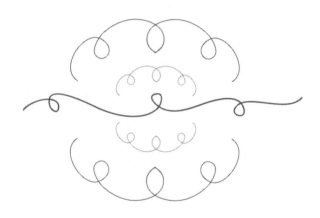

Acknowledgments

Very grateful thanks to Dr. John Young, a Morris Minor enthusiast who allowed me access to his little moggie called—um, Roger the Wreck. Any resemblance between his Roger the Wreck and mine is purely coincidental. Gratitude, too, to Ron and Innes, my local garagemen, who have not just kept my old banger running for the best part of twenty years but who will also, if you slip them the odd doughnut, tell you about crankshafts and timing chains. Any errors are obviously mine.

My thanks to the Brighton Buddhist Centre and to Padmavajri (Lotus Diamond Thunderbolt) in particular, for her time and her generosity.

And then there's Peter Tabern. Peter was the first person to notice that Jess was a girl. It's a long story, which he read on several different occasions in several different incarnations, each time holding up a lantern so I could see what I'd actually written. Thank you very much, Peter. Every writer needs a Peter Tabern, but they don't all get as lucky as me.

There's also Charles Boyle. He didn't allow me to thank him for what he did on my last book (*Knight Crew*), because he published it and he's ludicrously modest. But he's not in charge of this book, so here are the thanks, belated but very sincere. Tough luck, Charles; you can't win them all.

Last but not least is Rachel Denwood. She decided she wanted to be my new editor before she'd seen a word of *The Flask*. It's this sort of faith that keeps a writer going.